AN AMERICAN LEGAL ALMANAC
Law in all States: Summary and Update

by JOAN ROBINSON, LL.B.

1978 Oceana Publications, Inc.
Dobbs Ferry, New York

58980

Library of Congress Cataloging in Publication Data

Robinson, Joan
   An American legal almanac.

   (Legal almanac series)
   1. Law—United States—Compends. 2. Law—
United States—Popular works. I. Title.
KF387.R55   340'.0973   78-58299
ISBN 0-379-11125-X

Manufactured in the United States of America

TABLE OF CONTENTS

Part One
LAW AND THE FAMILY

Chapter I
FAMILY LAW 1

Chapter II
WILLS, TRUSTS, ESTATES AND ESTATE PLANNING .. 89

iii

Part Two
LAW AND LIVELIHOOD

Part Three
LAW AND LIVING

iv

Part Four
THE INDIVIDUAL AND SOCIETY

TABLE OF CHARTS

Chapter V
LAW FOR HOMEOWNERS AND TENANTS

Chapter VI
THE CONSUMER AND THE LAW

Chapter VIII
WOMEN AND THE LAW

Chapter XI
PROTECTION THROUGH THE LAW: CIVIL

Chapter XII
CRIMINAL LAW

PUBLISHER'S FOREWORD

An American Legal Almanac is the amalgam of two concepts. For those who subscribe to the *Legal Almanac Series* it seeks to be a simultaneous and across-the-board update of the great majority of the seventy *Legal Almanacs* that have been published since the inception of the program more than thirty years ago. Those using the work essentially as an update to *Legal Almanacs* will find useful the back appendix relating chapter-by-chapter the specific *Almanacs* which are updated.

But perhaps more significantly, this new work is a popular statement of contemporary law in those subject matter areas which are of the essence of our everyday existence. To accomplish this, the work is set out in four major sections:

PART ONE: *Law and the Family,* covering the basic relationships among family members, including marriage and divorce as well as inheritance and estate planning.

PART TWO: *Law and Livelihood,* analyzes both business and commercial law and laws governing workers and labor relations.

PART THREE: *Law and Living,* deals with laws governing special interest relationships - as homeowners or tenants, as consumer, as youth, as women.

PART FOUR: *The Individual and Society,* deals with laws governing basic rights, privileges, duties and immunities of individuals in relation to each other and in relation to their government. Here, such issues as civil rights, criminal law and tort law are analyzed.

The method of presentation is encyclopedic in the sense that *keywords*, alphabetically arranged, provide the hard core around which the coverage of each chapter is set out.

Joan Robinson, the author of *An American Legal Almanac* is an attorney and writer whose research for this work has provided not only the substance of this volume but the basis for continuing update of those *Legal Almanacs* which the editorial board of the Publisher has determined will be revised, updated and continued in print.

Whether used as a popular legal summary by itself or in conjunction with previously published *Legal Almanacs*, the work has as its objective the imparting of information. In no sense is it intended or can it replace the services of an attorney where specific advice and legal guidance are sought.

Part One

LAW AND THE FAMILY

Chapter I

FAMILY LAW

The sixties and the seventies have been years of change and turbulence. Racial minorities and women's rights groups were demanding equality and an end to the discrimination practiced against them. Eighteen year olds sought rights previously reserved for those over twenty-one. Still others felt strongly that the individual should have control over his own affairs and sought less government control over their private lives. These influences have been reflected in the laws relating to marriage and the family.

ABORTION

The most dramatic change in the field of family law has been the legalization of abortion. Abortion was a criminal offense in most early state laws. Gradually some of the states adopted less restrictive laws governing abortion. Many of these laws were based on a model act adopted by the American Law Institute, which permitted abortion in certain unusual circumstances, such as rape or incest.

In the sixties various women's rights groups and population control enthusiasts had been pressing for "abortion on demand" laws, claiming that a woman should be in control of her own body and that only she and her physician had the right to decide whether she could have an abortion. Opposing this philosophy were "right to life" groups who claimed that the fetus was a human being and that the unborn child's right to life was superior to the mother's right of privacy and control over her own body. The conflict between the two groups was exacerbated when the New York legislature passed a law permitting abortion on demand.

The controversy climaxed when the United States Supreme Court decided *Roe* v. *Wade,* 410 U.S. 113 (1973) and *Doe* v. *Bolton* 410 U.S. 179 (1973). The court held that during the first trimester (12 weeks) of pregnancy the woman was free to choose to have an abortion. During

1

the second trimester, the state could pass laws regulating the abortion procedure, to protect the pregnant woman's health. In the last trimester, since the fetus is then viable, the state has the right to make laws for the protection of the fetus and even limit abortions only to those cases where it is necessary to protect the mother's health or life. It also held that state residency requirements for abortion were unconstitutional.

Now that abortion has been legalized, several additional questions must be settled. Chief among these is whether parental consent is required for minors' abortions. Approximately sixteen states have provided for this consent by statute and similar legislation has been introduced in several other states. However some state courts have held such laws unconstitutional. The Supreme Court has now decided that minors do not require parental consent; nor is spousal consent required. See *Planned Parenthood of Missouri v. Danforth,* 428 U.S. 52.

ADOPTION

Today, with many people concerned with the overgrowth of the population, some are considering adopting, rather than having natural children. The practice of adoption has been with us from earliest times, provision being made for it even in the *Code of Hammurabi.* It was practiced by the Romans and those European countries whose laws are based on the civil law. Adoption was unknown at common law, however, and in England and the United States is permitted only by statute. The laws vary somewhat from state to state. These variations are set forth in charts at the end of this chapter.

Adoption is a court procedure which is governed largely by state statutes. These procedures have remained fairly constant over the years. Recently a decision of the U.S. Supreme Court changed the requirements for consent to the adoption of an illegitimate child.

Obtaining the consent of the natural parents to an adoption has always been of the utmost importance. Failure to obtain the proper consent can later result in a rescission of the adoption with its attendant heartbreak and misery. Care must be taken that the consent is freely given, without fraud or duress, and that the parents are aware that they are consenting to a permanent adoption of their child.

Until recently if an illegitimate child was adopted, only the mother's consent was required. However in *Stanley* v. *Illinois,* the Supreme Court ruled that the consent of the father of an illegitimate child is also required. Since the Stanley decision many of the states have amended their adoption laws to require the consent of the putative father. Some do not require his consent in all instances. South Dakota requires his consent only if the father is known, or has acknowledged his paternity or had been adjudicated the father of the child. Michigan requires the consent only if the father has filed a claim of paternity or is married to, or living with, the mother.

Over the past decade there has been a pronounced change in the type of children being adopted and the qualifications of adoptive parents. With increased knowledge of contraceptives, the supply of adoptable babies has dwindled. Although the procedure to adopt is statutory, whether an adoption will be permitted, is left to the discretion of the court. In making their decisions, most judges rely on the recommendations of the adoption agencies investigating the case. Therefore, the rules and regulations of these agencies affect adoptions as much, if not more, than statutory regulations. These agencies are less rigid than they were in the past in determining which adoptions would be in the child's best interest.

Interracial adoptions are forbidden by law in only a few states but for years this type of adoption was frowned upon by most agencies. Now since many of the babies available for adoption belong to "minority" races or are racially mixed, these adoptions are permitted, if the agencies feel they have a reasonable chance of success.

Even some of the barriers relating to the religion of the parents are being lowered, although for the most part an attempt is still made to match the religious faith of the adopting parents to that of the child.

Single persons are permitted to adopt, as well as older couples. An Oregon court recently permitted an adoption by prospective parents aged fifty-seven and fifty-eight. If all other factors are favorable, the advanced age of prospective parents will not prevent adoption.

People are encouraged to adopt handicapped children. Some forty states have passed subsidized adoption legislation, which permits less affluent persons to adopt.

ALIMONY

There is a growing trend to eliminate the question of fault in granting alimony. In the past, to a certain extent the awarding of alimony was punitive in nature. Today, almost half the states do not consider the question of guilt in awarding alimony. The test is primarily the need of one spouse and the ability of the other to pay. Also some states have permitted the husband to be the recipient of alimony, when the situation warranted it.

BIRTH CONTROL

The initial federal statute prohibiting the use of contraceptives was the Comstock Act, which prohibited the importation, mailing and interstate transportation of birth control devices. The philosophy of this act was incorporated into many state laws.

Public opinion and governmental attitudes have changed greatly since the days of the Comstock Act. In 1965, in *Griswald* v. *Connecticut,* a law banning the use of contraceptives was declared unconstitutional as it violated the right of privacy of married persons. Later, in *Eisenstadt* v. *Baird,* such restrictions were declared unconstitutional as to single persons as well.

Now one of the main questions being considered is whether contraceptives may be made available to minors without parental consent. In California, an Attorney General's Opinion states that minor female are entitled to public health care services, including contraception, without parental consent. A United States District Court recently held in *Population Services International* v. *Wilson,* that New York's ban on the distribution of contraceptives to minors was unconstitutional. In all probability the United States Supreme Court will decide on this question in the near future.

CHILDREN

The relationship between children and their parents will be discussed in a later chapter dealing with Juvenile Law.

DISSOLUTION OF MARRIAGE

A marriage may be annulled if it is void or voidable. Parties may separate from one another without legally dissolving the marriage. The laws relating to annulments and separations have remained fairly constant. Charts at the end of the chapter show the grounds for annulment and separation in all the states. The law relating to divorce has undergone a tremendous change with the introduction of the concept of "no fault divorce."

Traditionally divorces have been granted because of the wrongdoing (e.g. adultery, cruelty) of one spouse towards the other innocent spouse. Gradually there had been a trend away from this type of divorce towards the concept of no-fault divorce. Some states permitted divorce on the grounds of incompatibility; others allowed it if a couple lived separate and apart for a specified number of years. Finally in 1970 California made "irreconcilable differences which have caused the irremediable breakdown of the marriage," one of the grounds for divorce. Since then approximately one third of the states have followed California's lead. Some, such as Iowa and Missouri, have made "no-fault" the sole grounds for divorce. In others, Texas and Connecticut, for instance, it is one of several grounds for divorce. In some quarters there still is a great deal of resistance to "no fault," particularly by those who feel it will further contribute to the breakdown of the family structure. One of the main reasons for this is that in more than three quarters of the cases the divorce is uncontested and there is no inquiry by the court as to whether in fact the marriage is irretrievably broken. "No-fault" divorce could be made more palatable to these objectors if some sort of conciliation or marriage counselling provisions were included, particularly when young children are involved.

One effect of "no fault" divorce has been the decline in number of out-of-state or country divorces by residents of states having that type of statute.

MARRIAGE

Age of Marital Consent—Most of the states have lowered the age of matrimonial consent from twenty-one to eighteen years. Whereas, formerly the age of consent differed for males and females, now in most states there is no discrimination between the sexes in this respect.

Miscegenation—All but eight states have now repealed laws forbidding interracial marriages. However, these laws are void and unenforcable due to a U.S. Supreme Court decision declaring them unconstitutional.

SUPPORT

The legal equality of the sexes is gradually becoming recognized in the family support laws. The husband still is responsible for the support of his wife in all of the states, but in approximately one third of them, the wife is required to support the husband if he is unable to do so himself or is likely to become a public charge. Over half the states regard the support of minor children as the joint obligation of husband and wife.

The mother was formerly regarded as the one responsible for the support of an illegitimate child, but the courts are beginning to look towards the putative father for support also.

Chart 1

WHO MAY ADOPT

STATE	Statutory Definition	Other Age Requirements
Alabama	Proper adult	—
Alaska	Any person	—
Arizona	Any adult	—
Arkansas	Any person of lawful age	—
California	Any adult	10 years older than child[1]
Colorado	Any person	Over 21[2]
Connecticut	Any person	18 years of age
Delaware	Any resident	Over 21 if unmarried
District of Columbia	Any person	—
Florida	A husband and wife jointly, unmarried adult, unmarried minor who is natural parent of the child. If the other spouse is also adoptee's parent, the other spouse may adopt. Also under special circumstances, the court may permit only one spouse to adopt	—
Georgia	Adult resident (married and living with spouse; 25 years of age if unmarried)	10 years older than child

[1]Provision not applicable in case of adoption by stepparents
[2]Court may permit a minor to adopt

STATE	Statutory Definition	Other Age Requirements
Hawaii	Any proper adult person not married, or any person married to child's father or mother or husband and wife jointly	—
Idaho	Any adult	If under 25 years of age, must be 15 years older than child (unless spouse of natural parent)
Illinois	Any reputable person	Of legal age, but minor may adopt by leave of court for good cause.
Indiana	Any resident	—
Iowa	Any person of lawful age (construed to include minors attaining majority by marriage)	—
Kansas	Any adult	—
Kentucky	Any adult resident	—
Louisiana	Any person	Over 21 if unmarried; person over 20 may adopt person over 17
Maine	Any person	—
Maryland	Any person	Over 18
Massachusetts	Person of full age	Older than adoptee
Michigan	Any person	—
Minnesota	Any resident of more than one year (unless requirement waived)	—

Chart 1 cont.

STATE	Statutory Definition	Other Age Requirements
Mississippi	Any proper unmarried adult, or spouses jointly	—
Missouri	Any person	—
Montana	Spouses jointly; either if other is child's parent; single person 18 years of age; unmarried parent of illegitimate child; married person of 18 and legally separated	—
Nebraska	Any adult	—
Nevada	Any adult	10 years older than child
New Hampshire	Any individual, not a minor	—
New Jersey	Any adult[2] U.S. citizen (or one who has declared intent to be)	10 years older than child[1] (15, if adult adoptee)
New Mexico	A married couple, and adult unmarried individual. If one spouse is parent of the adoptee, or if the couple is legally separated, one spouse may adopt.	20 years older if adopting adult
New York	Any adult (minor may adopt spouse's child born in or out of wedlock)	—

---

[1] May be waived in the case of certain relatives
[2] If husband and wife adopt, only one spouse must be of full age

STATE	Statutory Definition	Other Age Requirements
North Carolina	Any proper adult person or spouses jointly	—
North Dakota	Husband and wife jointly; either, if other spouse is natural parent, an unmarried adult, married adult legally separated from spouse	10 years older than adoptee
Ohio	Any proper person	—
Oklahoma	Spouses jointly; either if other is child's parent; single person 21 years of age; married parent of illegitimate child; married person of 21 and legally separated	—
Oregon	Any person	—
Pennsylvania	Any individual	—
Puerto Rico	Any person in full exercise of civil rights	Over 21 and 16 years older than adoptee (except in stepchild adoption by spouse of at least 5 years)
Rhode Island	Any person	Older than adoptee
South Carolina	Spouses jointly; either if other is parent of child; single person of legal age; married, of legal age and legally separated; any unmarried parent may adopt illegitimate child	Only adult may adopt adult
South Dakota	Any adult	10 years older than child

Chart 1 cont.

STATE	Statutory Definition	Other Age Requirements
Tennessee	Any U.S. citizen	Over 18
Texas	Any adult	—
Utah	Any adult	—
Vermont	Any person of age and sound mind	—
Virginia	Any natural person	—
Washington	Any person	—
West Virginia	Any person	—
Wisconsin	Any adult resident; resident spouses (or resident stepparent) may adopt minor	—
Wyoming	Any adult resident, (or spouses jointly, or either spouse, if one is stepparent)	—

Chart 2

RESIDENCE REQUIREMENTS FOR ADOPTING PARENTS

STATE	Are There Residence Requirements?	What Are They?
Alabama	No	—
Alaska	No	—
Arizona	Yes	Resident of State
Arkansas	No	—
California	Yes	Resident of County of Proceeding
Colorado	No	—
Connecticut	No	—
Delaware	Yes	Resident of State
District of Columbia	Yes	Legal Resident of District or Have Lived One Year in District (unless adoptee in legal custody or control of Commissioners or child-placement agency)
Florida	No	—
Georgia	Yes	Resident of State
Hawaii	No	—
Idaho	Yes	Resident of and residing in State
Illinois	Yes	6 Months Immediate Continuous Residence (no residence requirement if adoptee is "related child" or child placed by an "agency")

Chart 2 cont.

STATE	Are There Residence Requirements?	What Are They?
Indiana	Yes	Resident of State
Iowa	No	—
Kansas	No	—
Kentucky	Yes	Resident of State or lived 12 months next preceding in State
Louisiana	No	—
Maine	No	—
Maryland	No	—
Massachusetts	No	—
Michigan	Yes	Resident of State
Minnesota	Yes	Resident of State for at least One Year (waivable by Court for best interests of child)
Mississippi	Yes	Resident of State for 90 Days before filing Petition (unless child related to one of the petitioners within third degree under civil law)
Missouri	No	—
Montana	No	—
Nebraska	Yes	Resident of State
Nevada	Yes	Reside in State for Six months before Granting of Adoption

STATE	Are There Residence Requirements?	What Are They?
New Hampshire	No	(but probate court has jurisdiction only if either the adoptor or adoptee resided in the state for 6 months before the petition for adoption is filed, or the child is placed with the division of welfare or a licensed child placing agency in New Hampshire at the time of filing the petition)
New Jersey	No	—
New Mexico	No	—
New York	No	—
North Carolina	Yes	Resided in State or Federal Territory therein 6 months just before filing Petition (residence, but no 6 month requirement applies in stepchild or grandchild adoption or in adoptions by the putative father)
North Dakota	No	—
Ohio	No	—
Oklahoma	No	—
Oregon	No	—
Pennsylvania	No	—

Chart 2 cont.

STATE	Are There Residence Requirements?	What Are They?
Puerto Rico	Yes	Resided in Puerto Rico Six months before Date of Petition
Rhode Island	Yes	Resident of State
South Carolina	No	—
South Dakota	No	—
Tennessee	Yes	Lived or maintained regular Place of Abode in State for One Year, regardless of Legal Residence (if in military service—one year before entering service)
Texas	No (child adoption)	Adult Adoption of Adult (Resident of State)
Utah	No	—
Vermont	No	—
Virginia	Yes	Any natural person residing in Virginia or who has custody of a child placed by a Virginian child-placing agency
Washington	No	—
West Virginia	Yes	Resident of State
Wisconsin	Yes	Resident of State
Wyoming	Yes	Resident of State (but any person may adopt adult resident)

Chart 3

WHO MAY BE ADOPTED

STATE	Minors?	Adults?	Persons of Any Age?
Alabama	X		
Alaska	X	X	
Arizona	X		
Arkansas			X
California	X	X	
		(younger than adopter; can't adopt spouse)	
Colorado	X	X	
Connecticut	X	X	
		(younger than adopter) (must have consent of adoptee's adult spouse)	
Delaware	X	X	
District of Columbia	X	X	
Florida	X	X	
Georgia	X	X	
Hawaii	X		
Idaho	X	X	
		(where adoption not made during minority due to inadvertence, mistake or neglect and adopter has had relation of parent)	

Chart 3 cont.

STATE	Minors?	Adults?	Persons of Any Age?
Illinois	X	X (if lived in home of adopter at any time for two years continuously before adoption proceeding, or related in manner of a "related child")	
Indiana	X	X	
Iowa	X	X	
Kansas	X	X	
Kentucky			X
Louisiana	X	X	
Maine			X
Maryland	X	X	
Massachusetts			X (younger than adopter)
Michigan	X		
Minnesota	X	X	
Mississippi	X	X	
Missouri			X
Montana	X (any child parent in state when petition filed)	X	

STATE	Minors?	Adults?	Persons of Any Age?
Nebraska	X		
Nevada	X	X (younger than adopter)	
New Hampshire			X
New Jersey	X	X	
New Mexico	X	X	
New York			X
North Carolina	X	X	
North Dakota			X
Ohio	X		
Oklahoma	X		
Oregon			X
Pennsylvania	X	X	
Puerto Rico			X
Rhode Island			X (younger than adopter)
South Carolina	X	X (by adult)	
South Dakota	X	X (by adult with written consent of adoptee who has lived in adopter's home for six months during minority)	

Chart 3 cont.

STATE	Minors?	Adults?	Persons of Any Age?
Tennessee			X (for those over 18, only adoptee's consent required unless adjudicated non-compos mentis (guardian's consent required))
Texas	X	X	
Utah	X	X	
Vermont			X
Virginia	X	X (stepchild of at least one year; niece or nephew with no living parents who has lived in adopter's home for at least one year; any adult who has resided in adopter's home for at least two years before reaching majority)	
Washington			X
West Virginia	X	X	
Wisconsin			X
Wyoming	X	X (resident)	

Chart 4

PROPER COURT IN ADOPTION PROCEEDINGS

STATE	Court	Does Petitioner Have a Choice of Venue?	Where Petitioner Resides?	Where Child Resides?	Where Agency having Child Located?
Alabama	Probate	Yes	P	P[1]	P
Alaska	Superior	Yes	P (statewide venue)	P	P
Arizona	Superior	No	P		
Arkansas	Probate	No		P	
California	Superior	No	P		
Colorado	Juvenile[2]	Yes	P		P
Connecticut	Probate	No	P[3]		
Delaware	Superior	No	P		Ṗ
District of Columbia	Domestic Relations Branch of Court of General Sessions	No			

Chart 4 cont.

STATE	Court	Does Petitioner Have a Choice of Venue?	Where Petitioner Resides?	Where Child Resides?	Where Agency having Child Located?
Florida	Circuit	Yes	P	P	P
Georgia	Superior	No (generally)	P [4]		
Hawaii	Circuit	Yes	P	P	
Idaho	District	No	P		
Illinois	Circuit	Yes	P	P (or was born; or where parents reside; or any county if in custody of agency or has guardian)	
Indiana	County Ct. with Probate Jurisdiction	Yes	P		P
Iowa	District	Yes	P	P	
Kansas	Probate	No	P [5]	P [5]	
Kentucky	Circuit	No	P		

STATE	Court	Does Petitioner Have a Choice of Venue?	Where Petitioner Resides?	Where Child Resides?	Where Agency having Child Located?
Louisiana	Juvenile or District	Yes	P[6]		
Maine	Probate	Yes	P[7]	P[7]	
Maryland	Circuit Ct. sitting in Equity (8)	Yes	P	P[12]	
Massachusetts	Probate	No	P[7]	P[7]	
Michigan	Probate	Yes	P	P (or where child found)	
Minnesota	Juvenile	No	P		
Mississippi	Chancery	Yes	P	P (or where born or found when deserted or abandoned; or where home to which child surrendered located)	

Chart 4 cont.

STATE	Court	Does Petitioner Have a Choice of Venue?	Where Petitioner Resides?	Where Child Resides?	Where Agency having Child Located?
Missouri	Circuit (juvenile division)	Yes	P	P	
Montana	District	No	P		
Nebraska	County	No	P		
Nevada	District	Yes (child: any county; adult adoption: county of either adopter's or adoptee's residence)			
New Hampshire	Probate	Yes	P	P	
New Jersey	Superior, Juvenile and Domestic Relations, or County Ct. (must use Superior Ct. if parents were divorced in state, unless said court has awarded custody to agency or consented to proceeding in other said courts)	Yes	P	P (if adult adoptee)	P (where agency has principal office)
New Mexico	District	Yes [13]	P	P	
New York	Family	No	P[5]	P[5]	P[5]

STATE	Court	Does Petitioner Have a Choice of Venue?	Where Petitioner Resides?	Where Child Resides?	Where Agency having Child Located?
North Carolina	Superior	Yes	P	P[1]	P
North Dakota	District	Yes	P	P	P
Ohio	Probate	Yes	P[9]	P[9]	
Oklahoma	County Court	No	P		
Oregon	Probate	Yes	P	P	P
Pennsylvania Philadelphia—Family Division	Orphans' Ct. (in Family Division)	Yes	P	P[10]	P
Puerto Rico	Superior	No	no restrictions		
Rhode Island	Family (adoptee under 18); Probate (adoptee over 18)	No Yes (where adoptee over 18)	P	P	P
South Carolina	Common Pleas or court with concurrent jurisdiction	Yes	P	(whether petitioner resident or non-resident)	(if petitioner non-resident)

Chart 4 cont.

STATE	Court	Does Petitioner Have a Choice of Venue?	Where Petitioner Resides?	Where Child Resides?	Where Agency having Child Located?
South Dakota	Circuit Court	Yes	P	P	
Tennessee	Chancery (or Circuit)	Yes	P	P[1]	P
Texas	District	Yes	P	P	P
Utah	District	No	P		
Vermont	Probate	No	P[5]	P[5]	P[5]
Virginia with Chancery jurisdiction	Court of record	No[11]	P		P
Washington	Superior	Yes	P	P	
West Virginia court where Circuit Ct. does not sit as Juvenile Ct.	Circuit (Juvenile Ct. does not sit as Juvenile Ct.)	No	P		
Wisconsin	County	No	P (adoption of adults)	P (adoption of minors)	
Wyoming	District		(May be brought in any district court)		

FOOTNOTES TO CHART 4

[1] In the states so marked, it is provided that if the child is a public charge, the adoption proceeding may be brought at the place where the child resided when it became a public charge.

[2] In Colorado, the proper court for the adoption of adults is the county or district court of either the adopter's or adoptee's residence. In city and county of Denver, Juvenile Court has jurisdiction, elsewhere the Juvenile division of district courts.

[3] In Connecticut, if the child is in an institution, the petition is filed in the district where the institution is located. If not in an institution, the child may be adopted by proceedings in the district where the petitioner resides.

[4] In Georgia, the court may, for good cause, permit the petition to be filed in the county where the child placing agency is located or where the child is domiciled.

[5] In Kansas, New York and Vermont, the proceeding is brought in the county of residence of the petitioner; if he be a non-resident of the state, then in the county where the child resides (in Kansas and New York), or if the child is in or being adopted from an institution, then in the county where it is located.

[6] Or where parents (or legal custodian) reside.

[7] In these states, the proceeding is brought in the county where the petitioner lives, if a resident of the state, or in the county where the child lives, if the petitioner is a non-resident.

[8] In Baltimore City, the proceedings are brought in Equity Court.

[9] In Ohio, the proceeding may also be brought in the county where the child was born, has a legal settlement, or has become a public charge. If the child has been placed in a private institution with parents' approval, may also be brought in county where parents reside.

[10] With the court's permission.

[11] If the petitioner resides in the City of Richmond, and north of James River, the petition is brought in the Circuit Court of the City of Richmond, Division I; if petitioner resides south of James River, then in Circuit Court of the City of Richmond, Division II.

[12] If person adopted is an adult or if related by blood or marriage to the petitioner.

[13] If adoptee was placed by Health and Social Service Department, petition must be filed in county where placement is being supervised.

Chart 5

CHILD'S CONSENT TO ADOPTION—
AGE REQUIREMENTS

No Requirements

Louisiana
New Jersey
South Carolina

10 Years

Hawaii
Maryland
Michigan
New Mexico
North Dakota (court may waive)
Puerto Rico (unless incapacitated)

12 Years

Arizona
California
Colorado
Florida
Idaho
Kentucky (may be waived)
Massachusetts
Montana
New Hampshire
North Carolina
Ohio (but not if child has resided
   continuously in adopting home
   for eight years or more, im-
   mediately before filing petition)
Oklahoma
Pennsylvania
South Dakota
Texas
Utah
West Virginia

14 Years

Alabama
Alaska
Arkansas
Connecticut
Delaware (may be waived by
   court)
District of Columbia
Georgia
Illinois
Indiana
Iowa
Kansas (and of sound intellect)
Maine
Minnesota
Mississippi (or personal service
   of process on child)
Missouri (unless court finds in-
   sufficient mental capacity to
   consent)
Nebraska
Nevada
New York (may be waived by
   court)
Oregon
Rhode Island
Tennessee
Vermont
Virginia
Washington
Wisconsin
Wyoming

Chart 6
INVESTIGATION

STATE	Is Investigation Required?	Who Must Investigate?
Alabama	Yes	State Department of Pensions and Security
Alaska	Yes (no specification, but inferrable from provision that no investigation required in adult adoptions)	
Arizona	Yes	Court officer or approved agency licensed by him
Arkansas	Yes (if ordered by Court)	Child Welfare Division
California	Yes (may be waived if adoption is through a licensed agency)	Department of Social Welfare
Colorado	Yes (except in relative or stepparent adoptions)	Any licensed placement agency; any County department of social services, any public welfare dept.; or court's own probation dept.
Connecticut	Yes	Commissioner of Welfare
Delaware	Yes	Department of health and social services or an authorized agency

Chart 6 cont.

STATE	Is Investigation Required?	Who Must Investigate?
District of Columbia	Yes	D.C. Board of Commissioners, or licensed placement agency if supervising case
Florida	Yes	Division of family services, department of health and rehabilitative services
Georgia	Yes	Dept. of Human Resources
Hawaii	Yes (may be waived by Court)	Director of social services and housing (or nearest county administrator, or approved placement agency, if Director refers)
Idaho	Yes (in Court's discretion; unless petitioner related to child or married to natural parent)	Department of health and welfare or qualified child-placement agency
Illinois	Yes	A licensed placement agency, a probation officer or (in Cook County) the County Services Division of the Cook County Department of Public Aid
Indiana	Yes	Duly licensed child-placement agency approved by State Dept. of Public Welfare

STATE	Is Investigation Required?	Who Must Investigate?
Iowa	Yes (may be waived by Court)	State Dept. of Social Welfare, or qualified person or agency named by Court
Kansas	Yes (discretionary in step-parent adoptions)	State Dept. of Social Welfare
Kentucky	Yes	Dept. of Child Welfare, or person or agency designated by it or Court
Louisiana	Yes	Dept. of Public Welfare
Maine	Yes (unless child is blood relative of one of petitioners or given for adoption by Dept. of Health and Welfare or licensed adoption agency); (may be waived by Court)	Dept. of Social Welfare or licensed adoption agency
Maryland	Yes (unless agency adoption, or Court has personal knowledge)	Dept. of Public Welfare, licensed agency, probation officer or other person designated by Court
Massachusetts	Yes (if child under 14 and adoption not sponsored by agency and petitioner is not a stepparent of, or related to the child, or child's guardian)	Dept. of Public Welfare

Chart 6 cont.

STATE	Is Investigation Required?	Who Must Investigate?
Michigan	Yes	County agent, placement agency licensed by state, Michigan Children's Institute. State Dept. of Social Welfare, or County Social Welfare Bureau.
Minnesota	Yes (may be waived by Court)	Commissioner of Public Welfare; licensed adoption agency or (if adoption is by stepparent) welfare department
Mississippi	Yes	Division of Welfare of State
Missouri	Yes	Dept. of Public Health and Welfare, any child-placement agency, juvenile court officer or other suitable person appointed by Court
Montana	Yes (in Court's discretion)	State department of social and rehabilitation services
Nebraska	Yes (if Court deems advisable)	Department of Public Welfare or any child-placement agency licensed or approved by it
Nevada	Yes (Court may waive where a petitioner or spouse related to child within third degree)	Welfare Division of Dept. of Health, Welfare and Rehabilitation

STATE	Is Investigation Required?	Who Must Investigate?
New Hampshire	Yes (unless petitioner, or petitioner's spouse, is natural parent)	Division of Welfare or licensed child-placing agency
New Jersey	Yes (usually)	Approved agency having principal office in New Jersey
New Mexico	Yes	Department of Health and Social Services
New York	Yes	Qualified disinterested person or authorized agency)
North Carolina	Yes	County director of social services or authorized agency
North Dakota	Yes	Public Welfare Board, county welfare board, licensed child placement agency or other qualified agency or person designated by the court
Ohio	Yes	"next friend"
Oklahoma	Yes (except when child is natural or adopted child of either petitioner)	Agency with custody or legal guardianship; otherwise state Dept. of Public Welfare or person qualified by training or experience designated by Court

Chart 6 cont.

STATE	Is Investigation Required?	Who Must Investigate?
Oregon	Yes	State Child Services Division
Pennsylvania	Yes	A local public or consenting private child-care agency, State Dept. of Public Welfare, or appropriate person designated by Ct. (Ct. may accept the placing agency report in lieu)
Puerto Rico	Yes	A government public welfare agency.
Rhode Island	Yes (except certain relative adoptions)	State department of social and rehabilitative services. If child has been placed by a licensed child placing agency, court may accept agency's investigation
South Dakota	Yes	Division of child welfare, probation officer or other discreet and competent person
Tennessee	Yes	County Director of Public Welfare or licensed placement agency; Court may waive in relative or stepparent adoption
Texas	Yes	Any state agency, including State Dept. of Public Welfare, a private agency or person appointed by the court

STATE	Is Investigation Required?	Who Must Investigate?
Utah	Yes (unless licensed placement agency's consent is filed or petitioner is spouse of natural parent)	Dept. of Public Welfare
Vermont	Yes (Court may waive)	Dept. of Social and Rehabilitation Services (or licensed placement agency designated by it) (Dept. may waive on court's request)
South Carolina	Yes	S.C. Children's Bureau; private or public welfare organization which cares for and places children, or a representative designated by the court
Virginia	Yes	Commissioner of Public Welfare, or, in Ct.'s discretion, agency which placed child; on Commissioner's request, a local superintendent or other welfare agency of a county or city or agency that placed child must make the investigation
Washington	Yes	Approved agency, qualified salaried court employee or other suitable and proper person

Chart 6 cont.

STATE	Is Investigation Required?	Who Must Investigate?
West Virginia	Yes	Suitable person or agency designated by court
Wisconsin	Yes	State Dept. of Public Welfare, licensed child-welfare agency or a county welfare dept. or children's board (investigation not required when guardian required to make recommendation files favorable one and said guardian is either State department of health and social services, licensed child-welfare agency, county welfare dept. or children's board)
Wyoming	Yes	Dept. of Public Welfare or private agency appointed by Ct. (in court's discretion)

Chart 7

INTERLOCUTORY DECREES AND TRIAL RESIDENCE REQUIREMENTS

STATE	Interlocutory Decree?	Period Before Final Order	Intervening Supervision?	Other Trial Residence Required?	How Long?
Alabama	Yes	Six months	Yes	No	
Alaska	No			No	
Arizona	No			No	
Arkansas	Yes	Six months		No	
California	No			No	
Colorado	Yes [4]	Six months		No	
Connecticut	Yes [4]	12-13 months from application		No	
Delaware	No		Yes	Yes	One year (may be reduced to six months)
District of Columbia	Yes [4]	Six months	Yes	Yes	Six months

Chart 7 cont.

STATE	Interlocutory Decree?	Period Before Final Order	Intervening Supervision?	Other Trial Residence Required?	How Long?
Florida	No			Yes	Petition heard after 90 days residence under supervision of Department of health and rehabilitative services (with certain exceptions)
Georgia	No			No	
Hawaii	No[5]			Yes	(No set time, in the discretion of the court)
Idaho	No			No	
Illinois	Yes	Six months			
Indiana	No		By approved agency for period set by court		
Iowa	No			Yes	12 months (court may shorten or waive)

STATE	Interlocutory Decree?	Period Before Final Order	Intervening Supervision?	Other Trial Residence Required?	How Long?
Kansas	No			No	
Kentucky	No			Yes	Three months just before petition
Louisiana	Yes	At least six months	At least twice	Yes	One year
Maine	No		Court may require supervision	Yes	One year (in Ct.'s discretion)
Maryland	Yes (in Ct.'s discretion)	Not more than one year		No	
Massachusetts	No			Yes	6 months (Ct. may waive for cause)
Michigan	Yes	One year (Ct. may waive, or extend for a time not longer than two years, in best interests of child)	Yes	No	
Minnesota	No			Yes	Six months (Ct. may waive)

Chart 7 cont.

STATE	Interlocutory Decree?	Period Before Final Order	Intervening Supervision?	Other Trial Residence Required?	How Long?
Mississippi	Yes	Six months (except in adoption of stepchild or child related within third degree or any case where chancellor deems it unnecessary; period may also be shortened by time child in adopters' home before interlocutory decree)	Yes (discretionary with the court)	No	
Missouri	No			Yes	Nine months
Montana	Yes	Six months (in stepchild or blood relative adoptions, or if court finds it in child's best interests, court may, after examining investigative report		No	

STATE	Interlocutory Decree?	Period Before Final Order	Intervening Supervision?	Other Trial Residence Required?	How Long?
		waive interlocutory decree and six months period and grant final decree)			
Nebraska	No			Yes	Six months immediately preceding decree
Nevada	No			Yes	Six months
New Hampshire	Yes (not required if petitioner or spouse is natural parent of the child)	Six months	Yes	No	
New Jersey	No (agency adoption) Yes (otherwise, except where a-dopter is brother, sister, aunt, uncle, grandparent, step-parent (Ct. may waive)	One year (if adoptee lived continuously with adopter since before Jan. 1, 1954, period may be less)	Yes	Yes	Six months

Chart 7 cont.

STATE	Interlocutory Decree?	Period Before Final Order	Intervening Supervision?	Other Trial Residence Required?	How Long?
New Mexico	No			Yes	Six mos. (if child under one year, until that age is reached) (on motion, and for good cause shown, or where petitioner is non-resident, Ct. may make such residence requirements as may be convenient and proper)
New York	No			Yes	Six months (child under 18, but Ct. may waive)
North Carolina	Yes[1]	One year[2]	Yes	Yes	One year[1,2]
North Dakota	No			Yes	Six months (not required in stepparent adoptions)

STATE	Interlocutory Decree?	Period Before Final Order	Intervening Supervision?	Other Trial Residence Required?	How Long?
Ohio	Yes (except in stepchild adoptions or where child placed in adopter's home six months under agency supervision)	Six months	Yes	Yes	Six months
Oklahoma	Yes (May be waived by the court if child is a stepchild of, or a blood relative of one of the petitioners of if a waiver is in the child's best interest)	Six months		No	
Oregon	No			No	
Pennsylvania	No			Yes	Six months (except relative adoption or if adoptee is 18 years or older)

Chart 7 cont.

STATE	Interlocutory Decree?	Period Before Final Order	Intervening Supervision?	Other Trial Residence Required?	How Long?
Puerto Rico	Yes	Six months	Yes	No	
Rhode Island	No			Yes	Six months (waivable by Ct. for good cause)
South Carolina	Yes	Six months (interlocutory decree and waiting period waivable by Ct. in stepchild or relative adoptions or in best interests of child)	Yes	No	
South Dakota	No			Yes	Six months
Tennessee	Yes	One year from interlocutory decree and within two years of filing petition [3]	Yes	No	
Texas	No			Yes	Six months (Ct. may waive)

STATE	Interlocutory Decree?	Period Before Final Order	Intervening Supervision?	Other Trial Residence Required?	How Long?
Utah	No			Yes	One year
Vermont	No			Yes	Six months (Ct. may certify as unnecessary)
Virginia	Yes	Six months (except stepparent adoptions and agency adoptions where child in petitioners' home six mos. and visited three times, or where child 12 yrs. old and in home five years)		Yes	Six months
Washington	Yes			No	
West Virginia	No	Six months		Yes	Six months

Chart 7 cont.

STATE	Interlocutory Decree?	Period Before Final Order	Intervening Supervision?	Other Trial Residence Required?	How Long?
Wisconsin	No			Yes	Six months (unless petitioner is step-parent or blood relative, or guardian's approval filed)
Wyoming	Yes	Six months [6]		Yes	Six months

[1] May be waived if child is 6 years old and has lived with the petitioners at least five years.

[2] In placement agency adoptions, may deduct time child has been in petitioners' home.

[3] Court may waive in adoptions of stepchild, grandchild, nephew or niece, or if child in petitioners' home for more than one year before filing of the petition.

[4] In court's discretion.

[5] Court *may* postpone effective date of final decree until six months after it is rendered.

[6] Court may waive if child is a stepchild of, or a blood relative of one of the petitioners or if a waiver is in the child's best interest, and the child has resided in petitioners' home for six months.

Chart 8

COMMON LAW MARRIAGES

States which recognize Common Law Marriages

Alabama	Kansas[1]	Rhode Island
Colorado	Montana	South Carolina
Georgia	Ohio	Texas
Idaho	Oklahoma	District of Columbia
Iowa	Pennsylvania	

States in which Common Law Marriages are
Recognized Conditionally

Alaska	(if entered into before 1917)
California	(if entered into before 1895)
Florida	(if entered into before January 1, 1968)
Indiana	(if entered into before January 1, 1958)
Michigan	(if entered into before January 1, 1957)
Minnesota	(if entered into before April 26, 1941)
Missouri	(if entered into before March 31, 1921)
Nebraska	(if entered into before March 31, 1921)
New Jersey	(if entered into before December 1, 1939)
New York	(if entered into before April 29, 1933)
South Dakota	(if entered into before July 1, 1959)

States which do not recognize Common Law Marriage

Arizona	Maryland	Utah
Arkansas	Massachusetts	Vermont
California	Nevada	Virginia
Connecticut	New Hampshire	Washington
Delaware	New Mexico	West Virginia
Hawaii	North Carolina	Wisconsin
Illinois	North Dakota	Wyoming
Kentucky[2]	Oregon	Puerto Rico
Louisiana	Tennessee	

---

[1] But the parties are subject to punishment for not obtaining a license.

[2] In Kentucky, common law marriages are valid only for the purposes of the Workmen's Compensation Law.

Chart 9

LEGAL AGE FOR MARRIAGE AND LICENSE REQUIREMENTS

State	Minimum Age F	Minimum Age M	Parental Consent Required if Below Age of: F	Parental Consent Required if Below Age of: M	Medical Required for License	Waiting Period Before License	Waiting Period After License
Alabama	14	17	18	21	yes	no	no
Alaska	16	18	18	19	yes	yes--3 days	no
Arizona	16	16	18	18	yes	no	no
Arkansas	16	17	18	21	yes	yes--3 days	no
California	16	18	18	21	yes	no	no
Colorado	16	16	18	18	yes	no	no
Connecticut	16	16	18	18	yes	yes--4 days	no
Delaware	16	18	18	18	yes	no	yes*
District of Columbia	16	18	18	21	yes	yes--3 days	no
Florida	16	18	21	21	yes	yes--3 days	no
Georgia	16	18	18	18	yes	yes--3 days	3 days if under age

* 24 hours for residents; 96 hours for out-of-state residents

State	Minimum Age F	M	Parental Consent Required if Below Age of: F	M	Medical Required for License	Waiting Period Before License	Waiting Period After License
Hawaii	16	17	18	18	yes	no	no
Idaho	16	16	18	18	yes	no	no
Illinois	16	—	18	18	yes	no	no
Indiana	17	17	18	18	yes	yes--3 days	no
Iowa	16	18	18	18	yes	yes--3 days	no
Kansas	18	18	18	18	yes	yes--3 days	no
Kentucky	16	18	18	18	yes	yes--3 days	no
Louisiana	16	18	18	18	yes	no	yes--72 hours
Maine	16	16	18	18	yes	yes--5 days	no
Maryland	16	18	18	21	no	yes--48 hours	no
Massachusetts	12	14	18	18	yes	yes--3 days	no
Michigan	16	—	18	18	yes	yes--3 days	no
Minnesota	16	18	18	18	no	yes--5 days	no
Mississippi	15	17	21	21	yes	yes--3 days	no
Missouri	15	15	18	21	yes	yes--3 days	no
Montana	16	18	18	21	yes	yes--5 days	no
Nebraska	16	18	19	19	yes	yes--5 days	no
Nevada	16	18	18	18	no	no	no

Chart 9 cont.

State	Minimum Age F	Minimum Age M	Parental Consent Required if Below Age of: F	Parental Consent Required if Below Age of: M	Medical Required for License	Waiting Period Before License	Waiting Period After License
New Hampshire	13	14	18	18	yes	yes--5 days	no
New Jersey	16	16	18	18	yes	yes--72 hours	no
New York	14	16	18	21	yes	no	yes--24 hours
New Mexico	16	16	18	18	yes	no	no
North Carolina	16	16	18	18	yes	no	no
North Dakota	15	18	18	18	yes	no	no
Ohio	16	18	18	18	yes	yes--5 days	no
Oklahoma	15	18	18	21	yes	no	no
Oregon	15	18	18	18	yes	yes--7 days	no
Pennsylvania	16	16	18	18	yes	yes--3 days	no
Puerto Rico	16	18	21	21	yes	no	no
Rhode Island	16	18	18	18	yes	yes--5 days	no
South Carolina	14	16	18	18	no	yes--24 hours	no
South Dakota	16	18	18	18	yes	no	no
Tennessee	16	16	18	18	yes	yes--3 days	no
Texas	16	16	18	18	yes	no	no
Utah	14	16	18	21	yes	no	yes--5 days
Vermont	16	18	18	18	yes	no	no

State	Minimum Age		Parental Consent Required if Below Age of:		Medical Required for License	Waiting Period Before License	Waiting Period After License
	F	M	F	M			
Virginia	16	18	18	18	yes	no	no
Washington	17	17	18	18	no	yes--3 days	no
West Virginia	16	18	18	18	yes	yes--3 days	no
Wisconsin	16	18	18	18	yes	yes--5 days	no
Wyoming	16	18	21	21	yes	no	no

Chart 10

DEGREES OF RELATIONSHIP WITHIN WHICH MARRIAGES ARE PROHIBITED

Relationships within which a man (or woman within corresponding degrees) is prohibited from marriage:

	All States
	Grandmother
	Mother
	Daughter
	Granddaughter
	Aunt
	Niece
	Sister
	Half-sister
ALABAMA	Step-mother
	Step-daughter
	Wife's granddaughter
	Daughter-in-law
ALASKA	Grand-aunt
	First Cousin
	Grand-niece
	First Cousin once removed
	Second Cousin
ARIZONA	First Cousin
ARKANSAS	First Cousin
DELAWARE	First Cousin
DISTRICT OF COLUMBIA	Step-mother
	Step-daughter
	Step-grandmother
	Grandson's wife
	Mother-in-law
	Wife's grandmother
	Wife's granddaughter
	Daughter-in-law

GEORGIA	Step-mother Step-daughter Mother-in-law Grandmother Daughter-in-law
IDAHO:	First Cousin
ILLINOIS	First Cousin
INDIANA	Grand-aunt First Cousin Grand-niece First Cousin once removed
IOWA	First Cousin Step-mother Step-daughter Grandson's wife Mother-in-law Daughter-in-law
KANSAS	First Cousin
KENTUCKY	First Cousin Grand-aunt Grand-niece First Cousin once removed
LOUISIANA	First Cousin
MAINE	Step-mother Step-daughter Grandfather's wife Grandson's wife Mother-in-law Wife's grandmother Wife's granddaughter Daughter-in-law
MARYLAND	Step-mother Step-daughter Grandfather's wife

Chart 10 cont.

	Grandson's wife
	Mother-in-law
	Wife's grandmother
	Wife's granddaughter
	Daughter-in-law
MASSACHUSETTS	Step-mother
	Step-daughter
	Grandfather's wife
	Grandson's wife
	Mother-in-law
	Wife's grandmother
	Wife's granddaughter
	Daughter-in-law
MICHIGAN	First Cousin
MINNESOTA	Grand-aunt
	First Cousin
	Grand-niece
	First Cousin once removed
MISSISSIPPI:	First Cousin
	Step-mother
	Step-daughter
MISSOURI	First Cousin
MONTANA	First Cousin
NEBRASKA	First Cousin
NEVADA	First Cousin
	Grand-aunt
	Grand-niece
	First Cousin once removed
NEW HAMPSHIRE	First Cousin
	Step-mother
	Step-daughter
	Grandson's wife
	Mother-in-law
	Daughter-in-law

NORTH CAROLINA	First Cousin
	Double First Cousin
NORTH DAKOTA	First Cousin
OHIO	Grand-aunt
	First Cousin
	Grand-niece
	First Cousin once removed
OKLAHOMA	First Cousin
	Step-mother
	Step-daughter
OREGON	Grand-aunt
	Grand-niece
	First Cousin
PENNSYLVANIA	First Cousin
	Step-mother
	Step-daughter
	Wife's granddaughter
	Daughter-in-law
RHODE ISLAND	Step-mother
	Step-daugher
	Grandfather's wife
	Grandson's wife
	Mother-in-law
	Wife's grandmother
	Wife's granddaughter
	Daughter-in-law
SOUTH CAROLINA	Step-mother
	Step-daughter
	Grandfather's wife
	Grandson's wife
	Mother-in-law
	Wife's grandmother
	Wife's granddaughter
	Daughter-in-law

Chart 10 cont.

SOUTH DAKOTA	First Cousin
	First Cousin once removed
	Step-mother
	Step-daughter
TENNESSEE	Grand-niece
	Step-mother
	Grandfather's Wife
	Wife's Grandmother
	Wife's Granddaughter
	Daughter-in-law
	Grandson's wife
TEXAS	Step-mother
	Step-daughter
	Wife's Granddaughter
	Daughter-in-law
UTAH	Grand-aunt
	Grand-niece
	First Cousin
VERMONT	Step-mother
	Step-daughter
	Grandfather's Wife
	Grandson's Wife
	Mother-in-law
	Wife's Grandmother
	Wife's Granddaughter
	Daughter-in-law
VIRGINIA	Step-mother
	Daughter-in-law
	Step-daughter
	Wife's Niece
	Wife's Granddaughter
WASHINGTON	First Cousin
	First Cousin once removed
	Grand-aunt
	Grand-niece
WEST VIRGINIA	First Cousin
	Double First Cousin

WISCONSIN	First Cousin (unless female is 55 years old)
	Double First Cousin
	First Cousin once removed
WYOMING	First Cousin
PUERTO RICO	Adopted Daughter
	First Cousin
VIRGIN ISLANDS	Grandfather's wife
	Grandson's wife
	Wife's grandmother
	Wife's granddaughter
	Step-mother
	Step-daughter
	Mother-in-law
	Daughter-in-law

Chart 11

MARRIAGES WHICH ARE PROHIBITED ON RACIAL GROUNDS (PERSON OF CAUCASIAN RACE AND OTHER RACE)[1]

NEGRO	Alabama
	Arkansas
	Georgia
	Mississippi
	North Carolina
	South Carolina
	Tennessee
	West Virginia
ORIENTAL OR MONGOLIAN	Georgia
	Mississippi
AMERICAN INDIAN	Georgia
	North Carolina
	South Carolina

[1] These laws are now void and unenforcible.

Chart 12

STATES PERMITTING
MARRIAGES BY PROXY AND BY CONTRACT

**Proxy
Marriages**

**Marriages
By Contract**

KANSAS: Neither authorized or prohibited and sometimes performed.

NEBRASKA: Permitted if both parties are members of a religious sect recognizing proxy marriage and if performed in accordance with rules of sect.

NEW MEXICO: Opinion by Attorney General upholding validity of proxy marriages but not recommended.

NEW YORK: Not explicitly authorized but not contrary to public policy if valid in state where contracted.

TEXAS: Permitted where one party in Military Service.

PUERTO RICO: Permitted by means of mandate through special power of attorney.

MONTANA: Permitted if formerly acknowledged before a Clerk of Court and 2 witnesses and filed with premarital certificate attached.

NEW YORK: Expressly authorized.

SOUTH CAROLINA: Recognized.

Chart 13

GROUNDS FOR ANNULMENT BY STATES

States in which there are no specific statutory grounds for annulment but in which a court of equity may grant either a declaration of nullity of a void marriage or a decree of judgment annulling a voidable marriage:

ALABAMA
ARIZONA
CONNECTICUT
FLORIDA*
ILLINOIS
MISSOURI
OHIO
RHODE ISLAND

States authorizing specific grounds for granting of annulment:

ARKANSAS	Non-age, insanity at time of ceremony, fraud, force or duress, inability to consummate marriage.
CALIFORNIA	Marriage entered into as a jest or dare or while intoxicated. Non-age, insanity at time of ceremony, fraud, force or duress, previous marriage existing, inability to consummate marriage.
COLORADO	Intoxication, non-age, fraud, force, duress.
DELAWARE	Inability to give consent or consummate the marriage, non-age, prohibited marriage, fraud, coercion, venereal disease or habitual drunkeness or use of narcotic drugs.
DISTRICT OF COLUMBIA	Non-age, insanity at time of ceremony, fraud, force or duress, inability to consummate marriage, marriage within prohibitive degrees of relationship, previous marriage existing.

*A divorce is the remedy where the marriage is either void or voidable.

GEORGIA	Non-age, previous marriage existing, marriage within prohibitive degree of relationship. NOTE: No annulment will be granted when children are born or are to be born as a result of the marriage.
HAWAII	Non-age, insanity at time of ceremony, fraud, force or duress, inability to consummate marriage, marriage within prohibitive degrees of relationship, previous marriage existing, existence of "Loathsome Disease."
IDAHO	Non-age, insanity at time of ceremony, fraud, force or duress, inability to consummate marriage, previous marriage existing.
INDIANA	Non-age, insanity at time of ceremony, fraud or duress.
IOWA	Insanity at time of ceremony, inability to consummate marriage, marriage within prohibitive degrees of relationship, previous marriage existing. In the case of non-age, the marriage may be nullified within six months after the party attains the age of consent.
KANSAS	Previous marriage existing, inability to consummate marriage at the time of the marriage, fraud, marriage within prohibitive degrees of relationship.
KENTUCKY	Fraud, or duress, non-age, marriage prohibited by law, inability to consummate the marriage, inability to consent to the marriage because of mental incapacity or the influence of alcohol or drugs.
LOUISIANA	Force or duress, marriage within prohibitive degrees of relationship, previous marriage existing, mistaken identity.

Chart 13 cont.

MARYLAND	Incest, existing marriage.
MAINE	Incest, insanity, existing marriage, non-age.
MASSACHUSETTS	Prior marriage existing, non-age, marriage within prohibitive degrees of relationship.
MICHIGAN	Non-age, insanity, fraud, force, duress, marriage within prohibitive degrees of relationship.
MINNESOTA	Non-age, lack of understanding at time of marriage, fraud, duress, incest.
MISSISSIPPI	Previous marriage existing, marriage between Caucasian and person of color, marriage within prohibitive degrees of relationship, incurable impotency, insanity or idiocy, failure to procure valid license (if there has been no subsequent cohabitation), fraud, force or duress, inability to consummate marriage at time of marriage provided no ratification of condition, wife pregnant by one other than husband (if no ratification of condition).
MONTANA	Non-age, existing marriage, insanity, fraud, incest, duress, physical incapacity.
NEBRASKA	Non-age, force or duress, fraud, insanity, imbecility or feeble-mindedness, inability to consummate marriage, existing marriage, venereal disease, marriage within prohibited degrees of relationship.
NEVADA	Non-age, inability to consent, fraud, duress, or any ground sufficient to annul an ordinary civil contract such as mutual mistake, impossibility of performance, etc.

NEW HAMPSHIRE	Non-age, and any other ground deemed applicable by court sitting in equity.
NEW JERSEY	Existing marriage, marriage within prohibitive degrees of relationship, inability to consummate marriage, (when not ratified by other party) lack of understanding at time of ceremony due to insanity, alcohol or drugs and not ratified, non-age, fraud, duress.
NEW MEXICO	Non-age, marriage within prohibitive degrees of relationship.
NEW YORK	Non-age, insanity at time of ceremony, fraud, force, duress, physical incapacity and inability to consummate marriage, incurable insanity occuring after marriage and continuing for five years.
NORTH CAROLINA	Impotency, interracial marriages, incestuous marriages, insanity, non-age, mistaken belief that female is pregnant.
NORTH DAKOTA	Non-age, former spouse surviving and marriage in force, unsound mind, fraud, force, physical incapability which incapability seems incurable, incestuous marriage.
OHIO	Non-age, existing marriage, insanity, fraud, duress, or marriage unconsummated.
OKLAHOMA	Non-age or lack of understanding.
OREGON	Injured party may sue for fraud, force, non-age, lack of understanding, or incestuous marriage.
PENNSYLVANIA	Marriages which are void for any reason may be annulled at suit of either party.

Chart 13 cont.

SOUTH CAROLINA

Lack of consent or other cause showing no real contract of marriage entered (provided there is no cohabitation).

SOUTH DAKOTA

Non-age where parents did not consent and the party did not consent or cohabit after coming of age, living spouse, unsound mind (unless after reason there is cohabitation), fraud (unless cohabitation after knowledge of fraud), force unless cohabitation is free, physical incapability which seems to continue and seems to be incurable.

TENNESSEE

Mental incapacity, non-age, duress by actual force or threat, marriage prohibited by law.

TEXAS

Natural or incurable impotency at time of entering marriage or other impediment which renders marriage void.

UTAH

Marriage is prohibited by law (e.g. incestuous), insanity, existing marriage, communicable venereal disease, marriage was not solemnized by an authorized person (may not be annulled if both parties believed the authority existed), non-age, any ground that existed at common law.

VERMONT

Non-age if action started after plaintiff reaches age (cohabitation after age bars the action) idiocy or lunacy, physical incapacity if action started within two years, force or fraud.

VIRGINIA

Living spouse, physical or mental causes deter entering into marriage state, lawful adjudication of insanity, or feeblemindedness, prohibitive degrees of relationship, and for any reason for which the marriage might be declared void.

WASHINGTON	There is no specific statute dealing with annulment, but marriages may be declared invalid for non-age, prior undissolved marriage, incest, inability to consummate the marriage, fraud, duress.
WEST VIRGINIA	Former spouse living and undivorced at marriage, consanguinity, insane, feeble-minded, idiot, imbecile, epileptic or venereal disease at time of marriage, natural or incurable impotency, non-age, spouse without knowledge of other convicted of an infamous crime, wife pregnant by other than husband and husband doesn't know, notorious prostitute, husband licentious without knowledge of spouse.
WISCONSIN	Incurable impotency or incapacity of copulation at suit of either party, provided suing party was ignorant at time of marriage, consanguinity, previous spouse living, fraud, force, coercion at suit of innocent, lack of understanding unless after reason person affirms marriage, under 16 years unless validated by compliance, at suit of guardian or party if marriage occurred without consent, provided suit started before party reaches 18 and within one year of marriage, any other marriages void or prohibited.
WYOMING	Non-age if parties separate during non-age and do not cohabit thereafter, force or fraud and no voluntary cohabitation after force or knowledge of fraud, physical incapacity at time of marriage.
PUERTO RICO	No specific statute for annulment: governed by general laws of contract.

Chart 13 cont.

VIRGIN ISLANDS   If ceremony performed in the district and plaintiff is an inhabitant when action is commenced, or if performed elsewhere, when the plaintiff has been an inhabitant for 6 weeks prior to commencement of action, on equitable grounds, or of void or prohibited marriages (e.g. incest, existing marriage, non-age, fraud, duress, impotency).

Chart 14

GROUNDS FOR SEPARATION BY STATES

ALABAMA	Cruelty or any cause justifying divorce, if plaintiff desires separation only.
ALASKA	No statutory right to separation.
ARIZONA	Any ground for absolute divorce, if other party does not object to separation decree.
ARKANSAS	No statutory right to separation, but support proceeding may be maintained.
CALIFORNIA	Any ground for divorce and willful desertion for periods not sufficiently long to authorize divorce.
COLORADO	Any ground authorizing a divorce.
CONNECTICUT	Any ground authorizing a divorce.
DELAWARE	No statutory right to separation.
DISTRICT OF COLUMBIA	Any grounds justifying an absolute divorce and cruelty.
FLORIDA	No statutory right to separation.
GEORGIA	No statutory right to separation.
HAWAII	Separation for a period not to exceed two years may be decreed for any ground on which an absolute divorce may be granted.
IDAHO	No statutory right to a separation, but wife may apply for an order of support.
ILLINOIS	Living separate and apart.
INDIANA	No statutory right to separation.
IOWA	Any ground authorizing a divorce.
KANSAS	Any ground authorizing a divorce.

Chart 14 cont.

KENTUCKY	Any ground authorizing a divorce or any other reason which the Court may deem sufficient.
LOUISIANA	Adultery, conviction of felony and imprisonment, habitual intemperance, cruelty, public defamation of other spouse, abandonment, attempt on life of other spouse, indictment for felony and flight from the state, intentional non-support, one year actual separation.
MAINE	Desertion for one year or living apart for one year for justifiable cause.
MARYLAND	Cruelty, excessively vicious conduct, abandonment and desertion, separation without hope of reconciliation.
MASSACHUSETTS	Non-support, desertion, living apart for justifiable cause.
MICHIGAN	Extreme cruelty, desertion for two years, failure to support.
MINNESOTA	No statutory right to separation.
MISSISSIPPI	No statutory right to separation.
MISSOURI	No statutory right to separation, but Court may permit action for separate maintenance.
MONTANA	Any ground authorizing a divorce.
NEBRASKA	No statutory provision.
NEVADA	No action for separation, but wife may sue for separate maintenance if she has been deserted for 90 days or has grounds sufficient to authorize a divorce.
NEW HAMPSHIRE	Any ground authorizing a divorce.
NEW JERSEY	Any ground authorizing a divorce.

NEW MEXICO	Parties permanently separated and no longer cohabiting.
NEW YORK	Cruel and inhuman treatment, conduct rendering cohabitation unsafe, abandonment, non-support, adultery, confinement in prison (3).
NORTH CAROLINA	Abandonment, maliciously turning other spouse out of doors, cruel and barbarous treatment endangering life, indignities rendering life burdensome and conditions incorrigible and habitual drunkenness, excessive use of drugs.
NORTH DAKOTA	Any grounds sufficient to authorize a divorce.
OHIO	No statutory right to separation.
OKLAHOMA	Any ground authorizing a divorce.
OREGON	Same as for divorce.
RHODE ISLAND	Any cause authorizing a divorce, or any cause deemed by the Court to be sufficient, or support without divorce when either party insane, or where condition exists which if continued will authorize divorce.
SOUTH CAROLINA	No statutory right to separation.
SOUTH DAKOTA	Any grounds authorizing a divorce and in addition, in an action for divorce, the Court may provide maintenance of wife and children although denying a divorce.
TENNESSEE	Cruel and inhuman treatment, indignities rendering cohabitation intolerable abandonment or turning out of doors, failing to provide.
TEXAS	No statutory right to separation although proceeding may be brought to fix legal

Chart 14 cont.

	custody and support of children.
UTAH	Desertion, non-support, wife living apart without fault.
VERMONT	Any cause justifying a divorce.
VIRGINIA	Cruelty, reasonable apprehension of bodily harm, abandonment or desertion.
WASHINGTON	No statutory right to separation.
WEST VIRGINIA	No statutory right to separation.
WISCONSIN	Any grounds authorizing a divorce.
WYOMING	Any grounds authorizing a divorce.
PUERTO RICO	No statutory right to separation.
VIRGIN ISLANDS	Any grounds authorizing a divorce.

Chart 15

TIME OF RESIDENCE

(minimum time of residence required before
divorce proceedings may be instituted)

ALABAMA	Six months if defendant non-resident; no requirement if plaintiff and actual domiciliary and Court has jurisdiction of defendant.
ALASKA	One year
ARIZONA	Ninety days
ARKANSAS	Sixty days
CALIFORNIA	Six months
COLORADO	Ninety days
CONNECTICUT	One year (None if cause of action arose in the state or plaintiff lived in the state at the time of marriage and has returned with the intention of remaining permanently).
DELAWARE	One year
DISTRICT OF COLUMBIA	One year
FLORIDA	Six months
GEORGIA	Six months
HAWAII	One year
IDAHO	Six weeks
ILLINOIS	One year except where offense committed in Illinois in which event six months will suffice.
INDIANA	Six months
IOWA	One year (except where defendant is a resident of Iowa and is served personally within the State)

Chart 15 cont.

KANSAS	Six months
KENTUCKY	One hundred and eighty days
LOUISIANA	Two years where divorce sought on grounds of two years' living separate and apart. On other grounds no specific requirement.
MAINE	Six months (If parties married in Maine or cohabited there after marriage, or if defendant is a resident, there would be no residence requirements).
MARYLAND	One year where cause of action arose outside the state, otherwise actual residence suffices. Two years where insanity is ground.
MASSACHUSETTS	Two years
MICHIGAN	One hundred and eighty days unless parties married in state and resided in state from time of marriage until time for filing of divorce.
MINNESOTA	One year except for adultery committed while plaintiff a resident of the State.
MISSISSIPPI	One year
MISSOURI	Ninety days
MONTANA	One year
NEBRASKA	One year, but may be waived in marriage solemnized within state and one of the parties has resided in state since marriage.
NEVADA	Six weeks
NEW HAMPSHIRE	One year except where both parties domiciled in state when action commenced or plaintiff actually domiciled and defendant served personally with process within the state.
NEW JERSEY	One year except for adultery.

NEW MEXICO	Six months
NEW YORK	Action may be brought if both parties reside in N.Y. and the cause of action arose there. If the marriage took place in N.Y. or parties resided as husband or wife there, or the cause of action arose in N.Y., it may be brought after either party has resided in N.Y. for one year. Otherwise either party must be a N.Y. resident for two years.
NORTH CAROLINA	Six months
NORTH DAKOTA	One year except on grounds of insanity (and respondent is confined outside the state) where five years required.
OHIO	Six months
OKLAHOMA	Six months
OREGON	Six months
PENNSYLVANIA	One year
RHODE ISLAND	Two years, but if defendant a resident for two years preceding commencement of action and served personally within state, no residence requirement for plaintiff.
SOUTH CAROLINA	One year, either plaintiff or defendant.
SOUTH DAKOTA	Plaintiff must be resident of the state until the decree is entered.
TENNESSEE	Six months
TEXAS	Six months
UTAH	Three months
VERMONT	Six months before commencement of action and one year before final hearing, two years if on grounds of insanity.

Chart 15 cont.

VIRGINIA	Six months
WASHINGTON	Plaintiff must reside in state.
WEST VIRGINIA	None on grounds of adultery, if defendant is personally served; otherwise one year. For any other cause one year.
WISCONSIN	Two years
WYOMING	Sixty days
PUERTO RICO	One year
VIRGIN ISLANDS	Six weeks

Chart 16

GROUNDS FOR DIVORCE BY STATE

(The figures in parentheses indicate the number of years for
which the condition complained of must have existed.)

ALABAMA

Irretrievable breakdown of the marriage, adultery, impotence or incapacity, physical violence, abandonment (1), imprisonment (for 2 years under a sentence of 7 years), habitual drunkenness or drug addiction, crime against nature, insanity (5), pregnancy of the wife at the time of marriage without the knowledge or agency of the husband, nonsupport (2), complete incompatibility, legal separation (2).

ALASKA

Adultery, impotence, conviction of a felony, willful desertion (1), cruelty, personal indignities, incompatibility of temperament, habitual and gross drunkenness (1), incurable mental illness and confinement to institution (1½), drug addiction.

ARIZONA

The marriage is irretrievably broken.

ARKANSAS

Adultery, impotence, desertion (1), prior undissolved marriage, conviction of felony or infamous crime, habitual drunkenness (1); cruelty, indignities, living separate and apart without cohabitation and regardless of consent (3); willful non-support, living apart due to incurable insanity (3).

CALIFORNIA

Irreconcilable differences and incurable insanity.

COLORADO

Irretrievable breakdown of the marriage.

CONNECTICUT

Marriage is irretrievably broken, living apart (1½), adultery, fraud in the marriage contract, willful desertion and neglect (1); disappearance or unexplained absence (7); habitual intemperance, intolerable cruelty, sentence to life imprisonment, imprisonment for infamous crime involving violation of conjugal duty, legal confinement due to mental illness (5).

Chart 16 cont.

DELAWARE
Court will grant divorce if it finds that the marriage is irretrievably broken because of separation, incompatibility, insanity or misconduct of the other party, (adultery, bigamy, conviction of crime, homosexuality, venereal disease, excessive use of alcohol or drugs or other grave offenses).

DISTRICT OF COLUMBIA
Adultery, desertion (1); voluntary separation from bed and board without cohabitation (1); felony conviction and sentence (2); separation under decree of separation (1); on application by innocent spouse.

FLORIDA
Marriage is irretrievably broken, mental incompetence (3).

GEORGIA
Adultery, incestuous marriage, mental incapacity at the time of marriage, impotence, force, coercion or fraud in obtaining the marriage; pregnancy at marriage unknown to husband; willful desertion (1); conviction of felony (2); habitual intoxication, cruelty, adjudication of incurable insanity and confinement to a mental institution (2), habitual use of drugs, marriage irretrievably broken.

HAWAII
Marriage irretrievably broken, living apart either voluntarily or pursuant to separation decree (2).

IDAHO
Adultery, extreme cruelty, willful desertion, willful neglect, habitual intemperance, conviction of a felony, permanent insanity plus confinement (3); living separate and apart without cohabitation (5), irreconcilable differences.

ILLINOIS
Adultery, impotence, prior existing marriage, desertion (1); habitual drunkenness (2); attempt upon life of the other spouse, extreme and repeated cruelty, conviction of a felony or infamous crime; communication of venereal disease, excessive use of drugs (2).

INDIANA
Marriage irretrievably broken, impotency at the time of the marriage, conviction after marriage of an infamous crime, commitment to a hospital or asylum for incurable insanity (2).

IOWA
Irretrievable breakdown of the marriage.

KANSAS
Adultery, abandonment (1); extreme cruelty, fraud, habitual drunkenness, gross neglect of duty, conviction of felony and imprisonment, incurable insanity (3), imcompatibility.

KENTUCKY
Irretrievable breakdown of the marriage.

LOUISIANA
Divorce granted immediately for adultery or conviction of felony and sentence to death or imprisonment at hard labor, or actual physical separation for two years. Divorce granted after living apart following decree of separation for adultery, conviction of felony and sentence to imprisonment, habitual intemperance and cruelty, public defamation, abandonment, attempt on life of spouse, flight from state after indictment for felony, non-support, one year actual separation.

MAINE
Adultery, impotence, extreme cruelty, desertion (3); habitual intoxication or use of drugs, cruel and abusive treatment; non-support, irreconcilable differences.

MARYLAND
Adultery, impotence, void marriage, abandonment without reasonable expectation of reconciliation (1), voluntary separation without possibility of reconciliation (1), conviction of a felony or misdemeanor and imprisonment (18 months); permanent and incurable insanity (3), separation (3).

MASSACHUSETTS
Adultery, impotence, desertion (1); confirmed intoxication (drugs or liquor); cruel or abusive treatment; non-support, imprisonment (5).

MICHIGAN
Irretrievable breakdown of the marriage.

MINNESOTA
Irretrievable breakdown of the marriage.

Chart 16 cont.

MISSISSIPPI

Adultery, impotence, sentence to penitentiary, desertion (1); habitual drunkenness; habitual excessive use of drugs; habitual cruel and inhuman treatment, insanity or idiocy at the time of marriage, prior undissolved marriage, pregnancy by a person other than the husband at the time of marriage, consanguinity, incurable insanity (3).

MISSOURI

Marriage is irretrievably broken.

MONTANA

Adultery, extreme cruelty consisting of an infliction or threat of infliction of grievous bodily injury or personal violence, false charges against the chastity of the wife, infliction of grievous mental suffering (1); willful desertion (1); willful neglect (1); habitual intemperance (1); conviction of a felony, irreconcilable differences causing breakdown of the marriage (6 months), incurable insanity coupled with confinement to an institution (5).

NEBRASKA

Marriage is irretrievably broken.

NEVADA

Insanity (2); living separate and apart without cohabitation (1), incompatibility.

NEW HAMPSHIRE

Irreconcilable differences causing irremediable breakdown of the marriage, adultery, impotence, extreme cruelty, conviction and imprisonment for felony (1); cruelty as to endanger health or seriously endanger reason, unheard of absence (2); habitual drunkenness (2); joining any religious sect or society which professes to believe the relation of husband and wife unlawful and refusal to cohabit (½); abandonment and refusal to cohabit (2); absence of either party without the consent of the other (2); absence of the husband without making provision for support of the wife (2); absence of the wife beyond State without husband's consent (10); husband, non-support and absence (2), husband leaving country without leaving means of support to wife.

NEW JERSEY

Adultery, desertion (1), cruelty (3 mos.), separation (1½), drug addiction (1), drunkenness (1), confined to mental institution (2), imprisonment (1½), deviant sexual behavior without spouse's consent.

NEW MEXICO
Adultery, impotence, cruel or inhuman treatment, incompatibility, abandonment.

NEW YORK
Cruel and inhuman treatment; desertion of the plaintiff by the defendant (1); confinement of the defendant to prison after the marriage (3); the voluntary commission of an act of adultery (including deviate sexual intercourse), living apart pursuant to a decree of separation (1); living separate and apart pursuant to a separation agreement, (1).

NORTH CAROLINA
Adultery, impotence, pregnancy of the wife by another, continuous separation (1); separation without cohabitation by reason of incurable insanity (5); commission of a crime against nature.

NORTH DAKOTA
Adultery, extreme cruelty, willful desertion (1); willful neglect (1); conviction of a felony; incurable insanity coupled with confinement in an institution (5); irreconcilable differences.

OHIO
Prior undissolved marriage, willful absence (1); adultery, impotence, extreme cruelty, fraud in the marriage contract, gross neglect of the marital duty, habitual drunkenness, imprisonment in penitentiary, procurement of a divorce outside the state; confinement to mental institution (4), living apart (2).

OKLAHOMA
Abandonment (1); adultery, impotence, pregnancy of the wife by another, extreme cruelty, fraudulent marriage contract, incompatability; habitual drunkenness, gross neglect of the marital duties, imprisonment under sentence for a felony at the time of the filing of the petition; procurement of a final decree of divorce without the state, insanity and confinement in a mental institution (5).

OREGON
Irreconcilable differences causing breakdown of marriage.

Chart 16 cont.

PENNSYLVANIA

Adultery, incapacity to procreate, an existing prior marriage, desertion (2); cruel and barbarous treatment endangering the life of the other, indignities to the other rendering conditions intolerable and life burdensome, uncondoned force, fraud or coercion, conviction of certain statutory crimes with a sentence of two years or more, incest, insanity with confinement (3).

RHODE ISLAND

Marriage originally void or voidable, incestuous marriage, either party a convicted criminal, deemed to be or treated as if civilly dead, impotence, adultery, extreme cruelty, willful desertion of either of the parties (5), or for a shorter period of time in the court's discretion, continued drunkenness; habitual and excessive use of drugs, non-support, any other gross misbehavior repugnant to and in violation of the marriage covenant, in the discretion of the court, where the parties have lived separate and apart (5); conviction of felony.

SOUTH CAROLINA

Desertion (1); physical cruelty, habitual use of drugs, habitual drunkenness, separation (3).

SOUTH DAKOTA

Adultery, extreme cruelty, willful desertion (1); willful neglect (1); habitual intemperance (1); conviction of felony, incurable insanity while confined by court order to an institution (5).

TENNESSEE

Adultery, impotence, prior undissolved marriage, desertion (1); conviction of infamous crime, conviction of a felony and sentence to a penitentiary; attempt upon the life of the other by means showing malice, wife's refusal to move with husband to this state while absenting herself from him (2); pregnancy at the time of marriage by another, habitual drunkenness, or use of drugs, living apart pursuant to a decree of separation, without any reconciliation (2).

TEXAS

Adultery, cruel and inhuman treatment, abandonment (3); living separate and apart without cohabitation (7); conviction

TEXAS (continued)
of felony and imprisonment (1); confinement to a mental institution with probability that the spouse will not recover (5), marriage irretrievably broken.

UTAH
Impotence, adultery, willful desertion (1); willful neglect to support, habitual drunkenness, conviction of a felony; extreme cruelty, legally adjudicated permanent insanity, separation under a decree of separate maintenance (3).

VERMONT
Adultery, confinement to State prison (3); extreme cruelty, willful desertion; absence without being heard of (7); non-support, incurable insanity with confinement to institution (5); living separate and apart without fault (6 mos.).

VIRGINIA
Adultery, unnatural acts, impotence, sentence to penitentiary; conviction of an infamous offense prior to marriage unknown to the other spouse, willful desertion (1); pregnancy of wife by another, prostitution by the wife before marriage, separation without cohabitation and without interruption (2).

WASHINGTON
Irretrievable breakdown of the marriage.

WEST VIRGINIA
Adultery, sentence to imprisonment for a felony, desertion (1); extreme cruelty, habitual drunkenness, habitual drug addiction, living separate and apart (2), permanent and incurable insanity.

WISCONSIN
Adultery, sentence and imprisonment (3); willful desertion (1); curel and inhuman treatment; habitual drunkenness (1); voluntarily living separate and apart (1); living separate and apart pursuant to a judgment of legal separation (1), non-support (1), committed to mental institution (1).

WYOMING
Adultery, impotence, conviction of felony and sentence to imprisonment, willful desertion (1); habitual drunkenness, extreme cruelty, neglect and failure to provide for the wife (1); indignities

Chart 16 cont.

WYOMING (continued)

rendering the conditions intolerable, vagrancy of the husband, conviction of a felony or infamous crime prior to the marriage when the facts were unknown at the time of the marriage; pregnancy of the wife by another, incurable insanity and confinement to institution (2); living separate and apart without cohabitation (2).

PUERTO RICO

Adultery, conviction of felony which may involve loss of civil rights, habitual drunkenness or excessive use of drugs, cruel and inhuman treatment, abandonment (1); incurable impotence (before or after marriage); attempt by spouse to corrupt son or prostitute daughter, attempt by husband to prostitute wife, living separate and apart (3); incurable insanity (7).

VIRGIN ISLANDS

Breakdown of the marriage and no likelihood that it can be saved.

Chart 17

GROUNDS FOR DIVORCE BY SUBJECT

(The figures in parentheses indicate the number of years
for which the condition complained of must have existed.)

ABANDONMENT (See ahead, DESERTION)
Alabama (1), Arkansas (1), Idaho, Kansas (1), Maine (3), Maryland (1), Montana (1), New Hampshire (2), North Dakota (1), Ohio (1), Oklahoma (1), Rhode Island (5 or less at discretion of judge), Texas (1), Virginia (1), West Virginia (1), Wyoming (1).

ADULTERY
All jurisdictions (except Indiana, Nevada and South Carolina) that have specific "fault" grounds for divorce. (The definitions and amount of proof required, and nature of defenses including condonation vary from state to state).

ATTEMPT ON LIFE OF SPOUSE OR ENDANGERING LIFE OF SPOUSE
Illinois, Rhode Island, Tennessee.

ATTEMPT TO CORRUPT SON OR DAUGHTER
Puerto Rico.

ATTEMPT TO PROSTITUTE WIFE
Puerto Rico.

CRUELTY
The statutes of the individual states should be examined for definitions of cruelty, extreme cruelty, intolerable cruelty and cruel and inhuman treatment. Often grounds for divorce expressly stated in certain state statutes are able to be included in cruelty and intolerable cruelty in others. For specific coverage as to MENTAL CRUELTY and PHYSICAL CRUELTY, see the captions.

CONVICTION OF FELONY AND IMPRISONMENT
Alabama (for 2 years under a sentence of 7), Arizona (1), Arkansas, Connecticut, District of Columbia, Georgia (2), Idaho, Illinois, Indiana, Kansas, Louisiana, Maryland (18 mos.), Massachusetts (5), Mississippi, Montana, New Hampshire (1), New Jersey (1½), New York (3), North Dakota, Tennessee, Texas (1), Utah, Vermont (3), Virginia, West Virginia, Wisconsin (3), Wyoming, Puerto Rico.

Chart 17 cont.

DEFAMATION OF OTHER SPOUSE
Louisiana (defamation of either spouse), Montana (defamation by husband of wife's chastity).

DESERTION (See definitions for distinction between ABANDONMENT and DESERTION)
THREE YEARS: Maine, Texas, Vermont.
TWO YEARS: Alabama (wife only), Massachusetts.
EIGHTEEN MONTHS: Maryland.
ONE YEAR: Alaska, Arizona, Arkansas, Connecticut, District of Columbia, Georgia, Illinois, Massachusetts, Mississippi, Montana, New York, North Dakota, Ohio, Oklahoma, Puerto Rico, South Carolina, South Dakota, Tennessee, Utah, Virginia, Washington, West Virginia, Wisconsin, Wyoming.
NO TIME LIMIT: Idaho, Louisiana, New Mexico, New Jersey, North Carolina, Vermont.
SPECIAL: Rhode Island (5 years or less in discretion of judge).

DISAPPEARANCE
Connecticut (7), New Hampshire (2), New York (5—this proceeding is called a dissolution rather than a divorce), Vermont (7).

DIVORCE OUT OF STATE BY OTHER PARTY
Ohio, Oklahoma.

FORCE OR DURESS
Georgia, Pennsylvania, Rhode Island.

FRAUD
Connecticut, Georgia, Kansas, Missouri, Ohio, Oklahoma, Pennsylvania, Rhode Island.

HABITUAL DRUNKENNESS
Alabama, Alaska (1), Arkansas (1), Connecticut, Delaware, Georgia, Idaho, Illinois (2), Kansas, Maine, Massachusetts (1), Mississippi, Montana (1), New Hampshire (2), New Jersey (1), North Dakota (1), Ohio, Oklahoma, Oregon (1), Rhode Island, South Carolina, South Dakota (1), Tennessee, Utah, West Virginia, Wisconsin (1), Wyoming, Puerto Rico. In Texas and Washington habitual drunkenness may be alleged under cruelty.

HABITUAL USE OF DRUGS
Alabama, Alaska, Arizona, Arkansas (1), Colorado (1), Connecticut,

HABITUAL USE OF DRUGS (Continued)
Delaware, Georgia, Idaho, Illinois (2), Maine, Massachusetts, Mississippi, New Jersey (1), North Dakota (1), Rhode Island, South Carolina, Puerto Rico, Tennessee, Texas, West Virginia, Wyoming.

INSANITY
Alabama (5), Alaska (1½), Arkansas (3), Connecticut (5), California (5), Delaware (5), Georgia (2), Idaho (3), Indiana (2), Kansas (3), Maryland (3), Mississippi (3), Montana (5), Nevada (2), New Jersey (2), New York (5) Note: In New York this is a "dissolution proceeding" and not a divorce. North Carolina (5), North Dakota (5), Ohio (4), Texas (5), Vermont (5), West Virginia, Wisconsin (1), Wyoming (2), Puerto Rico (7).

IMPOTENCE OR PHYSICAL INCAPACITY
Alabama, Alaska, Arkansas, Georgia, Illinois, Indiana, Maine, Maryland, Massachusetts, Mississippi, New Hampshire, North Carolina, Ohio, Oklahoma, Pennsylvania, Rhode Island, Tennessee, Utah, Virginia, Wyoming, Puerto Rico.

INCESTUOUS MARRIAGE
Georgia, Maryland, Mississippi, Pennsylvania, Rhode Island.

INCOMPATABILITY OF TEMPERAMENT
Alabama, Alaska, Delaware, Kansas, Nevada, New Mexico, Oklahoma, Virgin Islands.

INDIGNITY
Alaska, Arkansas, Montana (grievous mental suffering), Pennsylvania, Wyoming.

JOINING SECT BELIEVING COHABITATION UNLAWFUL
New Hampshire.

LIVING APART
FIVE YEARS: Idaho, Rhode Island.
THREE YEARS: Arkansas, Hawaii, Maine, Maryland, North Dakota, Puerto Rico, South Carolina, Texas.

TWO YEARS: Hawaii, Louisiana, New Hampshire, Ohio, Virginia, West Virginia, Wyoming.
EIGHTEEN MONTHS: Connecticut, New Jersey.
ONE YEAR: District of Columbia, Maryland, Nevada, North Carolina, Wisconsin.

Chart 17 cont.

LIVING APART (Continued)
SIX MONTHS: Vermont.
NO PARTICULAR TIME STATED: Alabama.

LIVING APART UNDER SEPARATION AGREEMENT
New York (1).

LIVING APART PURSUANT TO SEPARATION DECREE OR SEPA-
RATE MAINTENANCE ORDER
Alabama (2), Colorado (3), District of Columbia (1) only on applica-
tion of innocent spouse, Hawaii (2), Louisiana (1) for innocent party;
(14 months) for guilty party, New York (1), Tennessee (2), Utah (3),
Wisconsin (1).

MALFORMATION PREVENTING SEXUAL INTERCOURSE (exten-
sion of impotence or incapacity)
Alabama, New Hampshire, Pennsylvania (if concealed), Rhode Island,
Vermont (if concealed), Wyoming (only within 2 years from marriage).

MENTAL CRUELTY
Alaska, Arkansas, Connecticut, Georgia, Idaho, Illinois, Kansas,
Maine, Mississippi, Montana (1 yr.), New Hampshire, New Jersey,
New Mexico, New York, North Dakota, Ohio, Oklahoma, South
Dakota, Texas, West Virginia, Wisconsin, Wyoming.

MENTAL INCAPACITY
Florida, Georgia, Maryland, Mississippi, Rhode Island, Washington.

"NO FAULT" DIVORCE
Alabama, Arizona, California, Colorado, Connecticut, Delaware,
Florida, Georgia, Hawaii, Idaho, Indiana, Iowa, Kentucky, Maine,
Michigan, Minnesota, Missouri, Montana, New Hampshire, North
Dakota, Oregon, Texas, Washington, Virgin Islands.
See also LIVING APART categories, listed above.

NON-SUPPORT
Alabama (2), Alaska (1), Arizona (1), Arkansas, California (1), Colorado
(1), Delaware (check statute), Hawaii (60 days), Idaho, (described as
wilful neglect), Indiana (2), Kentucky, Maine, Massachusetts, Michigan,
Missouri, Montana (willful neglect - 1), Nebraska, Nevada (1), New
Hampshire (2 - absence also required), New Mexico, North Dakota
(willful neglect - 1), Ohio (gross neglect of marital duty), Rhode Island
(1), South Dakota (willful neglect - 1), Tennessee, Texas, Utah, Vermont,
Washington, Wisconsin, Wyoming (1).

PHYSICAL CRUELTY

All states which have specific "fault" grounds for divorce, except California, Florida, Indiana, Louisiana, North Carolina, Virginia, and Tennessee.

PRIOR UNDISSOLVED MARRIAGE

Arkansas, Delaware, Illinois, Maryland, Mississippi, Ohio, Pennsylvania, Rhode Island, Tennessee, Wyoming.

REFUSAL BY WIFE TO MOVE TO NEW RESIDENCE

Tennessee.

REFUSAL TO COHABIT

New Hampshire.

STERILITY

Mississippi, Utah.

UNNATURAL BEHAVIOR OR CRIME AGAINST NATURE

Alabama, Delaware, New Jersey, North Carolina.

VAGRANCY

Wyoming.

VENEREAL DISEASE

Delaware, Idaho, Illinois (if communicated), Texas (if undisclosed at time of marriage), West Virginia, Wyoming.

VIOLENT TEMPER

Alabama, Montana.

WIFE'S LACK OF CHASTITY

Idaho, Utah, Virginia.

WIFE PREGNANT BY ANOTHER AT TIME OF MARRIAGE (unknown to husband)

Alabama, Georgia, Mississippi, North Carolina, Oklahoma, Rhode Island, Tennessee, Utah, Virginia.

WILLFUL NEGLECT

Connecticut, Idaho, Kansas, Massachusetts, Montana, North Dakota, Ohio, Oklahoma, Rhode Island, South Dakota, Utah, Vermont, Wisconsin, Wyoming.

Chart 18

REMARRIAGE OF DIVORCED SPOUSES

1. States in which there are no restrictions on remarriage:

ALASKA	ILLINOIS	NORTH CAROLINA
ARIZONA	KENTUCKY	OHIO
ARKANSAS	MAINE	RHODE ISLAND
CALIFORNIA	MARYLAND	SOUTH CAROLINA
COLORADO	MISSOURI	SOUTH DAKOTA
CONNECTICUT	MONTANA	TENNESSEE
DELAWARE	NEBRASKA	VERMONT
DISTRICT OF	NEVADA	WASHINGTON
COLUMBIA	NEW HAMPSHIRE	WEST VIRGINIA
FLORIDA	NEW JERSEY	WYOMING
HAWAII	NEW MEXICO	VIRGIN ISLANDS
IDAHO	NEW YORK	

2. Restrictions on remarriage regulated by the Court:

GEORGIA—Judge or jury decides on restrictions, if any.

IOWA—One year restriction unless the Court consents to earlier marriage.

LOUISIANA—Remarriage regulated by the Court, except that wife may not remarry for ten months after decree and where divorce is granted by reason of adultery, the guilty party may never marry the corespondent.

MICHIGAN—Restrictions, if any, provided in decree.

MISSISSIPPI—Court may prohibit guilty party from remarrying.

NORTH DAKOTA—No remarriage allowed by either party unless the Court decree contains provisions permitting remarriage.

UTAH—No remarriage during pendency of appeal, or time allowed for appeal.

3. Remarriage prohibited for fixed period of time:

ALABAMA—Sixty days except that spouses may remarry.

KANSAS—Sixty days.

MASSACHUSETTS—Two years*.

MINNESOTA—Six months.

OKLAHOMA—Six months.

OREGON—Sixty days.

TEXAS—Six months.

---

*MASSACHUSETTS, innocent party may remarry any time, guilty party prohibited from remarrying for two years.

VIRGINIA—Four months restriction against either party, six months restriction against defendant guilty of adultery.

WISCONSIN—Six months.

PUERTO RICO—No restrictions on husband, 301-day restriction on wife.

4. Restrictions against guilty parties:

MASSACHUSETTS—Two years.

NEW YORK—Three years, and then only by Court permission.

LOUISIANA—Party guilty of adultery may never marry corespondent.

PENNSYLVANIA—Party guilty of adultery may never marry corespondent during lifetime of innocent party.

5. Other restrictions.

INDIANA—No license will be issued to a man with dependent children from a prior marriage unless he furnishes proof that he is contributing to their support.

Chapter II
WILLS, TRUSTS, ESTATES
AND ESTATE PLANNING

Through the years there have been changes in the estate laws. They have not been as dramatic as those in other fields such as Family law and have occurred more gradually. Most have been of too technical a nature to cover in a book such as this. Some others of more general interest are dealt with in this chapter.

ALIENS

For some time, most states have had restrictions on the rights of aliens to inherit and dispose of their property. Gradually, as attitudes towards aliens became more temperate, these limitations were abolished in the various states. In 1968 the U.S. Supreme Court ruled on the matter in *Zchernig v. Miller*. There, the court held that an Oregon statute restricting inheritance rights of aliens was unconstitutional, as it constituted undue interference by a state with the federal government's power to conduct foreign affairs. A short summary of state laws relating to inheritance rights of aliens is found in the Chart section.

ANATOMICAL GIFTS

The efficiency of modern scientific and medical technology has resulted in a new field of law relating to the donation of the body or parts of the human body for scientific research. Most states have enacted, with some variations, the Uniform Anatomical Gifts Act. Anyone over eighteen years of age make such gifts. They may be made in a will, but are usually made in a separate document, signed by the donor in the presence of two witnesses. This document may be a card which is carried on the person of the donor. Since many of the donated organs are used for transplants, it is urgent that the donee receive them as soon as possible after the donor's death. Recognizing this, some states permit a notation on a driver's license that he has donated organs for transplants.

Anatomical gift may be revoked in the manner specified by statute, usually by notifying the donee or by destroying the document making the gift.

The next of kin, in the order of priority set forth in the law, may donate a deceased person's organs. They may do so only in the absence of actual notice that the decedent did not wish this done. Their action may also be effectively opposed by next of kin having prior rights.

CHARITABLE GIFTS

Donations to charity were once given only by the very wealthy, motivated by philanthropic motives, tinged with a desire to diminish their estates by tax free gifts. Today, even the average man makes tax free gifts to charity.

The major change over the past twenty years has been in the laws governing the objects of the gifts, the charities themselves. Most large charities are non-profit corporations. Formerly these corporations were subject to laws which related mainly to business corporations and only a few random sections of the law related directly to non-profit corporations. It was usually a hit-and-miss proposition as to which sections of the business corporation law applied to charitable organizations, and to what extent they applied.

Today most states have a separate corporation law for non-profit corporations. They are only allowed to organize for certain specific purposes, and, as in the case of business corporations, must file their charters and amendments and various other reports with state officials. In addition, individuals and corporations soliciting funds for charitable purposes must file reports in most states. Although there are still fraudulent charities, on the whole they are subject to stricter government supervision than they were in the past.

CHILDREN

The rights of children under the laws of intestacy are noted under INTESTACY and have remained fairly constant over the years. Most of the changes relate to the inheritance rights of adopted and illegitimate children.

Adopted Children

For many years the various state laws did not explicitly define the inheritance rights of adopted children. That has changed, now that adoption is becoming more prevalent. Most states have laws stating that adopted children have the same inheritance rights from their adoptive parents and the kin of these parents, as if they were natural children. In addition some states have a provision similar to the one in Oregon, stating that if a will uses phrases such as "issue", "heirs of the body", or similar terms, they will include adopted children, unless a contrary intent is clearly indicated.

In most states a child who has been adopted may not inherit from his natural parents or their kin nor they from him. An exception is made in some states, if one of the natural parents dies, the other remarries and the child is adopted by his stepparent. In such a case the child's inheritance rights from and through his deceased natural parent (and the living one also) would not be affected.

Illegitimate Children

The general rule that the illegitimate child may inherit from his mother and her kin and vice versa, has been codified in most of the state laws. His rights of inheritance from his father and his kin is not so well defined. Some states, such as Indiana, permit inheritance from or through the putative father, if he marries the mother, acknowledges the child as his own, or if the father's paternity is established, during his lifetime, by a court of law. In others, such as California, if the child is acknowledged by the father, in writing, before competent witnesses, he may inherit from his father, but not from the father's kin. Still other states have laws similar to the one in Iowa which provides that an illegitimate child may inherit from his father if he is recognized by the father, as his child, during his lifetime. If the recognition is mutual, then the father can also inherit from the child.

CURTESY

Most states have abolished the common law concept of curtesy (a husbands right to a life estate in his wife's property upon her death).

DOWER

At common law, a wife was entitled to a life estate in one third of her husband's property. This right could not be defeated by a transfer of the property during the husband's life, nor by will. At one time the right of dower existed in all but a few states. Gradually, the concept of dower has been abolished in over three fourths of the states. The spouse still can not be disinherited, as most states give the spouse a right of election against a will. See below. Also see Charts for a summary of state laws relating to curtesy and dower.

ESTATE PLANNING

The estate planning field is a highly complex one, involving a great number of factors which vary from individual to individual. Once the concern of only the very wealthy, in these days of the shrinking dollar, this field is now of great interest to the average man. The prime aim of any estate plan would be to provide the planner and his family with a secure income throughout his life, (particularly during his retirement years) and to provide adequately for his spouse and family after his death.

For the average citizen, his social security benefits and pension fund from the core of his retirement fund. The laws covering both of these have changed greatly during the last two decades. These changes will be covered in a later chapter. In addition, an individual may add to his assets by adequate insurance plans and by a systematic system of saving and investing.

Decreasing the amount of estate taxes which will be paid is another aim of estate planning. Prior to the passage of the Tax Reform Act of 1976, one of the most common methods of doing this was by making lifetime gifts. Under the former law, there were separate rates for gift and estate taxes, the gift tax being the lesser of the two. Also individuals were entitled to an annual exclusion of $3,000 per gift and a lifetime exemption of $30,000, which could be credited against the gift tax. (In the case of a married couple, they could join together in making gifts and have an annual exclusion of $6,000, or a lifetime one of $60,000).

As indicated under TAXES, the Tax Reform Act, which became effective January 1, 1977, enacted a unified schedule for both estate and gift taxes. Although the yearly exclusion of $3,000 is still available under the present law, the making of lifetime gifts is not quite as advantageous as it once was. There are still advantages, however. There may be an income tax saving as presumably the recipient of the gift will be in a lower tax bracket than the donor. Although the gift will be included in the estate of the decedent, for purposes of taxation, the valuation of the gift will be its worth at the time the gift was made. Any appreciation in value between the time it was given and the death of the decedent will not be included in the tax valuation. Also, although the gift is included in the decedent's estate, the gift tax paid will not be so included. As under the former law any gift made within three years of decedent's death shall be considered to have been made in contemplation of death and treated as a testamentary disposition.

We have been discussing federal taxes here. In addition, many states impose these types of taxes and should be checked into before the gifts are made. As you can see the estate planning field is not an ideal one for a do-it-yourselfer. It is fraught with all sorts of legal technicalities, and competent legal advice should be obtained.

GUARDIANS

If a minor's parents die, a guardian must be appointed for him. If a guardian is not appointed by will, the court will appoint one. The guardian is responsible for both the person and property of the minor. If desired, separate guardians may be apppointed, one having control and custody of the child and the other being responsible for his property. The laws concerning guardians vary from state to state. Charts, outlining these laws are found in the Chart Section.

HOMESTEAD EXEMPTION

Most states exempt a certain portion of the land belonging to the head of the family from taxation or attachment by creditors. This exemption usually passes to the surviving spouse. The amount of the exemption has been gradually increasing in the various states. Twenty years ago the homestead allowance in Arkansas and Louisiana was $4,000, now it's $15,000; in Massachusetts it was $4,000, now it's $24,000. The current homestead allowances for all the states are found in the Chart Section.

INTESTACY

If a person dies without a will, he is said to have died intestate. Every state has laws governing the disposition of a person's property if he dies without a will. These laws, sometimes referred to as the "cannons of descent", have remained fairly constant over the years.

To establish intestate rights, the degree of relationship of the claimant to the deceased must be determined. In the United States, the civil law method of computation is used, counting from the decedent up to the common ancestor and then down to the claimant. For instance, a decedent's uncle would be related to him in the third degree.

	1st degree		2nd degree	
Decedent	⟶	Parent	⟶	Grandparent
		3rd degree		↓
				Uncle

An illustration of this method of computation is found in the Chart section.

The general rule is that when persons of equal degree survive, they share equally. Usually in cases of direct descent, if they are of unequal degree, the lesser degree share by representation. Thus, if the decedent was survived by two children and two grandchildren the property would be divided as follows; 1/3 to each of the surviving children and

1/6 to each of the grandchildren (who divide their parent's share).

Although these general rules are followed in most of the states, the intestate rights of spouses, children, parents and brothers and sisters vary from state to state and have undergone some changes over the years.

Rights of Spouse and Children

In all states, the spouse must share the intestate estate with the children of the marriage. The shared portion varies from state to state. In some, such as Colorado, the spouse receives one half of the estate and the children the other half. In others, such as Connecticut, the proportion is 1/3 to the spouse, 2/3 to the children. Some states allow a specific amount to be set aside for the spouse and if there is anything above this amount, it is shared with the children. New York has this type of statute. The spouse is entitled to $2,000 and if one child survives, the residue is shared equally between the spouse and child; if other children survive, the proportion is 1/3 to the spouse, 2/3 to the children. In most community property states, the spouse receives all of the community property and shares the decedent's separate estate with the children in varying proportions.

Rights of Spouse vs. Parents

In most states, the existence of surviving children precludes parents from inheriting any of the decedent's estate. In approximately half the states, even if there are no surviving issue of the decedent, the spouse will inherit the entire estate. In the remaining states the parents and spouse share the varying proportions. Approximately half of these remaining states allow the spouse a specific sum and the rest of the estate is shared with the parents, usually in equal shares. Over the years, the initial sum allowed to the spouse has been gradually increasing. Fifteen years ago the spouse was allowed $5,000 in New York, $10,000 in New Hampshire, $8,000 in Vermont and $25,000 in North Dakota. Now the allowances are $50,000 in New York, New Hampshire, and North Dakota and $20,000 in Vermont.

In the rest of the remaining states, the spouse and the parents share the entire estate in equal portions.

The rights of the surviving spouse and parents are superior to those of brothers and sisters in most of the states. In over one third of the states (if no children or parents survive) the spouse must share the estate with the brothers and sisters of the decedent. In approximately one fifth of the states (if no children or spouse survive) the estate must be shared by the decedent's parents and brothers and sisters.

MARITAL DEDUCTION

The federal law grants a special deduction to surviving spouses. Formerly a deduction up to one half the adjusted estate was allowed. Under the present law which was effective for estates of those dying after January 1, 1977, the deduction is for either one half of the adjusted estate or $250,000, whichever is greater. Depending on the size of the estate, skillful use of this exemption can result in the elimination of all or a substantial amount of federal estate tax. See discussion below under TRUSTS.

1976 Tax Reform Bill, many attorneys used a fairly standard marital deduction clause in wills leaving 50% of the estate to the surviving spouse, many attorneys have found it advisable to check through wills in their files to determine whether they should be amended to qualify for a larger deduction than 50% of the estate. Wills drafted prior to the Tax Reform Act of 1976 should be reviewed to assure that, for estates of less than $500,000, the full benefit of the new law is being utilized.

RIGHT OF ELECTION

In most states if a surviving spouse is dissatisfied with the provisions of a deceased spouse's will, he or she may elect to disregard the will and take a statutory allotment instead of his or her bequest. How this right of election is exercised and what constitutes a spouse's statutory share varies from state to state. See the Chart section for analysis of these laws in each state.

SIMULTANEOUS DEATH ACTS

Most states have adopted the uniform simultaneous death act. Under this act, if the survivor of a common disaster cannot be determined, then each of the decedents is presumed to be the survivor and the property is distributed accordingly. This presumption can be rebutted by a contrary provision in a will. It is usually advisable to insert a provision in joint wills, as to which spouse is to be considered the survivor. This is particularly true if the estate is to have the advantage of the marital deduction, which is predicated on a surviving spouse. (See below, under TAXES.)

TAXES

Even in death you cannot escape taxes. With the exception of Nevada, all the states impose an inheritance or estate tax of some kind. The type of tax as well as the rates vary greatly from state to state.

The Tax Reform Act of 1976 made sweeping changes in the estate and gift tax provisions of the Internal Revenue Code. These are the first major revisions in these fields in 28 years. Most of the law has been essentially unchanged since the twenties.

Nor is the change all bad! For estates whose gross value is $350,000 and less, most of the news is very good indeed. Their potential transfer taxes have been substantially reduced. Skillful planning together with your attorney may result in exempting combined husband and wife estates of $250,000 to over $400,000 from federal estate tax. Individual estates grossing less than $120,000 will virtually all pass to beneficiaries without any federal estate tax, and comparatively little change will be necessary to achieve this end.

While no attempt will be made here to detail the changes brought about by this landmark tax legislation, it might prove helpful to the reader for us to describe the unification of estate and gift taxes provisions.

Although the federal estate and gift tax laws have always been loosely interrelated, until now they have constituted two separate, essentially independent taxes. The federal gift tax rates were substantially lower than the federal estate tax rates; lifetime gifts— unless made within three years of death and held to have been in contemplation of death— would remove the amount of the gift from taxation at the donor's highest estate tax brackets and reallocate it to the bottom of the gift tax rate schedule.

Effective January 1, 1977, the separate estate and gift tax schedules were combined into a single, new, transfer tax.

As this transfer tax is a *unified* gift and estate tax, the cumulative amount of post-1976 taxable gifts is added to the value of the taxable estate in determining the amount of the estate tax.

The present law to a large extent eliminates the tax savings generated by the use of so called generation skipping trusts. Formerly, a wealthy individual could set up a trust for the benefit of his children, the remainder to go upon his death to his grandchildren. The interest of the trust, would not pass into their estates, hence escaping taxation. An estate tax would not be imposed until the grandchildren's death. This is no longer true. The present law now treats each intervening life beneficiary who belongs to a generation younger than the grantor as a "deemed transferor". Although the property in this example, would not be considered part of a child's estate for purposes of probate, a tax would be imposed on the child's interest based on the new uniform rate schedule. There is however a $250,000 exclusion provided for each child.

Finally, henceforth gifts coming within the $3,000 annual gift tax exclusion per donee will be much more important. These gifts will *not* be included in computing one's estate tax, even if made on one's deathbed. Thus, in many situations, these $3,000 gifts should be made to each child and grandchild, and perhaps his spouse, as soon as conveniently possible each year, normally in January.

TRUSTS

The trust, once only the instrument of the very wealthy, is coming into more universal use. In a general work such as this it would be impossible to examine the various types of trusts and the special rules relating to them. Our discussion will be confined to comments on trusts in general, and testamentary and *inter vivos* trusts in particular.

Basically a trust occurs when someone gives a third party, assets which are to be held for another. In legal terminology, the one making the gift is referred to as the settlor, the holder as the trustee and the person for whose benefit the gift is held, the beneficiary.

Testamentary Trusts

The testamentary trust, as the name implies, is created in a will and takes effect upon the testator's death. One of the more common testamentary trusts is the so called marital deduction trust.

Usually marital deduction trusts are employed in a will when a testator wishes to take full advantage of the marital deduction but is hesitant about giving his spouse outright control of a large portion of his estate. This might occur if most of the assets of an estate consisted of stock in a closely held family corporation and a husband did not have confidence in his wife's ability to run the business. In such a case he would set up a marital deduction trust consisting that part of his estate qualifying for the marital deduction. He would appoint someone whose business judgment he trusted, as trustee, with the instruction that his wife be given income for life, (coupled, if desired, with power to invade capital when necessary). The wife would also be given the power to designate in her will who would be the ultimate beneficiaries of the trust. This last power of appointment is crucial, as it gives the wife enough dominion over the trust for it to qualify for the unconditional gift required by the marital deduction.

The property received from this trust by the wife will escape taxation by virtue of the marital deduction. However upon the wife's death the property will pass into her estate. Assuming that she has outlived her husband, beyond the period when taxes paid on his estate would be credited against her estate, and that the assets in the trust remain infact, a possibility of double taxation arises, as the assets would be liable to tax as part of her estate.

Thus in a situation where a spouse wishes to leave property in trust to a surviving spouse who is considerably younger, and wishes to leave the entire estate to the spouse, that property qualifying for the marital deduction should be left in the form of trust described above.

The remainder may be left in a trust which brings about the opposite result of the marital deductin trust. Instead of giving the wife the power to name the ultimate beneficiaries, the husband specifies in his will that upon his wife's death the assets of the trust will pass to his children. Again the trusts will be considered part of the husband's estate and taxed accordingly. However, depending on the size of the estate, the necessity of paying the tax will either be eliminated or at least abated by the tax credit received by husband's estate. Since the wife is only an income beneficiary and had been given no control over the trust, on her death the assets of the trust will not be considered part of her estate, and the possibility of the double taxation inherent in the marital deduction type of trust will be avoided.

Inter Vivos Trust

An *inter vivos* trust is created, not in a will, but usually in a trust indenture made during the settlor's lifetime. This type of trust may be either irrevocable or revocable.

The irrevocable *inter vivos* trust usually has the consequences of an outright gift, provided the settlor does not retain too many incidents of ownership. It has several advantages over the testamentary trust. If correctly drafted it permits the assets of the trust to go directly to the beneficiary, without the necessity of going through probate proceedings. Also where a testamentary trust is subject to the tax laws of the testator's domiciliary state, an *inter vivos* trust is not. The settlor can decide which state tax laws would be most advantageous for him, and specify in the trust indenture, that the trust will be governed by the laws of that state.

If the trust is revocable, it has another advantage in addition to those listed above. The settlor will be able to judge for himself of the trustee's ability to manage the assets of the trust. If dissatisfied with the trustee, he can always revoke the trust and set up another.

Skillful drafting and use of revocable and irrevocable *inter vivos* trusts can bring you the same tax benefits as the testamentary trusts discussed above. However the trust field is definitely not one for a do-it-yourselfer. If you wish the results of your trusts to be as planned, you must obtain competent legal advice to eliminate possible costly and irreversible errors.

UNIFORM GIFT OF SECURITIES TO MINORS ACT

This act provides for a simple, inexpensive method of making gifts of securities to minors, by registering them in the name of the donor or another adult, as custodian for the minor. Most of the states have gradually been adopting this act through the years. Now it has been adopted by all the states except Georgia.

WILLS

You may not be able to take it with you, but if you leave a will you will at least be able to say what is to be done with it.

In general, rules relating to the execution and validity of will have for the most part remained unchanged. Most of the states have lowered the age for making a will to 18 years. All but five states require two witnesses to a will. (The other five require three witnesses.) The various states are still undivided on the legality of a holographic will (a will entirely in the handwriting of the testator, but unwitnessed). Comparison of state laws are found in the charts at the end of the chapter.

As indicated in the sections relating to estate planning, taxes and trusts, wills are becoming increasingly complex. If a will is to have the effect desired by the testator, it is evident that not only his will, but that of his spouse must be carefully planned and drawn with the advice of a competent attorney.

Chart 1

SUMMARY OF STATE LAWS RELATING TO ALIENS

ALABAMA
Any resident or non-resident alien may take and transmit real and personal property in the same manner as a native citizen.

ARIZONA
Aliens eligible to citizenship may take real property by descent.

ARKANSAS
Resident aliens may inherit property the same as citizens. All real property owned by an alien passes on his death in the same manner as property owned by citizens. Personal property owned by a resident alien is distributed in the same manner as if he were a citizen.

CALIFORNIA
Any person, whether citizen or alien, may take and dispose of real or personal property.

COLORADO
All aliens may inherit and transmit real and personal property the same as citizens

CONNECTICUT
Resident aliens may inherit and transmit real estate in the manner and to the same extent as citizens.

DELAWARE
All real and personal property located in the state may be inherited by and through an alien in the same manner as by a citizen of the state.

DISTRICT OF COLUMBIA
Aliens are entitled to inherit realty to the same extent as citizens. A good title by descent may be derived by those claiming through an alien ancestor.

FLORIDA
An alien may devise, inherit and transmit inheritance in real and personal property as if he were a citizen of the United States.

GEORGIA

Aliens, subjects of governments at peace with the United States, shall be entitled to all the rights of citizens of other states resident in this state.

IDAHO

No restrictions on inheritance by aliens.

ILLINOIS

All aliens may inherit and transmit real property by inheritance. No person shall be deprived of his right to inherit real property from any deceased person because he may be an alien or be compelled to trace his relationship to such deceased person through one or more aliens. An alien may not hold property for more than six years, at which time he must convey or become a citizen of the United States. All aliens may acquire and hold personal property in the same manner as citizens of the United States.

INDIANA

All aliens residing in the state who have declared their intention to become citizens of the United States may acquire and hold real estate in the same manner as citizens. All other aliens may inherit real estate, but must convey the same within five years after taking the property.

IOWA

Resident aliens enjoy the same rights in respect to descent of property as native-born citizens. Nonresident aliens may not acquire title to real property by inheritance except that heirs of naturalized citizens, and of aliens who have acquired real property by inheritance may hold such lands for twenty years, at the end of which time they must be sold or they revert to the state; this provision does not apply to the distribution of personal property.

KANSAS

All aliens eligible to citizenship under the law of the United States may transmit and inherit real estate in this state, in the same manner and to the same extent as citizens of the United States. Other aliens may only inherit to the same extent as

Chart 1 cont.

provided in the treaty between the United States and the alien's country.

KENTUCKY

Any alien, not an enemy, after declaring his intention to become a citizen of the United States, may inherit any interest in real or personal property, in the same manner as if he were a citizen of this state. If real estate passes to a nonresident alien by descent, such property may be held and alienated by such alien for eight years after the final settlement of the decedent's estate. An alien may inherit personal property in the same manner as a citizen. A person may inherit even though the ancestor through whom he claims is an alien.

LOUISIANA

No alien who is ineligible to citizenship of the United States may acquire any interest in real property by inheritance.

MAINE

An alien may take, hold, convey, and devise real estate or any interest therein.

MARYLAND

Aliens, not enemies, may inherit and transmit by inheritance real property in the same manner as citizens.

MASSACHUSETTS

Aliens may take and transmit real property, and no title to real property shall be invalid on account of the alienage of a former owner.

MICHIGAN

Any alien may acquire and hold real property by inheritance, and if he shall die intestate, his realty descends to his heirs; and in all cases realty passes in the same manner as if such alien were a native citizen.

MINNESOTA

Aliens may inherit real property in the same manner as citizens.

MISSISSIPPI

Resident aliens may acquire, hold and transmit real property by descent, as citizens of the state may.

MISSOURI
Aliens are capable of acquiring by descent, real estate, and of alienating the same as if they were citizens of the United States and residents of the state.

MONTANA
Residents aliens may take property by inheritance the same as citizens. A nonresident alien entitled to inherit property must appear and claim the same within two years. Nonresident aliens may not inherit property unless the foreign country of his residence would reciprocally permit a resident of the United States to inherit.

NEBRASKA
Aliens may not hold any land for more than five years, except that a resident alien may acquire land by inheritance provided that he shall sell the same within five years from the date of acquiring and if he fails to do so the property escheats to the state.

NEVADA
Any nonresident alien may take, hold and enjoy any real property within the State the same as any resident citizen. However, the rights of aliens not residing within the United States to take real or personal property by inheritance are dependent in each case upon the existence of a reciprocal right upon the parts of citizens of the United States to take real and personal property in like manner within the countries of which said aliens are inhabitants or citizens.

NEW HAMPSHIRE
An alien, resident in this state, may take, hold, or devise real estate; and it may descend in the same manner as if he were a citizen.

NEW JERSEY
Alien friends have the same rights with respect to real property as native-born citizens. In taking title to real or personal property, it shall be no bar to a person that he or any ancestor or other person through whom he traces his title, is or has been an alien.

Chart 1 cont.

NEW MEXICO
Aliens, except those ineligible to citizenship, may acquire and hold real estate. All aliens may inherit and transmit personal property in the same manner as citizens.

NEW YORK
Aliens are empowered to take, hold transmit and dispose of real property within this state in the same manner as native-born citizens and their heirs and devisees take in the same manner as citizens.

NORTH CAROLINA
Resident aliens may inherit and transmit real property in the same manner as citizens. Non-resident aliens may only inherit if a reciprocal right exists in the citizens or residents of the United States.

NORTH DAKOTA
Aliens may take, hold and depose of property, real or personal, within this state. Aliens may take by inheritance as well as citizens; and no person is precluded from inheriting by reason of the alienage of any relative.

OHIO
No person capable of inheriting shall be deprived of an inheritance by reason of the alienage of any of his ancestors. Aliens may hold realty by descent as fully and completely as any citizen of the United States.

OKLAHOMA
Aliens may take in all cases, by succession, as well as citizens; and no person is precluded from such succession by reason of the alienage of any relative. However, non-resident aliens may only hold title to real estate for five years.

OREGON
No statutory provision.

PENNSYLVANIA
Real and personal estate shall descend without regard to whether the decedent or any person otherwise entitled to take is, or has been, an alien.

RHODE ISLAND

Aliens may take, hold and transmit real and personal property in the same manner as citizens. Where it appears that a non-resident alien would not have the benefit or control of his inheritance, the probate court may direct that such inheritance he paid into the registry of the probate court for the non-resident's benefit.

SOUTH CAROLINA

Real and personal property may be acquired and disposed of, by an alien in the same manner and in all respects as by a natural born citizen; and title to real and personal property may be derived from, through, or in succession to an alien, in the same manner, in all respects, as though, from or in succession to a natural born citizen. Except that aliens or corporations controlled by aliens may not own or control more than $50,000 acres of land within the state. Alien widows of United States citizens have the same property rights as citizens.

SOUTH DAKOTA

Aliens may inherit and transmit property in this state and dispose of or transmit the same as a citizen.

TENNESSEE

An alien, resident or nonresident of the United States may take and hold real and personal property in this state and dispose of or transmit the same as a native citizen. The heirs of such aliens may take by inheritance as if citizens of the United States.

TEXAS

Same rights as citizens.

UTAH

Aliens may, in all cases, take by succession and no person is precluded from inheriting by reason of the alienage of any relatives.

VERMONT

Aliens, not enemies, may acquire real or personal property the same as citizens.

Chart 1 cont.

VIRGINIA

Any alien, not an enemy, may acquire and transmit real estate by descent in the same manner as property held by citizens. In taking title by descent, it is no bar to a party that any ancestor through whom he inherits is, or has been, an alien.

WASHINGTON

No restrictions.

WEST VIRGINIA

An alien may inherit and transmit by inheritance in the same manner as if he were a citizen. In taking title by descent, it is no bar to a party that any ancestor through whom he inherits is, or has been an alien.

WISCONSIN

Aliens may inherit and transmit by inheritance in the same manner and to the same extent as citizens.

WYOMING

Resident aliens may inherit and transmit property the same as citizens. The alienage of the legal heirs shall not invalidate any title to real estate which shall descend or pass from the decedent except that no non-resident alien who is a citizen of any country foreign to the United States of America shall by any manner or means acquire real property in this state by succession or testamentary disposition if the laws of the country of which such non-resident alien is a citizen do not allow citizens of the United State of America to take real property by succession or by testamentary disposition.

Chart 2

RIGHT OF DOWER, CURTESY AND STATUTORY SUBSTITUTIONS

STATE	Husband	Wife
Alabama	Life estate in wife's real property and one-half of all personal property, absolutely	Life estate in 1/3 of husband's real property if husband survived by lineal descendants and life estate in 1/2 if not survived by lineal descendants
Alaska	Abolished	Abolished
Arizona	Abolished	Abolished
Arkansas	Life estate in 1/3 of wife's real property and 1/3 of all personal property absolutely [1]	Life estate in 1/3 of husband's real property and 1/3 of all personal property absolutely
California	None	None
Colorado	None	Abolished
Connecticut	None	None
Delaware	Abolished	Abolished
District of Columbia	Abolished	Abolished
Florida	Abolished	Abolished
Georgia	None	Abolished
Hawaii	Life estate in 1/3 of wife's real property and 1/3 of all personal property absolutely	Life estate in 1/3 of husband's real property and 1/3 of all personal property absolutely

STATE	Husband	Wife
Idaho	Abolished	None
Illinois	Abolished	Abolished
Indiana	Abolished	Abolished
Iowa	Abolished	Abolished
Kansas	One-half absolutely, of all wife's real property	One-half absolutely, of all husband's real property
Kentucky	Life estate in 1/3 of wife's real property	Life estate in 1/3 husband's real property
Louisiana	None	None
Maine	Abolished	Abolished
Maryland	Abolished	Abolished
Massachusetts	Life estate in 1/3 wife's real property	Life estate in 1/3 husband's real property
Michigan	Abolished	Life estate in 1/3 husband's real property
Minnesota	Abolished	Abolished
Mississippi	Abolished	Abolished
Missouri	Abolished	Abolished
Montana	None	Abolished
Nebraska	Abolished	Abolished
Nevada	Abolished	Abolished
New Hampshire	Abolished	Abolished
New Jersey	Life estate in 1/2 real property	Life estate in 1/2 husband's real property
New Mexico	None	None

STATE	Husband	Wife
New York	Abolished	Abolished [2]
North Carolina	Abolished	Abolished
North Dakota	None	Abolished
Ohio	Life estate in 1/3 of wife's real property	Life estate in 1/3 of husband's real property
Oklahoma	Abolished	Abolished
Oregon	Abolished	Abolished
Pennsylvania	None	None
Rhode Island	Life estate in all wife's real property	Life estate in 1/3 of husband's real property
South Carolina	Abolished	Life estate in 1/3 of husband's real property
South Dakota	Abolished	Abolished
Tennessee	Life estate in all wife's real property	Life estate in 1/3 of husband's real property
Texas	None	None
Utah	Abolished	One-third, in value, of all husband's real property [3]
Vermont	One-third in value of wife's real property [4]	One-third in value of husband's real property [4]
Virginia	1/3 of wife's real property	1/3 of husband's real property
Washington	Abolished	Abolished

STATE	Husband	Wife
West Virginia	Life estate in 1/3 of wife's real property	Life estate in 1/3 of husband's real property
Wisconsin	Life estate in 1/3 of property owned by wife at death	Life estate in 1/3 of husband's real property
Wyoming	Abolished	Abolished

---

[1] Husband's interest may be defeated by will or conveyance by his wife.
[2] Wife takes a life estate in 1/3 husband's real property if marriage and ownership of property took place prior to September 1, 1930.
[3] See Uniform Probate Code, effective July 1, 1977 (75-1-101 et seq).
[4] Surviving spouse entitled to ½ in value of the real property if decedent was survived by issue or heir by adoption.

Chart 3

TERMINATION OF GUARDIANSHIP

STATE	Age of Majority	Marriage removes disability of infancy — Female	Male	Judicial Emancipation allowed by statute
ALABAMA	21	yes, if over 18	yes, if over 18	yes, as to infants over 18
ALASKA	19	yes	no	. . . .
ARIZONA	18	yes	no	yes, as to veterans
ARKANSAS	21(m) 18(f)	yes, as to person	yes, as to person	yes, in certain cases 18(m); 16(f)
CALIFORNIA	18	yes [1]	yes [1]	. . . .
COLORADO	21	yes	yes	. . . .
CONNECTICUT	18	C.L.	C.L.	yes, as to veterans
DELAWARE	18	yes	no	. . . .
DIST. of COL.	21	yes, as to person	no	. . . .
FLORIDA	18	yes	yes	yes

Chart 3 cont.

STATE	Age of Majority	Marriage removes disability of infancy — Female	Male	Judicial Emancipation allowed by statute
GEORGIA	18	......	......	......
HAWAII	18	yes, as to person	yes, as to person	......
IDAHO	18	yes	yes	......
ILLINOIS	18	yes, as to person	......	......
INDIANA	18	yes, in Court's discretion	yes, in Court's discretion	......
IOWA	18	yes	yes	......
KANSAS	18	yes, as to person	yes, as to person	yes
KENTUCKY	18	no	no	......
LOUISIANA²	18	yes	yes	yes
MAINE	18	yes	no	......
MARYLAND	18	no	no	......
MASSACHUSETTS	18	yes	yes	......

STATE	Age of Majority	Marriage removes disability of infancy — Female	Marriage removes disability of infancy — Male	Judicial Emancipation allowed by statute
MICHIGAN	18	yes, as to person	no	. . . . . .
MINNESOTA	18	yes, as to person	no	. . . . . .
MISSISSIPPI	21	yes, if over 18 (in Court's discretion)	yes, if over 18 (in Court's discretion)	yes
MISSOURI	21	yes	yes	yes, as to veterans over 18
MONTANA	18	yes	yes	. . . . . .
NEBRASKA	19	yes	yes	. . . . . .
NEVADA	21(m) 18(f)	no	no	. . . . . .
NEW HAMPSHIRE	18	no	no	. . . . . .
NEW JERSEY	18	. . . . . .	. . . . . .	. . . . . .
NEW MEXICO	18	yes	yes	. . . . . .
NEW YORK	18	yes, as to person	no	. . . . . .

Chart 3 cont.

STATE	Age of Majority	Marriage removes disability of infancy — Female	Male	Judicial Emancipation allowed by statute
N. CAROLINA	18	no	no	......
N. DAKOTA	18	yes, as to person	yes, as to person	......
OHIO	18	yes, as to person	......	......
OKLAHOMA	18	no, except as to property acquired after marriage	no, except as to property acquired after marriage	yes
OREGON	18	yes	yes	......
PENNSYLVANIA	18	no	no	......
RHODE ISLAND	18	no	no	......
S. CAROLINA	21	no	no	......
S. DAKOTA	18	yes	yes	......
TENNESSEE	18	no	no	yes
TEXAS	18	yes	yes	yes, as to veterans at 18; others, 19

STATE	Age of Majority	Marriage removes disability of infancy — Female	Male	Judicial Emancipation allowed by statute
UTAH	21(m) 18(f)	yes[3]	yes[3]	. . . .
VERMONT	18	yes	yes	. . . .
VIRGINIA	18	yes	no	. . . .
WASHINGTON	21	no	no	. . . .
WEST VIRGINIA	21	no	no	. . . .
WISCONSIN	21	no	no	. . . .
WYOMING	21	yes	yes	yes

[1] In specified cases only.
[2] Louisiana also allows a parental emancipation of infants over 15.
[3] Guardianship may, in court's discretion, continue as to property.

Chart 4

COURTS, ACCOUNTS AND INVENTORIES

STATE	COURT HAVING JURISDICTION	FILING REQUIREMENTS Accounting	Inventory
ALABAMA	Probate	every 3 years	3 months after appt.
ALASKA	Superior Court	one year after appt. annually thereafter	required
ARIZONA	Superior Ct. of County	annually	3 months after appt.
ARKANSAS	Probate	annually	2 months after appt.
CALIFORNIA	Superior Ct. of County	one year after appt. and as the court directs	3 months after appt.
COLORADO	County	......	1 month after appt.
CONNECTICUT	Probate	annually	required
DELAWARE	Court of Chancery	one year after appt. and as the court directs	......
DIST. OF COL.	Supreme Court (Probate Division)	at least once a year	3 months after appt.

STATE	COURT HAVING JURISDICTION	FILING REQUIREMENTS Accounting	Inventory
FLORIDA	Circuit	April 1 each year	. . . . . .
GEORGIA	Courts of Ordinary	annually	. . . . . .
HAWAII	Circuit	one year after appt., annually, thereafter	required
IDAHO	District	as the court directs	90 days after appt.
ILLINOIS	Circuit	one year after appt. and as court directs	60 days after appt.
INDIANA	Probate	biennially	required
IOWA	Probate	annually	. . . . . .
KANSAS	Probate	annually	30 days after appt.
KENTUCKY	County	one year after appt. then biennially	60 days after appt.
LOUISIANA	Parish	annually	required
MAINE	Probate	every 3 years, then as court directs	required

Chart 4 cont.

STATE	COURT HAVING JURISDICTION	FILING REQUIREMENTS Accounting	Inventory
MARYLAND	Equity, Orphan's	60 days after appt.	annually thereafter
MASSACHUSETTS	Probate	annually	required
MICHIGAN	Probate	annually	30 days after appt.
MINNESOTA	Probate	annually	. . . . . .
MISSISSIPPI	Chancery	annually	3 months after appt.
MISSOURI	Probate	annually	. . . . . .
MONTANA	District	1 year after appointment: thereafter as required by court	3 months after appt.; annually thereafter
NEBRASKA	County	1 year after appointment; annually thereafter	3 months after appt.
NEVADA	Any court having jurisdiction over persons and estates of minors	annually	60 days after appt.
NEW HAMPSHIRE	Probate	annually	required

STATE	COURT HAVING JURISDICTION	FILING REQUIREMENTS Accounting	Inventory
NEW JERSEY	Surrogate's Superior	1 year after appt., then as the court directs	permitted; required only if courts directs
NEW MEXICO	Children's or family court	annually	90 days after appt.
NEW YORK	Surrogate's Supreme	annually[1]	. . . . . .
NORTH CAROLINA	Superior	annually	3 months after appt.
NORTH DAKOTA	County	Under $3,000 as court directs; between $3,000-$20,000, annually; semi-annually, if over	3 months after appt.
OHIO	Probate	biennially	3 months after appt.
OKLAHOMA	District	1 year after appt.; there-after as court directs	3 months after appt.; if estate over $20,000, semi-annually, otherwise an-nually
OREGON [2]	Probate	annually	90 days after appt.
PENNSYLVANIA	Orphan's	as court directs	3 months after appt.

Chart 4 cont.

STATE	COURT HAVING JURISDICTION	FILING REQUIREMENTS Accounting	Inventory
RHODE ISLAND	Probate	annually	30 days after appt.
SOUTH CAROLINA	Probate	annually	3 months after appt.
SOUTH DAKOTA	Circuit	3 months after appt. thereafter as court directs	as court orders
TENNESSEE	County, Chancery	annually	next term of the court
TEXAS	County and Probate	annually	90 days after appt.
UTAH	District	annually, if estate under $20,000; semiannually, if over	3 months after appt.
VERMONT	Probate	1 year after appt; thereafter as court directs	60 days after appt.
VIRGINIA	Equity Courts	annually	4 months after appt.
WASHINGTON	Superior	annually	3 months after appt.
WEST VIRGINIA	Circuit	annually	2 months after appt.

STATE	COURT HAVING JURISDICTION	FILING REQUIREMENTS Accounting	Inventory
WISCONSIN	County	annually, before March 1, each year	6 months after appt.
WYOMING	District	annually	3 months after appt.

[1] Required of guardians in N.Y.C. and Nassau, Orange, Suffolk and Westchester counties.

[2] In Oregon a distinction is made between the guardian who has the responsibility for care of the ward's personal property. The conservatory must file accountings and make inventories. The guardian is not required to do so.

Chart 5

UNIFORM VETERANS GUARDIANSHIP ACT

(Adoption by states)

yes — State has adopted
no — State has not adopted

ALABAMA — no	MONTANA — no
ALASKA — no	NEBRASKA — yes
ARIZONA — no	NEVADA — no
ARKANSAS — yes	NEW HAMPSHIRE — no
CALIFORNIA — yes	NEW JERSEY — no
COLORADO — yes	NEW MEXICO — yes
CONNECTICUT — no	NEW YORK — no
DELAWARE — no	NORTH CAROLINA — yes
DIST. OF COL. — no	NORTH DAKOTA — no
FLORIDA — no	OHIO — yes
GEORGIA — no	OKLAHOMA — yes
HAWAII — yes	OREGON — no
IDAHO — no	PENNSYLVANIA — no
ILLINOIS — no	RHODE ISLAND — yes
INDIANA — yes	SOUTH CAROLINA — no
IOWA — yes	SOUTH DAKOTA — no
KANSAS — no	TENNESSEE — yes
KENTUCKY — yes	TEXAS — no
LOUISIANA — yes	UTAH — no
MAINE — yes	VERMONT — yes
MARYLAND — yes	VIRGINIA — no
MASSACHUSETTS — no	WASHINGTON — yes
MICHIGAN — no	WEST VIRGINIA — no
MINNESOTA — no	WISCONSIN — yes
MISSISSIPPI — yes	WYOMING — no
MISSOURI — yes	

Chart 6

NOMINATION OF GUARDIAN BY INFANT

	Age *		Age *
ALABAMA	14	MISSISSIPPI	14
ALASKA	14	MISSOURI	14
ARIZONA	14	MONTANA	14
ARKANSAS	14	NEBRASKA	14
CALIFORNIA	14	NEVADA	14
COLORADO	14	NEW HAMPSHIRE	14
but may nominate		NEW JERSEY	14
guardian only if		NEW MEXICO	14
parents are dead		NEW YORK	14
CONNECTICUT	14	NORTH CAROLINA	...
DELAWARE	14	NORTH DAKOTA	14
DIST. OF COL.	14	OHIO	14
FLORIDA	14	OKLAHOMA	14
notice must be		OREGON	14
given to infant of		PENNSYLVANIA	14
proposed appoint-		RHODE ISLAND	14
ment		SOUTH CAROLINA	...
GEORGIA	14	SOUTH DAKOTA	14
HAWAII	16	TENNESSEE	...
IDAHO	14	TEXAS	14
ILLINOIS	14	UTAH	14
INDIANA	14	VERMONT	14
IOWA	14	VIRGINIA	14
KANSAS	14	WASHINGTON	...
KENTUCKY	14	infant must con-	
LOUISIANA	...	sent to court's ap-	
MAINE	14	pointment	
MARYLAND	16	WEST VIRGINIA	14
MASSACHUSETTS	14	WISCONSIN	14
MICHIGAN	14	WYOMING	14
MINNESOTA	14		

* The age at which infant is permitted to select his own guardian.

Chart 7

FOREIGN AND ANCILLARY GUARDIANS

P — Permitted

	Foreign Guardian Recognized or permitted to become ancillary guardian	Removal of Property from State
ALABAMA	yes, may be appointed for resident ward	P
ALASKA	yes	P
ARIZONA	yes, except foreign corporations	P
ARKANSAS	yes; foreign corporation need not qualify to do business in state	P
CALIFORNIA	yes	P
COLORADO	yes	P
CONNECTICUT	yes, except foreign corporations	P
DELAWARE	yes	P
DIST. OF COL.	may be appointed ancillary	after appt. as ancillary
FLORIDA	yes	P
GEORGIA	yes	P
HAWAII	yes	P
IDAHO	yes	P
ILLINOIS	limited recognition only	
INDIANA	yes	P
IOWA	yes	P

P — Permitted

	Foreign Guardian Recognized or permitted to become ancillary guardian	Removal of Property from state
KANSAS	yes	P
KENTUCKY	yes, on application to court	P
LOUISIANA	yes	P, on proof of payment of infant's debts
MAINE	may qualify to act in state	P
MARYLAND	yes	P
MASSACHUSETTS	yes	P
MICHIGAN	yes, if ward is also non-resident	P
MINNESOTA	yes	P
MISSISSIPPI	yes, if ward also non-resident & reciprocity exists	yes, on petition to court if ward non-resident
MISSOURI	yes, but guardian must be resident	P
MONTANA	non-resident may appt. local guardian	P
NEBRASKA	yes, if reciprocity exists	P
NEVADA	yes	P
NEW HAMPSHIRE	non-resident may be appointed ancillary guardian	. . .
NEW JERSEY	non-resident may be appointed ancillary	P

Chart 7 cont.

P — Permitted

	Foreign Guardian Recognized or permitted to become ancillary guardian	Removal of Property from state
NEW MEXICO	no, but may be appointed ancillary	P
NEW YORK	yes	P
NORTH CAROLINA	yes	P
NORTH DAKOTA	yes	P
OHIO	no	yes, on notice to local custodian
OKLAHOMA	yes, if both ward and guardian are non-residents	P, if ward and guardian are non-residents
OREGON	yes, if both ward and guardian are non-residents	P, if ward and guardian are non-residents
PENNSYLVANIA	yes, unless local guardianship exists	P, unless local guardianship exists
RHODE ISLAND	yes, if both are non-residents and on application, local guardian may be removed	P. if both ward and guardian are non-residents
SOUTH CAROLINA	yes	P
SOUTH DAKOTA	yes	P
TENNESSEE	yes	P
TEXAS	yes	P
UTAH	yes	yes
VERMONT	no, but on application may be appointed guardian of property only	no
VIRGINIA	yes	P

P — Permitted

	Foreign Guardian Recognized or permitted to become ancillary guardian	**Removal of Property from State**
WASHINGTON	yes	P
WEST VIRGINIA	may be appointed ancillary	P
WISCONSIN	yes	P
WYOMING	yes	P

Chart 8

COMMISSIONS

STATE		AMOUNT
		(s) — Same as commissions paid executors and administrators of estates T — Thousand dollars
ALABAMA	(s)	as court determines, but not more than 2½% on receipts and 2½% on distributions
ALASKA	...	reasonable fee
ARIZONA	(s)	7% on first T; 5% on excess
ARKANSAS	(s)	up to 10% on first T; 5% on next 4 T; 2% on balance
CALIFORNIA	(s)	7% of first T; 4% on next 9 T; 3% on next 40 T; 2% on next 100 T; 1½% on next 350 T; 1% on excess over 500 T
COLORADO	(s)	not exceeding 6% on amounts under 25 T; 4% on next 75 T; 3% on balance
CONNECTICUT	(s)	reasonable rates, as court allows
DELAWARE	(s)	reasonable rates, not to exceed 10%
DIST OF COL.	...	5% of amounts collected, if and when disbursed
FLORIDA	(s)	6% on first T; 4% on next 4 T; 2% on all over 5 T
GEORGIA	(s)	2½% on all received and all paid out
HAWAII	...	reasonable amount
IDAHO	(s)	reasonable amount
ILLINOIS	(s)	reasonable amount

STATE		AMOUNT
		(s) — Same as commissions paid executors and administrators of estates
		T — Thousand dollars

STATE		AMOUNT
INDIANA	(s)	just and reasonable
IOWA	(s)	just and reasonable
KANSAS	(s)	just and reasonable
KENTUCKY	(s)	5% of income collected plus annual commission of 1/5 of 1% of fair value of real and personal property
LOUISIANA	...	10% of annual revenues from ward's property
MAINE	(s)	Provisions ambiguous. Court decisions vary in interpretation
MARYLAND	(s)	court's discretion decides — not more than 10% on amounts under 20 T; 4% on amounts over 20 T
MASSACHUSETTS	(s)	court decides; customary fees range from 2½% to 3%, up to 500 T and 1% on balance
MICHIGAN	(s)	5% on first T; 2½% on excess to 5 T; 2% on balance
MINNESOTA	(s)	just and reasonable
MISSISSIPPI	(s)	just and reasonable (to 7%)
MISSOURI	(s)	court's discretion decides — minimum scale specified
MONTANA	(s)	reasonable; not more than 3% on first 40 T and 2% on excess

Chart 8 cont.

STATE		AMOUNT
		(s) — Same as commissions paid executors and administrators of estates T — Thousand dollars
NEBRASKA	(s)	5% on first T; 2½% on next 4 T; 2% on all over 5 T
NEVADA	...	reasonable amount
NEW HAMPSHIRE	...	no statutory provisions; reasonable fee allowed
NEW JERSEY	(s)	5% on first 100 T; as court allows on excess not exceeding 5%
NEW MEXICO	(s)	10% on first 3T; 5% on excess
NEW YORK	(s)*	4% on first 25 T; 3½% on next 125 T; 3% on next 150 T; 2% on balance
NORTH CAROLINA	(s)	reasonable amount, to 5%, of receipts and disbursements
NORTH DAKOTA	...	reasonable amount
OHIO	...	6% on first T; 4% on next 4 T; 2% on remainder
OKLAHOMA	...	reasonable amount not to exceed 10% of interests and rents on real property; 3% of oil and gas royalties; 10% on all other property
OREGON	(s)	7% on first T; 4% on next 9 T; 3% on 10 T to 50 T; 2% on excess
PENNSYLVANIA	(s)	no specific provisions (customary 5% on small estates; 3% on large)
RHODE ISLAND	...	reasonable amount
SOUTH CAROLINA	(s)	2½% on personal assets received and 2½% on amounts paid

STATE		AMOUNT
		(s) — Same as commissions paid executors and administrators of estates
		T — Thousand dollars
SOUTH DAKOTA	(s)	5% on first T; 4% on next 4 T; 2½% on all over 5 T
TENNESSEE	(s)	Court allows reasonable fee
TEXAS	(s)	5% of gross income and 5% of money paid out
UTAH	(s)	5% on first T; 4% on next 4 T; 3% on excess to 10 T 2% on excess to $50 T: 1½% on 100 T; 1% on excess over 100 T
VERMONT	(s)	$4 per day when performing duties plus additional allowance
VIRGINIA	(s)	reasonable amount, as court allows, usually 5% but may be less
WASHINGTON	(s)	reasonable
WEST VIRGINIA		reasonable
WISCONSIN	(s)	2% of inventory value of the property less mortgages and liens plus net corpus gains
WYOMING	(s)	10% on first T; 5% on next 4 T; 3% on excess to 20 T; 2% on excess over 20 T

---

* In cases of veterans incompetent and wards, court fixes the amount, not to exceed 5% of income for year.

Chart 9

HOMESTEAD

State	Limit of Value	Limit of Area
ALABAMA	$6,000 (widow or minor children) $2,000 (others)	160 acres
ALASKA	$12,000	1/4 acre in town or city, 160 acres elsewhere
ARIZONA	$15,000	None
ARKANSAS	$2,500	1/4 acre in city, town or village; 80 acres elsewhere
CALIFORNIA	$20,000 (head of family or over 65 years of age) $10,000 (others)	No limitation
COLORADO	$7,500	No limitation
FLORIDA	None	1/2 acre in city or town; 160 acres elsewhere
GEORGIA	$500 (in town or city) $200 (elsewhere)	50 acres outside of town or city
HAWAII	$20,000 (head of family or over 65 years of age) $10,000 (others)	1 acre in "one piece of land"
IDAHO	$10,000 (head of family) $4,000 (others)	No limitation
ILLINOIS	$10,000	No limitation
IOWA	$500	1/2 acre in city or town; 40 acres elsewhere
KANSAS	None	1 acre in city of town; 160 acres of farm land

State	Limit of Value	Limit of Area
KENTUCKY	$1,000	None
LOUISIANA	$15,000	160 acres
MAINE	$3,000	No limitation
MASSACHUSETTS	$30,000	No limitation
MICHIGAN	$3,500	1 lot in city, town or village; 40 acres elsewhere
MINNESOTA	None	1/3 acre in city, village or borough over 5,000 population; ½ acre if less than 5,000 population; 80 acres elsewhere
MISSISSIPPI	$5,00	160 acres
MISSOURI	$1,500 in country $3,000 in city in city	160 acres in country; 30 sq. rods to 5 acres in city (depending on population)
MONTANA	$2,500	¼ acre in city or town; 320 acres of agricultural land
NEBRASKA	$2,000	2 lots in city or village; 160 acres in country
NEVADA	$10,000	None
NEW HAMPSHIRE	$1,000	None
NEW JERSEY	$1,000	None
NEW MEXICO	$1,000	None
NEW YORK	$1,000	None
NORTH CAROLINA	$1,000	None

State	Limit of Value	Limit of Area
NORTH DAKOTA	$25,000 in town No limit in country.	2 acres in town; 160 acres in country
OHIO	$1,000	None
OKLAHOMA	$5,000	160 acres if rural
OREGON	$5,000	1 block in city; 160 acres elsewhere
PENNSYLVANIA	No law	—
RHODE ISLAND	No law	—
SOUTH CAROLINA	$1,000	None
TEXAS	$10,000 in city, town or village; no limit in rural areas	200 acres for family; 100 acres for single adult
UTAH	$4,000 plus $1,500 for wife and $600 for each other member of family	No limitation
VERMONT	$5,000	No limitation
VIRGINIA	$3,500	No limitation
WASHINGTON	$10,000	No limitation
WEST VIRGINIA	$1,000	No limitation
WISCONSIN	$25,000	40 acres of agricultural land; 1/4 acre otherwise
WYOMING	$4,000	No limitation

Chart 10

DEGREES OF CONSANGUINITY UNDER THE CIVIL LAW

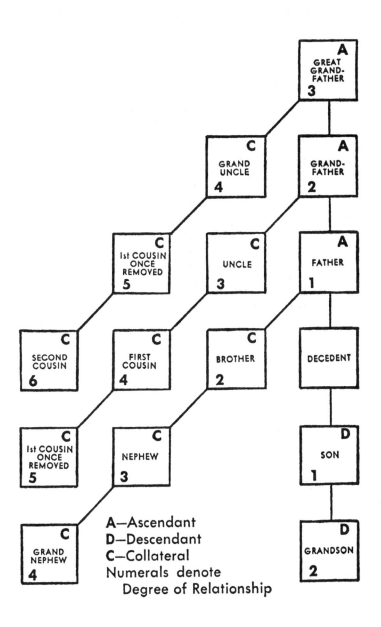

A—Ascendant
D—Descendant
C—Collateral
Numerals denote
Degree of Relationship

Chart 11

HOLOGRAPHIC WILLS

STATE	Holographic Wills Permitted	STATE	Holographic Wills Permitted
Alabama	No	New York	Valid only for military personnel and mariners at sea.
Alaska	Yes		
Arkansas	Yes		
Arizona	Yes		
California	Yes	North Carolina	Yes
Colorado	Yes	North Dakota	Yes
Connecticut	Not valid if made in Conn.; Yes, if valid where made.	Ohio	No
		Oklahoma	Yes
		Oregon	No
		Pennsylvania	Yes
Delaware	No	Rhode Island	No
Dist. of Columbia	No	South Carolina	No
Florida	No	South Dakota	Yes
Georgia	No	Tennessee	Yes
Hawaii	No, if made in Hawaii; Yes, if valid where made.	Texas	Yes
		Utah	Yes
		Vermont	No
		Virginia	Yes
Idaho	Yes	Washington	No
Illinois	No	West Virginia	Yes
Indiana	No	Wisconsin	No
Iowa	No	Wyoming	Yes
Kansas	No		
Kentucky	Yes		
Louisiana	Yes		
Maine	No		
Maryland	No		
Massachusetts	No		
Michigan	No		
Minnesota	No		
Mississippi	Yes		
Montana	Yes		
Nebraska	No		
Nevada	Yes		
New Hampshire	No		
New Jersey	No		
New Mexico	No		

Chart 12

NUMBER OF WITNESSES REQUIRED FOR VALID EXECUTION OF A WILL

The following States Require Three Witnesses:

Louisiana	New Hampshire
Maine	South Carolina
Massachusetts	Vermont

The following States Require Two Witnesses:

Alabama	Montana
Alaska	Nebraska
Arizona	Nevada
Arkansas	New Jersey
California	New Mexico
Colorado	New York
Connecticut	North Carolina
Delaware	North Dakota
District of Columbia	Ohio
Florida	Oklahoma
Georgia	Oregon
Hawaii	Pennsylvania
Idaho	Rhode Island
Illinois	South Dakota
Indiana	Tennessee
Iowa	Texas
Kansas	Utah
Kentucky	Virginia
Maryland	Washington
Michigan	West Virginia
Minnesota	Wisconsin
Mississippi	Wyoming
Missouri	

Chart 13

MINIMUM AGE REQUIREMENT FOR THE EXECUTION OF A WILL

STATE	AGE	STATE	AGE
Alabama	21(real property) 18(personal property)	Missouri	18
		Montana	18
Alaska	19	Nebraska	19
Arizona	21 or married	Nevada	18
Arkansas	18	New Hampshire	18 or married
California	18	New Jersey	18
Colorado	18	New Mexico	18
Connecticut	18	New York	18
Delaware	18	North Carolina	18
D. of Columbia	21	North Dakota	18
Florida	18	Ohio	18
Georgia	14	Oklahoma	18
Hawaii	20	Oregon	18
Idaho	18	Pennsylvania	18
Illinois	18	Rhode Island	18
Indiana	18	South Carolina	18
Iowa	18	South Dakota	18
Kansas	18	Tennessee	18
Kentucky	18	Texas	18 or married
Louisiana	16	Utah	18
Maine	18 or married	Vermont	18
Maryland	18	Virginia	18
Massachusetts	18	Washington	18
Michigan	18	West Virginia	18
Minnesota	18	Wisconsin	18
Mississippi	18	Wyoming	21

Chart 14

SPOUSE'S RIGHT OF ELECTION

State	Election by		Limitation or share Under the Right of Election	Period for Filing Election
	Husband	Wife		
ALABAMA	No	Yes	Intestate share; if no children or descendants limited to $50,000	Within 6 months after probate
ALASKA	Yes	Yes	One-third of augmented net estate	Within 6 months after publication of first notice to creditors
ARKANSAS	Yes, if Will executed prior to marriage	Yes	Intestate share	Within 1 month after expiration for filing claims
COLORADO	Yes	Yes	One-half of augmented net estate	Within 6 months after notice for filing claims or 1 year after death
CONNECTICUT	Yes	Yes	One-third of estate for life	Within 2 months after expiration for filing claims
DELAWARE	Yes	Yes	$20,000 or 1/3 of estate, whichever is less	Within 6 months after grant of Letters Testamentary or of Administration

State	Election by		Limitation or Share Under the Right of Election	Period for Filing Election
	Husband	Wife		
DISTRICT OF COLUMBIA	Yes	Yes	Intestate share up to 1/2 of estate	Within 6 months after probate
FLORIDA	Yes	Yes	30% of net assets	Within 4 months of notice of administration
GEORGIA	No	No		
HAWAII	Yes	Yes	Dower or curtesy	Within 6 months after death
IDAHO	Yes	Yes	One-half of quasi community property	Within 6 months after publication of first notice to creditors
ILLINOIS	Yes	Yes	If descendants survive, one-third of entire estate; if not, one-half of entire estate	Within 7 months after probate
INDIANA	Yes	Yes	One-third of entire estate [1]	Within 10 days after time for filing claims
IOWA	Yes	Yes	Intestate share	Within 2 months after second notice of probate; 4 months after notice by executor

State	Election by Husband	Election by Wife	Limitation or Share Under the Right of Election	Period for Filing Election
KANSAS	Yes	Yes	Intestate share	Within 4 months after probate
KENTUCKY	Yes	Yes	Dower, limited to 1/3 of real property	Within 6 months after probate
MAINE	Yes	Yes	Intestate share, limited to 1/2 of the estate	Within 6 months after probate
MARYLAND	Yes	Yes	Intestate share	Within 30 days after expiration of time for filing claims
MASSACHUSETTS	Yes	Yes	One-third of estate if issue survives[2]	Within 6 months after probate
MICHIGAN	No	Yes	Intestate share limited to 1/2 of realty absolutely and 1/2 subject to legacies; personal property up to $5,000 and half of remainder	Within 60 days after entry or order closing estate to claims
MINNESOTA	Yes	Yes	Intestate share limited to 1/2 of entire estate if no surviving issue	Within 6 months after probate, or 9 months after death
MISSISSIPPI	Yes	Yes	Intestate share limited to 1/2 of entire estate[3]	Within 90 days after probate

State	Election by		Limitation or Share Under the Right of Election	Period for Filing Election
	Husband	Wife		
MISSOURI	Yes	Yes	One-third of estate if lineal descendants survive, otherwise one-half	10 days after time limited for contesting Will or within 90 days after final determination of litigation
MONTANA	Yes	Yes	One-third of augmented estate	Within 6 months after publication of first notice to creditors, or within one year of death, whichever is sooner
NEBRASKA	Yes	Yes	Intestate share	Within 1 year after issuance of letters testamentary
NEW HAMPSHIRE	Yes	Yes	Intestate share	Within 6 months after appointment of Executor
NEW JERSEY	Yes	Yes	Dower, Curtesy	Within 6 months after probate
NEW YORK	Yes	Yes	Intestate share limited to 1/2 of net estate; one-third if issue survive [4]	Within 6 months after issue of letters testamentary or letters of administration
NORTH CAROLINA	Yes	Yes	Intestate share, limited to 1/2 of the estate	Within 6 months after issuance of letters testamentary or of administration

State	Election by Husband	Wife	Limitation or Share Under the Right of Election	Period for Filing Election
NORTH DAKOTA	Yes	Yes	One-third of augmented estate	Within 6 months after publication of first notice to creditors
OHIO	Yes	Yes	Intestate share limited to 1/2 of estate	Within 1 month after service of citation to elect, if no citation issued within 7 months after appointment of executor or administrator
OKLAHOMA	Yes	Yes	Intestate share	No fixed period
OREGON	Yes	Yes	One-fourth of net estate [5]	Within 90 days after admission of will to probate or 30 days after filing inventory
PENNSYLVANIA	Yes	Yes	One-third of estate if lineal descendants survive, otherwise one-half	Within 6 months after probate
RHODE ISLAND	Yes	Yes	Dower or curtesy	Within 6 months after probate
SOUTH CAROLINA	No	Yes	Dower	Prior to distribution of estate, or when called to renounce her dower interest

State	Election by		Limitation or Share Under the Right of Election	Period for Filing Election
	Husband	Wife		
TENNESSEE	Yes	Yes	Dower or curtesy plus one-third of personal property if no child or not more than two survive; a child's part of personal property if more than two children survive	Within 6 months after probate of will
UTAH	No	Yes	One-third in value of all husband's real property	Within 4 months after probate
VERMONT	Yes	Yes	Dower or curtesy	Within 8 months after probate
VIRGINIA	Yes	Yes	Dower or curtesy plus one-third of personal property if issue or adopted child survive, otherwise one-half	Within 1 year after death or probate
WEST VIRGINIA	Yes	Yes	Dower or curtesy and one-third of the personal property	Within 8 months of probate
WISCONSIN	Yes	Yes	Dower and up to one-third of the personal property	Within 6 months after death

State	Election by		Limitation or Share Under the Right of Election	Period for Filing Election
	Husband	Wife		
WYOMING	Yes	Yes	Intestate share of entire estate, limited to 1/4 if children survive; 1/2 if no children survive	Within 3 months after probate

1 If surviving spouse is a second or subsequent spouse who did not have children by the decedent and the decedent left a child or descendant, then the share is limited to one-third the net personal estate plus a life estate in one-third of the real property.

2 If testator leaves no issue or kindred surviving spouse takes $25,000 plus one-half of remainder. If testator leaves kindred but no issue, surviving spouse takes $25,000 plus income of one-half of the personal property in trust and income from one-half of real property.

3 If the surviving spouse has separate property amounting to more than a one-fifth share of the estate, the survivor can only elect to take the difference between the separate property and the share entitled under the election

4 Depending on the size of the estate, certain absolute legacies or trust provisions may defeat the right of election (see E.P.T.L. §5-1.1).

5 The net estate may be reduced by the value of certain property given under the will.

Part Two

LAW AND LIVELIHOOD

Chapter III
COMMERCIAL LAW

Most of the changes in the commercial law field were made to accommodate our growing technological expertise and availability and rapidity of communication and transportation. The Uniform Commercial Code recognizes that no longer are commercial transactions always within one state, but may encompass many. Hence the need for uniformity in commercial dealings. An outmoded copyright law has been renovated to take into account our sophisticated instrument for communication and reproduction of ideas.

CONTRACTS

In general principles of contract law have been modified in recent years by the provisions of the Uniform Commercial Code (See below under Commercial Code, and below under Sales). These principles have been modified also in certain consumer transactions. (See the Chapter herein relating to the Consumer and the Law.) Some states have also amended sections of their laws relating to Statute of Limitations on contracts (the time in which a suit may be brought on a contract). See Charts at the end of this chapter.

COPYRIGHT

Effective January 1, 1978, the United States will have a new copyright law. This has been the first complete major revision of the Copyright law (Title 17 of the U.S. Code) since 1909.

One of the major changes of the law is the elimination of the common law right of copyright. Under the present law, a statutory copyright dates from the time of publication. It lasts for twenty-eight years and may be renewed for another twenty-eight years. If a work is not published, the author has a common law right of copyright, which is perpetual, unless the author publishes the work.

This common law right will no longer exist under the new law. The right of copyright comes into existence, when the work is "created". In section 101, the "definitions" section of the act, it is stated, "A work is created when it is fixed in a copy . . . for the first time; where a work is prepared over a period of time, the portion of it that has been fixed at any particular time constitutes the work as of that time, and where the work has been prepared in different versions, each version constitutes a separate work."

The term of duration under the new law is fifty years after the death of the author, or if the book is jointly authored after the death of the last surviving author. Anonymous works and works made for hire are protected for seventy-five years after publication or one hundred years after creation, whichever is sooner. Works published and copyrighted prior to the new law, which have not entered into the public domain, will continue under the old copyright duration of twenty eight years, but the renewal term will be extended from twenty-eight years to forty seven years. Unpublished works, created before January 1, 1978, which were protected by a common law copyright, will be protected after the effective date of the new law for seventy five years from publication or one hundred years from creation, whichever is the shorter period of time.

The new law also codifies the case law rulings which have become known as the "fair use doctrine." Sec. 107 provides that the fair use of a copyrighted work, including use "for purposes such as criticism, comment, news reporting, teaching, (including multiple copies for classroom use), scholarship or research" is not an infringement of copyright. The factors that may be considered in determining fair use would be the nature and character of the use (e.g. whether for commercial or educational, non-profit purposes), the nature of the copyrighted work, the substantiality of the portion used in relation to the whole, together with the effect of the use on the potential market for, or the value of the work. However, this section is not meant to limit the meaning of "fair use". The House Report, accompanying the new Copyright law, states that Section 107 merely restates the present judicial doctrine of "fair use", and was not passed with the intent of changing, narrowing it or enlarging it in any way.

The new law also takes up the problem of photocopying by libraries. Section 108 of the law sets forth those circumstances and the manner in which such photocopying may be done without violation of a copyright. Section 108 reads as follows:

Limitations on exclusive rights: Reproduction by libraries and archives

(a) Not withstanding the provisions of section 106, it is not an infringement of copyright for a library or archives, or any of its employees acting within the scope of their employment, to reproduce no more than one copy or phonorecord of a work, or to distribute such copy

or phonorecord, under the conditions specified by this section, if—
(1) the reproduction or distribution is made without any purpose of direct or indirect commercial advantage;
(2) the collections of the library or archives are (i) open to the public, or (ii) available not only to researchers affiliated with the library or archives or with the institution of which it is a part, but also to other persons doing research in a specialized field; and
(3) the reproduction or distribution of the work includes a notice of copyright.

(b) The rights of reproduction and distribution under this section apply to a copy or phonorecord of an unpublished work duplicated in facsimile form solely for purposes of preservation and security or for deposit for research use in another library or archives of the type described by clause (2) of subsection (a), if the copy or phonorecord reproducted is currently in the collections of the library or archives.

(c) The right of reproduction under this section applies to a copy or phonorecord of a published work duplicated in facsimile form solely for the purpose of replacement of a copy or phonorecord that is damaged, deteriorating, lost, or stolen, if the library or archives has, after a reasonable effort, determined that an unused replacement cannot be obtained at a fair price.

(d) The rights of reproduction and distribution under this section apply to a copy, made from the collection of a library or archives where the user makes his or her request or from that of another library or archives, of no more than one article or other contribution to a copyrighted collection or periodical issue, or to a copy or phonorecord of a small part of any other copyrighted work, if—
(1) the copy or phonorecord becomes the property of the user, and the library or archives has had no notice that the copy or phonorecord would be used for any purpose other than private study, scholarship, or research; and
(2) the library or archives displays prominently, at the place where orders are accepted, and includes on its order form, a warning of copyright in accordance with requirements that the Register of Copyrights shall prescribe by regulation.

(e) The rights of reproduction and distribution under this section apply to the entire work, or to a substantial part of it, made from the collection of a library or archives where the user makes his or her request or from that of another library or archives, if the library or archives has first determined, on the basis of a reasonable investigation, that a copy or phonorecord of the copyrighted work cannot be obtained at a fair price, if—
(1) the copy or phonorecord becomes the property of the user, and the library or archives has had no notice that the copy or phonorecord would be used for any purpose other than private study, scholarship, or research; and
(2) the library or archives displays prominently, at the place

where orders are accepted, and includes on its orders form, a warning of copyright in accordance with requirements that the Register of Copyrights shall prescribe by regulation.

(f) Nothing in this section—
(1) shall be construed to impose liability for copyright infringement upon a library or archives or its employees for the unsupervised use of reproducing equipment located on its premises: *Provided,* That such equipment displays a notice that the making of a copy may be subject to the copyright law;
(2) excuses a person who uses such reproducing equipment or who requests a copy or phonorecord under subsection (d) from liability for copyright infringement for any such act, or for any later use of such copy or phonorecord, if it exceeds fair use as provided by section 107;
(g) The privileges prescribed by subsections (a) and (b) do not, unless authorized by the copyright owner, extend to any person who has acquired possession of the copy or phonorecord from the copyright owner, by rental, lease, loan, or otherwise, without acquiring ownership of it.

The remedies under the new act are substantially the same as those under the old, and as under the former act, registration is a condition precedent to bringing an infringement suit.

COMMERCIAL CODE

The Uniform Commercial Code (hereinafter referred to as "the Code" was a massive task undertaken by the American Law Institute and the National Conference of Commissioners on Uniform State Laws. Its purpose, as stated in the Code, was to simplify the rules of commercial law and to unify the various state laws on the subject. Prior to the Code, not only were there different laws governing commercial transactions in the various states, but differences existed in intrastate laws. Most states had separate laws governing sales, negotiable instruments, bills of lading. Hence, even a simple sales transaction, completed within one state, could involve as many as five different laws. It was this duplication of laws, with the resulting delays and inefficiencies, which the UCC sought to supplant.

It is also interesting to note that the UCC recognizes the duty of each party to a business dealing to act in good faith. It specifically incorporates this concept into the Code by Section 203 which reads as follows: "Any contract or duty within this Act imposes an obligation of good faith in its performance or endorsement." This concept of "morality" in business dealings is also evidenced in the provision permitting courts to void a sales contract for being unconscionable. This is discussed more fully under SALES below.

The framers of the Code also recognized the importance of usual trade and business practices, as well as prior business dealings, in business transactions. It specifically provides that such factors should be taken into consideration in interpreting disputed contracts. Section 1-205 relating to Course of Dealing and Usage of Trade reads as follows:

(1) A course of dealing is a sequence of previous conduct between the parties to a particular transaction which is fairly to be regarded as establishing a common basis of understanding for interpreting their expressions and other conduct.

(2) A usage of trade is any practice or method of dealing having such regularity of observance in a place, vocation or trade as to justify an expectation that it will be observed with respect to the transaction in question. The existence and scope of such a usage are to be proved as facts. If it is established that such a usage is embodied in a written trade code or similar writing the interpretation of the writing is for the court.

(3) A course of dealing between parties and any usage of trade in the vocation or trade in which they are engaged or of which they are or should be aware give particular meaning to and supplement or qualify terms of an agreement.

(4) The express terms of an agreement and an applicable course of dealing or usage of trade shall be construed wherever reasonable as consistent with each other; but when such construction is unreasonable express terms control both course of dealing and usage of trade and course of dealing controls usage of trade.

(5) An applicable usage of trade in the place where any part of performance is to occur shall be used in interpreting the agreement as to that part of the performance.

(6) Evidence of a relevant usage of trade offered by one party is not admissible unless and until he has given the other party such notice as the court finds sufficient to prevent unfair surprise to the latter.

In 1953, Pennsylvania was the first state to enact the Uniform Commercial Code. Her action has since been followed by all her sister states except Louisiana. Not all of the states have identical statutes. Many have adopted the Code with some of their own variations, but still the laws have a uniformity which was absent in the pre-Code era.

CORPORATIONS

One of the stronger trends in the recent developments in corporation law has been the recognition of the special needs of corporations, which require restrictions on the voluntary transfer of the shareholders' stock. Such restrictions are imposed upon so called "close" corporations and upon professional corporations. A "close" corporation is one in which the people who actively manage the corporation and the few people who own most of the shares of the corporation are substantially identical. It is sometimes said that fundamentally a close corporation has a very strong resemblance to a partnership.

A common method of providing a corporation with some of the attributes of a partnership is through the use of so called stockholders agreements. Some states require corporations to restrict the transfer of its shares in its articles of incorporation or shareholders agreements before it is granted a close corporation status. Such agreements usually set forth the extent of the participation of the shareholders in the activities of the corporation and how the shares will be distributed among the shareholders. Restrictions are usually placed upon the powers of both directors and shareholders of the corporation to protect all connected with the corporation. Veto power is usually given with respect to the admission of new shareholders, restrictions on the transfer of shares and provisions for the purchase of shares of deceased shareholders are spelled out. To ease this later burden and to prevent the forced sale of stock of closely held corporations in order to pay Federal Estate Taxes, the Internal Revenue Code permits deferral of payments in accordance with law. The Small Business Tax Revision Act of 1958 amended the code to permit estates taxes to be paid in ten annual installments if the value of the "close" corporation business exceeds thirty five per cent of the gross estate or fifty percent of the taxable estate. The Tax Reform Act of 1976 allows fifteen year extensions in the Federal Estate Tax payments if the value of the close corporation is at least 50% of the gross estate.

Prior to 1963, no state had any completely separate law relating specifically to close corporations, although the general corporation laws frequently had scattered sections applicable to this type of corporation. The following states have since adopted separate close corporation statutes: Arizona, California, Delaware, Kansas, Maine, Maryland, Pennsylvania and Texas. For a better understanding of the nature of these statutes, let us look at some of the applicable Delaware statutes. Title 8, section 343 of the Delaware Code provides that the certificate of incorporation shall contain a statement by a corporation that is a close corporation, if it is to have such status, and must contain the provisions required by section 342. Such additional mendatory requirements specified in Section 343 are as follows:

> (1) All of the corporation's issued stock of all classes, exclusive of treasury shares, shall be held of record by not more than a specified number of persons, not exceeding thirty; and
> (2) All of the issued stock of all classes shall be subject to one

or more of the restrictions on transfer permitted by section 202 of this title; and

(3) The corporation shall make no offering of any of its stock of any class which would constitute a "public offering" within the meaning of the United States Securities Act of 1933, as it may be amended from time to time.

By perfecting its close corporation status in Delaware, the certificate of incorporation may confer management directly upon the shareholders. If this is not done the stockholders may restrict the power of directors. It is also provided that should the directors of a close corporation become deadlocked as to the management of the corporation, then a provisional director may be appointed by the Court of Chancery.

Since the enactment of the Delaware close corporation provisions, the features of the Delaware statutes have been used as the model for similar laws in other states.

One other factor which influences the organization of close corporation is that if they meet the statutory requirements, the corporation may elect to become a "tax option" corporation or as they are sometimes called, a "Subchapter S" corporation. If qualified, a tax option corporation may elect by the unanimous consent of its stockholders to avoid payment of corporate income tax and instead have income tax paid by the stockholders, as if the income had been received by the stockholders in proportion to their share holdings. However, to make the "tax option" election a corporation may not have more than ten stockholders who must be individuals, estates or certain types of trusts. (After a specified period the corporation may have as many as fifteen stockholders.) In addition, other statutory requirements must be met.

Another type of corporation which is gaining in prominence is the Professional Corporation. For some time professionals had been requesting their local legislatures to adopt a new type law to permit them to organize as a corporation. The first state to do so was Tennessee, in 1961. Although initially opposed to such legislation, the Internal Revenue Service resigned itself to such corporations in 1969 and accorded them a corporate tax status. At the present time all states allow professionals to either form a corporation or an association with the characteristics of a corporation. Some states permit both types of organizations.

Professional corporations may only be organized to render one type of professional service. No stock in a professional corporation may be issued or transferred to any person, not licensed to perform the professional service involved. To preserve the professional corporation, most state laws require the remaining stockholders to purchase shares of a stockholder who has died, retired or been professionally disqualified. Despite the fact that he is involved in a corporation, each professional still is held to standards of professional conduct and his professional responsibility to patients or clients is in no way limited.

Furthermore, since one of the prime motives in the organization of a professional corporation is the tax advantage of that ensures, a corporate form of organization must be strictly followed. Thus, even though several professionals incorporate a professional corporation, if they were to maintain separate accounting books, have individual incomes, rather than shares income among the shareholders, pay their own separate rents and not follow a corporate form in their other activities, the Internal Revenue Service would challenge whether such individuals were truly incorporated within the meaning of the tax laws.

Heretofore we have been concerned with only two special types of corporations, namely close corporations and professional corporations. Now let us turn to some new developments in the law relating to corporations in general.

Model Business Corporation Act

Since 1946 over half of the states have adopted complete new corporatin laws. Most of the states have based their new corporation laws on the Model Business Corporation Act, originally sponsered by the section on Corporations, Banking and Business Law of the American Bar Association. The model act does not require total uniformity in all the states that have adopted it, but such states that have adopted it, have similar laws with similar terminology.

Since the Model Act was initially drafted, it has been revised several times, extensively in 1969 and more recently in 1973. Let us examine the 1969 amendments first.

The number of individuals required to act as incorporators in forming a corporation were changed from a minimum of three to one or more. Corporations were given the power to enter into partnerships and joint ventures. A modernized "indemnification" provision was adopted based upon a law originated by the State of Delaware. Indemnification is a legal procedure whereby someone, who is an officer, director, employee or agent of a corporation or one of its subsidiaries, may be reimbursed for legal expenses, including judgments and fines, for which he becomes liable in the course of performing his duties for the corporation. The legal expense may be incurred in an actual legal action involving the person seeking to be indemnified or such expenses may be incurred in connection with a threatened legal action. The person seeking indemnification must meet the statutory requirement before such indemnification may take place.

Additional amendments concerned the powers and duties of directors. One new amendment permits the articles of incorporation to provide that the business of the corporation may be managed by other than the board of directors. The former requirement that there must be at least three directors was supplanted by the requirement of only one or more directors. A statutory procedure was set forth for legalizing contracts or other transactions between the corporation and one or more of its directors (or another corporation or business in which its directors or officers have a financial interest.) If the financially interested director was present at the board meeting to approve the contract or transaction and if his vote was counted for approval, then the contract or transaction may be validated, if:

(a) the fact of such relationship or interest is disclosed or known to the board of directors or committee which authorizes, approves or ratifies the contract or transaction by a vote or consent sufficient for the purpose without counting the votes or consents of such interested directors; or

(b) the fact of such relationship or interest is disclosed or known to the shareholders entitled to vote and they authorize, approve or ratify such contract or transaction by vote or written consent; or

(c) the contract or transaction is fair and reasonable to the corporation.

Additional amendments gave the corporation the power to lend money to its directors (if approved by the stockholders) and to use its credit to assist employees (if the board of directors decides that such assistance will benefit the corporation.) Directors and shareholders were also given authority to take action by unanimous written consent without a meeting.

One of the most important changes was made with regard to the purposes which a corporation intends to pursue. These purposes must be specified in the Articles of Incorporation. Formerly, the Articles had to specify the exact type of business which the corporation intended to pursue (e.g. operation of a restaurant or the manufacture of chairs). Under the new provision the purpose or purposes of the corporation may be stated to be, or to include the transaction of any or all lawful business for which corporations may be incorporated in the state in which the corporation is organized.

There were some more amendments in 1973, including a provision which allows directors to participate in board meetings and committee meetings by means of a conference telephone or other communication equipment whereby all the participants can hear one another.

Delaware Corporation Law

While the Model Act is important because so many states have adopted it, of equal importance is the Delaware Corporation Law, as a great number of corporations choose it as their state of incorporation. Other states, such as Kansas have patterned their laws after the Delaware Law.

A complete revision of the Delaware law occured several years efore the Model Act revision. Some consider that provisions of the Delaware law are more progressive and liberal than the Model Act. A brief discussion of these provisions may highlight some of the current and future changes that may be found in the corporation laws of the various states.

When a corporate document such as the Certificate of Incorporation or an Amendment or Merger is filed in Delaware, the document may specify therein on what date the document shall become effective. Under prior law the date of filing was the effective date of the instrument. Under the new law the document could be made effective on a holiday when filings usually can not be made, January 1, for instance. However the law states that the effective date of the instrument may not be later than ninety days after its filing with the Secretary of State of Delaware.

You will recall that in the discussion of the Model Act it was mentioned that it permits stockholders to take action by unanimous written consent, without a meeting. The Delaware law permits stockholders to approve action by written consent which may be less than unanimous, unless the Certificate of Incorporation provides otherwise. The consent in writing must be signed by the holders of outstanding stock constituting not less than the minimum number of votes required to authorize such actin. For example by statute an amendment to the Certificate of Incorporation must be approved by a majority of the stock. In the case mentioned above the written consent of a majority of the stockholders would be required. However if action is taken by written consent and there is less than an unanimous vote, prompt notice of such action must be given to stockholders who did not consent.

In Delaware, the office of president and secretary of the corporation may be held by the same person. This is not permitted in the Model Act.

In Delaware, in the absence of a contrary provision in the Certificate of Incorporation, a merger may be approved without the vote of stockholders of the surviving corporation, if no amendments are made to the Certificate of Incorporation of the survivor and there are no substantial changes in capital, as specified in the statute.

However if no vote of the stockholders is required in connection with the merger, one other important consequence flows therefrom. Delaware, as do many other states, has a procedure whereby stockholders who do not vote their shares in favor of a merger and who comply with the procedure outlined in the statute, may have their shares appraised by a court procedure. A value is placed on the shares and the stockholder who "dissents" to the merger will be paid this value, rather than receiving the shares or securities he would have received after the merger. Such value it should be kept in mind, may be greater or less than the value of shares issued in the merger, so that the stockholder takes some risk in requesting appraisal rights for his shares. However, stockholders do not have appraisal rights in the case of a merger which may be approved without stockholder vote. Appraisal rights are also withdrawn from stockholders when the shares held by said stockholder are listed on a natinal securities exchange or held by more than 2,000 stockholders. While there are certain statutory exceptions to the foregoing, they do not apply in most cases because the stockholder has a ready market for the sale of his shares in the event he disapproves of the merger. This would give him a quicker and less cumbersome method of recovering value for his shares as opposed to the appraisal method. Where appraisal is available, the corporation is required to send copies of the Delaware statutes relating to appraisal rights of stockholders. This type of notification is a growing trend. It was most recently adopted in the new California Corporation law, which went into effect on January 1, 1977.

In closing note must be made that Delaware has enactd a type of law which has rapidly been adopted in approximately twenty three states. This is the so called, "tender, offer disclosure" statute. When a corporation offers to purchase for cash, stock or other securities, the stock of another corporation, it is called a "tender offer". In the past such offers have often come as a complete surprise to those in the management of the corporations whose shares were sought to be bought. To remedy this situation, statutes have been passed requiring that management receive at least one or two months notice prior to the time in which stock purchases are allowed to be made. This permits the management ample time to allow different views on the tender offer, to be given. As a further precaution against possible fraud, some states require the Attorney General to receive notice of the proposed offer.

Many states have followed Delaware's lead in adopting some of the trends outlined above.

SALES

Contracts for the sale of personal property are governed by the Uniform Commercial Code. Prior to this time sales were governed by various state laws, in many cases, the Uniform Sales Act. In a book of this scope it is impossible to do more than highlight a few of the changes resulting from the adoption of the UCC. The reader who is particularly interested in the UCC provisions is referred to the Code itself and to the Legal Almanac, Lloyd, *Understanding the Uniform Commercial Code.*

Changes have been made in the law relating to the formation of contracts. The formalities of acceptance have been somewhat curtailed. For instance, Section 2-207(2) indicates that even if the writings of the parties do not establish a contract, if both parties act as if a contract has been made, then the court will find one. The terms of the contract will be found from the various writings of the parties and supplemented by provisions found in the UCC itself.

As any middle-aged lawyer can tell you, for years it has been a fundamental principle of contract law that a counter offer has the effect of killing the initial offer. For a valid contract to be consummated, the counteroffer must be accepted by the original offeror. This is not true under the UCC. Section 2-207 reads as follows:

§ 2-207. Additional Terms in Acceptance or Confirmation.-

"(1) A definite and seasonable expression of acceptance or a written confirmation which is sent within a reasonable time operates as an acceptance even though it states terms additional to or different from those offered or agreed upon, unless acceptance is expressly made conditional on assent to the additional or different terms.

(2) The additional terms are to be construed as proposals for addition to the contract. Between merchants such terms become part of the contract unless:

(a) the offer expressly limits acceptance to the terms of the offer;

(b) they materially alter it; or

(c) notification of objection to them has already been given or is given within a reasonable time after notice of them is received.

(3) Conduct by both parties which recognizes the existence of a contract is sufficient to establish a contract for sale although the writings of the parties do not otherwise establish a contract. In such case the terms on which the writings of the parties agree, together with any supplementary terms incorporated under any other provisions of this Act."

The importance of consideration, which has traditionally been an essential part of a contract has been considerably diminished by the UCC in some instances, as shown by the following examples.

Traditionally an offer may be revoked at any time. If one desired an irrevocable or "firm" offer he had to pay a consideration for it. Generally this is true under the UCC, but it is expressly provided in Section 2-205, that a signed written firm offer by a merchant may be enforceable without compensation, for the time stated in the offer, or if none has been stated, for three months. Note this rule applies only to merchants. If the offeror is not a merchant, he is liable under the same circumstances, only if he has a full understanding of what he is doing.

Under the UCC, (Sec. 2-305) the parties may consummate a contract even though the price has not been fixed. The parties can agree to fix the price in the future, or if the contract is silent regarding price, it will be the reasonable price at the time of delivery. Of course, despite this provision, the parties are free to provide in the agreement that there will be no contract until the price has been agreed upon.

Statute of Frauds

Under prior laws to be enforceable a contract had to be in writing. This requirement was generally referred to as the statute of frauds. Sales for goods valued over $500 (the figure varies from state to state) are not enforceable under the UCC unless there is a writing indicating that a contract has been entered into and signed by the party sought to be charged. However under the Code, there are exceptions. If goods are specially made for the buyer and are not able to be sold in the ordinary course of trade, and the seller has substantially completed his part of the contract, the contract will not fail because it was not in writing. Nor will a contract fail for lack of writing, where payment has been made and accepted, goods have been delivered and accepted, or the party sought to be charged admits to the contract in a subsequent legal proceeding.

A memorandum signed by the party sought to be charged, giving some evidence that a contract has been entered into and specifying the quantity of goods involved would also be sufficient to establish a contract under the UCC.

Warranties

The UCC provides for express and implied warranties. Care must be taken to determine whether the statement made by the seller is an expression of fact or opinion. In the first instance the statement may be regarded as an express warranty. In the case of the mere expression of an opinion, a warranty does not arise. In cases where a model is used to demonstrate the goods to be sold, the seller does not warrant that the goods will conform exactly to the specifications of the model, unless he specifically say so. The Code also provides for an implied warranty of fitness for a particular purpose, which occurs when the seller has reason to know any particular purpose for which the goods are required and that the buyer is relying on the seller's skill or judgment to select the goods. There is also an implied warranty of merchantability. It is implied in a contract of sale, if the seller is a merchant of goods of that kind.

Implied warranties can be excluded or limited under the Code. Sec. 2-316(3) provides that the use of words such as "as is" or "without fault" or any other words customarily used to call the buyer's attention to the fact that a warranty is not given, has the effect of excluding a warranty. Of course if the buyer has the opportunity to inspect the goods and the defect is one that could have been detected by him, there is no warranty as to those defects. If it is customarily done in the course of trade, warranties may be limited or modified by trade practices.

The implied warranty of merchantability can also be modified or excluded. To do so it must be specifically stated that the warrant of merchantability is being modified or excluded. It is pretty well settled by case law that to be effective the term merchantability must be used in the modifying or exclusionary statement. If the statement is written, the language curtailing the warranty must be conspicuous.

Risk of Loss

One of the more troublesome questions in any sale, is which party bears the loss if the goods are destroyed. Under former laws this usually involved determining the exact moment at which title passes. The UCC, in Section 2-509 lists the various contingency situations and sets forth who will bear the risk of loss.

§ 2-509. Risk of Loss in the Absence of Breach.—

(1) Where the contract requires or authorizes the seller to ship the goods by carrier

(a) if it does not require him to deliver them at a particular destination, the risk of loss passes to the buyer when the goods are duly delivered to the carrier even though the shipment is under reservation (Section 2-505); but

(b) if it does require him to deliver them at a particular destination and the goods are there duly tendered while in the possession of the carrier, the risk of loss passes to the buyer when the goods are there duly so tendered as to enable buyer to take delivery.

(2) Where the goods are held by a bailee to be delivered without being moved, the risk of loss passes to the buyer.

(a) on his receipt of a negotiable document of title covering the goods; or

(b) on acknowledgment by the bailee of the buyer's right to possession of the goods; or

(c) after his receipt of a non-negotiable document of title or other written direction to deliver, as provided in subsection (4) (b) of Section 2-503.

(3) In any case not within subsection (1) or (2), the risk of loss passes to the buyer on his receipt of the goods if the seller is a merchant; otherwise the risk passes to the buyer on tender of delivery.

(4) The provisions of this section are subject to contrary agreement of the parties and to the provisions of this Article on sale on approval (Section 2-327) and on effect of breach on risk of less (Section 2-510)."

Remedies of Buyer and Seller

The UCC has made some changes with respect to the remedies of the seller and the buyer. Many of these focus on the buyer's insolvency. When a seller learns that the buyer is insolvent, he may refuse to deliver goods to the buyer on credit. If the goods have already been shipped but have not been received by the buyer or his agent, the seller may stop the goods in transit. If the buyer has received the goods and they have not been paid for, the seller may reclaim them within ten days of learning about the buyer's insolvency. If the buyer has ever in writing, to the seller, represented himself to be solvent, the ten day limitation does not apply. Of course if the buyer has already transferred the goods to an innocent third party, for value, the goods cannot be reclaimed by the seller.

Another of the remedies of the seller under the UCC, is an unrestricted right to resell the goods on learning of the buyers default (or in the case of an anticipatory breach). Under some earlier laws he was limitd to taking such action only when the goods involved were perishible or the buyer had been in default an unreasonable length of time.

Unconscionability of Contract

One of the more interesting provisions in the Code relating to sales is Sec. 2-302 which empowers a court to refuse to enforce a contract or any part of it which it deems unconscionable. Usually the courts will invoke this provision when it is obvious that one party is taking unfair advantage of another, particularly in dealings between experienced merchants and not so knowledgeable non-merchants. Section 2-302 reads as follows:

§ 2-302. Unconscionable Contract or Clause.—

"(1) If the court as a matter of law finds the contract or any clause of the contract to have been unconscionable at the time it was made the court may refuse to enforce the contract, or it may enforce the remainder of the contract without the unconscionable clause, or it may so limit the application of any unconscionable clause as to avoid any unconscionable result.

(2) When it is claimed or appears to the court that the contract or any clause thereof may be unconscionable the parties shall be afforded a reasonable opportunity to present evidence as to its commercial setting, purpose and effect to aid the court in making the determination."

SECURITIES

Congress in its wisdom has granted to the Securities and Exchange Commission vast administrative powers in connection with the sale of securities. These powers provide the greatest protection and safeguard for an investor in securities. The Commission was created by the Securities Exchange Act of 1934, which outlines many of its powers. It also contains much of the substative law, which it administers.

The broadest of the antifraud provisions of the securities law for the protection of investors are found in Section 10(b) of the act, as reinforced by a 1942 rule promulgated by the S.E.C. (Rule 10b-5).

Those provisions, designed to curb manipulative and deceptive devices in the trading of securities, are as follows:

Section 10(b) of the Securities Exchange Act of 1934

"Regulation of the Use of Manipulative and Deceptive Devices

Sec. 10. It shall be unlawful for any person, directly or indirectly, by the use of any means or instrumentality of interstate commerce or of the mails, or of any facility of any national . . . securities exchange—

(b) To use or employ, in connection with the purchase or sale of any security registered on a national securities exchange or any security not so registered, any manipulative or deceptive device or contrivance in contravention of such rules and regulations as the Commission may prescribe as necessary or appropriate in the public interest or for the protection of investors.

RULE 10b-5—EMPLOYMENT OF MANIPULATIVE AND DECEPTIVE DEVICES

"It shall be unlawful for any person, directly or indirectly, by the use of any means or instrumentality of interstate commerce, or of the mails, or of any facility of any national securities exchange,

(1) to employ any device, scheme, or artifice to defraud,

(2) to make any untrue statement of a material fact or to omit to state a material fact necessary in order to make the statements made, in the light of the circumstances under which they were made, not misleading, or

(3) to engage in any act, practice or course of business which operates or would operate as a fraud or deceit upon any person, in connection with the purchase or sale of any security."

Most cases involving an investor who is alleging fraud will claim a violation of these provisions. However, state laws and common law rules also may apply against such practice but do not cover as broad an area as the federal law.

The area covered by the cases which define and apply the provision of section 10(b) in tainted transactions cover the broad panorama of a changing spectrum. The following is a discussion of some of the cases including some which have made front page headlines in many newspapers.

In the case of *Kardon v. National Gypsum Co.* 75 F. Supp. 795, two plaintiffs, Morris and Eugene B. Kardon owned all the stock of Western Board and Paper Co. and its affiliate corporation Michigan Paper Stock. Co. with two of the defendants Leon Slavin and William Slavin. Each of the four parties owned a one fourth interest in the corporations and were all officers and directors therein. The two Slavin brothers purchased the plaintiff's stock on March 18, 1946. Prior to that date they had worked out an agreement to sell the corporate assets to one of the defendants, the National Gypsum Company. At the time of the sale of the stock, Leon Slavin was asked by the plaintiff's attorney if he had made any agreement with respect to the sale of the stock.

The reply was no. Nevertheless, the sale of asssets to the National Gypsum Company was later completed.

The plaintiffs brought an action alleging violation of Section 10(b) of the Securities and Exchange Act of 1934, asking for an account of profits realized through the sale of the corporate assets.

The court found a sale by the directors (the two Slavin brothers) of the corporate assets which was in their own interest and that they had not disclosed the important facts to the stockholders. The court held that even though Section 10(b) did no more than forbid certain conduct in general terms, the conduct of the defendents came within the act and the remedy sought was one provided by the law. Accordingly the court entered a decree for the accounting requested by the plaintiffs.

It was found in the case of *Speed v. Transmission Corp.* 135 F. Supp. 176, modified 235 F. 2d 369, that plaintiffs were minority shareholders in a subsidiary of the defendant corporation. They had sold their stock to defendant pursuant to a written offer by the defendant. The offer grossly underestimated the inventory value of the subsidiary. Sales and profit expectation was reported as being poor. A violation of the 10b-5 rule was found. The defendants were held to have breached their obligation as a fiduciary owned by them a majority stockholders.

Full disclosure of so called "inside information", which would affect the value of a security transaction is often involved in violations of the anti-fraud provisions of the securities laws. One case involving a stockbroker was *The Matter of Cody, Roberts & Co.* 40 S.E.C. 907. A partner in the firm of Cody, Roberts & Co. was a director of Curtiss-Wright Corporation. At a dividend meeting of the board of Curtis-Wright, it was voted to cut the dividend. Before such news became public, the partner allegedly called an employee of the stockbroker advising him of the dividend cut. The emloyee allegedly sold out the stock of his customers and went short on the Curtis-Wright stock. The Securities and Exchange Commission found this to be a deceit upon the purchasers.

Another case involved the largest stockbroker, Merrill Lynch. In the case of *Shapiro v. Merrill, Lynch, Pierce, Fenner & Smith, Inc.* 495 F. 2d 228, it was alleged that Merril Lynch had certain confidential information, concerning Douglas Aircraft company stock and it was also allegedly that this information was disclosed to certain customers of the broker. Plaintiff brought action as a purchaser of Douglas stock. The court held that while there was no duty to disclose confidential information, there was a duty to abstain from trading in such stock unless the stockbroker did disclose such information to the public.

The most famous case in the area under discussion is the landmark decision in *Securities and Exchange Commission v. Texas Gulf Sulpher Co.,* 401 F. 2d 833. The defendant conducted drilling operations for metal ores between November 8, 1963 and April 15, 1964. All the holes, except one were drilled after March 30, 1964. The first revealed a substantial quantity of minerals. However a gloomy press release was issued on the matter on April 12, 1964. On April 16, 1964, a fantastic ore strike was announced. From November 12, 1963 through April 16, 1964, officers, directors and their relatives and friends purchased a substantial amount of the defendant's shares. The S.E.C. brought a suit claiming a violation of Rule 10-b—5. It was held by the court that the rule had been violated, in that: (a) Material inside information which affected the price of the stock was not revealed, (b) the insiders acted on said information prior to its revelation to the public, (c) no specific intent to defraud is required to establish a violation of the rule and (d) the April 12, 1964, press release was misleading.

Investors and the Reform Law of 1976

Security holders will find certain changes enacted by the new tax reform law of 1976 to be of interest to them as investors. Under the old law the holding period for a security to quality as a long term capital gain or loss was six months. An increase in the holding period has been evaded which will go into effect in two stages. From January 1, 1977 through December 31, 1977 the holding period has been dropped from six months to nine months. On or after January 1, 1978 the holding period will be one full year.

While these changes work against the investor, there are some modifications that can be of some aid. Everyone knows that no matter how long or how small an investors gain is on the sale of a security he will have to pay taxes to Uncle Sam on the gain. Yet the same investor finds limitations placed upon him when he sells a security at a loss if such capital loss exceeds any capital gains or if there are no capital gains. Thus under the old tax law if an investor had a capital loss on the sale of a security which exceeded his capital gain, he could only deduct up to a total of $1,000 of said loss against ordinary income. The amount which an investor may deduct under the provisions of the new tax law will be increased to $2,000 in 1977 and will be increased to $3,000 from 1978 on.

Investors and Corporate Annual Reports

To aid investors, much of the thrust of the securities laws of the United States is aimed at furnishing adequate information about any corporation's operations, if such corporation's securities are publicly traded. As the years have gone by more and more information and red tape have been involved with the registration of securities. However, the information requirement most used by investors and security analysts has enjoyed comparative freedom from government regulation in the past. This useful tool is the Annual Report of the corporation. In 1974, the Securities and Exchange Commission institute a number of new requirements which apply to annual reports.

Under the previous law, the annual report was required to set forth financial statements of the corporation for the last two fiscal years. The financial statement for the most recent fiscal year must also be certified. Any deviations from normal accounting practice in these reports had to be explained in footnotes. Seven copies of the Annual Report are required to be sent to the S.E.C.

In addition to the seven copies of the annual report, corporations were, and still are, required to file a Form 10-K report with the S.E.C. The 10-K report contains similar information to that found in the annual report. One of the new S.E.C. requirements is that a corporation shall furnish to any shareholder upon written request and without charge, a copy of form 10-K. Some corporations put a glossy cover over a form 10-K report and use it as an annual report. Others employ the 10-K report as an appendix to the annual report.

Let us now consider the new annual report requirements. Now, both of the financial statements must be certified, rather than just the most recent year as was formerly required. Now the annual report must contain a breakdown of the various lines of business engaged in by the corporation for the last five fiscal years. These operations must be summarized and analyses made thereof by the management of the corporation. In addition the report must give the names and addresses. of the officers and directors of the corporation as well as their principal occupations and the principal business of their employers. The principal market in which the shares of voting stock of the corporation are traded and must be listed as well as the dividends and market price range of such stock for two fiscal years.

Chapter IV
THE WORKER AND THE LAW

In the last decades, greater interest has been shown in the need for regulation of internal affairs of unions. The number of public employees has been increasing, and the problems inherent in the unionization of such workers are being considered by the legislatures and the courts. As life expectancy rates begin to increase, workers have become more interested in pension rights and old age benefits. Legislation during the past decade has reflected these concerns.

DISCRIMINATION

The subject of job discrimination has been a particularly sensitive area in the sixties and seventies. Federal law and the laws of more than half the states prohibit job discrimination because of race, creed, sex or national origin. (Discrimination because of sex and race is discussed elsewhere in this book.). The Federal Age Discrimination Act, and many state laws, prohibit individuals between the ages of 40 and 65 from being refused employment because of age. The fact that the employer's pension plan would not cover individuals over a particular age is no defense for refusing to hire anyone in this age group. These laws are administered on the state level by the various designated state agencies. On the federal level the law is administered by the U.S. Department of Labor, Wage-Hour Division.

The federal government and several states have laws prohibiting discrimination against handicapped persons unless it can be shown that they would be unable to function because of their disability, in the particular job involved.

Discrimination on the basis of ethnic group, religion or sex is prohibited by the Civil Rights Act of 1964. This act is administered in part by the Equal Employment Opportunities Commission (EEOC). Anyone who feels he has been discriminated against must file charges with the EEOC, within 180 days of the alleged discrimination. A complaint must also be lodged with the state agency which administers the state fair employment practices act.

Within ten days after receiving the complaint, the EEOC will notify the accused party of the charges made against him (not disclosing the name of the complainant).

Usually the EEOC lets the state agency take whatever action it deems fit. If the action taken by the state is not satisfactory, the EEOC should be so informed and requested to take action. This notice to the EEOC should be given within 300 days after the discrimination occurred.

If the EEOC is unable to complete its investigation or dispose of the matter satisfactorily within 180 days after receiving notice of it, the EEOC will notify the complainant of this in a "suit letter". An individual may bring a suit on his own behalf in a federal district court within ninety days after this notification is received.

Some municipalities also have ordinances forbidding discrimination, and the EEOC may require charges filed with such agencies and a subsequent attempt by the agency to settle the matter, before it takes any action on the alleged injury.

Besides the statutory remedies provided by the Civil Rights Act, one may also bring a discrimination suit on constitutional grounds or pursuant to earlier civil rights acts passed in the eighteen hundreds, but these remedies are usually more costly and time consuming.

INDIVIDUAL RETIREMENT ACCOUNTS: KEOUGH PLANS

The federal Pension Reform Act permits an individual employee not covered by any other pension plan to set up his own individual retirement account. He may pay into a fund in his own name up to 15% of his earnings with a maximum of $1500 each year. He can continue to pay into his IRA, even upon changing jobs, always with the proviso that he is not covered by any other retirement plan.

Self-employed individuals may also establish a Keough Plan whereby they pay 15% of their earnings (maximum, $7500), each year into a savings and investment account.

Individuals participating in such plans receive certain tax benefits and income taxes on the interest and earnings accumulated under the plans are usually deferred until the person retires.

ERISA

The Employment Retirement Income Security Act (ERISA) was signed into law by the president on September 2, 1974. It sets forth the substantive provisions designed to govern pension and profit sharing plans that will be accepted as qualified plans under federal law. It marks the first major revision in this type of law since 1942.

The new law specifies how individuals may participate in such plans, what rights they have under such plans, how the plans are to be administered, and how the annual reports and other disclosures to the persons who participate in such plans are to be made.

In order for an employee to be covered under the new law, he or she must be at least 25 years old and must have completed at least one year's service during which he or she worked at least 1000 hours. If on the date of employment, the employee is within five years of the age at which employees ordinarily retire (many companies require mandatory retirement at 65 years of age), he or she may be excluded from the plan. Otherwise age may not be used to exclude an employee under a qualified plan. Employees who have their retirement benefits provided under a collective bargaining agreement resulting from good faith bargaining with a labor union may be excluded from a qualified plan.

For the purpose of determining the qualification of a plan, corporations under common control are to be treated as a single unit.

The jurisdiction to administer qualified plans has been granted to both the Internal Revenue Service and the Department of Labor in addition to the corporation or other firm whose employees are covered. Some differences in the procedure to qualify a plan can result from such split authority. The following discussion will apply in most cases to both the Tax titles and the Labor titles of the Act.

A qualified plan must specify when the basic benefits of the plan will vest in the employee. In order for a plan to be qualified, its vesting provision must be at least as liberal as one of the three types of vesting standards provided by the law.

The simplest standard of the three types contained in the law is the ten year vesting schedule. Under this type of provision, a qualified plan may set forth that a participant has no vested right to any benefits provided by the plan up until the time he completes ten years of employment. After ten years of employment, the employee has a 100% interest in all the benefits derived from the employer's contributions. Any qualified plan covered by the labor provisions of the act must provide that an employee will be fully vested for accrued benefits derived from his own contributions.

The second type of standard contained in the law is the five to fifteen year option which provides for a gradual vesting in the employer's contribution when the worker completes five years of service. Full vesting will take place when the worker completes fifteen years of service.

Under this option there is no vesting prior to the completion of five years of service. When the five years are completed the worker is vested in at least twenty-five percent of the employer's contributions. Thereafter the vested interest increases at the rate of five percent per year of service until the worker has a 50 per cent vested interest upon the completion of ten years of service. From then on vesting increases at the rate of ten per cent per year until the worker is fully vested at the end of fifteen years of service.

The third type of standard contained in the law is the so called "rule of 45." This standard of vesting is based upon two factors: the employee's years of service and the age of the employee. An alternative not involving age must be provided, and will be discussed later.

The rule of forty-five is derived from the fact that if an employee has at least five years of service and his age when added thereto equals or exceeds forty-five, he then has a fifty percent vested interest in the employer's contributions. The following chart shows the vesting schedule.

Years of service equals or exceeds	The sum of service and age equals or exceeds	% Vested
5	45	50
6	47	60
7	49	70
8	51	80
9	53	90
10	55	100

As an alternative, this type of standard must provide that, regardless of age, an employee has a fifty percent vested interest after ten years of service, and that the percent will increase ten percent for each year of service thereafter until the employee is fully vested.

In each of the foregoing standards, once an employee is covered initially he is granted a year of additional service if he renders 500 hours of service during such period.

Once a plan has been drafted, a booklet written in language understandable to the average participant must be sent to all covered by the plan and filed with the Secretary of Labor. This booklet must be provided within ninety days after an employee becomes a participant or one hundred twenty days after the plan is established, whichever is later.

The administrators of the assets of the plan must have independant public accountants examine its financial statements and an actuary must supervise the preparation of actuarial statements.

An annual report containing financial and actuarial statements is filed with the Secretary of Labor within 210 days after the plan year. The annual report must be made available for inspection by plan participants or beneficiaries, and additional financial information on assets and liabilities must be furnished in statements to plan participants within 210 days after the close of the plan year.

MEDICARE

In 1965, the federal government began a medicare program designed to furnish basic health insurance for persons over sixty-five, consisting of hospital and medical insurance plans.

Hospital insurance (sometimes called Part A) is financed by funds withheld from employee's salaries and matching contributions from employers. Everyone entitled to social security benefits is automatically entitled to hospital insurance under medicare. The medical insurance portion of medicare (sometimes referred to as Part B) is financed not only by the federal government, but also by monthly premiums paid by recipients. This portion of medicare is voluntary and is received only by those who have enrolled for it and are paying premiums.

Both types of insurance are available to everyone over sixty-five, even if they have not worked long enough to obtain enough quarters to be eligible for social security benefits. In addition to the monthly premiums on the medical insurance coverage, they must also pay a premium for hospital insurance coverage. It is essential that anyone wishing to be certain of medicare coverage contact his social security office at least three months prior to attaining the age of sixty-five. to insure his obtaining coverage in time for his birthday. It is especially important for those not covered by social security to contact the office. There is only a limited seven month enrollment period for the medical insurance coverage, which begins three months before the month of the recipient applicant's birthday and ends three months after that month. If enrollment is not done during this period, one can register thereafter only in the first three months of the year and protection will not start until the following July. Premiums are increased 10% for every year one could enroll but did not.

Medicare's medical insurance plan helps pay for such expenses as physicians services, outpatient hospital services and other health and medical expenses such as therapy and diagnostic services. Each year Medicare will pay eighty percent of the reasonable charges, (up to $60 - the annual deductible), for any additional covered services you receive during the year.

Medicare's hospital insurance covers hospitalized costs and certain follow-up care when a person leaves a hospital. In general, the plan pays for up to ninety days of inpatient care in any participating hospital per benefit period. (The period generally starts with entrance into a hospital and ends sixty days after discharge from the hospital or any follow-up care unit.). There is a deductible of $124 for the first sixty days. Thereafter, through the ninetieth day, medicare pays for all covered services up to $31 a day. This type of insurance also covers 100 days of care in a skilled nursing facility or 100 home health "visits" from a home health agency. Certain conditions must be met and deductibles paid. More detailed information about coverage under both plans may be found in *Your Medicare Handbook*, which is available at local Social Security offices.

Since its inception, medicare coverage has been expanded to include others besides senior citizens. In 1973, it began to cover disabled persons who have been entitled to social security disability payments for two years. Protection will end when the person (if under sixty-five) is no longer eligible for disability payments.

The program was also expanded recently to include almost anyone (under sixty-five years of age) with permanent kidney failure who needed maintenance dialysis treatments or a kidney transplant. An applicant for benefits must have enough work credits to be eligible for social security, or be the spouse or dependent child of one who has enough credits. Only the member of the family with the kidney failure is eligible for the medicare. Other members are not. Medicare coverage ends twelve months after the month maintenance dialysis treatments are no longer necessary or a kidney transplant is received.

SOCIAL SECURITY

There are few people today who will not eventually be covered by social security. As originally conceived, social security was designed to provide retirement benefits to industrial and business workers. Gradually coverage was expanded to include members of the armed forces, clergy, houseworkers and farm workers and the self employed. Most people who work today are eligible for Social Security.

To be covered by social security the worker must accumulate a certain number of quarters. A quarter is three months of a year. During each quarter an individual must earn at least $50. Self-employed persons must earn more. The number of quarters for which you must have worked to become eligible for social security varies depending on the age of the person involved. In any case, no one is required to have been covered by social security for more than 10 years (40 quarters).

A certain proportion of an employee's wages are withheld for Social Security, up until a specified maximum salary is reached. In 1976 employers were required to hold 5.85% of workers' incomes for social security, and also required to pay an equal amount into the fund. The maximum amount of salary on which social security can be assessed is now $16,500. Since he must pay the entire amount himself, different rates of deductions apply to a self-employed person. In 1976 such individuals were required to withhold 7.9%. These rates, as well as the amount of money to which one is entitled under social security, should be checked at your local office. Both will undoubtedly continue to be raised from time to time, particularly in the light of 1972 legislation which provides for automatic increases in Social Security benefits as the cost of living increases.

Under Social Security, a worker may retire at age sixty-two. If he does so, he will receive a lesser amount than he would if he waits until sixty-five to retire. The amount of Social Security a person will receive generally can not be determined until the benefits are actually applied for. However they can be estimated. Anyone may obtain a pamphlet entitled "Estimating Your Social Security Retirement Check", from the nearest Social Security Office.

Conversely, if a person delays retirement until after age sixty-five, he may receive more benefits. He will receive an additional one percent for each year (1/12 of one percent per month) worked after sixty-five up to seventy-two years of age. This additional credit applies only with respect to months after 1970.

Even if one elects to receive Social Security at sixty-five, he may continue to work and still receive Social Security benefits provided he does not earn more than $2,760 a year. If anyone earns in excess of this amount he must forfeit $1. in benefits for each $2. earned in excess of $2,760. However no matter how much a person earns annually, if he does not receive $230. in wages for any month, he can collect Social Security benefits for that month. Once a person reaches seventy-two, there is no limit on the earnings he can make to be eligible for Social Security — he is entitled to Social Security in any case.

Although originally established to provide security after retirement, coverage was extended in the fifties to protect workers who were unable to continue in the job because of disabilities. Under the Social Security law, a person is considered disabled if he has a condition (mental or physical) which makes him unable to work and which is expected to last (or has lasted) for at least twelve months, or is expected to result in death. Disabled persons can start receiving checks at the end of six months after the disability has begun and continues for the length of the disability.

Spouses of those covered by social security are entitled to benefits also. At sixty-five, they are entitled to benefits amounting to half of those received by the worker. Less will be received if they elect to receive benefits at sixty-two. A wife under sixty-two, is entitled to benefits if she is caring for a worker's unmarried child under eighteen, (or one who was disabled before reaching twenty-two years of age). Unmarried children under eighteen, (or full-time students under twenty-two) are entitled to benefits, as are children over 18 but disabled, provided they became disabled before twenty-two.

Upon the worker's death a lump sum payment (maximum of $225) may be applied for by his surviving spouse or anyone who can prove that he or she paid the funeral bill. Monthly payments will also be made to a widow or dependent widower sixty years or older. Benefits accrue to children under eighteen or disabled children over eighteen (see rules above). A wife not eligible for benefits because she is too young is entitled to benefits if she is caring for a worker's disabled child or one under eighteen. Checks may also be sent to a widow or dependent widower fifty years or older who become disabled not later than seven years after a worker's death, or in the case of a widow caring for dependent children, within seven years after she stopped receiving checks for caring for dependent children. In 1975, a United States Supreme Court decision held that a father can receive checks on the same basis as widowed mothers. A new pamphlet issued by the Social Security Administration indicates that benefits can be paid to a father if he is the widower of a woman who died while insured under social security and has not remarried and has in his care dependant children (i.e. married, under eighteen or disabled) who are entitled to benefits. Dependent parents of the deceased may also be entitled to benefits. To collect them, the parents must be sixty-two years of age or older.

With the prevalence of divorce today, the benefits of a divorced wife under social security are of greater interest. If the marriage lasted twenty years, a divorced wife sixty-two years of age or over, a surviving divorced wife of a deceased worker, sixty years or over, or a disabled surviving divorced wife of fifty years, are entitled to social security benefits.

The provisions of the social security law have generally been amended to reflect the needs of the times. As indicated earlier, coverage has been expanded and it is hoped that benefits will keep abreast with the cost of living. When it became necessary, the medical needs of senior citizens were served by the passage of Medicare, described above under a separate heading. No doubt additional changes will occur in the future. One impetus for this will be the women's rights, movement, which already has stimulated discussions concerning placing housewives' services within the purview of the law. Changes may also be made concerning supplementary income which may be obtained by senior citizens, as it becomes evident that social security payments alone are not sufficient for support.

UNIONS

The history of the labor movement in the United States has been a long and sometimes stormy one. In its earlier days, workers labored under unbelievable hardships and employers (sometimes aided by the courts) exercised almost dictatorial power over their employees. It was apparent that if unions were to become established in the United States, legislative help would be needed.

One of the main obstacles to the development of the unions was the almost unrestrained use of injunctions by employers to force them to return to work. In the early thirties the Norris La Guardia Act was passed. Although earlier legislation had sought to curb the use of injunctive power of employers, this act was the first effective anti-injunction statute and clearly defined non enjoinable actions by labor unions. It also recognized the unions' right to organize workers, to strike and establish picket lines. Later court decisions have indicated that the picketing must be for a lawful purpose and conducted in a peaceful manner, in a way that will not deprive others of their constitutional rights.

The main nucleus of the legislation designed to aid unions and to insure their right to bargain collectively is found in the National Labor Relations Act, which was originally enacted in the 1930's and known as the Wagner Act. Later, in the forties, it was amended by the Taft-Hartley Act.

This act is administered by the National Labor Relations Board (NLRB) and applies to businesses involved in interstate business.

The main thrust of the National Labor Relations Act is to insure that employees are represented by the union of their choice, to guarantee the right of unions to bargain collectively with employees and to prevent unfair labor practices.

Section 8(a) of the act lists those activities which constitute unfair labor practices on the part of an employer. These include such activities as trying to intimidate or coerce employees from joining a particular union, trying to dominate a union, and discriminating in employment because an employee is (or is not) a union member. Also prohibited is taking action against an employee who has filed charges or given testimony under the NLRA. Of course, failure to bargain in good faith with a duly authorized union is a direct violation of the act.

Unfair labor practices by unions are listed in Section 8(b) of the act. These practices include restraining employees from exercising rights granted to them by the act, refusal to bargain collectively, featherbedding (i.e. requiring employer to hire more workers than he needs or to pay for services not received), and collection of excessive or discriminatory membership fees.

In September of 1971, the U.S. Department of Labor published a layman's guide to federal labor laws and practices.

Approximately one third of the states have state labor relations acts which provide for state boards similar in nature to the NLRB and whose duties include insuring fair elections for unions to represent workers and taking action against either unions or employers for unfair trade practices.

Now, with the rights of workers to unionize and bargain collectively firmly established, the most recent changes in the law are concerned with internal affairs and practices of the unions themselves and the development of unions in the public sector of labor.

The chief federal legislation, regulating internal union matters is The Landrum Griffen Act (Labor Management and Disclosure Act of 1959), which sets forth a so called "Bill of Rights" for union members. Unions are required to make known the contents of collective bargaining agreements to their membership. Members of unions are assured of their voting rights by secret ballot. Dues and assessments may not be raised without the consent of the membership. The law also prescribes certain rules for disciplinary procedures. Various information and reports as to the financial affairs of the union and its officers must be filed with the government.

The issue of whether government employees could unionize and enter into collective bargaining agreements, has been paramount during the sixties, up until the present time.

The increase of employees on both the federal and state government payrolls has led to increased dissatisfaction with the traditional rules of treating public employees and has led to their unionization on both state and federal levels.

Impetus to such unionization on the federal level was given by President Kennedy's executive order 10988. Under this order some organizations were entitled to obtain "exclusive recognition." Certain conditions had to be met (e.g. the union must show that it represented at least ten percent of the employees involved and must be designated or elected by a majority of the employees within the bargaining unit). Once these requirements were met, the union was authorized to enter into collective bargaining with the government agency, and, what was even more significant, the agency was required to negotiate with the union. However no employee's union or association was considered lawful, if it asserted the right to strike against the government or advocated its overthrow. Membership in the union may not be denied because of race, creed, color or national origin.

President Nixon's Executive Order 1491, which became effective in 1970, extended the collective bargaining rights of federal employees and established a Federal Labor Relations Council to administer the program instead of the Civil Service Commission, as was the case under the former Order. The Assistant Secretary of Labor for Labor Management Relations was given authority to resolve disputes and to supervise elections. Unions representing government employees were required to furnish information similar to that required by the Landrum-Griffin Act, (discussed above).

The attitude of state governments towards public employees' right to unionize, varies from state to state. At one end of the spectrum are those states which will not permit government employees to unionize or bargain collectively. At the other end are those which make collective bargaining for state employees compulsory. Most states however are somewhere in the middle. Some permit only certain employees (such as school teachers) to unionize, while forbidding others to do so. All of the states have laws prohibiting strikes against state agencies. This is the crux of the problem concerning unionization of government employees. Their ultimate employer is the general public, and to permit strikes, particularly by employees rendering essential services to the public (police and firemen, for example) is considered by many to be contrary to the common good. However given the increasing number of public employees and the considerable agitation on the part of most to unionize and bargaining collectively, it is certain that the problem will not disappear and that an adequate solution, possibly that of agreements for submitting disputes to binding arbitration, must be found in the very near future.

Part Three

LAW AND LIVING

Chapter V

LAW FOR
HOMEOWNERS AND TENANTS

The shortage of land and the rapidly rising costs of housing have occasioned many of the current changes in the law relating to the homeowner and tenant.

The traditional laws relating to acquiring land by deed (or by adverse possession — see chart at the end of this chapter) remain substantially unchanged. However, new types of housing more consistent with the quickened pace of living have become popular. Today, many do not wish to spend their leisure time mowing lawns, pruning trees, and performing the myriad tasks that confront the traditional homeowner, yet they also wish to avoid the potential hazards of renting; many are therefore turning to the cooperative and the condominium.

Still there are those who, for financial or other reasons, must be tenants. Chafing under high rents and inadequate services they are rebelling against the tyranny of landlords. They are demanding that the law consider their rights and needs as well as those of the landlord, and gradually the courts are beginning to listen to them.

ATTRACTIVE NUISANCE

A homeowner is not usually responsible for accidental injuries to trespassers on his land. His only duty towards a trespasser is not to injure him deliberately, although if he wishes he can use reasonable force to eject him from his property.

Over the years some courts have been making an exception to this rule. In those instances where children have been the trespassers, they have applied the so called "attractive nuisance" doctrine.

The theory is based on the belief that children are both naturally curious and incautious. If you have something on your property, which is unsafe and which might lure a child on your land to investigate, you will be liable to any injury befalling the child as a result of the investigation.

Not all states follow this doctrine, but over the years it has been gaining in acceptance. Such things as uncovered wells, unprotected pools and defective gym equipment have been classified as attractive nuisances. Even if your state is not one of those following the doctrine, it is wise to "child proof" your home and grounds against potential dangers to children.

CONDOMINIUMS

The last decade has seen an increase in popularity in the condominium. This type of housing has been familiar in other parts of the world for some time, but it is relatively new in the United States. Here, the first law authorizing the use of condominiums was the Puerto Rico Horizontal Property Act. Since then all the states have enacted laws regulating the use of condominiums.

One reason for their popularity is the rising cost of private homes. Condominiums are usually much cheaper and confer many of the benefits of the individual homeowner on the buyer. In a well-managed condominium, the benefits of increased leisure time and freedom from maintenance worries, usually associated with apartment dwellers, accrue to him as well.

When someone buys a condominium, he takes title to his own individual unit. In addition, he owns certain common areas and accommodations jointly with other members of the complex.

Since he holds title to the unit, the condominium buyer is able to secure a mortgage to help finance his purchase. Most banks are willing to give him a mortgage and in addition both the FHA and VA are authorized to aid in this type of financing. Since he is primarily liable for the mortgage loan payment and interest, the owner may deduct the interest payments from his income taxes. Should he later default on the mortgage, his unit is the only one which would be foreclosed, as the other unit owners are not responsible for his mortgage.

There are other tax advantages to the condominium owner as well. He may deduct local property taxes paid by him and may apply for a homestead exemption. Should he later sell the condominium, any profit made by him may be deferred if he uses the proceeds to pay for another home.

Just as the deed is the fundamental document upon which an individual home owner's rights rest, the Declaration and Bylaws of the Condominium and the Individual Unit Deed embodies the Condominium owner's rights.

The Declaration sets forth a description of the land on which the condominium is built as well as a description of the buidling or buildings and the plans for the various individual units. The individual units are specifically identified by mailing address, detailed description, and monetary value. The common areas and facilities are described and the percentage of interest each unit owner has in them is specified. The Declaration also contains a statement of purposes for which the building or buildings in the complex are intended and of any restrictions on their use. Voting rights and procedures are usually contained in the Declaration, although many of these procedures are statutory in most states.

The bylaws outline the policies and procedures which will govern the administration, management and maintenance of the complex, such as provisions for election of the board of directors and officers of the owners' association and for the collection of management and operating fees.

The Individual Unit Deed contains a description of the individual unit, its number and mailing address and more or less restates the provisions in the Declaration relating to the rights of the individual unit owner. Samples of these three documents may be found at the end of this chapter.

In most cases the owners' association, through its officers and board of directors, controls the management of the condominium complex. If the condominium is smoothly run and all the owners are compatible, condominium living can be quite satisfying. Unfortunately this is not always the case. The individual owner may discover that his annual maintenance fees have increased (at a time when he is least able to afford it) because the other owners, sometimes over his dissent, have voted for additional improvements to the jointly owned areas. He may even discover that he can not make what he considers necessary improvements or alterations on his own unit, because they might involve breaking through jointly owned areas, without the consent of other owners.

From this it can be seen that before purchasing a condominium, the buyer and/or his lawyer should carefully examine the Declaration, Bylaws and local laws relating to condominiums. He should know what is his individual property and what is jointly owned. Knowledge of his voting rights and how to exercise them is a necessity. Finally he should acquaint himself with his future neighbors and make certain their life style is compatible with his own.

COOPERATIVES

Another type of housing similar to the condominium is the co-operative. Cooperatives have existed in the United States for many years, but until recently they have been associated mainly with the very wealthy.

Unlike the condominium owner, the cooperative dweller does not receive title to his unit. Instead, his purchase price buys stock in the corporation holding title to the land on which the cooperative is built. By virtue of owning these shares of stock, he is entitled to a lease.

This lease is basically the same as any other, except that its duration is longer, usually expiring (or capable of being renewed for) many years in the future, or whenever the lesee's stock is sold, whichever is sooner. No rent is provided for; instead there is a maintenance fee which is fixed yearly by the directors of the cooperative corporation. Other provisions in the lease may be inserted, relating to such matters as renewal provisions, inspections, rights and duties of the lessee and lessor, and additional maintenance fees to be charged in case of emergency repairs. A sample lease may be found at the end of this chapter.

Besides the lease, two other documents of vital importance to the prospective cooperative buyer are the certificate of incorporation and bylaws of the corporation holding title to the cooperative. These documents contain, among other things, the purpose and capitalization of the corporation, the rights of stockholders, details concerning their meetings and duties, meeting and voting rights, and election of directors and officers. As in the case of condominiums, the buyer should be aware of his rights before committing himself, and these documents should be carefully studied.

The owner of a cooperative unit does not have all of the tax advantages of a condominium owner. The individual owner is not permitted to deduct that portion of his maintenance fee which is set aside for interest and tax payments from his federal income tax. He is not permitted to do so because he is not primarily liable for these payments; the corporation is. He is permitted, like the condominium owner, to defer profits from a sale if he uses them to buy a new residence.

Some state laws do permit the co-op owner to deduct for interest and tax payments if he lives in a qualified cooperative. In order for a cooperative to qualify, several requirements must be fulfilled, one of which is that the apartment house must derive most of its income (usually a 4/5 ratio) from cooperative apartments rather than regular rentals. However sometimes it is more profitable for someone to live in an unqualified cooperative since the lower maintenance fee (resulting from the corporation receiving a substantial amount of income from rentals), more than offsets an income tax deduction.

REAL ESTATE SETTLEMENT PROCEDURES ACT

A real estate closing is generally a confusing and mystifying ritual to the average person. He makes out checks but sometimes he is not certain what they are for. Sometimes to his dismay, he discovers that his closing costs are somewhat greater than he anticipated.

To remedy this situation, in 1974 Congress enacted the Real Estate Settlement Procedures Act. The purpose of the act was to insure that buyers will be more completely informed of settlement costs, escrow accounts, etc.

One way of doing this is to require the distribution of booklets, by the lender bank, explaining to the prospective buyer the purpose and nature of each cost incident to real estate settlements. Estimated closing costs are given and some of the unfair practices and unnecessary charges to be avoided by the buyer are explained.

A seller is prohibited from requiring that a certain title company be used. Title companies may no longer give commissions or rebates (at the buyer's expense) to attorneys unless they perform other services for the company besides recommending that the buyer use that particular company.

Limitations are also set on the amount required to be placed in escrow accounts for the purpose of paying future taxes and insurance payments. The law states that in jurisdictions where taxes and insurance premiums are post-paid, the borrower could not be required to deposit more than the amount of taxes and insurance premiums that will be due and payable on the date of settlement plus the pro rata portion of such taxes and premiums that has already accrued. In those jurisdictions where the taxes and insurance premiums are pre-paid, the borrower could not be asked to deposit more than the pro rata portion of the estimated taxes and insurance premiums based on the number of months from the last payment date to date of settlement. Additionally, in all jurisdictions lenders may also require one-sixth of the taxes and premiums estimated to become due and payable during the twelve months following the day of closing.

There were great hopes for the law, particularly among consumer advocates, but it was suspended shortly after its effective date, as some jurisdictions found that some of its provisions were causing too many delays. It has since been further amended and became effective again in June of 1976. Just how useful it will be in bringing about much needed reforms will be left for the future to determine.

TENANTS' RIGHTS

Traditionally, the landlord has held a favored position in the eyes of the law. While his tenant owed him rent, he had to do virtually nothing in return, except to furnish the land or dwelling place. He could usually terminate the tenancy upon proper notice to the tenant. The state requirements relating to the formality of leases and their termination are found in charts at the end of this chapter.

The first curtailment of the landlord's power came with the rent control laws which were promulgated during the World War II era. These laws imposed duties upon the landlord, placed a ceiling on rents he could charge and severely limited his right to terminate a lease. These rent control laws have been eliminated in most states, but they are still in effect with respect to certain apartments in some cities such as Boston and New York.

In more recent times the power of the landlord has been gradually curtailed, particularly in those urban areas where nearly everyone is a tenant. Many tenants are poor and would be unable to find other lodgings if the landlord failed to provide necessary services.

Recently the courts have held that the landlord has the duty of making the premises habitable for the tenants. The tenant has been permitted to withhold the rent until the condition complained of has been improved. Usually the neglect has to be that which results in affecting the health of the tenant adversely. This ruling has been applied to instances where the landlord did not supply sufficient heat or a proper water supply, where the premises had become rat-infested or there has been improper garbage disposal. Some courts have extended this doctrine to require a landlord in a high crime area to take necessary safety precautions, such as installing proper locks on the entrance doors and repairing broken windows in common hallways.

In some states the right to withhold rent is statutory and the procedure for doing so is set forth. Some states provide that the tenant pay the rent money into court until the landlord makes the necessary repairs or alterations; others permit a receiver to be appointed by the court. Tenants pay the rent money to him and he uses it, (or a specified portion of it) to make the repairs that the landlord has neglected.

Only a minority of the states permit withholding of rent and if a tenant is tempted to do so, he should consult a lawyer first to determine just what his rights are.

Chart 1

ADVERSE POSSESSION

STATE	TIME REQUIRED	STATE	TIME REQUIRED
Alabama [1]	20 years	Montana	5 years
Alaska	7 years	Nebraska	10 years
Arizona[1]	10 years	Nevada[1]	5 years
Arkansas	7 years	New Hampshire	20 years
California	5 years	New Jersey	30 years
Colorado[1]	18 years	New Mexico	10 years
Connecticut	15 years	New York	10 years
Delaware	20 years	North Carolina[1]	20 years
District of Columbia	15 years	North Dakota[1]	20 years
Florida	7 years	Ohio	21 years
Georgia[1]	20 years	Oklahoma	15 years
Hawaii	20 years	Oregon	10 years
Idaho	5 years	Pennsylvania	21 years
Illinois[1]	20 years	Rhode Island	10 years
Indiana	20 years	South Carolina	10 years
Iowa	10 years	South Dakota	20 years
Kansas	15 years	Tennessee[1]	20 years
Kentucky	7 years	Texas	25 years
Louisiana[1]	30 years	Utah	7 years
Maine	20 years	Vermont	15 years
Maryland	20 years	Virginia	15 years
Massachusetts	20 years	Washington[1]	10 years
Michigan[1]	15 years	West Virginia	10 years
Minnesota	15 years	Wisconsin	20 years
Mississippi	10 years	Wyoming	10 years
Missouri	10 years		

[1] *In some special situations the duration is shorter. The statute should be consulted.*

NOTE: In most states special rules apply if the owner is an infant or incompetent. If either of these disabilities exist, the statutes should be consulted.

Chart 2

TENANCIES AND THEIR TERMINATION

NOTE

In the following chart, reference is made to the common law rule. To avoid repetition, the common law rules are set forth herein:

A *year to year tenancy* requires six months' notice to the tenant before the expiration of the year. This originated with agricultural tenancies but came to be extended to other types of rentals as well.

Month to month tenancy requires one month's notice to the tenant.

Week to week tenancy requires one week's notice.

Tenancy at will requires one month's notice to the tenant.

Where a lease is for a set period of time, no notice is required to be given to a tenant.

ALABAMA

Where *no time is specified* for the termination of a tenancy, the tenancy is construed to run from December 1 to December 1 of the following year. An *express tenancy at will is terminable* by either the landlord or the tenant upon ten (10) days' notice in writing to the other. A *month to month tenancy* may be terminated by ten (10) days' notice in writing. *Lodgings* or dwelling houses hired for an unspecified period of time are deemed to have been rented for a term equivalent to the interval of time for which rent is required to be paid or, if there is no agreement, monthly tenancy is presumed and the rule specified above for such tenancy applies.

ALASKA

Has adopted the Uniform Residential Landlord and Tenant Act.

ARIZONA

Year to year tenancy terminates at the end of the year, unless written permission to continue in possession is given. *Month to month tenancy* is terminated by ten days' notice to either the landlord or tenant, by the other. *Semimonthly tenancy* is terminated by five days' notice by the tenant; failure to give notice renders the tenant liable for ten days' rent. *Tenant for definite period,* written or oral lease, shall surrender the premises at the expiration of the term—no notice required.

ARKANSAS

Common law rules apply. *Yearly tenancy* begins anew each year. *Monthly tenancy* is terminated by one month's notice. *Tenancy at will is terminated by an act of either party inconsistent with continuance of tenancy. Tenancy at sufferance* is terminated by the landlaord's entry into premises. *Holdover tenant:* Tenant who holds over after giving landlord notice of his intention to quit the premises is liable to the landlord for double rent. *Tenant for like or term of years:* If he holds over after thirty days' notice to quit the premises, he is liable for double rent after expiration of period in notice, or expiration of term. When rent is unpaid, holding over after ten days to vacate the premises is a misdemeanor.

CALIFORNIA

Tenancy at will is terminated by thirty days' notice by either party (except as to tenants in mobile homes, who shall be given sixty days' notice). *Month to month tenancy* is terminated by thirty days' notice, unless a shorter period of time is agreed upon between the parties. Where there is no usage or contract provision to the contrary, rent is payable at the end of the term when it does not exceed one year. If holding is by the day, week, month, quarter, or year, rent is due as each respective period expires. A hiring of premises for an unspecified period is presumed to be for the same period of time as the rent interval.

COLORADO

Term Certain: Notice is not required when rental is for a term certain. *Year to year* requires three months' notice to the tenant. *Six months' tenancy* requires one month's notice to the tenant. *Month to month tenancy* requires ten days' notice. Tenancy at will requires 3 days notice. The required notice shall describe the premises, the time of termination and shall be signed by the party giving the notice or his agent.

Chart 2 cont.

CONNECTICUT

Conviction of lessee or tenant for illegal use of the premises renders the lease void and subjects the tenant to ouster without any notice. Under an oral lease, rent is payable at stated intervals, and, if it remains unpaid for more than nine days, the lease terminates at the option of the lessor or landlord on notice to the lessee tenant.

DELAWARE

Where no term is provided, the term is for one month, except for farm units. Rental agreements for all but farm units may be terminated by sixty days' notice prior to the expiration of the term of tenancy. Thirty days' notice is required if the tenant is required to move because of employment, death, or serious ailment of tenant or immediate family member; sixty days' notice is required for farmlands.

DISTRICT OF COLUMBIA

No notice is required if premises are leased for a specific period of time. Month to month and quarter to quarter tenancies and tenancies by sufferance require thirty days' notice to the tenant.

FLORIDA

Any lease not in writing signed by lessor is deemed a tenancy at will, for the term of the interval of rent payments. *Year to year tenancy* requires three months notice prior to end of year. *Quarterly tenancy* requires notice of not less than forty-five days prior to expiration of the quarter. *Month to month tenancy* requires notice of not less than fifteen days prior to the end of the month. *Week to week tenancy* requires seven days notice.

GEORGIA

Where no time is specified, the tenancy is construed to be one at will; the landlord must give the tenant sixty days' notice and the tenant must give the landlord thirty days' notice.

HAWAII

Periodic tenancy is terminable on twenty-five days' notice prior to expiration of the period. *Oral tenancy* is terminated by ten days' notice. *Month to month tenancy:* holding over creates valid enforceable tenancy for additional period.

IDAHO

Tenancy at will may be terminated by giving not less than one month's notice, in writing, time to vacate to be specified in notice. After service of notice and expiration of time specified in notice, the landlord may enter and repossess the premises.

ILLINOIS

No notice required if tenancy expires by its own terms. When default is made in any of the terms of the lease, it may be terminated on ten days' written notice. *Year to year tenancy* requires sixty days' notice at any time within the four months preceding the last sixty days of the year. Certain farm tenancies require four months' notice. *Week to week tenancy* requires seven days prior notice. In all other cases of tenancies for less than one year, thirty days' notice in writing is required.

INDIANA

Tenancy at will can only be created by writing and may be terminated by one month's notice in writing. *Year to year tenancy* requires three months' notice. *Tenancy for period to period of less than three months' interval,* requires notice equal to the rent interval. Where the tenancy is for a definite period of time, or where the time for termination of the tenancy is specified, or in case of a tenancy by sufferance, no notice to quit is required.

IOWA

Tenancy at will requires thirty days' notice unless rent is paid at intervals of less than thirty days, in which case the notice is the same as the rent interval.

KANSAS

Tenant in possession without express agreement is considered a tenant at will; if tenancy continues for more than one year he is considered a year to year tenant, unless contrary is shown. *Tenancy at will* requires thirty days' notice in writing by either party. *Year to year tenancy* requires thirty days' notice. When rent is payable at intervals of three months or less, the rent interval is the length of time required for notice. Where tenant is employee of landlord, ten days' notice is required to be given to tenant. In farm tenancies the notice must fix the time to quit as March 1, or for fall crops, the day following the harvest or August 1; when a tenant holds over after a lease for a year, the date of termination must be the same as that in the original lease.

Chart 2 cont.

KENTUCKY

Tenancy at will or by sufferance requires one month's written notice by landlord to tenant. No notice is required when premises are leased for a definite term. *Tenancy for a term of one year:* When the tenant holds over more than ninety days the lease is renewed by operation of the law, and so by year to year. *Tenancies for less than one year:* When tenant holds over for more than thirty days, the lease is automatically renewed for sixty days.

LOUISIANA

Where there is no fixed term, a month to month tenancy is construed in city property, and ten days' notice by either party terminates the tenancy. If the tenant holds over for one week, the lease is presumed renewed. In country property, a term is considered to be for one year if there is no fixed term. If the tenant remains in possession with the landlord's consent for one month past the year, the term is deemed renewed for one year.

MAINE

Tenancy at will: Thirty days' notice by either party, or by mutual consent, terminates the tenancy. Thirty days' notice must be made to terminate on a rent day unless the tenant is in arrears. When tenancy expires, the tenant is liable for forcible entry and detainer unless he has paid rent after service of notice. A tenancy at will may also be terminated by sale or lease.

MARYLAND

Tenancy at will and for definite terms requires one month's written notice in counties. In farm lands, six months' written notice is requred. *Month to month tenancy* requires one month's notice. *Week to week notice* requires one week's notice. *Year to year tenancy* requires three months' notice. In Baltimore City special rules prevail: Thirty days' notice to a tenant for less than one year term and ninety days for a year to year tenant. A tenant must give the landlord thirty days' notice of intention to quit the premises. Emergency regulations require one-hundred and twenty days' notice when the tenancy is for dwelling purposes for one year or less, a tenancy at will or on sufferance, or for a term measured by the life of another person. Agreement between the landlord and the tenant may prevail over statutory provisions.

MASSACHUSETTS

Tenancy at will may be terminated by 3 months notice by either party, unles rent is payable for less than 3 month period. Then the notice shall be equal to the interval between days of payment. If the interval is less than 30 days then 30 days notice must be given. *Tenancy by sufferance* may be terminated at any time at the desire of the landlord. Where no term is specified, no notice is necessary. *Month to month, week to week, tenancy* etc.: The notice required is the same length of time as the rent interval.

MICHIGAN

Tenancy at will or by sufferance requires one month's notice by either party. *Periodic tenancies* (for periods of less than three months) require notice as long as the rent interval. *Nonpayment of rent* requires seven days' notice. *Year to year tenancy* may be terminated at any time upon one year's notice. When rental is for a specific term, no notice is required.

MINNESOTA

Tenancy at will requires three months' notice in writing by either party. *Year to year tenancy* requires three months' notice prior to the end of second and subsequent years. *Terms of less than three months.* The time of notice must be as long as the rent interval.

MISSISSIPPI

Year to year tenancy requires two months' notice. *Semi- or quarter- annual tenancy* requires one month's notice. *Monthly or weekly tenancy* requires one week's notice. No notice is required when the lease is set to expire at a definite time.

MISSOURI

Year to year tenancy requires sixty days' notice. *At will or by sufferance or tenancy for less than one year* requires one month's notice in writing by landlord. No notice is required where the term is specified.

MONTANA

Year to year, quarter to quarter, month to month, week to week, and *day to day tenancies* are terminated by the end of the agreed term, mutual consent, or tenant-in-possession's acquisition of of title superior to that of his landlord, or notice as long as the

Chart 2 cont.

rent interval. *Holding over* renews the original term, if the landlord agrees. When hiring is terminated before the time originally
agreed upon, the tenant must pay porportionate rental for time
hired.

NEBRASKA
Uniform Residential Landlord and Tenanct Act adopted.

NEVADA
Common law applies. *Holdover:* A tenant who has held over
for sixty days beyond term is entitled to renewal of original
period.

NEW HAMPSHIRE
Every tenant is deemed to be a tenant at will unless a contract
to the contrary is shown. Notice to quit may be given by the
landlord, specifying any day he chooses; notice must, however,
be for the same length of time as the rent interval, if for less than
three months. *Holdover tenants:* Seven days' notice must be
given to person holding over after term has expired.

NEW JERSEY
Tenancy at will and from year to year may be terminated on
three months' notice in writing from the landlord to the tenant
and on six months' written notice from the tenant to the landlord. *Tenancy at sufferance* requires notice, but no time is specified.
Month to month and week to week tenancies require one month's
and one week's notice respectively.

NEW MEXICO
Common law rules apply.

NEW YORK
Tenancy at will and by sufferance may be terminated by thirty
days' written notice by the landlord to the tenant. *Monthly
tenancy,* outside of New York City, may be terminated by either
party on thirty days' notice to the other. In New York City,
thirty days' notice by the landlord to the tenant is required. The
tenant is not required to give notice.

NORTH CAROLINA
Tenancy for years or at will is terminated by one month's notice.
Month to month tenancy requires seven days' notice. *Week to
week tenancy* requires two days' notice.

NORTH DAKOTA

Tenancies for years and at will are terminable by one month's written notice served on the person residing in the premises. *Other tenancies* may be terminated by destruction of property, lessee's acquisition of title superior to that of his lessor, by mutual consent, property damage, or when the landlord fails to fulfill his obligations. A lease on property, other than lodgings, in places where there is no established usage is presumed to be for one year.

OHIO

Common law applies. Notice to quit premises is not necessary when the tenant holds over after a year to year lease.

OKLAHOMA

A tenant is deemed to be a tenant at will unless contrary can be shown. *Tenancy at will* requires thirty days' notice to quit. *Tenant for three months or less* requires thirty days' notice unless the rent interval is less, in which cases the rent interval is used. *Year to year tenancy* requires three months' notice. No notice is required when specific term has expired or when tenant commits waste.

OREGON

Tenancy at will requires notice equal to length of rent interval. *Year to year tenancy* requires sixty days' notice. *Month to month tenancy:* Requires 30 days. Agricultural land tenancy requires ninety days' notice. Lease terminates on date specified in lease without notice, where lease mentions specific date.

PENNSYLVANIA

Landlord may repossess premises when term ends, when lease is forfeited because of breaches, or because of the tenant's failure to pay rent. *Lease for indefinite period of time* requires thirty days' notice. *Lease for one year or more* requires three months' notice.

PUERTO RICO

Leases without fixed terms may be terminated by notice in the same length of time as the rent interval.

Chart 2 cont.

RHODE ISLAND

Tenancy at will or by sufferance terminates on the day specified by the landlord. *Year to year tenancy* requires three months' notice. *Terms of less than one year* require notice equal to one half of the rent interval, but not more than three months.

SOUTH CAROLINA

Tenancy at will requires twenty days' notice. *Month to month tenancy* requires thirty days notice. All other tenancies are considered month to month tenancies. Tenancies for specific periods require no notice to be given. No tenancy may ripen into a tenancy for year to year.

SOUTH DAKOTA

Tenancies are presumed to be for one year, unless otherwise specified. Tenancy may be terminated by the landlord when the tenant misuses the premises or fails to make necessary repairs; it may be terminated by the tenant when the landlord does not make the premises fit for use or when premises are destroyed. Tenancy terminates by expiration of term, by mutual consent, or tenant's acquisition of superior title to landlord's.

TENNESSEE

Year to year tenancy requires six months' notice prior to termination of year. *Quarter to quarter, month to month or week to week tenancy* requires notice the same length of time as the tenancy—quarterly, monthly or weekly, respectively.

TEXAS

Tenancy at will or by sufferance is terminated by the landlord's demand. *Month to month tenancy* is terminated by one month's notice. *Other shorter terms* require notice in the same amount of time as the term; if otherwise adequate, the time in the notice does not have to coincide with the end of the period.

UTAH

A tenancy for a specified term terminates without notice at the end of the term. Holding over constitutes unlawful detainer.

VERMONT

Tenancy at will is terminated by any act that amounts to a demand for possession. Common law rules apply.

VIRGINIA

Year to year tenancy may be terminated by either party by notice in writing three months before the end of any term of one year. *Month to month tenancy* requires thirty days' written notice. Notice may be waived. Notice is not required if the term ends at a specified time.

WASHINGTON

Year to year tenancies are abolished except when created by express written contract. When premises are rented for an indefinite period of time with monthly or other periodic rent dates reserved, such tenancy shall be construed as tenancy for the period of time for which rent is paid. *Month to month or period to period tenancy* requires thirty days' notice or more before the end of the period to be given by lessee, twenty days' notice when given by lessor. Tenancy for specific term terminates at end of the term without notice.

WEST VIRGINIA

Year to year tenancy requires three months' notice in writing by either party unless there is an agreement that no notice be given. If a tenant for an indefinite period of time receives notice, he may hold until the end of the current term.

WISCONSIN

Tenancy at will or by sufferance is terminated by twenty-eight days' notice in writing by either party. *Periodic tenancy of less than one month* requires notice equivalent to the time of rent interval. Other periodic tenancies require twenty-eight days' notice.

WYOMING

Tenancy by sufferance is the only kind that can exist without a lease and this is terminated by an affirmative act on the part of the landlord. There is no implied renewal. The only notice is a three-day notice before the quitting time.

Chart 3

STATUTORY REQUIREMENTS FOR LEASES AND LIMITATIONS ON TERMS

ALABAMA

Leases for over one year must be in writing. A lease cannot be for a term of more than ninety-nine years. A lease for more than twenty years is void as to the excess period unless acknowledged before a notary and recorded within one year of its execution.

ALASKA

Lease for one year or more is void as against a subsequent innocent purchaser for value unless it is recorded.

ARIZONA

A lease for more than one year must be in writing. Instruments affecting real property are void as against purchasers and creditors unless recorded.

ARKANSAS

A lease for more than one year must be in writing. Tenant's possession is notice of unrecorded lease. A lease which is to be recorded must be acknowledged before a notary public by the parties.

CALIFORNIA

A lease for more than one year must be in writing subscribed by the party to be charged with it. An unrecorded lease is valid between the parties to it and those who have notice of it; if it is for more than one year, it is void as against purchaser or mortgagee in good faith if their deed or mortgage is first recorded. A lease must be acknowledged before notary before it can be recorded.

COLORADO

A lease for more than one year must be in writing. Recording is not necessary ever as to innocent third parties if the tenant is in possession; recording is never necessary as between the parties or persons with notice.

CONNECTICUT

A lease for life or for more than one year or which contains renewal provisions or options to purchase are not effective as against any persons other than the lessor or his heirs unless the lease or a notice thereof is written, acknowledged and recorded as a deed. Actual possession by a tenant probably is not notice to third parties. A reasonable time is allowed to record a lease. A lease for more than one year is not enforceable against either party if not in writing and subscribed by the party to be charged or his agent.

DELAWARE

A lease for more than one year must be in writing and recorded. A lease must be acknowledged before it can be recorded; otherwise, it is not effective. Lease for more than 5 years must be recorded.

DISTRICT OF COLUMBIA

A lease for more than one year must be in writing. Lack of recording does not affect the validity of a lease between the parties to the lease or persons with notice of the lease; but it is required for constructive notice as to innocent third parties.

FLORIDA

A lease for more than one year must be in writing and witnessed by two persons. A lease for more than one year must be recorded to be effective against creditors and subsequent purchasers of property.

GEORGIA

A lease for more than one year must meet the requirements of deeds. Contracts creating landlord and tenant relationship may be oral if for not more than one year.

HAWAII

A lease for more than one year must be in writing and acknowledged and recorded or it is not valid as against bona fide purchasers.

IDAHO

Leases for more than one year must be acknowledged and recorded as deeds. Tenant's possession is generally considered sufficient to put third party on inquiry as to his rights.

ILLINOIS

A lease for more than one year must be acknowledged and recorded as a deed. Tenant in possession is considered sufficient to put third party on inquiry as to his rights.

INDIANA

A lease for more than three years must be in writing and recorded. A lease is void as against subsequent purchaser or mortgagee whose grant is recorded before the lease is.

Chart 3 cont.

IOWA
A lease for more than one year must be in writing. A lease need not be acknowledged before a notary, nor does it have to be recorded.

KANSAS
A lease for more than one year must be in writing by deed or note, and signed by the party assigning or granting the same (i.e., the landlord). Leases may be recorded as deeds.

KENTUCKY
A lease for more than one year should be in writing. A lease conveying an interest in real property (if for more than five years) must be recorded and acknowledged to be effective as against a bona fide purchaser of real property. Tenant's possession is notice to the world, putting it on inquiry as to tenant's rights.

LOUISIANA
A lease may be oral or written but must be recorded to affect a bona fide purchaser. Possession is not notice.

MAINE
A lease for more than two years, or for an indefinite period of time, must be in writing, acknowledged, and recorded to be valid as against third parties without notice. Possession under an unrecorded lease does not give constructive notice of the tenant's rights.

MARYLAND
A lease for less than three years may be parol (verbal). A lease for three years or more must be in writing. A lease for seven years or more must be recorded as a deed (although a memorandum of the deed may be filed instead of the full lease). Tenant's possession under a lease for less than seven years, although unrecorded, gives notice of his rights. Even in cases of leases for seven years or more, the lease is valid as between the original parties, their creditors and others though the lease is not recorded.

MASSACHUSETTS
An unwritten lease creates only a tenancy at will. A lease for over seven years (or notice thereof) must be recorded to be valid against innocent persons. A lease must be acknowledged before it can be recorded.

MICHIGAN
A contrct for leasing for more than one year must be in writing and

signed by the party by whom the lease was made or his legal representative or authorized person. A lease for more than three years must be acknowledged and recorded as a deed. Possession by a tenant under a lease for three years or less is notice to the world of his interest.

MINNESOTA

Leases for more than one year must be in writing. A lease for more than three years must be executed, acknowledged, and recorded as a deed to be valid against third parties without notice. Possession under unrecorded lease puts third parties on notice to inquire into the rights of the person in possession.

MISSISSIPPI

A lease for more than one year must be writing signed, and delivered and, to constitute notice to third parties, must be recorded. Possession under an unrecorded lease constitutes notice.

MISSOURI

A lease for more than one year is required to be in writing. All leases not in writing create tenancies at will, which may be terminated by one month's notice. This does not apply to leases of real property for agricultural uses other than gardening purposes. A parol lease for more than one year when followed by entry and payment of rent is converted into tenancy from year to year. There is no statute requiring leases to be recorded, but they may be. Actual possession puts third persons on notice.

MONTANA

A lease for more than one year is required to be in writing. Lease must be acknowledged to be entitled to be recorded. Unrecorded leases are void as against subsequent purchasers or mortgagees. Open and notorious possession of the property is constructive notice to all persons. An unrecorded lease is also notice as to all persons having actual notice.

NEBRASKA

A lease for more than one year must be in writing, acknowledged and recorded to be valid except as between the parties to the lease. Tenant's possession under an unrecorded lease is notice of all that inquiry would elicit.

NEVADA

A lease for more than one year must be in writing. Agricultural lands

Chart 3 cont.

may not be leased for a period of more than twenty-five years. No land
may be leased for a period of more than ninety-nine years—a lease for
excess period is void as to excess. Possession of tenant in possession
is notice. Lease is not required to be recorded.

NEW HAMPSHIRE
No lease for more than seven years is valid except against the grantor,
his heirs and successors in interest, unless executed, attested, acknowledged, and recorded as a deed.

NEW JERSEY
A lease for more than three years must be in writing. A lease for life or
term of not less than two years may be recorded; if not recorded it is
void as against judgment creditors without notice and bona fide purchasers and mortgagees for value without notice, whose deeds are first
recorded. Open, notorious possession constitutes notice of the right
under which a person is in possession.

NEW MEXICO
A lease for more than three years must be in writing.

NEW YORK
A parol lease for more than one year is void but the landlord may recover
for use and occupancy of the premises. A lease for more than three years
must be in writing and comply with the recording statutes. Unrecorded
leases are void as against subsequent purchasers.

NORTH CAROLINA
A lease for more than three years must be in writing and, in order to
be effective as against third parties, must be recorded. (A memorandum
of lease may be recorded instead of the full lease.) One who enters
premises under a void lease is a tenant at will.

NORTH DAKOTA
A lease for more than one year must be in writing and subscribed by
the party to be charged or agent whose authority is in writing. Leases
are valid between parties without acknowledgement before notary but
leases may not be recorded unless acknowledged. Unless possession is
is taken by the tenant, lease must be recorded to protect against the
rights of third parties without notice.

OHIO

All leases are required to be in writing but oral leases for three years or less are effective if possession is taken and rent is paid. Entry under a lease for more than three years and the payment of rent creates a tenancy from year to year, except as to the duration of the lease. A lease may be recorded (or a memorandum of it).

OKLAHOMA

A lease for more than one year must be in writing. A lease is not valid as against third parties unless acknowledged and recorded. Open and actual possession of the property gives notice to the world of the interest of the person in possession.

OREGON

Lease must be in writing if for more than one year and must be recorded to be effective as against bona fide purchaser without notice of the lease. Possession under a lease is notice to third parties.

PENNSYLVANIA

A lease for more than three years must be in writing signed by the parties or their authorized agents; otherwise a tenancy at will is created; if such a tenancy is created and continues for over one year, the tenancy becomes a year to year tenancy. A lease for not more than three years may be parol or written. A lease for more than three years need not be acknowledged before a notary or recorded. A lease for more than twenty-one years must be acknowledged and recorded as a deed. (A memorandum of lease may be recorded instead of the full lease.)

RHODE ISLAND

A lease for more than one year is void unless in writing, acknowledged, delivered, and recorded, except as to persons with notice and between the parties and their successors in interest. Parol lease for one year or less is valid.

SOUTH CAROLINA

A lease for more than one year is not valid as against third parties who do not have actual notice, unless lease is in writing and recorded. Court has not passed on question of whether a bona fide purchaser without notice is bound by a verbal lease made by the seller where tenant is not in possession.

Chart 3 cont.

SOUTH DAKOTA

A lease for a term of more than one year must be in writing. A lease must be recorded to be effective against subsequent bona fide purchaser or incumbrancer whose instrument is first recorded. No lease for agricultural land may be for a period longer than ten years. No lease for city or town property may be for more than ninety-nine years, and is invalid if for more.

TENNESSEE

A lease for more than one year must be in writing and signed by the party to be charged with it or by a duly authorized agent. Tenant taking possession under a parol lease for more than one year becomes a tenant for year to year term. Leases for more than three years must be registered in the county where the property is located.

TEXAS

A lease for more than one year must be in writing and signed by the person to be charged therewith or his authorized agent. A lease for more than one year must be recorded in order to be effective against third parties without notice. Possession is notice to third parties.

UTAH

A lease for over one year must be in writing and acknowledged and recorded to impart constructive notice to third parties. Leases must be recorded as deeds are.

VERMONT

Lease must be signed, sealed, and witnessed, acknowledged and recorded as deed to impart constructive notice to third parties.

VIRGINIA

A lease for more than one year must be in writing. A lease for more than five years must be in writing and recorded to be notice to purchasers for value and creditors. Tenant's possession under oral lease for less than five years puts others on notice to inquire into his rights.

WASHINGTON

A lease for more than one year is required to be in writing and acknowledged before a notary. An unacknowledged lease for more than one year is void. An oral lease is treated as a month-to-month tenancy. A lease for more than two years is void as to bona fide subsequent purchasers and mortgagees, unless recorded. Possession of tenant is enough to put persons on notice to inquire.

WEST VIRGINIA

A lease for over one year must be in writing and signed by the person to be charged with it. An estate in land for over five years must be recorded; it must be conveyed by deed or will.

WISCONSIN

A lease for more than one year must be signed and executed as a deed if it is to constitute notice to third parties. A lease for less than one year may be recorded if in proper form for recording.

WYOMING

A lease for more than one year must be in writing. A lease for over three years must be excecuted and recorded as a deed.

APPENDIX A

CONDOMINIUM

The sample forms in this appendix were prepared by the Federal Housing Administration, which is administered by the U.S. Department of Housing and Urban Development.

ENABLING DECLARATION
ESTABLISHING A PLAN FOR
CONDOMINIUM OWNERSHIP

WHEREAS, _____ , (hereinafter referred to as "Grantor") owns certain real property herein described; and

WHEREAS, said Grantor has improved said property by constructing thereon a _____ unit multifamily structure known as _____ , said structure having been constructed in accordance with plans and specifications prepared by _____ , said plans being on record in the _____ of the City of _____ _____ State of _____ , and styled _____ , FHA Project No. _____ , and consisting of sheets _____ through _____ , _____ through _____ , etc., all inclusive; and

WHEREAS, said Grantor hereby establishes by this declaration a plan for the individual ownership of the real property estates consisting of the area or space contained in each of the apartment units in said multifamily structure, and the co-ownership by the individual and separate owners thereof, as tenants in common, of all of the remaining real property which is hereinafter defined and referred to herein as the "common areas and facilities."

NOW, THEREFORE, said Grantor, the fee owner of the following described real property, to-wit:

(Land description)

hereby makes the following declaration as to divisions, covenants, restrictions, limitations, conditions and uses to which the above described real property and improvements thereon, consisting of a _____ unit multifamily structure and appurtenances, may be put, hereby specifying that said declaration shall constitute covenants to run with the land and shall be binding on said Grantor, its successors and assigns, and all subsequent owners of all or any part of said real property and improvements, together with their grantees, successors, heirs, executors, administrators, devisees or assigns:

A. Said Grantor, in order to establish a plan of condominium ownership for the above-described property and improvements, hereby covenants and agrees that it hereby divides said real property into the following separate freehold estates:

1. The _____ separately designated and legally described freehold estates consisting of the spaces or areas, being the area or space contained in the perimeter walls of each of the _____ apartment units in said multifamily structure constructed on said property, said spaces being defined, and referred to herein, as "apartment spaces."

2. A freehold estate consisting of the remaining portion of the real property is described and referred to herein as the "common areas and facilities," which definition includes the multifamily structure and the property upon which it is located, and specifically includes, but is not limited to, the land, roof, main walls, slabs, elevator, elevator shaft, staircases, lobbies, halls, parking spaces, storage spaces, community and commercial facilities, swimming pool, pumps, water tank, trees, pavement, balconies, pipes, wires, conduits, air conditioners and ducts, or other public utility lines.

B. For the purpose of this declaration, the ownership of each "apartment space" shall include the respective undivided interest in the common areas and facilities specified and established in "E" hereof, and each "apartment space" together with the undivided interest is defined and hereinafter referred to as "family unit."

C. A portion of the "common areas and facilities" is hereby set aside and allocated for the restricted use of the respective "apartment spaces," as is hereinafter designated, and as shown on survey attached hereto, and said areas shall be known as "restricted common areas and facilities."

D. The _____ individual "apartment spaces" hereby established and which shall be individually conveyed are described as follows:

(Legal description of apartment spaces)

E. The undivided interest in the "common areas and facilities" hereby established and which shall be conveyed with each respective "apartment space" is as follows:

(Apartment number - Percentage of undivided interest)

The above respective undivided interests established and to be conveyed with the respective "apartment spaces" as indicated above, cannot be changed, and said Grantor, its successors and assigns, and grantees, convenant and agree that the undivided interests in the "common areas and facilities" and the fee titles to the respective "apartment spaces" conveyed therewith, shall not be separated or separately conveyed, and each said undivided interest shall be deemed to be conveyed or encumbered with its respective "apartment space" even though the description in the instrument of conveyance or encumbrance may refer only to the fee title to the "apartment space."

F. The proportionate shares of the separate owners of the respective "family units" in the profits and common expenses in the "common areas and facilities," as well as their proportionate representation for voting purposes in the Association of Owners, is based on the proportionate value that each of the "family units," referred to herein, bears to the value of $, * which represents the total value of all of the "family units." The value of the respective "family units," their respective interests for voting purposes, and their proportionate shares in the common profits and expenses shall be as follows:

(Family unit number - value * - Proportionate representation for voting and share in common profits and expenses)

G. The "restricted common areas and facilities" allocated for the restricted uses of the respective "family units" are as follows:

FAMILY UNIT 1: That portion of the parking area designated as parking space No. 1; storage space No. 1; together with balcony adjoining the "apartment space" associated with family unit 1 on the south. Said restricted areas are further described, located, and shown on survey attached hereto. **

H. That attached hereto and made a part hereof as Exhibit "A" is a survey consisting of _____ sheets as prepared by _____ , dated _____.

I. Said Grantor, its successors and assigns, by this declaration, and all future owners of the "family units," by their acceptance of their deeds, covenant and agree as follows:

1. That the "common areas and facilities" shall remain undivided; and no owner shall being any action for partition, it being agreed that this restriction is necessary in order to preserve the rights of the owners with respect to the operation and management of the condominium.

2. That the "apartment spaces" shall be occupied and used by the respective owners only as a private dwelling for the owner, his family, tenants and social guests and for no other purpose.

3. The owner of the respective "apartment spaces" shall not be deemed to own the undecorated and/or unfinished surfaces of the perimeter walls, floors and ceilings surrounding his respective "apartment space," nor shall said owner be deemed to own pipes, wires, conduits or other public utility lines running through said respective "apartment spaces" which are utilized for, or serve more than one "apartment space," except as tenants

---

* Value to correspond with FHA appraised value.

** Descriptive material for guidance only; conform to actual facts.

in common with the other "family unit" owners as heretofore provided in "E". Said owner, however, shall be deemed to own the walls and partitions which are contained in said owner's respective "apartment space," and also shall be deemed to own the inner decorated and/or finished surfaces of the perimeter walls, floors and ceilings, including plaster, paint, wallpaper, etc.

4. The owners of the respective "apartment spaces" agree that if any portion of the "common areas and facilities" encroaches upon the "apartment spaces," a valid easement for the encroachment and for the maintenance of same, so long as it stands, shall and does exist. In the event the multifamily structure is partially or totally destroyed, and then rebuilt, the owners of "apartment spaces" agree that minor encroachment of parts of the "common areas and facilities" due to construction shall be permitted and the valid easement for said encroachment and the maintenance thereof shall exist.

5. That an owner of a "family unit" shall automatically, upon becoming the owner of a "family unit or units," be a member of _____ , hereinafter referred to as the "Association," and shall remain a member of said Association until such time as his ownership ceases for any reason, at which time his membership in said Association shall automatically cease.

6. That the owners of "family units" covenant and agree that the administration of the condomimium shall be in accordance with the provisions of this Declaration, the By-Laws of the Association which are made a part hereof and attached as Exhibit "B", and shall be subject to the terms of a Regulatory Agreement executed by the Association and the Commissioner of the Federal Housing Administration, which Agreement is made a part hereof and is attached as Exhibit "C".

7. That each owner, tenant or occupant of a "family unit" shall comply with the provisions of this Declaration, the By-Laws, decisions and resolutions of the Association or its representative, and the Regulatory Agreement, as lawfully amended from time to time, and failure to comply with any such provisions, decisions, or resolutions, shall be grounds for an action to recover sums due, for damages, or for injunctive relief.

8. That this Declaration shall not be revoked or any of the pro-

visions herein amended unless all of the owners and the mortgagees of all of the mortgages covering the "family units" unanimously agree to such revocation or amendment by duly recorded instruments.

9. That no owner of a "family unit" may exempt himself from liablity for his contribution towards the common expenses by waiver of the use or enjoyment of any of the common areas and facilities or by the abandonment of his "family unit."

J. All sums assessed by the Association but unpaid for the share of the common expenses chargeable to any family unit shall constitute a lien on such family unit prior to all other liens except only (1) tax liens on the family unit in favor of any assessing unit and special district, and (2) all sums unpaid on the first mortgage of record. * Such lien may be foreclosed by suit by the manager or Board of Directors, acting on behalf of the owners of the family units, in like manner as a mortgage of real property. In any such foreclosure the family unit owner shall be required to pay a reasonable rental for the family unit, if so provided in the by-laws, and the plaintiff in such foreclosure action shall be entitled to the appointment of a receiver to collect the same. The manager or Board of Directors, acting on behalf of the owners of the family units, shall have power, unless prohibited herein, to bid in the unit at foreclosure sale, and to acquire and hold, lease, mortgage and convey the same. Suit to recover a money judgment for unpaid common expenses shall be maintainable without foreclosing or waiving the lien securing the same.

K. Where the mortgagee of a first mortgage of record or other purchaser of a family unit obtains title to the unit as a result of foreclosure of the first mortgage, such acquirer of title, his successors and assigns, shall not be liable for the share of the common expenses or assessments by the Association chargeable to such family unit which became due prior to the acquisition of title to such family unit by such acquirer. Such unpaid share of common expenses or assessments shall be deemed to be common expenses collectible from all of the family units including such acquirer, his successors and assigns.

---

* The list of liens having priority over the assessments by the Association for common expenses may be expanded provided the approval of FHA is obtained.

L. The respective "family units" shall not be rented by the owners thereof for transient or hotel purposes, which shall be defined as (a) rental for any period less than thirty (30) days; or (b) any rental if the occupants of the "family unit" are provided customary hotel services, such as room service for food and beverage, maid service, furnishing laundry and linen, and bellboy service. Other than the foregoing obligations, the owners of the respective "family units" shall have the absolute right to lease same provided that said lease is made subject to the covenants and restrictions contained in this Declaration and further subject to the By-Laws and Regulatory Agreement attached hereto.

M. In the event the property subject to this Enabling Declaration is totally or substantially damaged or destroyed, the repair, reconstruction, or disposition of the property shall be as provided for

_____ *

N. In a voluntary conveyance of a family unit the grantee of the unit shall be jointly and severally liable with the grantor for all unpaid assessments by the Association against the latter for his share of the common expenses up to the time of the grant or conveyance, without prejudice to the grantee's right to recover from the grantor the amounts paid by the grantee therefor. However, any such grantee shall be entitled to a statement from the manager or Board of Directors of the Association, as the case may be, setting forth the amount of the unpaid assessments against the grantor due the Association and such grantee shall not be liable for, nor shall the family unit conveyed be subject to a lien for, any unpaid assessments made by the Association against the grantor in excess of the amount therein set forth.

O. All agreements and determinations lawfully made by the Association in accordance with the voting percentages established in the _____ _____ , ** this Declaration or in the By-Laws, shall be deemed to be binding on all owners of family units, their successors and assigns.

_____

* Insert applicable statutory reference; or, in the absence of statute, insert the following "an Agreement approved by _____, % of the votes."

** Identify state law establishing family unit ownership, if any.

P. That the Board of Directors of the Association of Owners, or the Management Agent, or Manager shall obtain and continue in effect blanket property insurance in form and amounts satisfactory to mortgagees holding first mortgages covering family units but without prejudice to the right of the owner of a family unit to obtain individual family unit insurance.

Q. That insurance premiums for any blanket insurance coverage shall be a common expense to be paid by monthly assessments levied by the Association of Owners; and that such payments shall be held in a separate escrow account of the Association of Owners and used solely for the payment of the blanket property insurance premiums as such premiums become due.

R. That so long as said Grantor, its successors and assigns, owns one or more of the family units established and described herein, said Grantor, its successors and assigns shall be subject to the provisions of this Declaration and of Exhibits "A", "B", and "C" attached hereto; and said Grantor covenants to take no action which would adversely affect the rights of the Association with respect to assurances against latent defects in the property or other right assigned to the Association, the members of such association and their successors in interest, as their interests may appear, by reason of the establishment of the condominium.

S. The terms "Declaration" and "Condominium Ownership" as used herein shall mean and include the terms "Master Deed" and "Apartment Ownership" respectively.

    (Execution and Acknowledgement in Accordance with Requirements of Jurisdiction)

BY-LAWS ———————————— CONDOMINIUM

ARTICLE I
PLAN OF APARTMENT OWNERSHIP

Section 1. *Apartment Ownership.* The project located at ——————
Street, City of ——————————— , State of ——————————— ,
known as " ——————————————— Condominium" is submitted
to the provisions of *, ————————————————— .

Section 2. *By-Laws Applicability.* The provisions of these By-Laws
are applicable to the project. (The term "project" as used herein shall
include the land).

Section 3. *Personal Application.* All present or future owners, tenants,
future tenants, or their employees, or any other person that might use
the facilities of the project in any manner, are subject to the regulations
set forth in these By-Laws and to the Regulatory Agreement, attached
as Exihibit "C" to the recorded Plan of Apartment Ownership.

The mere acquisition or rental of any of the family units (hereinafter
referred to as "units") of the project or the mere act of occupancy of
any of said units will signify that these By-Laws and the provisions of
the Regulatory Agreement are accepted, ratified, and will be complied
with.

ARTICLE II
VOTING, MAJORITY OF OWNERS, QUORUM, PROXIES

Section 1. *Voting.* Voting shal be on a percentage basis and the percentage of the vote to which the owner is entitled is the percentage
assigned to the family unit or units in the Master Deed.

Section 2. *Majority of Owners.* As used in these By-Laws the term
"majority of owners" shall mean those owners holding 51% of the
votes in accordance with the percentages assigned in the Master Deed.

Section 3. *Quorum.* Except as otherwise provided in these By-Laws,
the presence in person or by proxy of a "majority of owners" as defined
in Section 2 of this Article shall constitute a quorum.

———————
* Idenity state law establishing apartment ownership.

Section 4. *Proxies.* Votes may be cast in person or by proxy. Proxies must be filed with the Secretary before the appointed time of each meeting.

ARTICLE III

ADMINISTRATION

Section 1. *Association Responsibilities.* The owners of the units will constitute the Association of Owners (hereinafter referred to as "Association") who will have the responsibility of administering the project, approving the annual budget, establishing and collecting monthly assessments and arranging for the management of the project pursuant to an agreement, containing provisions relating to the duties, obligations, removal and compensation of the management agent. Except as otherwise provided, decisions and resolutions of the Association shall require approval by a majority of owners.

Section 2. *Place of Meetings.* Meetings of the Association shall be held at the principal office of the project or such other suitable place convenient to the owners as may be designated by the Board of Directors.

Section 3. *Annual Meetings.* The first annual meeting of the Association shall be held on _____(Date)*. Thereafter, the annual meetings of the Association shall be held on the _____ (1st, 2nd, 3rd, 4th) _____(Monday, Tuesday, Wednesday, etc.) of _____(month) each succeeding year. At such meetings there shall be elected by ballot of the owners a Board of Directors in accordance with the requirements of Section 5 of Article IV of these By-Laws. The owners may also transact such other business of the Association as may properly come before them.

Section 4. *Special Meetings.* It shall be the duty of the President to call a special meeting of the owners as directed by resolution of the Board of Directors or upon a petition signed by a majority of the owners and having been presented to the Secretary, or at the request of the Federal Housing Commissioner or his duly authorized representative. The notice of any special meeting shall state the time and place of such meeting and the purpose thereof. No business shall be transacted at a special meeting except as stated in the notice unless by consent of four-fifths of the owners present, either in person or by proxy.

Section 5. *Notice of Meetings.* It shall be the duty of the Secretary to mail a notice of each annual or special meeting, stating the purpose thereof as well as the time and place where it is to be held, to each owner

---

* This date must be approved by the FHA Insuring Office.

of record, at least 5 but not more than 10 days prior to such meeting. The mailing of a notice in the manner provided in this Section shall be considered notice served. Notices of all meetings shall be mailed to the Director of the local insuring office of the Federal Housing Administration.

Section 6. *Adjourned Meetings.* If any meeting of owners cannot be organized because a quorum has not attended, the owners who are present, either in person or by proxy, may adjourn the meeting to a time not less than forty-eight (48) hours from the time the original meeting was called.

Section 7. *Order of Business.* The order of business at all meetings of the owners of units shall be as follows:

(a) Roll call.
(b) Proof of notice of meeting or waiver of notice.
(c) Reading of minutes of preceding meeting.
(d) Reports of officers.
(e) Report of Federal Housing Administration representative, if present.
(f) Report of committees.
(g) Election of inspectors of election.
(h) Election of directors.
(i) Unfinished business.
(j) New business.

ARTICLE IV

BOARD OF DIRECTORS

Section 1. *Number and Qualification.* The affairs of the Association shall be governed by a Board of Directors composed of _____ person,* all of whom must be owners of units in the project.

Section 2. *Powers and Duties.* The Board of Directors shall have the powers and duties necessary for the administration of the affairs of the Association and may do all such acts and things as are not by law or by these By-Laws directed to be exercised and done by the owners.

Section 3. *Other Duties.* In addition to duties imposed by these By-Laws or by resolutions of the Association, the Board of Directors shall be

---

* The number should be an odd number not less than five.

responsible for the following:

(a) Care, upkeep and surveillance of the project and the common areas and facilities and the restricted common areas and facilities.

(b) Collection of monthly assessments from the owners.

(c) Designation and dismissal of the personnel necessary for the maintenance and operation of the project, the common areas and facilities and the restricted common areas and facilities.

Section 4. *Management Agent.* The Board of Directors may employ for the Association a management agent at a compensation established by the Board to perform such duties and services as the Board shall authorize including, but not limited to, the duties listed in Section 3 of this Article.

Section 5. *Election and Term of Office.* At the first annual meeting of the Association the term of office of two Directors shall be fixed for three (3) years. The term of office of two Directors shall be fixed at two (2) years, and the term of office of one Director shall be fixed at one (1) year. At the expiration of the initial term of office of each respective Director, his successor shall be elected to serve a term of three (3) years. The Directors shall hold office until their successors have been elected and hold their first meeting. (If a larger Board of Directors is contemplated, the terms of office should be established in a similar manner so that they will expire in different years.)

Section 6. *Vacancies.* Vacancies in the Board of Directors caused by any reason other than the removal of a Director by a vote of the Association shall be filled by vote of the majority of the remaining Directors, even though they may constitute less than a quorum; and each person so elected shall be a Director until a successor is elected at the next annual meeting of the Association.

Section 7. *Removal of Directors.* At any regular or special meeting duly called, any one or more of the Directors may be removed with or without cause by a majority of the owners and a successor may then and there be elected to fill the vacancy thus created. Any Director whose removal has been proposed by the owners shall be given an opportunity to be heard at the meeting.

Section 8. *Organization Meeting.* The first meeting of a newly elected Board of Directors shall be held within ten (10) days of election at such place as shall be fixed by the Directors at the meeting at which such Directors were elected, and no notice shall be necessary to the newly elected Directors in order legally to constitute such meeting, providing a majority of the whole Board shall be present.

Section 9. *Regular Meetings.* Regular meetings of the Board of Directors may be held at such time and place as shall be determined, from time to time, by a majority of the Directors, but at least two such meetings shall be held during each fiscal year. Notice of regular meetings of the Board of Directors shall be given to each Director, personally or by mail, telephone or telegraph, at least three (3) days prior to the day named for such meeting.

Section 10. *Special Meetings.* Special meetings of the Board of Directors may be called by the President on three days notice to each Director, given personally or by mail, telephone or telegraph, which notice shall state the time, place (as hereinabove provided) and purpose of the meeting. Special meetings of the Board of Directors shall be called by the President or Secretary in like manner and on like notice on the written request of at least three Directors.

Section 11. *Waiver of Notice.* Before or at any meeting of the Board of Directors, any Director may, in writing, waive notice of such meeting and such waiver shall be deemed equivalent to the giving of such notice. Attendance by a Director at any meeting of the Board shall be a waiver of notice by him of the time and place thereof. If all the Directors are present at any meeting of the Board, no notice shall be required and any business may be transacted at such meeting.

Section 12. *Board of Director's Quorum.* At all meetings of the Board of Directors, a majority of the Directors shall constitute a quorum for the transaction of business, and the acts of the majority of the Directors present at a meeting at which a quorum is present shall be the acts of the Board of Directors. If, at any meeting of the Board of Directors, there be less than a quorum present, the majority of those present may adjourn the meeting from time to time. At any such adjourned meeting, any business which might have been transacted at the meeting as originally called may be transacted without further notice.

Section 13. *Fidelity Bonds.* The Board of Directors shall require that all officers and employees of the Association handling or responsible for Association funds shall furnish adequate fidelity bonds. The premiums on such bonds shall be paid by the Association.

ARTICLE V
OFFICERS

Section 1. *Designation.* The principal officers of the Association shall be a President, a Vice President, a Secretary, and a Treasurer, all of whom shall be elected by and from the Board of Directors. The Directors may appoint an assistant treasurer, and an assistant secretary, and such other officers as in their judgment may be necessary. (In the case of an Association of one hundred owners or less the offices of Treasurer and Secretary may be filled by the same person.)

Section 2. *Election of Officers.* The officers of the Association shall be elected annually by the Board of Directors at the organization meeting of each new Board and shall hold office at the pleasure of the Board.

Section 3. *Removal of Officers.* Upon an affirmative vote of a majority of the members of the Board of Directors, any officer may be removed, either with or without cause, and his successor elect d at any regular meeting of the Board of Directors, or at any special meeting of the Board called for such purpose.

Section 4. *President.* The President shall be the chief executive officer of the Association. He shall preside at all meetings of the Association and of the Board of Directors. He shall have all of the general powers and duties which are usually vested in the office of president of an Association, including but not limited to the power to appoint committees from among the owners from time to time as he may in his discretion decide is appropriate to assist in the conduct of the affairs of the Association.

Section 5. *Vice President.* The Vice President shall take the place of the President and perform his duties whenever the President shall be absent or unable to act. If neither the President nor the Vice President is able to act, the Board of Directors shall appoint some other member of the Board to so do on an interim basis. The Vice President shall also perform such other duties as shall from time to time be imposed upon him by the Board of Directors.

Section 6. *Secretary.* The Secretary shall keep the minutes of all meetings of the Board of Directors and the minutes of all meetings of the Association; he shall have charge of such books and papers as the Board of Directors may direct; and he shall, in general, perform all the duties incident to the office of Secretary.

Section 7. *Treasurer.* The Treasurer shall have responsibility for Association funds and securities and shall be responsible for keeping full and accurate accounts of all receipts and disbursements in books belonging to the Association. He shall be responsible for the deposit of all moneys and other valuable effects in the name, and to the credit, of the Association in such depositaries as may from time to time be designated by the Board of Directors.

ARTICLE VI
OBLIGATIONS OF THE OWNERS

Section 1. *Assessments.* All owners are obligated to pay monthly assessments imposed by the Association to meet all project communal expenses, which may include a liability insurance policy premium and an insurance premium for a policy to cover repair and reconstruction work in case of hurricane, fire, earthquake or other hazard. The assessments shall be made pro rata according to the value of the unit owned, as stipulated in the Master Deed. Such assessments shall include monthly payments to a General Operating Reserve and a Reserve Fund for Replacements as required in the Regulatory Agreement attached as Exhibit "C" to the Plan of Apartment Ownership.

Section 2. *Maintenance and Repair.*

(a) Every owner must perform promptly all maintenance and repair work within his own unit, which if omitted would affect the project in its entirety or in a part belonging to other owners, being expressly responsible for the damages and liabilities that his failure to do so may engender.

(b) All the repairs of internal installations of the unit such as water, light, gas, power, sewage, telephones, air conditioners, sanitary installations, doors, windows, lamps and all other accessories belonging to the unit area shall be at the owner's expense.

(c) An owner shall reimburse the Association for any expenditures incurred in repairing or replacing any common area and facility damaged through his fault.

Section 3. *Use of Family Units - Internal Changes.*

(a) All units shall be utilized for residential purposes only.

(b) An owner shall not make structural modifications or alterations in his unit or installations located therein without previously notifying the Association in writing, through the Management Agent, if any, or through the President of the Board of Directors, if no management agent is employed. The Association shall have the obligation to answer within   days and failure to do so within the stipulated time shall mean that there is no objection to the proposed modification or alteration.

Section 4. *Use of Common Areas and Facilities and Restricted Common Area and Facilities.*

(a) An owner shall not place or cause to be placed in the lobbies, vestibules, stairways, elevators and other project areas and facilities of a similar nature both common and restricted, any furniture, packages or objects of any kind. Such areas shall be used for no other purpose than for normal transit through them.

(b) The project shall have _____ elevators, _____ devoted to the transportation of the owners and their guests and _____ for freight service, or auxiliary purposes. Owners and tradesmen are expressly required to utilize exclusively a freight or service elevator for transporting packages, merchandise or any other object that may affect the comfort or well-being of the passengers of the elevator dedicated to the transportation of owners, residents and guests.

Section 5. *Right of Entry.*

(a) An owner shall grant the right of entry to the management agent or to any other person authorized by the Board of Directors or the Association in case of any emergency originating in or threatening his unit, whether the owner is present at the time or not.

(b) An owner shall permit other owners, or their representatives, when so required, to enter his unit for the purpose of performing installations, alterations or repairs to the mechanical or electrical services, provided that requests for entry are made in advance and that such entry is at a time convenient to the owner. In case of an emergency, such right of entry shall be immediate.

Section 6. *Rules of Conduct.*

(a) No resident of the project shall post any advertisements, or posters of any kind in or on the project except as authorized by the Association.

(b) Residents shall exercise extreme care about making noises or the use of musical instruments, radios, television and amplifiers that may disturb other residents. Keeping domestic animals will abide by the Municipal Sanitary Regulations.

(c) It is prohibited to hang garments, rugs, etc., from the windows or from any of the facades of the project.

(d) It is prohibited to dust rugs, etc., from the windows, or to clean rugs, etc., by beating on the exterior part of the project.

(e) It is prohibited to throw garbage or trash outside the disposal installations provided for such purposes in the service areas.

(f) No owner, resident or lessee shall install wiring for electrical or telephone installation, television antennae, machines or air conditioning units, etc., on the exterior of the project or that protrude through the walls or the roof of the project except as authorized by the Association.

ARTICLE VII
AMENDMENTS TO PLAN OF APARTMENT OWNERSHIP

Section 1. *By-Laws.* These By-Laws may be amended by the Association in a duly constituted meeting for such purpose and no amendment shall take effect unless approved by owners representing at least 75% of the total value of all units in the project as shown in the Master Deed.

ARTICLE VIII
MORTGAGES

Section 1. *Notice to Association.* An owner who mortgages his unit, shall notify the Association through the Management Agent, if any, or the President of the Board of Directors in the event there is no Management Agent, the name and address of his mortgagee; and the Association shall maintain such information in a book entitled "Mortgagees of Units."

Section 2. *Notice of Unpaid Assessments.* The Association shall at the request of a mortgagee of a unit report any unpaid assessments due from the owner of such unit.

ARTICLE IX
COMPLIANCE

These By-Laws are set forth to comply with the requirements of*

In case any of these By-Laws conflict with the provisions of said statute, it is hereby agreed and accepted that the provisions of the statute will apply.

---

* Identify state law establishing apartment ownership.

MODEL FORM OF
MANAGEMENT AGREEMENT FOR CONDOMINIUMS
(Section 234)

Agreement made this _____ day of _____, 19___, between the
*_____ for the _____ Condomin-
ium, hereinafter called the "Association", organized and established
in accordance with the Plan of Apartment Ownership executed and
recorded in the Office of the Recorder of the County of _____,
State of _____, in Book of _____ Deeds at
page _____, having its principal office at _____, and _____,
having its principal office at _____, hereinafter called the
"Agent".

WITNESSETH:

In consideration of the terms, conditions, and covenants hereinafter set forth, the parties hereto mutually agree as follows:

FIRST.   (a) The Association hereby appoints the Agent, and
the Agent hereby accepts appointment, on the terms and conditions
hereinafter provided, as exclusive managing agent of the condominium known as _____ , located in the County of
_____ State of _____, and consisting of _____
dwelling units.

(b) The Agent fully understands that the function of
the Association is the operation and management of the Condominium; and the Agent agrees, notwithstanding the authority given to
the Agent in this Agreement, to confer fully and freely with the Directors of the Association in the performance of its duties as herein set
forth and to attend membership or Director's meetings at any time
or times requested by the Association. It is further understood and
agreed that the authority and duties conferred upon the Agent hereunder are confined to the common areas and facilities and the restricted common areas and facilities as defined in the Plan of Apartment
Ownership. Such authority and duties do not and shall not include
supervision or management of family units except as directed by the
Association.

---

* Name of association, cooperative or corporation of unit owners.

SECOND. In order to facilitate efficient operation, the Association shall furnish the Agent with a complete set of the plans and specifications of the Condominium as finally approved by the Federal Housing Administration, and with the aid of these documents and inspection made by competent personnel, the Agent will inform itself with respect to the layout, construction, location, character, plan and operation of the lighting, heating, plumbing, and ventilating systems, as well as elevators, if any, and other mechanical equipment in the Condominium. Copies of guarantees and warranties pertinent to the construction of the Condominium and in force at the time of the execution of this Agreement shall be furnished to the Agent.

THIRD. The Agent shall hire in its own name all managerial personnel necessary for the efficient discharge of the duties of the Agent hereunder. Compensation for the services of such employees shall be the responsibility of the Agent. Those employees of the Agent who handle or are responsible for the handling of the Association's monies shall, without expense to the Association, be bonded by a fidelity bond acceptable both to the Agent and the Association.

FOURTH. Under the personal and direct supervision of one of its principal officers, the Agent shall render services and perform duties as follows:

(a) On the basis of an operating schedule, job standards, and wage rates previously approved by the Association on the recommendation of the Agent, investigate, hire, pay, supervise, and discharge the personnel necessary to be employed in order properly to maintain and operate the Condominium. Such personnel shall in every instance be in the Association's and not in the Agent's employ. Compensation for the services of such employees (as evidenced by certified payrolls) shall be considered an operating expense of the Condominium.

(b) Immediately ascertain the general condition of the property, and if the accommodations there afforded have yet to be occupied for the first time, establish liaison with the general contractor to facilitate the completion by him of such corrective work, if any, as is yet to be done; also, cause an inventory to be taken of all furniture, office equipment, maintenance tools and supplies, including a determination as to the amount of fuel on hand.

(c) Coordinate the plans of owners of family units in the condominiums, hereinafter referred to as "Members" for moving their personal effects into the Condominium or out of it, with a view towards scheduling such movements so that there shall be a minimum of inconvenience to other Members.

(d) Maintain businesslike relations with Members whose service requests shall be received, considered and recorded in systematic fashion in order to show the action taken with respect to each. Complaints of a serious nature shall, after thorough investigation, be reported to the Association with appropriate recommendations. As part of a continuing program, secure full performance by the Members of all items and maintenance for which they are responsible.

(e) Collect all monthly assessments due from Members, all rents due from users of garage spaces and from users or lessees of other non-dwelling facilities in the Condominium; also, all sums due from concessionaires in consequence of the authorized operation of facilities in the Condominium maintained primarily for the benefit of the Members. The Association hereby authorizes the Agent to request, demand, collect, receive, and receipt for any and all charges or rents which may at any time be or become due to the Association and to take such action in the name of the Association by way of legal process or otherwise as may be required for the collection of deliquent monthly assessments. As a standard practice, the Agent shall furnish the Association with an itemized list of all delinquent accounts immediately following the tenth day of each month.

(f) Cause the buildings, appurtenances and grounds of the Condominium to be maintained according to standards acceptable to the Association, including but not limited to interior able to the Association, including but not limited to interior and exterior cleaning, painting, and decorating, plumbing, steamfitting, carpentry, and such other normal maintenance and repair work as may be necessary, subject to any limitations imposed by the Association in addition to those contained herein. For any one item of repair or replacement the expense incurred shall not exceed the sum of _____* unless specifically authorized by the Association; excepting, however, that emergency repairs, involving manifest danger to life or property, or immediately necessary for the preservation and safety of the property, or for the safety of the Members, or required to avoid the suspension of any necessary service to the Condominium, may be made by the Agent irrespective of the cost limitation imposed by this paragraph. Notwithstanding this authority as to emergency repairs, it is understood and agreed that the Agent will, if at all possible, confer

---

* From $100 to $500, depending upon the size of the Condominium.

immediately with the Association regarding every such expenditure. The Agent shall not incur liabilities (direct or contingent) which will at any time exceed the aggregate of _____ *, or any liability maturing more than one year from the creation thereof, without first obtaining the approval of the Association.

(g) Take such action as may be necessary to comply promptly with any and all orders or requirements affecting the premises placed thereon by any federal, state, county, or municipal authority having jurisdiction thereover, and orders of the Board of Fire Underwriters or other similar bodies, subject to the same limitation contained in Paragraph (f) of this Article in connection with the making of repairs and alterations. The Agent, however, shall not take any action under this Paragraph (g) so long as the Association is contesting, or has affirmed its intention to contest any such order or requirement. The Agent shall promptly, and in no event later than 72 hours from the time of their receipt, notify the Association in writing of all such orders and notices of requirements.

(h) Subject to approval by the Association, make contracts for water, electricity, gas, fuel oil, telephone, vermin extermination, and other necessary services, or such of them as the Association shall deem advisable. Also, place orders for such equipment, tools, appliances, materials and supplies as are necessary properly to maintain the Condominium. All such contracts and orders shall be made in the name of the Association and shall be subject to the limitations set forth in Paragraph (f) of this Article. When taking bids or issuing purchase orders, the Agent shall act at all times under the direction of the Association, and shall be under a duty to secure for and credit to the latter any discounts, commissions, or rebates obtainable as a result of such purchases.

(i) When authorized by the Association in writing, cause to be placed and kept in force all forms of insurance needed adequately to protect the Association, its members, and mortgagees holding mortgages covering family units, as their respective interests appear (or as required by law), including but not limited to workmen's compensation insurance, public liability insurance, boiler insurance, fire and extended coverage insurance, and burglary and theft insurance. All of the various types of insurance coverage required shall be placed with such companies, in such amounts, and with such beneficial interests appearing therein as shall be acceptable to the Association and to mortgagees holding mortgages covering family units. The placed with such companies, in such amounts, and with such beneficial

---

* From $1,000 to $5,000, depending upon the size of the Condominium.

interests appearing therein as shall be acceptable to the Association and to mortgagees holding mortgages covering family units. The Agent shall promptly investigate and make a full written report as to all accidents or claims for damage relating to the management, operation and maintenance of the Condominium, including any damage or destruction to the Condominium, the estimated cost of repair, and shall cooperate and make any and all reports required by any insurance company in connection therewith.

(j) From the funds collected and deposited in the special account hereinafter provided, cause to be disbursed regularly and punctually (1) salaries and any other compensation due and payable to the employees of the Association, and the taxes payable under paragraph (k) of this Article, (2) fire and other property insurance premiums and the amount specified in the Regulatory Agreement for allocation to the Reserve Fund for Replacements and to the General Operating Reserve, and (3) sums otherwise due and payable by the Association as operating expenses authorized to be incurred under the terms of this Agreement, including the Agent's commission. After disbursement in the order herein specified, any balance remaining in the special account may be disbursed or transferred from time to time, but only as specifically directed by the Association in writing, but such balance must be within the limits of the fidelity bond which shall be in an amount equal to the gross monthly collections.

(k) Working in conjunction with an accountant, prepare for execution and filing by the Association all forms, reports, and returns required by law in connection with unemployment insurance, workmen's compensation insurance, disability benefits, Social Security, and other similar taxes now in effect or hereafter imposed, and also requirements relating to the employment of personnel.

(l) Maintain a comprehensive system of office records, books, and accounts in a manner satisfactory to the Association and to the consenting parties, which records shall be subject to examination by their authorized agents at all reasonable hours. As a standard practice, the Agent shall render to the Association by not later than the tenth of each succeeding month a statement of receipts and disbursements as of the end of every month.

(m) On or about _____ and thereafter at least 60 days before the beginning of each new fiscal year, prepare with the assistance of an accountant, if need be, an operating budget setting forth an itemized statement of the anticipated receipts and disbursements for the new fiscal year based upon the then current schedule of monthly assessments, and taking into account the general condition of the Condominium. Each such budget, together with a statement from the Agent outlining a plan of operation and justifying the estimates made in every important particular, shall be submitted to the Association in final draft at least 30 days prior to the commencement of the annual period for which it has been made, and following its adoption by the Association, copies of it shall be made available, upon request, for submission to the consenting party. The budget shall serve as a supporting document for the schedule of monthly assessments proposed for the new fiscal year. It shall also constitute a major control under which the Agent shall operate, and there shall be no substantial variances therefrom, except such as may be sanctioned by the Association. By this is meant that no expenses may be incurred or commitments made by the Agent in connection with the maintenance and operation of the Condominium in excess of the amounts allocated to the various classifications of expense in the approved budget without the prior consent of the Association, except that, if necessary because of an emergency or lack of sufficient time to obtain such prior consent, an overrun may be experienced, provided it is brought promptly to the attention of the Association in writing.

(n) The Agent shall actively handle the renting of any garage spaces or other non-dwelling accommodation, arranging for the execution of such leases or permits as may be required.*

(o) It shall be the duty of the Agent at all times during the term of this Agreement to operate and maintain the Condominium according to the highest standards achievable consistent with the overall plan of the Association and the interests of the consenting party. The Agent shall see that all Members are informed with respect to such rules, regulations and notices as may be promulgated by the Association from time to time. The Agent shall be expected to perform such other acts and deeds as are reasonable, necessary and proper in the discharge of its duties under this Agreement.

FIFTH.   Everything done by the Agent under the provisions of Article FOURTH shall be done as Agent of the Association, and all obligations or expenses incurrred thereunder shall be for the account, on behalf, and at the expense of the Association, except that the Association shall not be obligated to pay the overhead expenses

---

* If desired, a clause may be included whereby the Agent, upon the request of the owner of any family unit, agrees to serve as broker or agent in the sales or rentals of individual family units for a specified commission.

of the Agent's office. Any payments to be made by the Agent hereunder shall be made out of such sums as are available in the special account of the Association, or as may be provided by the Association. The Agent shall not be obliged to make any advance to or for the account of the Association or to pay any sum, except out of funds held or provided as aforesaid, nor shall the Agent be obliged to incur any liability or obligation for the account of the Association without assurance that the necessary funds for the discharge thereof will be provided.

SIXTH   The Agent shall establish and maintain, in a bank whose deposits are insured by the Federal Deposit Insurance Corporation and in a manner to indicate the custodial nature thereof, a separate bank account as Agent of the Association for the deposit of the monies of the Association, with authority to draw thereon for and payments to be made by the Agent to discharge any liabilities or obligations incurred pursuant to this Agreement, and for the payment of the Agent's fee, all of which payments shall be subject to the limitations in this Agreement.

SEVENTH The sole compensation which the Agent shall be entitled to receive for all services performed under this Agreement shall be a fee computed and payable monthly in an amount equivalent to _____ (%) of gross collections, exclusive of all surcharges.

EIGHTH.   (a) Unless cancelled pursuant to section (b), (c), or (d) of this Article, this Agreement shall be in effect for a term of _____ from the date of execution, provided that in no event shall it be of any force and effect until there is endorsed hereon the consent of the consenting party.

(b) This Agreement may be terminated by mutual consent of the parties as of the end of any calendar month, but not without prior written notice to the consenting party.

(c) In the event a petition in bankruptcy is filed by or against Agent, or in the event that he shall make an assignment for the benefit of creditors or take advantage of any insolvency act, either party hereto may terminate this Agreement without notice to the other, but prompt advice of such action shall be given to the consenting party.

(d) It is expressly understood and agreed by and between the parties hereto that the Federal Housing Administration shall have the right to terminate this Agreement at the end of any calendar month, with or without cause, on 30 days' written notice to the Association and the Agent of its intention so to do. It is further understood and agreed that no liability shall attach to the Federal Housing Administration in the event of termination of this Agreement pursuant to this section.

(e) Upon termination, the contracting parties shall account to each other with respect to all matters outstanding as of the date of termination, and the Association shall furnish the Agent security, satisfactory to the Agent, against any outstanding obligations or liabilities which the Agent may have incurred hereunder.

NINTH.   As used in this Agreement:

(a) The term "consenting party" shall mean the Federal Housing Administration acting through its Commissioner or his duly authorized representatives.

(b) The term "assessments" shall mean those monthly rates established by the Association which the Members are bound to pay as their share of the common expenses under the Master Plan of Apartment Ownership.

(c) The term "gross collections" shall mean all amounts actually collected by the Agent, either as assessments or as rents.

(d) The term "Association" as used herein shall mean an association, cooperative or corporation consisting of all of the owners of family units in the Condominium organized and existing under state law for the purpose of administering the Condominium established by the Plan of Apartment Ownership.

TENTH.   (a) This Agreement, which is made subject and subordinate to all rights of the Federal Housing Administration as insurer of mortgages on family units in the Condominium, shall inure to the benefit of and constitute a binding obligation upon the contracting parties, their respective successors and assigns; and to the extent that it confers rights, privileges, and benefits upon the consenting party, the same shall be deemed to inure to its benefit, but without liability, in the same manner and with the same force and effect as though the Federal Housing Administration was a signatory to this Agreement.

(b) This Agreement shall constitute the entire Agreement between the contracting parties, and no variance or modification thereof shall be valid and enforceable, except by supplemental agreement in writing, executed and approved in the same manner as this Agreement.

(c) For the convenience of the parties, this Agreement

has been executed in several counterparts, which are in all respects similar and each of which shall be deemed to be complete in itself so that any one may be introduced in evidence or used for any other purpose without the production of the other counterparts. Immediately following endorsement of the consenting parties, counterparts will be furnished to the consenting parties so that each may be advised of the rights, privileges, and benefits which this Agreement confers.

IN WITNESS WHEREOF, the parties hereto have executed this Agreement the day and year first above written.

_____

(Association)

By _____

_____

(Agent)

By _____

The Federal Housing Administration hereby consents to the foregoing Management Agreement and the Managing Agent designated therein.

DATE: _____   _____

(Federal Housing Commissioner)

By _____

(Authorized Agent)

APPENDIX B COOPERATIVE FORMS

The sample forms in this appendix were prepared by the Federal Housing Administration, which is administered by the U.S. Department of Housing and Urban Development.

MODEL FORM OF
CERTIFICATE OF INCORPORATION[1]

(For Sales Type Cooperative Corporations Organized on a Stock Basis under Section 213 Involving Community Facilities and One or More Project Mortgages)

This is to certify:

That we, the subscribers: _____ ,

(Name)

whose post office address is _____ ;

_____ , whose post office address is

(Name)

_____ ; and

_____ , whose post office address is

(Name)

_____ , all being of full legal age, do, under and by virtue of the general laws of the State of _____ _____ , authorizing the formation of corporations, associate ourselves with the intention of forming a Corporation pursuant to the following:

ARTICLE I - NAME

The name of the Corporation is _____ .

---

[1] Should be drawn in a format to conform to laws of jurisdiction in which filed.

ARTICLE II - PURPOSES

The purpose for which the Corporation is formed and the business and objects to be carried on and promoted by it are as follows:

(a) to create a corporation to provide housing on a cooperative basis and to provide on a cooperative basis the community facilities as described in Appendix A and such additions or changes thereto as are approved by the Preferred Stockholders, to be regulated by the Federal Housing Commissioner (hereinafter called the "Commissioner") as to sales, charges, capital structure, and methods of operation in the manner and for the purposes provided in Section 213 of Title II of the National Housing Act, as amended, (hereinafter called the "Act") and the Administrative Regulations thereunder; to enable the financing of such housing and community facilities with the assistance of mortgage insurance under the Act, as amended, in accordance with the provisions of any state or local laws prohibiting discrimination in housing on the basis of race, color, creed, or national origin, and with the Regulations of the Federal Housing Administration providing for nondiscrimination and equal opportunity in housing, on the understanding that failure or refusal to comply with any such provisions shall be a proper basis for the Commissioner to take any corrective action he may deem necessary including, but not limited to, the rejection of future applications for FHA mortgage insurance and the refusal to enter into future contracts of any kind with which the corporation, corporate officers, directors, trustees, managers or stockholders are identified; and as such housing corporation, to acquire any real estate or interest or rights therein or appurtenant thereto and any and all personal property in connection therewith. So long as any of the dwellings or property listed and described in Appendix B hereof is owned by this corporation or by a shareholder of this corporation or is encumbered by a Mortgage or Deed of Trust insured under the Act or held by the Commissioner, or so long as any such property or dwelling is owned by the Commissioner, the corporation shall engage in no other business than the construction and operation of a housing development and the described community facilities, all on a non-profit cooperative basis.

(b) to construct, operate, maintain and improve, and to sell, convey, assign, mortgage or lease any real estate and any personal property necessary to the operation of such development and community facilities;

(c) to borrow money and issue evidence of indebtedness in furtherance of any or all of the objects of its business; to secure the same by mortgage, deed of trust, pledge or other lien;

(d) to enter into, perform and carry out contracts of any kind necessary to, or in connection with, or incidental to the accomplishment of any one or more of the purposes of the corporation; and

(e) to make patronage refunds to stockholders, occupants of living units, or others as provided for the by-laws.

ARTICLE III - ADDRESS

The Post Office address of the place at which the principal office of the Corporation in this State will be located is _____ _____ . The resident agent of the Corporation on whom process may be served is _____, whose Post Office address is _____.

ARTICLE IV
DIRECTORS AND OFFICERS

The number of directors of the corporation shall be as provided in the by-laws. The directors shall be elected by the regular members except as herein otherwise provided, and shall act as such until their successors are duly chosen and qualified. Officers shall be elected as provided for in the by-laws.

ARTICLE V - CAPITAL STOCK

The total amount of the capital stock of the Corporation shall be _____ shares, of which 5 shares having a par value of $20.00

per share shall be designated as Preferred Stock[2], and _____ shares having a par value of $ _____ per share shall be designated as Common Stock [3].

Section 1. Provisions of Preferred Stock Power and Authority of Holders Thereof

Subsection 1. Upon insurance by the Commissioner of a certain Mortgage or Deed of Trust (hereinafter called the Mortgage) said Preferred Stock shall be issued to the Federal Housing Administration (hereinafter called the "Administration") or to its designated representatives, and delivered to the Commissiner in order that the Commissioner, in connection with the insurance of said Mortgage under the Act, may regulate and restrict the Corporation as to rents or sales, charges, capital structure, rate of return and methods of operation as provided in this Certificate of Incorporation and to enable the Commissioner to protect the contingent liability of the Administration as insurer of such mortgage or of subsequent insured mortgages covering any of the dwellings or property described in Appendix B. So long as any mortgage insurance pertaining to any of the said dwelling units or property shall be in effect, or any mortgage covering any of said dwelling units or property shall be held by the Commissioner, or any said dwelling units or property shall be owned by the Commissioner, said Preferred Stock shall be held by the Commissioner or his successors and shall be registered upon the books of the Corporation in the name of the Administration or its nominees. During such period the Corporation shall not be required to recognize any persons other than the Administration, or representatives of the Administration, as the holders of the Preferred Stock.

Subsection 2. The Preferred Stock at any time outstanding may be redeemed by the Corporation at par, provided, however, that such stock shall not be redeemed (1) if any of the dwellings or property described in Appendix B is covered by an FHA insured mortgage,

---

[2] This stock must be registered in the name of the Federal Housing Administration; it must be par stock; the value and number of shares (not less than 5) may vary from that designated herein but the consideration paid for it will always be $100. The certificate should contain a statement of the rights, privileges and restrictions pertaining to this stock.

[3] The "common stock" may be par or no par and may provide for such classes or preferences as are deemed appropriate. The total number of shares of common stock should equal the total number of units covered by the commitment.

(2) if the Commissioner is the holder of a mortgage on any of said dwellings or property, or (3) if the Commissioner is the owner of any of said dwellings or property. Notwithstanding the above provisions, the Preferred Stock shall be redeemed by the Corporation at par when the request for same has been received from the Preferred Stockholder. Preferred Stock, so redeemed, shall be retired or cancelled.

Section 2. Rights in Case of Default

In the event of any default by the Corporation, as hereinafter defined, and during the period of such default or at any time during the period between initial and final endorsement of any mortgage executed by the Corporation for mortgage insurance by the Commissioner whether or not a default has occurred, the holder or holders of the Preferred Stock, voting as a class and for the purpose of making effective the regulation and restriction set forth in this Certificate of Incorporation, and to protect the interest of the Administration, shall be entitled to remove all existing directors of the Corporation and to elect a new board of directors in their stead consisting of three members, through either of the following procedures: [4]

Subsection 1. The president or the secretary, or either of them, as may be required by law, shall, at the request in writing of the holders of record of a majority of shares of the Preferred Stock, addressed to him at the office of the Corporation and stating the purpose of the meeting, forthwith call a special meeting, to take place within ten days after such call, of the Preferred Stockholders for the purpose of removal of existing directors and officers and the election of new directors and officers. If such officer shall fail to issue a call for such meeting within three days after the receipt of such request, then the holders of a majority of the shares of the Preferred Stock may do so by giving notice as provided by law, or, if not so provided, then by giving ten days' notice of the time, place and object of the meeting by advertisement inserted in any newspaper published in the county or city in which the principal office of the Corporation is situated;

OR

Subsection 2. Such meeting may be called pursuant to the statutes of the jurisdiction under which the Corporation was organized, or

---

[4] In Insurance Upon Completion cases, delete the phrase "or at any time during the period between initial and final endorsement for mortgage insurance by the Commissioner whether or not a default has occurred."

pursuant to the Statutes of the jurisdiction in which the property described in Appendix B is situated;

OR

Subsection 3. Notwithstanding either of the foregoing Subsection 1 or 2, the holders of the Preferred Stock may, by waiver of notice, or by three days' notice by registered mail given on behalf of the Commissioner, call and hold a meeting either in the offices of the Administration in Washington, D.C., or in the offices of the Insuring Office in the state in which the property described in Appendix B is situated.

Subsection 4. At the meeting held pursuant to such notice or call, without regard to whether such call is issued pursuant to the provisions of Subsection 1, 2 or 3 of this Section, the holders of the Preferred Stock shall proceed to elect three new directors (the number being limited to three under either of said provisions), any or all of whom may be Preferred Stockholders, but one of whom, at the discretion of the Preferred Stockholders, may be a Common Stockholder.

Subsection 5. When such default shall have been cured, and the Commissioner shall have so advised the former president or secretary to that effect, and shall have advised either of them that satisfactory evidence has been submitted to the effect that any further defaults of a similar nature will not be permitted again to recur, if within the power of the officers or stockholders to prevent the same, or if there has been no default when the mortgage note has been finally endorsed for mortgage insurance, then the right again to elect directors of their own choosing shall be vested in the holders of the Common Stock who shall proceed to give notice to the holders of both the Common and the Preferred Stock of their intention to hold a meeting, stating the date and place of such meeting, for the purpose of removing existing directors and electing new directors.

Section 3. Powers, Duties and Rights of Holders of Common Stock

Subsection 1. Except as otherwise provided by law or as set forth in this Certificate of Incorporation, all voting rights shall be vested in the holders of the Common Stock.

Section 4. Dividends

Unless otherwise required by law no dividend shall be paid at any time upon any class of stock issued by the Corporation.

Section 5. Rights on Dissolution

In the event of any voluntary or involuntary liquidation or dissolution of the Corporation, the holders of the Preferred Stock shall be entitled to receive for each share held, out of the assets of the Corporation available for distribution to its stockholders, whether from capital, surplus or earnings, an amount equal to the par value of each share held, before any distribution of such assets shall be made to the holders of the Common Stock.

ARTICLE VI -REQUIRED RESERVES

Section 1. Reserve Fund or Funds for
Replacements

Commencing on the date of the first payment toward amortization of the principal of any FHA-insured mortgage executed by this Corporation unless a later date is approved in writing by the holders of the Preferred Stock, a Reserve Fund for Replacements for any such mortgage shall be established and maintained by the Corporation by the allocation thereto of an amount equal to 1/12th of the annual reserve required by the FHA commitment applicable to any such FHA-insured mortgage and a like amount monthly thereafter. At the election of the Corporation, any such Fund may be maintained in the form of cash or may be invested in obligations of, or fully guaranteed as to principal by the United States of America. Any such Fund shall be maintained in a separate account with the mortgagee (or in the case of a deed of trust, with the beneficiary) or under the control of the mortgagee in a safe and responsible depository designated by the mortgagee, and shall at all times be under the control of the mortgagee. Any such Fund shall be for the purpose of effecting the replacement of structural elements and mechanical equipment of the property covered by the respective mortgage and for such other purposes as may be agreed to in writing by the holders of the Preferred Stock. Disbursements from any such Fund may be made only after receiving the consent in writing of the holders of the Preferred Stock: Provided, however, that upon the payment in full of the respective FHA-insured mortgage executed by the Corporation, the Corporation shall cease to be obligated to make monthly payments to the respective Reserve

Fund for Replacements and disbursements from the respective Reserve Fund for Replacements shall be only for such purposes as may be agreed to in writing by the holders of the Preferred Stock. Upon completion of the community facilities as approved by the FHA and with the prior written consent of the holders of the Preferred Stock, the amount remaining in any Reserve Fund for Replacements shall be transferred to a new Reserve Rund for Replacements designated as the Community Facility Reserve Fund for Replacements which shall be under the control of the Corporation in such manner as the Corporation shall prescribe.

Section 2. Operating Reserve or Reserves

Commencing at occupancy of any of the dwelling units listed and described in Appendix B which are covered by an FHA-insured mortgage executed by the Corporation, a General Operating Reserve shall be established and maintained for the dwelling units covered by any such mortgage by allocation and payment thereto monthly of an amount equivalent to not less than 3% of the monthly amount otherwise chargeable to the members pursuant to their occupancy agreements. Such reserve shall remain in a special account and may be in the form of a cash deposit or invested in obligations of, or fully guaranteed as to principal by, the United States of America, and shall at all times be under the control of the Corporation. Such cumulative reserve or reserves are intended to provide a measure of financial stability during periods of special stress and may be used to meet deficiencies from time to time as a result of delinquent payment by individual cooperators, to provide funds for the re-puchase of stock of withdrawing members and other contingencies. Disbursements totaling in excess of 20% of the total balance of any such reserve as of the close of the preceding annual period may not be made during any annual period without the consent of the holders of the Preferred Stock. Reimbursements shall be made to any such account upon payment of delinquencies or sale of stock for which funds were withdrawn from the respective reserve: Provided, however, that upon payment in full of the respective FHA-insured mortgage executed by the Corporation, the Corporation shall cease to be obligated to make payments to the respective General Operating Reserve; and upon the completion of the community facilities as approved by the FHA and with the prior consent of the Preferred Stockholders, the amount remaining in any General Operating Reserve shall be transferred to a new General Operating Reserve designated as the Community Facility Operating Reserve, which shall be under the control of the Corporation in such manner as it shall prescribe.

ARTICLE VII - RULES FOR CONDUCT OF AFFAIRS

The following provisions are hereby adopted for the conduct of affairs of the Corporation and in regulation of the powers of the Corporation, the directors and stockholders:

> Section 1. Limitations on Alienation, Encumbrances, Remodeling, Occupancy, Changing Corporate Structure, Disposition of Excess Mortgage Funds.

The Corporation shall not without prior approval of the holders of the Preferred Stock, given in writing, (a) sell, assign, transfer, rent, lease, dispose of or encumber any real or personal property; (b) remodel, reconstruct, demolish or subtract from any property owned by the Corporation; (c) permit the occupancy of any of the dwelling accomodations of the Corporation except at the charges fixed by the schedule of charges provided for hereinafter; (d) permit occupancy of any of the dwelling accommodations of the Corporation except by a tenant-stockholder of the Corporation; (e) consolidate or merge the Corporation into or with any other Corporation; go into voluntary liquidation; carry into effect any plan of reorganization of the Corporation; cancel any of its shares of Preferred Stock, or effect any changes whatsoever in its capital structure; alter or amend this Certificate of Incorporation; or amend its by-laws; (f) fail to establish and maintain the Fund or Funds for Replacements and General Operating Reserve or Reserves or any other fund or reserve as set forth in this Certificate of Incorporation; (g) incur liabilities (direct or contingent) with respect to the particular dwellings and property covered by any mortgage executed by the Corporation which will exceed in the aggregate 1% of the FHA commitment amount applicable to the particular dwellings and property covered by any such mortgage, provided that this requirement shall be applicable only so long as any such mortgage executed by the Corporation is insured or held by the FHA; (h) fail to provide in a manner approved by the holders of the Preferred Stock for the management of any dwelling units or property covered by an FHA-insured mortgage or by a mortgage held by FHA and executed by the Corporation; (i) invest any funds of the Corporation in any property, real, personal or mixed, except obligations of, or fully guaranteed as to principal by, the United States of America as provided in this Certificate of Incorporation provided this requirement shall be applicable only so long as any mortgage executed by the Corporation is insured or held by the FHA.

Section 2. Limitations on Carrying Charges

Monthly carrying charges charged to members during the initial occupancy period shall be made by the Corporation in accordance with a schedule of charges filed with and approved in writing by the holders of the Preferred Stock prior to the opening of the development for occupancy. Such charges shall be in an amount sufficient to meet the FHA estimate of cooperative management expense, operating expense and maintenance expense, debt service, taxes, special assessments and ground rents, if any, reserves and all other expenses of the Corporation. Subsequent to the initial occupancy period, charges made by the Corporation for its accommodations shall be in accordance with a schedule of charges filed with and approved in writing by the holders of the Preferred Stock and shall be in amounts sufficient to meet the Corporation's estimate of expenses set forth in an operating budget which shall be prepared and submitted to the FHA sixty days prior to the beginning of each fiscal year. The operating budget shall set forth the anticipated income of the development and a sufficiently detailed estimate of expenses which will include separate estimates for administration expense, operating expense, maintenance expense, utilities, hazard insurance, taxes and assessments, ground rent, interest and amortization, mortgage insurance premium, replacement reserve and operating reserve. The Corporation shall not permit occupancy of its accommodations except in accordance with a schedule of charges approved by the holders of the Preferred Stock and such schedule shall not be changed except with the written approval of the Preferred Stockholders; nor shall occupancy be permitted by the Corporation except upon the execution of an occupancy agreement in a form approved by the holders of the Preferred Stock. The property of the Corporation shall not be rented as an entirety.

Section 3. Limitation on Payments

During the period between initial and final endorsement for mortgage insurance by the Administration, no compensation or fee shall be paid nor obligation therefor incurred by the Corporation except with the prior written approval of the holders of the Preferred Stock.

Thereafter[5] no compensation or fee shall be paid by the Corporation except for necessary services and except at such rate as is fair and reasonable in the locality for similar services, nor, except with the prior written approval of the holders of the Preferred Stock, shall any compensation be paid by the Corporation to its officers, directors or stockholders, or to any person, or corporation, for supervisory or managerial services; nor shall any compensation be paid by the Corporation to any employee in excess of $4,000 per annum, except with such prior written approval. No officer, director, stockholder, agent, or employee of the Corporation shall in any manner become indebted to the Corporation, except on account of approved occupancy charges: Provided, however, that upon the payment in full of all FHA-insured mortgages covering the property described in Appendix B and executed by the Corporation, the limitations herein shall not be applicable.

Section 4. Maintenance Requirements

The Corporation shall maintain its property, the grounds, buildings and equipment appurtenant thereto, in good repair and in such condition as will preserve the health and safety of its members.

Section 5. Requirements as to Corporate Property and Records

The Corporation, its property, equipment, buildings, plans, office, apparatus, devices, books, contracts, records, documents and papers shall be subject to inspection and examination by the holders of the Preferred Stock or their duly authorized agent at all reasonable times.

Section 6. Uniform Record System Required

The books and accounts of the Corporation shall be kept in accordance with the Uniform System of Accounting prescribed by the holders of the Preferred Stock. The Corporation shall file with the

---

[5] In Insurance Upon Completion cases, delete the first sentence of this section, the word "Thereafter," and begin the section with the words "No compensation . . . "

holders of the Preferred Stock and the mortgagee the following reports verified by the signature of such officers of the Corporation as may be designated and in such form as may be prescribed by the holders of the Preferred Stock.

(a) monthly or quarterly operating reports, when required by the holders of the Preferred Stock;

(b) semi-annual financial statement within sixty days after the the semi-annual period when required by the holders of the Preferred Stock;

(c) annual reports prepared by a certified public accountant or other person acceptable to the holders of the Preferred Stock, within sixty days after the end of each fiscal year, when required by the holders of the Preferred Stock;

(d) specific answers to questions upon which information is desired from time to time relative to the operation and condition of the property and the status of any mortgage;

(e) copies of minutes of all stockholders' meetings certified to by the secretary of the Corporation within thirty days after such meetings, and copies of minutes of directors' meetings, when required by the holders of the Preferred Stock.

Section 7. Limitations Against Racial Restrictions

The Corporation shall not execute or file for record any instrument which imposes a restriction upon the sale, leasing, occupancy, or use of the property described in Appendices A & B, or any part thereof, on the basis of race, color or creed.

ARTICLE VIII - CONTRACTUAL POWERS

No contract or other transaction between this Corporation and any other corporation, and no act of this Corporation, shall in any way be affected or invalidated by the fact that any of the directors or officers of this Corporation are pecuniarily or otherwise interested in, or are directors or officers of, such other corporations; any directors individually, or any firm of which any director may be a member, may be a party to, or may be pecuniarily or otherwise interested in, any contract or transaction of this Corporation, provided the fact that he or such firm is so interested, shall be disclosed on the minutes of this Corporation; and any director of this Corporation who is also a director or officer of such other corporation or who is so interested may be counted in determining the existence of a quorum at any meeting of the board of directors of this Corporation, which shall authorize any such contract or transaction, provided, however, such director may not vote thereat to authorize any such contract or transaction.

ARTICLE IX - EVENTS OF DEFAULT

The happening of any of the following events shall constitute a default within the meaning of that word as used in this Certificate of Incorporation: (1) the failure of the Corporation to have dismissed within thirty days after commencement of any bankruptcy, receivership, or any petition for reorganization filed by or against the Corporation under the provisions of any State insolvency law or under the provisions of the Bankruptcy Act of 1898, as amended, or upon the making by the Corporation of an assignment for the benefit of its creditors, unless said action is previously approved in writing by the holders of the Preferred Stock; (2) the failure of the Corporation to pay the principal, interest, or any other payment due on any note, bond, or other obligation executed by it, as called for by the terms of such instrument; (3) the failure of the Corporation to establish and maintain the Reserve Fund or Funds for Replacements and General Operating Reserve or Reserves or any other fund or reserve as provided in Article Sixth hereof or the use of such reserves except as permitted in said Article; (4) execution or filing for record by the Corporation of any instrument which imposes a restriction upon sale, leasing, occupancy, or use of the property or any part thereof, on the basis of race, color or creed; (5) the violation of any of the terms of this Certificate of Incorporation, or the failure of the Corporation to perform any of the covenants, conditions or provisions required by it to be performed by this Certificate, the By-laws of the Corporation, of any FHA-insured Mortgage or mortgage held by the FHA, and executed by the Corporation, or any contract to which the Corporation and the Commissioner shall be parties, or the failure to carry out in full the terms of any agreement whereby the loan covered by any FHA-insured Mortgage executed by the Corporation is to be advanced or the project is to be constructed and operated; (6) the attempt by the Corporation, its officers, directors or stockholders to accomplish by indirect methods that which they are not permitted by the terms hereof to do directly; (7) the failure of the Corporation to report to the holders of the Preferred Stock any changes in its officers and directors or in its official address to which mail is to be directed or notices sent; (8) the failure of the Corporation to complete the community facilities described in Appendix A within the time provided for in the FHA Commitment.

ARTICLE X - DURATION

The duration of the Corporation shall be _____ .[6]

(To be appropriately executed and acknowledged)

---

[6] In those states where the statutes do not permit corporations to have a perpetual duration, a clause substantially as follows should be added: "Six months prior to the period heretofore mentioned, this Corporation shall take the necessary steps to extend the life of this Certificate of Incorporation for such additional period of time as the FHA directs. Failure of the Corporation to extend the life of the Corporation for such additional period shall be considered an event of default in addition to the events enumerated in the preceding Article."

MODEL FORM OF BY-LAWS

ARTICLE I

NAME AND LOCATION OF CORPORATION

Section 1. The name of this Corporation is _____ _____. Its principal office is located at _____ _____ .

ARTICLE II

PURPOSE

Section 1. The purpose of this Corporation is to provide its members[1] with housing and community facilities, if any, on a nonprofit basis consonant with the provisions set forth in its Certificate of Incorporation.

ARTICLE III

MEMBERSHIP

Section 1. *Eligibility.* Any natural person approved by the Board of Directors shall be eligible for membership, provided that he or she executes a Subscription Agreement and Occupancy Agreement in the usual form employed by the Corporation covering a specific unit in the housing project.[2]

---

[1] In corporations organized on a stock basis, change the word "members" to "stockholders" and add thereafter the following parenthetical clause: "(hereinafter referred to as 'members')."

[2] In corporations organized on a stock basis, change the word "membership" to "stock ownership" and add thereafter the following parenthetical clause: "(hereinafter referred to as 'membership')."

Section 2. *Application for Membership.* Application for membership shall be presented in person on a form prescribed by the Board of Directors, and all such applications shall be acted upon promptly by the Board of Directors.

Section 3. *Subscription Funds.*[3] All subscription funds (except funds required for credit reports) received from applicants prior to the endorsement of the mortgage note by the Federal Housing Administration (hereinafter sometimes referred to as the "Administration") shall be deposited promptly without deduction in a special account or accounts of the Corporation as escrowee or trustee for the Subscribers to Membership, which monies shall not be corporate funds, but shall be held solely for the benefit of the Subscribers until transferred to the account of the Corporation as hereinafter provided. Such special account or accounts shall be established with _____ (name of institution) located at _____, whose deposits are insured by an agency of the Federal Government. Such account or accounts may be interest bearing, with the interest earned to be retained and owned by the Corporation. Such funds shall be subject to withdrawal, or transfer to the account of the Corporation or disbursed in a manner directed by the Corporation only upon certification by the President and Secretary of the Corporation to the above-named institution or institutions that:

(a) The Subscription Agreement of a named applicant has been terminated pursuant to its terms and such withdrawal is required to repay the amount paid by him under such agreement; or

(b) Applicants for _____[4] dwelling units have not been procured within the effective period of the FHA Commitment, or any extension thereof, and such withdrawal is required to repay to the applicants the amounts paid by them; or

---

[3] In view of the facts that certain sponsoring groups such as labor unions veterans' organizations, church groups, cooperative sponsoring organizations, may wish to use some other method of handling subscriptions or subscriptions funds, this section may be altered, subject to prior approval of the Administration.

[4] Insert number required by the applicable FHA Committment.

(c) Applicants for _____ [5] dwelling units (or such lesser number as may be approved by the Administration) have signed Subscription Agreements, have been approved as to their credit by the Administration, and have paid the subscription price in full. If these requirements have been met and the mortgage loan has been scheduled for closing with the approval of the Administration, the entire amount of the funds in the subscription escrow account may be transferred to the corporation, at which time the corporation shall issue and deliver membership certificates to all members.

If more than one mortgage is to be executed by the corporation, this section shall be deemed to be applicable to the specific subscription fund received from applicants with respect to the specific dwelling units to be covered by each mortgage and to require the creation of separate and specific escrow accounts with respect to each mortgage.

Section 4. *Members.* The members shall consist of the incorporators and such subscribers as have been approved for membership certificates. The status of the incorporators as members shall terminate at the first annual meeting of members unless they have executed Subscription Agreements and, where required by the Administration, Occupancy Agreements. The authorized membership of the Corporation shall consist of _____ regular memberships. [6]

Section 5. *Membership Certificates.* Each membership certificate shall state that the Corporation is organized under the laws of the State of _____ , the name of the registered holder of the membership represented thereby, the Corporation lien rights as against such membership as set forth in this Article, and the preferences and restrictions applicable thereto, and shall be in such form as shall be approved by the Board of Directors. Membership certificates shall be consecutively numbered, bound in one or more books, and shall be issued therefrom upon certification as to full payment. Every membership certificate shall be signed by the President or Vice President, and the Secretary, and shall be sealed with the corporate seal.

Section 6. *Lost Certificates.* The Board of Directors may direct a new certificate or certificates to be issued in place of any certificate or certificates previously issued by the Corporation and alleged to

---

[5] Insert number required by the applicable FHA Commitment.

[6] In cases where FHA control is via ownership of preferred stock, add "and _____ preferred memberships."

have been destroyed or lost, upon the making of an affidavit of that fact by the person claiming the share certificate to be lost or destroyed. When authorizing such issuance of a new certificate or certificates, the Board of Directors may, in its discretion, and as a condition precedent to the issuance thereof, require the registered owner of such lost or destroyed certificate or certificates, or his legal representative, to advertise the same in such manner as the Board of Directors shall require and to give the Corporation a bond in such sum as the Board of Directors may require as indemnity against any claim that may be made against the Corporation.

Section 7. *Lien.* The Corporation shall have a lien on the outstanding regular memberships in order to secure payment of any sums which shall be due or become due from the holders thereof for any reason whatsoever, including any sums due any occupancy agreements.

Section 8. *Transfer of Membership.* Except as provided herein, membership shall not be transferable and, in any event, no transfer of membership shall be made upon the books of the Corporation within ten (10) days next preceding the annual meeting of the members. In all transfers of membership the Corporation shall be entitled to a fee it deems appropriate to compensate it for the processing of the transfer.

(a) *Death of Member.* If, upon death of a member, his membership in the Corporation passes by will or intestate distribution to a member of his immediate family, such legatee or distributee may, by assuming in writing the terms of the Subscription Agreement and Occupancy Agreement, where required by the Administration, within sixty (60) days after member's death, and paying all amounts due thereunder, become a member of the Corporation. If a member dies and an obligation is not assumed in accordance with the foregoing, then the Corporation shall have an option to purchase the membership from the deceased member's estate in the manner provided in paragraph (b) of this Section, written notice of the death being equivalent to notice of intention to withdraw. If the Corporation does not exercise such option, the provisions of paragraph (c) of this Section shall be applicable, the references to "member" therein to be construed as references to the legal representative of the deceased member.

(b) *Option of Corporation to Purchase.* If the member desires to leave the project, he shall notify the Corporation in writing of such intention and the Corporation shall have an option for a period of thirty (30) days commencing the first day of the month following the giving of such notice, but not the obligation, to purchase the membership, together with all of the member's rights with respect to the dwelling unit, at an amount to be determined by the Corporation as representing the transfer value thereof, less any amounts due by the member of the Corporation under the Occupancy Agreement, and less the cost or estimated cost of all deferred maintenance, including painting, redecorating, floorfinishing, and such repairs and replacements as are deemed necessary by the Corporation to place the dwelling unit in suitable condition for another occupant. The purchase by the Corporation of the membership will immediately terminate the member's rights and the member shall forthwith vacate the premises.

(c) *Procedure Where Corporation Does Not Exercise Option.* If the Corporation waives in writing its right to purchase the membership under the foregoing option, or if the Corporation fails to exercise such option within the thirty (30) day period, the member may sell his membership to any person who has been duly approved by the Corporation as a member and occupant.

If the Corporation agrees, at the request of the member, to assist the member in finding a purchaser, the Corporation shall be entitled to charge the member a fee it deems reasonable for this service. When the transferee has been approved for membership and has executed the prescribed Occupancy Agreement, the retiring member shall be released of his obligations under his Occupancy Agreement, provided he has paid all amounts due the Corporation to date.

(d) *Transfer Value.* [7] Whenever the Board of Directors elects to purchase a membership, the term "transfer value" shall mean the sum of the following:

(1) The consideration (i.e. down payment) paid for the membership by the first occupant of the unit involved as shown on the books of the Corporation;

(2) The value, as determined by the Directors, of any improve-

---

[7] If desired, a provision may be added to the effect that the transfer value otherwise applicable may be increased and decreased pursuant to fluctuations in the economy as evidenced by a Cost of Living Index or a Construction Cost Index. The language of such provision must be cleared with the FHA.

ments installed at the expense of the member with the prior approval of the Directors, under a valuation formula which does not provide for reimbursement in an amount in excess of the typical initial cost of the improvements; and

(3) The amount of principal amortized by the Corporation on its mortgage indebtedness and attributable to the dwelling unit involved as paid by the member involved and previous holders of the same membership.[8] However, the amount of principal paid by the Corporation for a period of three (3) years after the Corporation has made its first principal payment on the mortgage shall not be included in this computation.

[9] Whenever a member who has received rent supplement assistance sells his membership, the amount of such assistance shall be deducted from the transfer value to which such member would otherwise be entitled as follows:

(i) A portion of that amount of principal amortized as determined in (d) (3), above, will not be made available to the member. The amount so withheld shall be determined by multiplying the amortized principal attributable to the unit by the quotient of the total rent supplement assistance to the member divided by the total monthly carrying charges the member was obligated to pay under his occupancy agreement and would have paid if he had not received rent supplement assistance.

(ii) In the event the corporation exercises its option to purchase the membership pursuant to paragraph (b), above, an amount computed in accordance with (i), above, shall be withheld from the proceeds of such sale and retained by the Corporation.

(iii) In the event the member sells his membership pursuant to paragraph (c), above, the selling member and

---

[8] In Section 221 below market interest rate cases in Section 236 cases the sentence following the asterisks should be added (A limitation which further restricts the amount payable to the retiring member in such cases may be imposed subject to the approval of FHA).

[9] Include this paragraph only in projects where rent supplements are contemplated.

the purchaser who purchases from such member shall jointly certify to the Corporation as to the sales price of the membership in such manner and in such form as may be required by the Corporation. An amount equal to the amount computed in accordance with (i) above, shall be paid to the Corporation prior to the Corporation's release of such member's obligation under his occupancy agreement and the transfer of his membership to the new owner; provided, however, that in the event the sales price does not exceed the total paragrphs d (1) and d (2), above, then the selling member shall be entitled to receive the full amount of the sales price.

(iv) All funds received by the Corporation representing withheld amortized principal attributable to Rent Supplement Payments shall be deposited in a special account by the Corporation and disbursed as directed by the Federal Housing Administration.

Section 9. *Termination of Membership for Cause.* In the event the Corporation has terminated the rights of a member under the Occupancy Agreement, the member shall be required to deliver promptly to the Corporation his membership certificate and his Occupancy Agreement, both endorsed in such manner as may be required by the Corporation. The Corporation shall thereupon at its election either (1) repurchase said membership at its transfer value (as hereinabove defined) or the amount the retiring member originally paid for the acquisition of his membership certificate, whichever is the lesser, or (2) proceed with reasonable diligence to effect a sale of the membership to a purchaser and at a sales price acceptable to the Corporation. The retiring member shall be entitled to receive the amount so determined, less the following amounts (the determination of such amounts by the Corporation to be conclusive):

(a) any amounts due to the Corporation from the member under the Occupancy Agreement;

(b) the cost or estimated cost of all deferred maintenance, including painting, redecorating, floor finishing, and such repairs and replacements as are deemed necessary by the Corporation to place the dwelling unit in suitable condition for another occupant; and

(c) legal and other expenses incurred by the Corporation in connection with the default of such member and the resale of his membership. In the event the retiring member for any reason should fail for a period of 10 days after demand to deliver to the Corporation his endorsed membership certificate, said membership certificate shall forthwith be deemed to be cancelled and may be reissued by the Corporation to a new purchaser.

[10] Section 10. *Sales Price.* Memberships may be sold by the Corporation or the member only to a person approved by the Board of Directors in accordance with the requirements of the Regulatory Agreement, and the sales price shall not exceed the transfer value as provided in this Article, except that in sales effected by the Corporation a service charge not in excess of $100 may be charged by the Corporation. Where the sale is accomplished by a member, a certificate in form approved by the FHA as to the price paid shall be executed by the seller and purchaser and delivered to the Corporation.

ARTICLE IV

MEETINGS OF MEMBERS

Section 1. *Place of Meetings.* Meetings of the membership shall be held at the principal office or place of business of the Corporation or at such other suitable place convenient to the membership as may be designated by the Board of Directors.

Section 2. *Annual Meetings.* The first annual meeting of the Corporation shall be held on _____. (Date) Thereafter, the annual meetings of the Corporation shall be held on the _____ (1st, 2nd, 3rd, 4th) _____ (Monday, Tuesday, Wednesday, etc.) of _____ (Month) each succeeding year. At such meeting there shall be elected by ballot of the members a Board of Directors in accordance with the requirements of Section 3 of Article V of these By-Laws. The members may also transact such other business of the Corporation as may properly come before them.

---

[10] Omit in Section 213 cases and market interest rate cases under Section 221 (d) (3).

Section 3. *Special Meetings.* It shall be the duty of the President to call a special meeting of the members as directed by resolution of the Board of Directors or upon a petition signed by twenty (20) percent of the members having been presented to the Secretary, or at the request of the Federal Housing Commissioner or his duly authorized representative. The notice of any special meeting shall state the time and place of such meeting and the purpose thereof. No business shall be transacted at a special meeting except as stated in the notice unless by consent or four-fifths of the members present, either in person or by proxy.

Section 4. *Notice of Meetings.* It shall be the duty of the Secretary to mail a notice of each annual or special meeting, stating the purpose thereof as well as the time and place where it is to be held, to each member of record, at his address as it appears on the membership book of the Corporation, or if no such address appears, at his last known place of address, at least _____ but no more than _____ days prior to such meeting (the number of days notice to comply with state statute). Service may also be accomplished by the delivery of any such notice to the member at his dwelling unit or last known address. Notice by either such method shall be considered as notice served. Notices of all meetings shall be mailed to the Director of the local insuring office of the Federal Housing Administration.

Section 5. *Quorum.* The presence, either in person or by proxy, of at least _____ [11] percent of the members of record of the Corporation shall be requisite for, and shall constitute a quorum for the transaction of business at all meetings of members. If the number of members at a meeting drops below the quorum and the question of a lack of quorum is raised, no business may thereafter be transacted.

Section 6. *Adjourned Meetings.* If any meeting of members cannot be organized because a quorum has not attended, the members who are present, either in person or by proxy, may, except as otherwise provided by law, adjourn the meeting to a time not less than forty-eight (48) hours from the time the original meeting was called, at which

---

[11] The figure to be inserted will vary with the size of the cooperative, for details see footnote 12.

subsequent meeting the quorum requirement shall be _____ [12]
percent.

Section 7. *Voting.*[13] At every meeting of the regular members,
each member present, either in person or by proxy, shall have the right
to cast one vote on each question and never more than one vote. (Note
If desired, a provision may be included to the effect that where a husband
and wife are joint members, each shall be entitled to cast one-half vote.)
The vote of the majority of those present, in person or by proxy, shall
decide any question brought before such meeting, unless the question
is one upon which, by express provision of statute or of the Certificate
of Incorporation or of these By-Laws, a different vote is required, in
which case such express provisions shall govern and control. No member
shall be eligible to vote or to be elected to the Board of Directors who
is shown on the books or management accounts of the Corporation
to be more than 30 days delinquent in payments due the Corporation
under his Occupancy Agreement.

Section 8. *Proxies.* A member may appoint as his proxy only a
member of his immediate family (as defined by the Board of Directors)
except that an unmarried member may appoint any other member as
his proxy. In no case may a member cast more than one vote by proxy
in addition to his own vote. Any proxy must be filed with the Secretary
before the appointed time of each meeting.

Section 9. *Order of Business.* The order of business at all regularly
scheduled meetings of the regular members shall be as follows:

(a) Roll Call.
(b) Proof of notice of meeting or waiver of notice.
(c) Reading of minutes of preceding meeting.
(d) Reports of officers.

---

[12] The figure to be inserted will vary with the size of the cooperative, as follows:

Number of Memberships	Quorum percentage to be inserted in Article IV, Sec. 5	Quorum percentage applicable to adjourned meetings to be inserted in Article IV, Sec. 6
20 or less	50	25
21 - 150	25	15
151 - 300	20	10
301 - 500	15	10
501 or more	10	5

[13] There will be no objection to including a provision permitting voting by mail, and this may be
desirable in the larger cooperatives.

(e) Report of committees.
(f) Election of inspectors of election.
(g) Election of directors.
(h) Unfinished business.
(i) New business.

In the case of special meetings, items (a) through (d) shall be applicable and thereafter the agenda shall consist of the items specified in the notice of meeting.

If present, a representative of the Administration will be given an opportunity to address any regular or special meeting.

ARTICLE V

DIRECTORS

Section 1. *Number and Qualification.* The affairs of the Corporation shall be governed by a Board of Directors composed of _____ persons [14] , a majority of whom shall be members of the Corporation.

Section 2. *Powers and Duties.* The Board of Directors shall have all the powers and duties necessary for the administration of the affairs of the Corporation and may do all such acts and things as are not by law or by these By-Laws directed to be exercised and done by the members. The powers of the Board of Directors shall include but not be limited:

(a) To accept or reject all applications for membership and admission to occupancy of a dwelling unit in the cooperative housing project, either directly or through an authorized representative;

(b) Subject to the approval of the Administration, to establish monthly carrying charges as provided for in the Occupancy

---

[14] Any convenient number of Directors (not less than three nor more than nine) may be provided.

Agreement, based on an operating budget formally adopted by such Board;

(c) Subject to the approval of the Administration, to engage an agent or employees for the management of the project under such terms as the Board may determine;

(d) To authorize in their discretion patronage refunds from residual receipts when and as reflected in the annual report; [15]

(e) To terminate membership and occupancy rights for cause;

(f) To promulgate such rules and regulations pertaining to use and occupancy of the premises as may be deemed proper and which are consistent with these By-Laws and the Certificate of Incorporation; [16] and

(g) [17] Pursuant to a plan approved by the Administration, to prescribe additional monthly carrying charges to be paid by families whose incomes exceed the limitations for continuing occupancy established from time to time by the Administration; or, at the Board's option, to terminate the membership and occupancy of such families.

Section 3. *Election and Term of Office.* The term of the Directors named in the Certificate of Incorporation shall expire when their successors have been elected at the first annual meeting or any special meeting called for that purpose. At the first annual meeting of the members the term of office of two Directors shall be fixed for three (3) years. The term of office of two Directors shall be fixed at two (2) years, and the term of office of one Director shall be fixed at one (1) year. At the expiration of the initial term of office of each respective Director, his successor shall be elected to serve a term of three (3) years. The Directors shall hold office until their successors have been elected and hold their first meeting. (If a larger Board of Directors is contemplated, the terms of office should be established in a similar manner so that they will expire in different years.)

Section 4. *Vacancies.* Vacancies in the Board of Directors caused by any reason other than the removal of a Director by a vote of the

---

[15] Delete in Section 236 cases.

[16] Add "and the Regulatory Agreement" where Regulatory Agreement is executed by the Corporation.

[17] Include this provision only in Section 221 below market rate cases.

membership or by the vote of the preferred members [18] shall be filled by vote of the majority of the remaining Directors, even through they may constitute less than a quorum; and each person so elected shall be a Director until a successor is elected by the members at the next annual meeting to serve out the unexpired portion of the term.

Section 5. *Removal of Directors.* At any regular or special meeting duly called, any Director may be removed with or without cause by the affirmative vote of the majority of the entire regular membership of record and a successor may then and there be elected to fill the vacancy thus created. Any Director whose removal has been proposed by the members shall be given an opportunity to be heard at the meeting. The term of any Director who becomes more than 30 days delinquent in payment of his carrying charges shall be automatically terminated and the remaining Directors shall appoint his successor as provided in Section 4, above.

Section 6. *Compensation.* No compensation shall be paid to Directors for their services as Directors. No remuneration shall be paid to a Director for services performed by him for the Corporation in any other capacity, unless a resolution authorizing such remuneration shall have been unanimously adopted by the Board of Directors before the services are undertaken. No remuneration or compensation shall in any case be paid to a Director without the approval of the Administration. A Director may not be an employee of the Corporation.

Section 7. *Organization Meeting.* The first meeting of a newly elected Board of Directors shall be held within ten (10) days of election at such place as shall be fixed by the Directors at the meeting at which such Directors were elected, and no notice shall be necessary to the newly elected Directors in order legally to constitute such meeting, providing a majority of the whole Board shall be present.

Section 8. *Regular Meetings.* Regular meetings of the Board of Directors may be held at such time and place as shall be determined, from time to time, by a majority of the Directors, but at least four such meetings shall be held during each fiscal year. Notice of regular meetings of the Board of Directors shall be given to each Director, personally or by mail, telephone or telegraph, which notice shall state the time, place (as hereinabove provided) and purpose of the meeting. Special meetings of the Board of Directors shall be called by the President

---

[18] Delete "or by a vote of the preferred members" where Corporation has executed Regulatory Agreement.

or Secretary in like manner and on like notice on the written request of at least three Directors.

Section 10. *Waiver of Notice.* Before or at any meeting of the Board of Directors, any Director may, in writing, waive notice of such meeting and such waiver shall be deemed equivalent to the giving of such notice. Attendance by a Director at any meeting of the Board shall be a waiver of notice by him of the time and place thereof. If all the Directors are present at any meeting of the Board, no notice shall be required and any business may be transacted at such meeting.

Section 11. *Quorum.* At all meetings of the Board of Directors a majority of the Directors shall constitute a quorum for the trans-action of business, and the acts of the majority of the Directors present at a meeting at which a quorum is present shall be the acts of the Board of Directors. If, at any meeting of the Board of Directors, there be less than a quorum present, the majority of those present may adjourn the meeting from time to time. At any such adjourned meeting, any business which might have been transacted at the meeting as originally called may be transacted without further notice.

Section 12. *Fidelity Bonds.* The Board of Directors shall require that all officers and employees of the Corporation handling or respon-sible for corporate or trust funds shall furnish adequate fidelity bonds. The premiums on such bonds shall be paid by the Corporation.

Section 13. *Safeguarding Subscription Funds.* It shall be the duty of the Board of Directors to see to it that all sums received in connection with membership subscriptions prior to the closing of the mortgage transaction covering the housing project of the Corporation, are deposited and withdrawn only in the manner provided for in Article III, Section 3 of these By-Laws.

ARTICLE VI

OFFICERS

Section 1. *Designation.* The principal officers of the Corporation shall be a President, a Vice President, a Secretary, and a Treasurer, all of whom shall be elected by and from the Board of Directors. [The remaining provisions of this article are omitted here. They generally cover the election, removal, and duties of each officer.]

ARTICLE VII

RIGHTS OF FEDERAL HOUSING ADMINISTRATION
[Omitted here.]

ARTICLE VIII

AMENDMENTS

Section 1. These By-Laws may be amended by the affirmative vote of the majority of the entire regular membership of record at any regular or special meeting, provided that no amendment shall become effective unless and until it has received the written approval of the Administration. Amendments may be proposed by the Board of Directors or by petition signed by at least twenty (20) percent of the members. A description of any proposed amendment shall accompany the notice of any regular or special meeting at which such proposed amendment is to be voted upon.

ARTICLE IX

CORPORATE SEAL

Section 1. *Seal.* The Board of Directors shall provide a suitable corporate seal containing the name of the Corporation, which seal shall be in charge of the Secretary. If so directed by the Board of Directors, a duplicate of the seal may be kept and used by the Treasurer or any assistant secretary or assistant treasurer.

ARTICLE X

FISCAL MANAGEMENT

Section 1. *Fiscal Year.* The fiscal year of the Corporation shall begin on the _____ day of _____ every year, except that the first fiscal year of the Corporation shall begin at the date of incorporation. The commencement date of the fiscal year herein established shall be subject to change by the Board of Directors should corporate practice subsequently dictate, but not without the prior written approval of the Administration.

Section 2. *Books and Accounts.* Books and accounts of the Corporation shall be kept under the direction of the Treasurer and in accordance with the Uniform System of Accounts prescribed by the FHA Commissioner. That amount of the carrying charges required for payment on the principal of the mortgage of the Corporation or any other capital expenditures shall be credited upon the books of the Corporation to the "Paid-In Surplus" account as a capital contribution by the members.

Section 3. *Auditing.* At the closing of each fiscal year, the books and records of the Corporation shall be audited by a Certified Public Accountant or other person acceptable to the Administration, whose report will be prepared and certified in accordance with the requirements of the Administration. Based on such reports, the Corporation will furnish its members with an annual financial statement including the income and disbursements of the Corporation. The Corporation will also supply the members, as soon as practicable after the end of each calendar year, with a statement showing each member's pro rata share of the real estate taxes and mortgage interest paid by the Corporation during the preceding calendar year.

Section 4. *Inspection of Books.* Financial reports such as are required to be furnished to the Administration and the membership records of the Corporation shall be available at the principal office of the Corporation for inspection at reasonable times by any members.

Section 5. *Execution of Corporate Documents.* With the prior authorization of the Board of Directors, all notes and contracts, including Occupancy Agreements, shall be executed on behalf of the Corporation by either the President or the Vice President, and all checks shall be executed on behalf of the Corporation by (1) either the President or the Vice President, and countersigned (2) by either the Secretary or Treasurer.

ARTICLE XI[19]

COMMUNITY FACILITY PROVISIONS

Section 1. *Applicable Provisions.* Notwithstanding any provision herein to the contrary, upon the payment in full of each FHA-insured

---

[19] This Article to be included only in Sales Type projects where community facilities are to be owned by the Corporation.

mortgage executed by the Corporation and the release of the dwelling units included therein to the respective members, the following provisions of these By-Laws shall not be applicable to such members:

(a) Article III; and

(b) Sections 2 and 13 of Article V; and

in lieu thereof the following provisions shall apply to such members, and to all members upon payment in full of all FHA-insured mortgages executed by the Corporation:

Section 2. *Membership.*

(a) *Members.* Members shall consist of the owners of the dwelling units listed in Appendix B of the Articles of Incorporation, a copy of which is attached hereto, who have been approved for membership by the Board of Directors, and who have paid for their membership and received membership certificates, and such other persons to whom memberships have been transferred as provided herein.

(b) *Transfer of Membership.* Except as herein provided, memberships are not transferable or assignable:

1. The Board of Directors shall determine the membership value (hereinafter called the "Membership Fee") at which same may be transferred.

2. Subject to the prior approval of the Board of Directors, memberships may be permanently transferred by members to any of the following, in the order listed:

a. To the puchaser or lessee of the member's home if same is listed in Appendix B of the Articles of Incorporation.

b. To the owner or lessee of any of the other houses listed in Appendix B of the Articles of Incorporation who does not already own a membership.

c. To the applicant for membership at the top of a waiting list maintained by the Board of Directors, who is a resident of the area, the confines of which shall be as determined by the Board of Directors.

d. To a non-resident of the area.

(c) *Temporary Transfers.* Subject to the prior approval of the

Board of Directors, a member may temporarily assign his membership to his lessee for a designated period of time provided, however, that the member making the temporary assignment remains obligated to the Corporation for the payment of all assessments and other charges approved by the membership, and for the payment of the lessee's dues. Any delinquency in payment of dues, assessment and such other charges shall be subject to the provisions of paragraph (d) hereof.

(d) *Termination of Membership.* Any member failing to pay annual dues, assessments or other charges duly approved by the Board of Directors within thirty (30) days after notification of delinquency has been mailed to him at the address appearing on the records of the Corporation shall be suspended by the Board of Directors. Any person thus suspended shall be notified promptly in writing by the Secretary of his suspension, and if the amounts due and payable are not paid within fifteen (15) days after the sending of such notice he shall cease to be a member of the Corporation and shall not be entitled to the privileges accorded to members. The Corporation shall be obligated, after reassignment and sale of said membership to return the Membership Fee less amounts due. (The Board of Directors, in its discretion, may reinstate any member upon request and payment of all amounts in arrearage.) The Board of Directors, at its discretion, may cancel the membership of any member upon the return of the Membership Fee provided, however, that the member may be reinstated upon appeal and approval of reinstatement by the majority of the members present at a regular or special meeting. The Corporation shall not be obligated to refund any membership fee to any member except as provided herein.

Section 3. *Directors.* The Board of Directors shall have the powers and duties necessary for the administration of the affairs of the Corporation and may do all such acts and things as are not by law or by these By-Laws directed to be exercised and done by the members. The powers of the Board of Directors shall include but not be limited:

(a) To promulgate such rules and regulations pertaining to the use and operation of the community facilities which are consistent with these By-Laws and the Certificate of Incorporation.

(b) To establish the annual dues, assessments and charges for the operation and maintenance of the community facilities and any other property, real or personal, owned by the Corporation.

MODEL FORM OF OCCUPANCY AGREEMENT

(For use by Sec. 213, Sec. 221 and Sec. 236 Cooperatives composed of one mortgage parcel. (Multi-Section cooperative should use FHA Form 3237-B.))

THIS AGREEMENT, made and entered into this _____day of _____, 19_____ , by and between _____ (hereinafter referred to as the Corporation), a corporation having its principal office and place of business at and_____(hereinafter referred to as Member);

WHEREAS, the Corporation has been formed for the purpose of acquiring, owning and operating a cooperative housing project to be located at _____, with the intent that its members in stock corporations change "members" to "stockholders" and add the following parenthetical clause "(hereinafter called members)" shall have the right to occupy the dwelling units thereof under the terms and conditions hereinafter set forth; and

WHEREAS, the Member is the owner and holder of a certificate of membership or _____ shares of common capital stock of the Corporation and has a bona fide intention to reside in the project;

[1] WHEREAS, the Member has certified to the accuracy of the statements made in his application and family income survey and agrees and understands that family income, family composition and other eligibility requirements are substantial and material requirements of his initial and of his continuing occupancy.

NOW, THEREFORE, is consideration of One Dollar ($1.00) to each of the parties paid by the other party, the receipt of which is hereby acknowledged, and in further consideration of the mutual promises contained herein, the Corporation hereby lets to the Member, and the Member hereby hires and takes from the Corporation, dwelling unit number _____ , located at _____;

TO HAVE AND TO HOLD said dwelling unit unto the Member, his executors, administrators and authorized assigns, on the terms

---

[1] Required only in Sec. 236 cases and in Sec. 221 (d)(3) below market interest rate cases.

and conditions set forth herein and in the corporate Charter and By-Laws of the Corporation and any rules and regulations of the Corporation now or hereafter adopted pursuant thereto, from the date of this agreement, for a term terminating on _____
19____ , [2] renewable thereafter for successive three-year periods under the conditions provided for herein.

ARTICLE 1. MONTHLY CARRYING CHARGES

Commencing at the time indicated in ARTICLE 2 hereof, the Member agrees to pay to the Corporation a monthly sum referred to herein as "Carrying Charges", equal to one-twelfth of the Member's proportionate share of the sum required by the Corporation, as estimated by its Board of Directors to meet its annual expenses, including but not limited to the following items:

(a) The cost of all operating expenses of the project and services furnished.
(b) The cost of necessary management and administration.
(c) The amount of all taxes and assessments levied against the project of the Corporation or which it is required to pay, and ground rent, if any.
(d) The cost of fire and extended coverage insurance on the project and such other insurance as the Corporation may effect or as may be required by any mortgage on the project.
(e) The cost of furnishing water, electricity, heat, air conditioning, gas, garbage and trash collection and other utilities, if furnished by the Corporation.
(f) All reserves set up by the Board of Directors, including the general operating reserve and the reserve for the replacements.
(g) The estimated cost of repairs, maintenance and replacements of the project property to be made by the Corporation.
(h) The amount of principal, interest, mortgage insurance premiums, if any, and other required payments on the hereinafter mentioned insured mortgage.
(i) Any other expenses of the Corporation approved by the Board of Directors, including operating deficiencies, if any, for prior periods.

---

[2] The termination date to be inserted should be three years from the date of the Occupancy Agreement.

The Board of Directors shall determine the amount of the Carrying Charges annually, but may do so at more frequent intervals, should circumstances so require. No member shall be charged with more than his proportionate share thereof as determined by the Board of Directors. That amount of the Carrying Charges required for payment on the principal of the mortgage of the Corporation or any other capital expenditures shall be credited upon the books of the Corporation to the "Paid-In Surplus" account as a capital contribution by the members.

[3] Notwithstanding the above provisions it is understood and agreed by the Member and the Corporation that where the annual family income of the Member is such that he is entitled to the benefit of the interest reduction payment made by the Secretary of Housing and Urban Development (hereinafter referred to as secretary) to the mortgage, the monthly Carrying Charges for the member shall be reduced to the extent required by the Secretary as set forth in the Regulatory Agreement.

Until further notice from the Corporation the Monthly Carrying Charges for the abovementioned dwelling unit shall be $_____ .

It is understood and agreed that if the annual family income of the Member is hereafter increased, his monthly Carrying Charges will be increased to the extent required by the Secretary as set forth in the Regulatory Agreement.

[4] The Member agrees, however, that if during the term of this agreement the total income of his family exceeds the limitations for occupancy which may be established from time to time by the Secretary of Housing and Urban Development (hereinafter referred to as Secretary) he will pay to the Corporation, at the option of the Corporation and upon 90 days' written notice, additional Monthly Carrying Charges in an amount commensurate with the amount of his family income in excess of the income limitations, pursutant to a plan previously developed by the Corporation and approved by the Secretary. In no event shall the total Monthly Carrying Charge, including such additional charges for excess income, exceed that which would have been applicable had the mortgage of the Corporation borne interest at the rate of 6 percent per annum and a mortgage insurance premium of 1/2 of 1 percent been required.

---

[3] Required only in Section 236 cases.
[4] Required only in Sec. 221 below market interest rate cases.

[5] The Member agrees that his family income, family composition and other eligibility requirements are substantial and material condition with respect to the amount of monthly carrying charges he will be obligated to pay and with respect to his continuing right of occupancy. The Member agrees to make a recertification of his income to the Corporation at least every two years from the date of this Agreement so long as he is receiving the benefit of interest reduction payments made by the Secretary to the mortgagee. The Member further agrees that the monthly carrying charges are subject to adjustment by the Corporation to reflect income changes which are disclosed on any of the Member's recertifications, as required by the Regulatory Agreement. Immediately upon making such adjustment, the Corporation agrees to give 30 days written notice to the Members stating the new amount the Member will be required to pay, which, until further notice shall then be the Member's monthly carrying charge.

The Member agrees to pay to the Corporation any Carrying Charge which should have been paid but for (a) Member's misrepresentation in his initial income certification or recertification, or any other information furnished to the Corporation: or (b) Member's failure to supply income recertifications when required or to supply information requested by the Corporation.

ARTICLE 2. WHEN PAYMENT OF CARRYING CHARGES TO COMMENCE.

After thirty days' notice by the Corporation to the effect that the dwelling unit is or will be available for occupancy, or upon acceptance of occupancy, whichever is earlier, the Member shall make a payment for Carrying Charges covering the unexpired balance of the month. Thereafter, the Member shall pay Carrying Charges in advance on the first day of each month.

ARTICLE 3. PATRONAGE REFUNDS.[6]

The Corporation agrees on its part that it will refund or credit to the Member within ninety (90) days after the end of each fiscal year,

---

[5] Required only in Section 236 cases.

[6] Omit this paragraph in Section 236.

his proportionate share of such sums as have been collected in antici- pation of expenses which are in excess of the amount need for expenses of all kinds, including reserves, in the discretion of the Board of Directors.

ARTICLE 4. MEMBER'S OPTION FOR AUTOMATIC RENEWAL.

It is convenanted and agreed that the term herein granted shall be extended and renewed from time to time by and against the parties hereto for further periods of three years each from the expiration of the term herein granted, upon the same covenants and agreements as herein contained unless; (1) notice of the Member's election not to renew shall have been given to the Corporation in writing at least four months prior to the expiration of the then current term, and (2) the Member shall have on or before the expiration of said term (a) endorsed all his (stock) (membership certificate) for transfer in blank and de- posited same with the Corporation, and (b) met all his obligations and paid all amounts due under this Agreement up to the time of said expiration, and (c) vacated the premises, leaving same in good state of repair. Upon compliance with provisions (1) and (2) of this Article, the Member shall have no further liability under this agreement and shall be entitled to no payment from the Corporation.

ARTICLE 5. PREMISES TO BE USED FOR RESIDENTIAL PURPOSES ONLY.

The Member shall occupy the dwelling unit covered by this agree- ment as a private dwelling unit for himself and/or his immediate family and for no other purpose, and may enjoy the use in common with other members of the corporation of all community property and facilities of the project so long as he continues to own a [membership certificate] [share of common stock] of the Corporation, occupies his dwelling unit, and abides by the terms of this agreement. Any sublessee of the Member, if approved pursuant to Article 7 hereof, may enjoy the rights to which the Member is entitled under this Article 5.

The Member shall not permit or suffer anything to be done or kept upon said premises which will increase the rate of insurance on the building, or on the contents thereof, or which will obstruct or interfere with the rights of other occupants, or annoy them by unreasonable noises or otherwise, nor will he commit or permit any nuisance on the premises or commit or suffer any immoral or illegal act to be committed thereon. The Member shall comply with all of the requirements of the Board of Health and of all other governmental authorities with respect to the said premises. If by reason of the occupancy or use of said premises by the Member the rate of insurance on the building shall be increased, the Member shall become personally liable for the additional insurance premiums.

ARTICLE 6. MEMBER'S RIGHT TO PEACEABLE POSSESSION.

In return for the Member's continued fulfillment of the terms and conditions of this agreement, the Corporation covenants that the Member may at all times while this agreement remains in effect, have and enjoy for his sole use and benefit the dwelling unit hereinabove described, after obtaining occupancy, and may enjoy in common with all other members of the Corporation the use of all community property and facilities of the project.

ARTICLE 7. NO SUBLETTING WITHOUT CONSENT OF CORPORATION.

The Member hereby agrees not to assign this agreement nor to sublet his dwelling unit without the written consent of the Corporation on a form approved by the Department of Housing and Urban Development (hereinafter referred to as HUD). The liability of the Member under this Occupancy Agreement shall continue notwithstanding the fact that he may have sublet the dwelling unit with the approval of the Corporation and the Member shall be responsible to the Corporation for the conduct of his sublessee. Any unauthorized subleasing shall, at the option of the Corporation, result in the termination and forfeiture of the member's rights under this Occupancy Agreement. Non-paying guest of the Member may occupy Member's unit under such conditions as may be prescribed by the Board of Directors in the rules and regulations.

ARTICLE 8. TRANSFERS.

Neither this agreement nor the Member's right of occupancy shall be transferrable or assignable except in the same manner as may now or hereafter be provided for the transfer of memberships in the By-Laws of the Corporation.

The Member hereby certifies that neither he nor anyone authorized to act for him will refuse to sell his membership, after the making of a bona fide offer, or refuse to negotiate for the sale of, or otherwise make unavailable or deny the membership to any person because of race, color, religion, or national origin. Any restrictive covenant or cooperative property relating to race, color, religion, or national origin is recognized as being illegal and void and is hereby specifically disclaimed. Civil action for preventive relief may be brought by the Attorney General in any appropriate U.S. District Court against any person responsible for a violation of this certification.

ARTICLE 9. MANAGEMENT, TAXES AND INSURANCE.

The Corporation shall provide necessary management, operation and administration of the project; pay or provide for the payment of all taxes or assessments levied against the project and pay or provide for the payment of fire insurance and extended coverage, and other insurance as required by any mortgage on property in the project, and such other insurance as the Corporation may deem advisable on the property in the project. The Corporation will not, however, provide insurance on the Member's interest in the dwelling unit or on his personal property.

ARTICLE 10. UTILITIES.

The Corporation shall provide water, electricity, gas, heat and air conditioning in amounts which it deems reasonable. (Strike out any of the foregoing items in this Article which are not applicable.) The Member shall pay directly to the supplier for all other utilities.

ARTICLE 11. REPAIRS.

(a) *By Member.* The Member agrees to repair and maintain his dwelling unit at his own expense as follows:

(1) Any repairs or maintenance necessitated by his own negligence or misuse;

(2) Any redecoration of his own dwelling unit; and

(3) Any repairs, maintenance or replacements required on the following items:

(Insert the items desired, subject to HUD approval.)

(b) *By Corporation.* The Corporation shall provide and pay for all necessary repairs, maintenance and replacements, except as specified in clause (a) of this Article. The officers and employees of the Corporation shall have the right to enter the dwelling unit of the Member in order to effect necessary repairs, maintenance, and replacements, and to authorize entrance for such purposes by employees of any contractor, utility company, municipal agency, or others, at any reasonable hour of the day and in the event of emergency at any time.

(c) *Right of Corporation to Make Repairs at Member's Expense.* In case the Member shall fail to effect the repairs, maintenance or replacements specified in clause (a) of this Article in a manner satisfactory to the Corporation and pay for same, the latter may do so and add the cost thereof to the Member's next month's Carrying Charge payment.

ARTICLE 12. ALTERATIONS AND ADDITIONS.

The Member shall not, without the written consent of the Corporation, make any structural alterations to the premises or in the water, gas or steampipes, electrical conduits, plumbing or other fixtures connected therewith, or remove any additions, improvements, or fixtures from the premises.

If the Member for any reason shall cease to be an occupant of the premises, he shall surrender to the Corporation possession thereof, including any alterations, additions, fixtures and improvements.

The Member shall not, without the prior written consent of the Corporation, install or use in his dwelling unit any air conditioning equipment, washing machine, clothes dryer, electric heater, or power tools. (Strike out any of the foregoing items which are not applicable.) The Member agrees that the Corporation may require the prompt removal of any such equipment at any time, and that his failure to remove such equipment upon request shall constitute a default within the meaning of Article 13 of this agreement.

ARTICLE 13. DEFINITION OF DEFAULT BY MEMBER AND EFFECT THEREOF.

It is mutually agreed as follows: At any time after the happening of any of the events specified in clauses (a) to (i)[7] of this Article the Corporation may at its option give to the Member a notice that this agreement will expire at a date not less than ten (10) days thereafter. If the Corporation so proceeds all of the Member's rights under this agreement will expire on the date so fixed in such notice, unless in the meantime the default has been cured in a manner deemed satisfactory by the Corporation, it being the intention of the parties hereto to create hereby conditional limitations, and it shall thereupon be lawful for the Corporation to re-enter the dwelling unit and to remove all persons and personal property therefrom, either by summary dispossess proceedings or by suitable action or proceeding, at law or in equity or by any other proceedings which may apply to the eviction of tenants or by force or otherwise, and to repossess the dwelling unit in its former state as if this agreement had not been made:

(a) In case at any time during the term of this agreement the Member shall cease to be the owner and legal holder of a membership [or share of the stock] of the Corporation.

(b) In case the Member attempts to transfer or assign this agreement in a manner inconsistent with the provisions of the By-Laws.

(c) In case at any time during the continuance of this agreement the Member shall be declared a bankrupt under the laws of the United States.

(d) In case at any time during the continuance of this agreement a receiver of the Member's property shall be appointed under any of the laws of the United States or of any State.

(e) In case at any time during the continuance of this agreement the Member shall make a general assignment for the benefit of creditors.

---

[7] Change "(i)" to "(k)" in Section 236 cases and in Section 221 below market interest rate cases.

(f) In case at any time during the continuance of this agreement any of the stock or membership of the Corporation owned by the Member shall be duly levied upon and sold under the process of any Court.

(g) In case the Member fails to effect and/or pay for repairs and maintenance as provided for in Article 11 hereof.

(h) In case the Member shall fail to pay any sum due pursuant to the provisions of Article 1 or Article 10 hereof.

(i) In case the Member shall default in the performance of any of his obligations under this agreement.

[8] (j) In case at any time during the term of this agreement the limitations for occupancy which may be established from time to time by HUD are exceeded.

[8] (k) In case at any time during the term of this agreement, the Member fails to comply promptly with all requests by the Corporation or HUD for information and certifications concerning the income of the Member and his family, the composition of the Member's family and other eligibility requirements for occupancy in the project.

The Member hereby expressly waives any and all right of redemption in case he shall be dispossessed by judgment or warrant of any Court or judge; the words "enter", "re-enter", and "re-entry", as used in this agreement are not restricted to their technical legal meaning, and in the event of a breach or threatened breach by the Member of any of the covenants or provisions hereof, the Corporation shall have the right of injunction and the right to invoke any remedy allowed at law or in equity, as if re-entry, summary proceedings, and other remedies were not herein provided for.

The Member expressly agrees that there exists under this Occupancy Agreement a landlord-tenant relationship and that in the event of a breach or threatened breach by the member of any of the covenants or provisions of this Agreement, there shall be available to the Corporation such legal remedy or remedies as are available to a landlord for the breach or threatened breach under the law[9] by a tenant of any provision of a lease or rental agreement.

The failure on the part of the Corporation to avail itself of any of the remedies given under this agreement shall not waive nor destroy the right of the Corporation to avail itself of such remedies for similar or other breaches on the part of the Member.

---

[8] Required only in Section 236 cases and in Section 221 below market interest rate cases.

[9] In some States it may be desirable to include reference to a particular State statute on this subject.

ARTICLE 14. MEMBER TO COMPLY WITH ALL CORPORATE REGULATIONS.

The Member covenants that he will preserve and promote the co-operative ownership principles on which the Corporation has been founded, abide by the Charter, By-Laws, rules and regulations of the Corporation and any amendments thereto, and by his acts of cooperation with its other members bring about for himself and his co-members a high standard in home and community conditions. The Corporation agrees to make its rule and regulations known to the Member by delivery of same to him or by promulgating them in such other manner as to constitute adequate notice.

ARTICLE 15. EFFECT OF FIRE LOSS ON INTERESTS OF MEMBER.

In the event of loss or damage by fire or other casualty to the above-mentioned dwelling unit without the fault or negligence of the Member, the Corporation shall determine whether to restore the damaged premises and shall further determine, in the event such premises shall not be restored, the amount which shall be paid to the Member to redeem the (membership) (common stock) of the Member and to reimburse him for such loss as he may have sustained.

If, under such circumstances, the Corporation determines to restore the premises, Carrying Charges shall abate wholly or partially as determined by the Corporation until the premises have been restored. If on the other hand the Corporation determines not to restore the premises, the Carrying Charges shall cease from date of such loss or damage.

ARTICLE 16. INSPECTION OF DWELLING UNIT.

The Member agrees that the representatives of any mortgagee holding a mortgage on the property of the Corporation, the offices and employees of the Corporation, and with the approval of the Corporation the employees of any contractor, utility company, municipal agency or others, shall have the right to enter the dwelling unit of the Member and make inspections thereof at any reasonable hour of the day and at any time in the event of emergency.

ARTICLE 17. SUBORDINATION CLAUSE.

The project, of which the above-mentioned dwelling unit is a part, was or is to be constructed or purchased by the Corporation with the assistance of a mortgage loan advanced to the Corporation by a private lending institution with the understanding between the Corporation and the lender that the latter woulda apply for mortgage insurance under the provision of the National Housing Act. Therefore, it is specifically understood and agreed by the parties hereto that this agreement and all rights, privileges and benefits hereunder are and shall be at all times subject to and subordinate to the lien of a first mortgage and the accompanying documents executed by the Corporation under date of _____, (or to be executed by the Corporation) payable to _____ in the principal sum of $_____ with interest at _____ per centum, and insured or to be insured under the provisions of the National Housing Act, and to any and all modifications, extenstions, and renewals thereof and to any mortgage or deed of trust made in replacement thereof and to any mortgage or deed of trust which may at any time hereafter be placed on the property of the Corporation or any part thereof. The Member hereby agrees to execute, at the Corporation's request and expense, any instrument which the Croporation or any lender may deem necessary or desirable to effect the subordination of this agreement to any such mortgage, or deed of trust, and the Membber hereby appoints the Corporation and each and every officer thereof, and any future officer, his irrevocable attorney-in-fact during the term hereof to execute any such instrument on behalf of the Member. The Member does hereby expressly waive any and all notices of default and notices of foreclosure of said mortgage which may be required by law.

In the event a waiver of such notices is not legally valid, the Member does hereby constitute the Corporation his agent to receive and accept such notices on the Member's behalf.

ARTICLE 18. LATE CHARGES AND OTHER COSTS IN CASE OF DEFAULT.

The Member covenants and agrees that, in addition to the other sums that have become or will become due, pursuant to the terms of this Agreement, the Member shall pay to the Corporation a late charge in an amount to be determined from time to time by the

Board of Directors for each payment of Carrying Charges, or part thereof, more than 10 days in arrears.

If a Member defaults in making a payment of Carrying Charges or in the performance or observance of any provision of this Agreement, and the Corporation has obtained the services of any attorney with respect to the defaults involved, the Member covenants and agrees to pay to the Corporation any costs or fees involved, including reasonable attorney's fees, notwithstanding the fact that a suit has not yet been instituted. In case a suit is instituted, the Member shall also pay the costs of the suit, in addition to other aforesaid costs and fees.

ARTICLE 19. NOTICES.

Whenever the provisions of law or the By-Laws of the Corporation or this agreement require notice to be given to either party hereto, any notice by the Corporation to the Member shall be deemed to have been duly given, and any demand by the Corporation upon the Member shall be deemed to have been duly made if the same is delivered to the Member at his unit or to the Member's last known address; and any notice or demand by the Member to the Corporation shall be deemed to have been duly given if delivered to an officer of the Corporation. Such notice may also be given by depositing in the United States mails addressed to the Member as shown in the books of the Corporation, or to the President of the Cooperative, as the case may be, and the time of mailing shall be deemed to be the time of giving of such notice.

ARTICLE 20. ORAL REPRESENTATION NOT BINDING.

No representations other than those contained in this agreement, the Charter and the By-Laws of the Corporation shall be binding upon the Corporation.

ARTICLE 21. RENT SUPPLEMENT (Insert only in cases involving Rent Supplements).

The Corporation has entered into a Rent Supplement Contract with the Secretary which provides that the Secretary will pay a portion of the the rent on behalf of qualified members. Pursuant to said Contract, the Secretary has approved the monthly Carrying Charge specified in Article 1 for the unit and has determined that the member is eligible for rent supplement payments in the amount of $ _____ per month. In addition, to the conditions recited above, the member agrees that the following special conditions shall be applicable so long as he receives the benefit of rent supplement payments:

(a) Of the monthly Carrying Charge, Member agrees to pay, as Member's share, the sum of $ _____ being the difference between the monthly Carrying Charge and the amount of monthly rent supplement payment to be made by the Secretary pursuant to the Rent Supplement Contract.

(b) Member agrees in the event the amount of monthly rent supplement payment is adjusted by the Secretary to reflect income change of the Member, to pay in lieu of the amount specified in the preceding paragraph, the difference between the monthly Carrying Charge and the adjusted amount of rent supplement payment. The Corporation agrees to give written notice to Member, by an addendum to be made a part of this Agreement, immediately upon such adjustment made by the Secretary, stating the new amount the Member will be required to pay as Member's share of the monthly Carrying Charge.

(c) Member agrees that the family income, family composition and other eligibility requirements shall be deemed substantial and material obligations of his occupancy with respect to the amount of rent supplement benefits for which Member is eligible and in determining Member's share of the monthly Carrying Charge.

(d) Member agrees to comply promptly with all requests by the Corporation or the Secretary for information and certification concerning the total current family income of the Member, composition of the Member's family and other requirements for occupancy.

(e) Member agrees to report immediately to the Corporation if his monthly income increases to or is more than $ (this amount is equal to four times the basic monthly Carrying Charge for the unit).

(f) Member, except in the case of Members who are 62 years of age or older, agrees that a recertification of income shall be made to the the Secretary each year from the date of the original certification by the Secretary.

(g) Member understands that the rent supplement payment and Member's share of the monthly Carrying Charge is subject to adjustment to reflect income changes and agrees to be bound by such adjustment.

(h) Corporation and Member understand that, where by reason of an increase in income, Member is no longer entitled to rent suplement benefits, Member may continue to occupy the unit by paying increased monthly Carrying Charges established by the Corporation with the approval of the Secretary.

(i) Member agrees to reiumburse the Secretary for any excess rent supplement payments made by the Secretary during any period when an appropriate adjustment or termination of payments was not made:

(1) because of Member's failure to report an increase in income to the Corporation, as required by paragraph (e) above;

(2) because of Member's misrepresentation of statements made in Member's application for rent supplement payments, recertification of income or any other information furnished to Corporation or Secretary; or

(3) because of Member's failure to supply information requested by the Corporation or the Secretary.

IN WITNESS WHEREOF, the parties hereto have caused this agreement to be signed and sealed the day and year first above writer.

(Corporation)

By _____ (Seal)

_____

_____

Member and Shareholder

To Be Duly Acknowledged

Chapter VI
THE CONSUMER AND THE LAW

The last decade has seen the steady rise in consumerism. For years the public has suffered shoddy products, inept repairs and their complaints being ignored. Now, led by consumer groups and activists, they are compelling manufacturers and sellers to listen to their demands, but even more important, they are convincing legislators to give them legal remedies which they may use when their demands go unanswered.

CONSUMER PROTECTION

The doctrine of caveat emptor is gradually being laid to rest. In simpler times it was easy for the buyer to examine the goods and obtain information from the seller concerning his intended purchase.

Today it is not so simple. The consumer rarely buys directly from the manufacturer. What he buys is usually packaged and the contents are not seen until he reaches home. If the product is defective, he usually gets no satisfaction from, and indeed in many cases, cannot even contact, the manufacturer.

In the past the consumer has been aided by private organizations such as the Better Business Bureau, but that has not been enought. Now, spurred on by various consumer groups and activists, lawmakers on both the federal and state level have passed laws designed to help the consumer. Some of these laws, such as the Consumer Credit Protection Act deal with obtaining credit and are discussed elsewhere in this chapter.

Some of the federal agencies involved in the protection of the consumer are the Food and Drug Administration, the Securities and Exchange Commission, the Public Health Service, and the Department of Justice, to mention a few.

The Federal Trade Commission, for instance, participates quite frequently in the field of consumer protection, holding hearings concerning unfair practices and enforcing laws relating to false advertising and unfair pricing practices.

However the federal government rarely attempts to enforce individual complaints. They are more concerned with the welfare and rights of the general public. If enough complaints are received, they may take action, but consumer rights are usually enforced by local and state agencies.

Nearly every state has some sort of consumer laws dealing with deceptive trade practices. Some of the deceptive practices which are prohibited are false and misleading advertising, not expressing guarantee terms clearly, disparaging an advertised lower price item or refusing to show it to a customer, hoping to switch his interest to a higher priced item, and falsely labeling goods.

One of the most common unfair practices, legislated against by many states, is the mailing of unsolicited merchandise. Usually the receiver forgets or neglects to return it and then the company sending it demands payment for the merchandise. States' legislation, similar to that in Massachusetts, now permits the recipient of such merchandise to treat it as an unconditional gift and dispose of it as he sees fit.

Another abuse legislated against has been the high pressure sales tactics used by door to door salesmen. Many a family has found itself legally bound to pay for an unwanted, or too expensive, item because of pressure exerted by a persuasive, friendly door to door salesman. Formerly nothing could be done, except to plead the usual defenses to a contract (infancy, fraud, etc.). Many persons could not afford a law suit over the matter.

After investigation of this practice by the Federal Trade Commission, now by law, customers in this type of sale must be given a three day decision period. They may cancel the order within the three days. All customers must be informed of this right and given blank cancellation forms, which the buyer can complete and return to the company should he decide to cancel.

How are consumer rights enforced? Procedures vary from state to state. Usually the state agency in charge of hearing consumer complaints (a consumer protection agency or the state's attorney general's office) is notified of the alleged wrongdoing. If there is a legitimate offense, an attempt is made to mediate the difference between the parties. At this point, most reputable firms try to correct the situation as soon as it is brought to their attention. If it is impossible to settle the dispute then the consumer pursues the legal remedies allowed by statute. These vary from state to state and from law to law. In some cases there is a criminal penalty or fine. Other statutes grant the consumer the right to bring a civil action for damages plus attorney's fees.

Before any action is taken the state and federal laws must be examined to determine the consumer's rights. The important thing to remember is that the consumer does have rights and should be aware of them.

CREDIT CARDS

Properly used, a credit card is a very convenient and useful financial device. There are some who feel they would be unable to function without one.

Before 1970, the loss of a credit card could be quite costly. The holder of one had unlimited liability for purchases made with it, until the issuing company had received written notice that the card had been lost or stolen. In many instances it was several days before the discovery of the loss or theft. By that time quite a bill could be accumulated. In addition, many unsolicited cards were being mailed to persons who really did not want them.

In 1970, Congress amended the Consumer Credit Protection Act to remedy these situations.

The law prohibited mailing unsolicited credit cards. It does not prohibit the renewal of existing cards by mail, but the issuer of the card must provide a method whereby the user can be properly identified (e.g. a signature, photograph or fingerprint) on the card.

Now the law provides that the holder is not liable for anything charged on his card after he has notified the person specified on his card of the loss or theft. With respect to charges made before the notice is given, his liability is limited to $50 for each card. The law also provides that the potential holder of the card must be given notice of this liability and furnished with stamped, self-addressed envelopes for the purpose of giving notice to the issuer.

The law has provided much needed relief to credit card holders, but it should be noted that the $50 limitation of liability applies to *each* card. In the case of one holding a great many cards in his wallet, the liability could be quite high if proper notification is not promptly given.

There is insurance coverage offered to cover liability on credit card loss. It is modestly priced and can serve to eliminate the last measure of anxiety.

ENFORCEMENT OF CREDITOR'S RIGHTS

A creditor who obtains a judgment may enforce it by executing against a debtor's property. Not all property may be executed against. Most states have statutes listing exempt property (such as necessary household furnishings or implements needed for employment). The nature of these exemptions vary from state to state. (See Chart 3 at the end of this Chapter.)

There are times when a creditor feels that a debtor is about to remove property from the state, or will conceal property from him. Sometimes the debtor is a non-resident, but has property within the state. In order to insure that the debtor will have assets in the state when he obtains a judgment, a creditor will seek to get a court order of attachment before the final judgment. The court will grant such an order provided proper notice is given to the debtor and there are grounds for attachment. The grounds for attachment vary from state to state and are listed in Chart 5 at the end of this Chapter.

Another remedy of creditors, and that which has undergone the most change in recent years, is that of garnishment. In a garnishment proceeding, a creditor brings an action against a third party who owes money to a judgment debtor, to compel the third party to pay the money owed, to the creditor, rather than the debtor.

Garnishments usually take place after the judgment has been obtained, although in a few states pre-judgment garnishments are permitted. The Supreme Court has ruled that unless proper notice is given to the debtor, they are unconstitutional because of lack of due process. (*Sniadach v. Family Finance*, 395 U.S. 337 (1969)). Today most states do not permit pre-judgment garnishments.

Most garnishments are made on the debtor's salary. These have been increasing in recent years. Congress became so concerned over the increase in salary garnishments and the personal bankruptcies accompanying them that they passed legislation which sought to remedy the situation.

The federal Consumer Credit Protection Act has provisions relating to garnishments and limiting the amount of a wage earner's salary which could be garnished. Previous to this state laws governed the amount of salary that could be garnished, and the law and the amount varied from state to state. The Consumer Credit Protection Act provides that "the maximum part of the aggregate disposable earnings of an individual for any work-week which is subjected to garnishment may not exceed (1) 25 per centum of his disposable earnings for that week, or (2) the amount by which his disposable earnings for that week exceed thirty times the Federal minimum hourly wage prescribed by section 206(a)(1) of title 29 in effect at the time the earnings are payable, whichever is less."

"Disposable earnings" are defined as those earnings which remain to the employee after deduction of any amounts required to be withheld by law (e.g. withholding taxes and social security payments.) Most state laws governing garnishment compute exemptions on the basis of gross income. The Consumer Credit Protection Act does not differentiate between exemptions granted to heads of households, as do many state laws. The same rule as to the amount that may be garnished applies to all wage earners.

The Consumer Credit Protection Act does not specifically set forth the procedure for enforcing garnishments. Procedures set forth in the states' laws are followed. As a rule a demand must be sent to the debtor for payment of what is owed. Upon failure to comply with this demand, service is made on the garnishee together with an affidavit setting forth facts and demanding an answer as to why the property sought should not be garnished. He is given an opportunity to answer and if he cannot furnish a valid reason against garnishment, an order will be made directing him to pay the amount owed to the creditor or to the court. With some variations this is the procedure followed in most of the states.

There have been some employers, who, annoyed by the inconvenience and paperwork involved in garnishment procedures, have discharged employees whose salaries have been garnished. They are now forbidden to do so by the Consumer Credit Protection Act which provides, "(a) No employer may discharge any employee by reason of the fact that his earnings have been subject to garnishment for any one indebtedness. (b) Whoever willfully violates subsection (a) of this section shall be fined not more than $1,000, or imprisoned not more than one year, or both."

The Consumer Credit Protection Act exempts support orders, orders under Chapter XIII of the Bankruptcy Act, and debts for state or federal taxes from its purview. The law also contains no reference to wage assignments. It is possible that now that there are restrictions on the amount that may be garnished, that creditors will try to obtain wage assignments from debtors. Chart 4 relating to state wage assignment laws, may be found at the end of this Chapter.

States also have passed laws governing garnishment. Before the passage of the federal act, they varied greatly from state to state. The Consumer Credit Protection Act provides that state laws which are substantially the same as, or more stringent than the federal act, will not be superseded by it.

It is to be hoped that this legislative effort to aid the debtor will be successful. As one author states, "*** the exact interpretation of the new federal legislation and newly enacted state statutes is still in doubt. As time passes, however, and the courts are given the opportunity to make such interpretations, an orderly process with some semblance of standardization will evolve throughout the United States. This writer anticipates a tremendous decline in the number of personal wage garnishments as creditors realize that the amount of wages which can be taken, when considered in the light of filing fees, attorney fees and the like, leaves little to apply on the outstanding obligation. Creditors will have to seek other means to satisfy their claims."

FAIR CREDIT REPORTING ACT

Due to the prevalence of the use of credit, credit reporting agencies have begun to profoundly influence the course of an individual's life. Based on information received from them, one is able to receive credit, finance a mortgage or obtain a job. Up to a relatively short time ago, many were at the mercy of these agencies. Computer and human errors have sometimes resulted in denials of credit or refusals of employment. Victims of these mistakes (if they ever found out about them) had only the remedy of a costly law suit.

Reform in this area came with the passage of subchapter 3 of the Consumer Credit Protection Act, which has come to be known as the Fair Credit Reporting Act.

The act regulates the purposes for which a consumer reporting agency may provide a consumer report and limits what may be contained in it.

For the purposes of this act, the term consumer report means "any communication of any type (written or oral) given to a consumer reporting agency. These reports pertain to credit worthiness, credit standing, credit capacity, character, general reputation, personal characteristics or mode of living. This information is to be used for determining a person's eligibility for credit or insurance or employment. A consumer reporting agency is "any person which for monetary fees, dues, or on a cooperative, non-profit basis, regularly engages in whole or in part in the practice of assembling or evaluating consumer credit information or other information on consumers for the purpose of furnishing consumer reports to third parties, and which uses any means or facility of interstate commerce for the purpose of preparing or furnishing consumer reports."

A consumer report may be furnished to any court having jurisdiction to order a report, or to any person who the agency has reason to believe intends to use the information for a proper purpose.

Usually information which is over seven years old may not be reported, except that bankruptcies may be reported for fourteen years. However if the information is for the purpose of credit transactions or life insurance policies, involving more than $50,000, there is no limitation on the age of the material to be reported, nor is there any limitation on the age of materials where the purpose of inquiry is for employment which would be for an annual salary of $20,000 or more.

If a person is denied credit or employment on the basis of a consumer report, he must be informed of this, and given the name of the credit reporting agency. He can then demand to see the credit agency report. If he feels that the report contains erroneous material, he may report this to the agency. The agency is given a reasonable amount of time in which to recheck the material. If it finds that the material is false, or cannot be verified, it must delete it from its report. If the information is disputed, the wronged consumer has the privilege of writing a statement in one hundred words or less, explaining his side of the story. This statement must be included in the reports on the consumer. Not only must future reports be corrected or amended by the consumer's statement, but if the consumer requests it, the corrected report (with his statement, if any) must be sent to any one who has had access to the information within the previous six months. If the material had been furnished in connection with employment inquiries, the time limitation is two years. The agency must also supply the consumer with the names of all that have receive erroneous reports about him, so that he may correct any erroneous impressions they might have, concerning him.

Anyone violating the provisions of the Act relating to false reporting is liable for damages suffered as a result of improper reporting or denial of the consumer's right of correction under the act. The consumer is entitled to reasonable attorneys fees incurred in enforcing his rights. There are also criminal penalties for persons who receive information from the consumer reporting agency under false pretenses. Criminal penalties are also imposed upon any officer or employee of an agency who supplies information to anyone not entitled to it.

Many states have passed fair credit reporting acts. State laws will take precedence over the federal act if they are substantially the same as or more restrictive than the federal law. The Federal Trade Commission is charged with the enforcement of the federal Fair Trade Reporting Act; the attorney general's office or the state consumer protection agency usually has jurisdiction over the state laws.

INTEREST

The rate of interest varies from state to state. Indeed it can vary within the state depending on its purpose. Most states have a legal interest rate. The rate is generally 6% but it fluctuates from state to state and generally ranges from 5½ to 8½%. Most states permit a different rate for contracts. These rates range from 6% to an unlimited amount. Charging an excessive amount of interest (usury) usually results in the loss of the interest or, in some states, a voiding of the contract. Chart 1 sets out the legal and contract rate of interest.

TRUTH IN LENDING

At some time in our lives most of us have been in a situation involving the use of credit. Used judicially, it is an aid to obtaining a more comfortable life style. Used incorrectly it can easily ruin one's life. Many persons, to their regret, have rushed into credit situations, not knowing exactly what they were signing, or how much money they would eventually have to pay their lenders.

Recognizing this, Congress passed the Consumer Credit Protection Act, the first part of which deals with Consumer Cost Disclosure and has come to be known as the "Truth in Lending Act". Congress set forth the purpose of the act as follows:

> "The Congress finds that economic stabilization will be enhanced and the competition among the various financial institutions and other firms engaged in the extension of consumer credit would be strengthened by the informed use of credit. The informed use of credit results from an awareness of the cost thereof by consumers. It is the purpose of this subchapter to assure a meaningful disclosure of credit terms so that the consumer will be able to compare more readily the various credit terms available to him and avoid the uninformed use of credit."

The "Truth in Lending" law specifies certain disclosures which must be made to the consumer by the one extending credit or the one arranging for the credit transaction. These disclosures must be made either in the contract or the document of indebtedness signed by the purchaser, or in a separate instrument.

One thing of which the consumer must be informed are what savings he earns if the purchase is paid for in cash. The exact charge for credit, expressed not only in monthly, but annual charges must be given. A buyer might be willing to finance a purchase at 1½% interest per month, but might reconsider if he realizes that the annual finance charge is 18% per year. Hidden charges, besides interest charges, such as those for insurance costs must now be revealed to the consumer.

The finance charge must be printed in readable, bold-faced type and should appear on all monthly statements. The number, the amount of each payment, the periods and due dates under the contract must be revealed to the consumer at the beginning of the transaction. Consumers must also be informed of any late or delinquent charges.

Also, the act provides that if a contract contains a final "balloon payment", this must be set forth in the contract in prominent type. A "balloon payment" transaction is one where all the payments, except the final one, are for a sum, which the consumer is able to pay. However the final payment is so much larger than the others, that the consumer finds himself unable to pay it and is often forced to obtain refinancing.

Under this act, a consumer may bring an action to recover twice the finance charge where proper disclosures have not been made, or false information given. The lendor is given 15 days to correct the error after he learns of it. If he does not, and a successful suit is brought, the consumer is granted reasonable costs and attorney fees. In any event, recovery is limited to $1,000.

The consumer is also given the right to rescind certain transactions under the act. Not only does he have this right, but the law requires that the creditor must give the consumer notice of this right, prescribing the manner in which the notice must be given.

Rescindable transactions involve the extension or arrangement of consumer credit where the loan or financing will be secured by a lien or mortgage on the principal residence of the consumer. In such situations, the consumer is given the right to think about the transaction, and if he wishes, rescind it within three business days after the consummation of the transaction, or after the consumer is informed of his right to rescind.

It should be noted though that the law specifically excepts the usual purchase money first mortgage situation from its purview.

Besides the federal law, almost two-thirds of the states have laws regulating credit and protecting the consumer in this area. Most of them deal with retail installment credit sales, although some such as Massachusetts have adopted Truth in Lending laws, somewhat similar to the federal legislation.

Chart 1

STATE USURY RATES*

STATE	Legal Rate %	Contract Rate %
Alabama	6	8
Alaska	6	9
Arizona	6	not over 10
Arkansas	6	10
California	7	10
Colorado	8	no maximum if in writing, 16% on loans over $2,000.
Connecticut	6	12
Delaware	6	9
District of Columbia	6	8
Florida	6	10
Georgia	7	8
Hawaii	6	1% per month
Idaho	8	10
Illinois	5	8 (9½% if secured by residential mtg.)
Indiana	8	8
Iowa	5	9
Kansas	6	10
Kentucky	6	8½
Louisiana	7	8
Maine	6	no max. if in writing to corp.
Maryland	6	8 (10% if secured by residential mtg.)
Massachusetts	6	no limit if in writing
Michigan	5	7
Minnesota	6	8

* This chart does not reflect all of the possible variables in the contract rate of interest. Many states have enacted legislation which provides a range of allowable interest charges by contract depending upon whether or not the contract is in writing and the amount of the loan. The chart does however reflect the most prevalent charges in consumer type transactions.

STATE	Legal Rate %	Contract Rate %
Mississippi	6	10
Missouri	6	10
Montana	6	10
Nebraska	6	10
Nevada	7	12 (If lowest prime rate at three largest banking institutions is 9% or more, may contract for interest not exceeding such lowest prime rate plus 3.5%)
New Hampshire	6	no limit if in writing
New Jersey	7½	7½
New Mexico	6	10 (secured), 12 (unsecured)
New York	7½	7½
North Carolina	6	8%, $50,000 or less (first realty mortgage); 10% $50,000 -$100,000 business loan; 12%, $100,000 to $300,000; 9%, less than $100,000; any rate, more than $300,000; single family dwelling mortgage, no limit
North Dakota	6	9½
Ohio	6	8
Oklahoma	6	10
Oregon	6	10
Pennsylvania	6	6
Rhode Island	6	21
South Carolina	6	8% plus additional interest on loans over $50,000.
South Dakota	6	10
Tennessee	6	10
Texas	6	10
Utah	6	10
Vermont	8½	8½
Virginia	6	8
Washington	6	12

STATE	Legal Rate %	Contract Rate %
West Virginia	6	8
Wisconsin	5	12
Wyoming	7	10

Chart 2

STATUTES OF LIMITATIONS
(In Years)

References in this chart are to general practice sections. A different
statute of limitation may apply to transactions governed by the Uniform Commercial Code.

STATE	Simple Contract	Sealed Instruments	Open Accounts	Promissory Notes
Alabama	6	10	3	6
Alaska	6	10	6	6
Arizona	6 written* 3 oral	6*	3	6
Arkansas	5 written 3 oral	5	3	5
California	4 written 2 oral	4	4	4
Colorado	6	6	6	6
Connecticut	6 written 3 oral	6	6	6
Delaware	3		3	6
District of Columbia	3	12	3	3
Florida	5 written 4 oral		4	5
Georgia	6 written 4 oral	20	4	6
Hawaii	6	6	6	6
Idaho	5 written 4 oral	5	4	5
Illinois	10 written 5 oral	10	5	10
Indiana	10 money 15 realty 20 all other types 6 oral	20	6	10
Iowa	10 written 5 oral	10	5	10

* Made within the state.

STATE	Simple Contract	Sealed Instruments	Open Accounts	Promissory Notes
Kansas	5 written 3 oral	5	3	5
Kentucky	15 written 5 oral	15	5	15
Louisiana	usually 10		3	5
Maine	6	20	6	6
Maryland	3	12	3	3
Massachusetts	6	20	6	6
Michigan	6	6	6	6
Minnesota	6	6	6	6
Mississippi	6 written 3 oral	6	3	6
Missouri	10 written for payment of money. 5 all others.	10	5	10
Montana	8 written 5 oral	8	5	8
Nebraska	5 written 4 oral	5	4	5
Nevada	6 written 4 oral	6	4	6
New Hampshire	6	20	6	6
New Jersey	6	16	6	6
New Mexico	6 written 4 oral	6	4	6
New York	6	6	6	6
North Carolina	3	10	3	3
North Dakota	6	6	6	6
Ohio	15 written 6 oral	15	6	15
Oklahoma	5 written 3 oral	5	3	5
Oregon	6		6	6
Pennsylvania	6	20	6	6
Rhode Island	6	20	6	6
South Carolina	6	20	6	6

STATE	Simple Contracts	Sealed Instruments	Open Accounts	Promissory Notes
South Dakota	6	20	6	6
Tennessee	6	6	6	6
Texas	4 written 2 oral	4	2	4
Utah	6 written 4 oral	6	4	6
Vermont	6	8	6	6
Virginia	5 written 3 oral	10	3	5
Washington	6 written 3 oral	6	3	6
West Virginia	10 written 5 oral	10	5	10
Wisconsin	6	20*	6	6
Wyoming	10 written 8 oral	10	8	10

* Made within the state.

Chart 3
PRIMARY FEATURES OF
STATE EXEMPTION STATUTES

State	Exemption (or maximum amount subject to garnishment)
ALABAMA	Exemption, 75% of wages, salaries or other compensation of laborers or employees.
ALASKA	Exemption, 25% of the disposable income for the week, subject to execution, or the sums by which income exceeds the amount of $114 for the week, whichever amount is less. Under certain circumstances child support may be exempt.
ARIZONA	Exemption, 50% of earnings for 30 days before service of garnishment — if necessary for support.
ARKANSAS	*Claimed exemption* for laborers and mechanics, 60 days of earnings up to $200 for single person and $500 for head of household. *Automatic exemption* — first $25 of net wages.
CALIFORNIA	*Head of Household* Exemption, 100% of earnings for 30 days prior to service of garnishment — if necessary for support of a family in California. A claim for family necessaries or wages of an employee of the debtor are treated as indicated under "all others". *All Others* Exemption, 50% of earnings for 30 days prior to service of garnishment.
COLORADO	*Head of Household* — 70% of earnings exempt. *Single Person* 25% of earnings exempt.
CONNECTICUT	Exemption, 100% of earnings.
DELAWARE	Exemption, 100% of wages, salaries, commission or remuneration except for the self employed. However wages extent of 85% are subject to attachment for debts due the State of Delaware.
DISTRICT OF COLUMBIA	Exemption, 25% of the disposable income for the week or 30 times the Federal Minimum Wage, whichever is less.

State	Exemption (or maximum amount subject to garnishment)
FLORIDA	100% exemption — head of household.
GEORGIA	Exemption, the greater of 75% of disposable earnings or 30 times Federal minimum hourly wage.
HAWAII	Exemption, 95% of first $100 per month; 90% of next $100; 80% of excess.
IDAHO	Maximum garnishment — the lesser of 25% of disposable earnings or excess of 30 times Federal minimum hourly wage.
ILLINOIS	*Exemption:* The greater of: Head of household — $65 per week; single person — $50 per week; or 85% of gross earnings, or the greater of 75% of disposable earnings or 30 times the Federal minimum wage.
INDIANA	Exemption, 25% of the disposable earnings above 30 times the Federal minimum wage.
IOWA	Exemption, 25% of disposable earnings or 30 times the Federal minimum hourly wage up to a maximum of $250.00 per year.
KANSAS	Exemption, the greater of 75% of disposable earnings, or 30 times the Federal minimum hourly wage.
KENTUCKY	Exemption, the greater of 75% of disposable earnings or 30 times the Federal minimum hourly wage.
LOUISIANA	Exemption, 75% of disposable earnings, but not less than $70 a week of disposable earnings.
MAINE	$40 of wages due and payable, $10 in any case exempt.
MARYLAND	Exemption, the greater of $120 times number of week's wages or 75% of same. *Specific Counties:* Greater of 75% of wages due or 30 times Federal minimum hourly wage are exempt.
MASSACHUSETTS	Exemption, $125 of wages per week, $100 per week of pension.

State	Exemption (or maximum amount subject to garnishment)
MICHIGAN	*First Garnishment: Exemption, Head of Household* — 60% of wages, maximum, $50; minimum, $30 for week. Pay period in excess of week, maximum, $90; minimum, $60. *Exemption, Others* — 40% of wages, minimum, $20; maximum, $50. *Subsequent Garnishments* — *Exemption, Head of Household* — 60% of wages, maximum, $30; minimum, $12 for week. Pay period over 16 days, maximum, $60; minimum, $30. *Others* — 30% of wages, maximum, $20; minimum, $10.
MINNESOTA	*Maximum Garnishment* — Lesser of 25% of disposable earnings, or excess of 8 times the number of business days and paid holidays (not exceeding 5 in any week) times the Federal minimum hourly wage. 100% exemption if earnings needed for family support.
MISSISSIPPI	75% of earnings for residents are exempt.
MISSOURI	May not exceed 25% or 30 times the current maximum federal wage, whichever is less. If head of household and resident, exemption is 10%.
MONTANA	*Head of Household or those over 60 years* — 100% of exemption for 45-day period before garnishment, but if debt is for necessaries or gasoline, 50% exempt.
NEBRASKA	*Maximum garnishment:* lesser of 25% of disposable earnings for one week (15%, if head of household), or 30 times federal minimum wage.
NEVADA	*Maximum Garnishment* — Lesser of 25% of disposable earnings or excess over 30 times Federal minimum hourly wage.
NEW HAMPSHIRE	Exemption, 100% of wages earned after service of garnishment. 100% of wages earned before service unless

State	Exemption (or maximum amount subject to garnishment)
	judgment rendered by a New Hampshire Court, then 50 times Federal minimum hourly wage per week.
	100% — earnings of wife and children exempt.
NEW JERSEY	Exemption, 10% of earnings over $48 per week. Court may increase percentage of garnishment on employee's earnings in excess of $7500 per year.
NEW MEXICO	Exemption, greater of 75% of disposable earnings of each pay or 40 times the Federal minimum hourly wage per week.
NEW YORK	*Court of Record.* Exemption, 90% of income where employee earns at least $85 per week, 100% if employee earns less.
	Court Not of Record. Exemption, 10% of earnings subject to garnishment of employee earning $30 or more per week if such employee resides or works in city of 250,000 or more, 10% of earnings of employees not meeting such residence or working locality test but earning $25 a week.
NORTH CAROLINA	*Head of Household* — 100% of earnings for 60 days before service are exempt.
NORTH DAKOTA	*Maximum garnishment:* lesser of 25% of disposable earnings for one week or 40 times federal minimum wage.
OHIO	Exemption, greater of 82.5% of disposable earnings for 30-day period, or 175 times Federal minimum hourly wage.
OKLAHOMA	*Consumer Obligations* — Garnishment can take lesser of 25% of disposable weekly earnings or excess of 30 times Federal minimum hourly wage.
	Other Obligations — 100% exemption for 90-day period, resident head of household; 75% if wages not required for support of family.
OREGON	*Maximum Garnishment* — Lesser of 25% of disposable earnings for one week, or excess

State	Exemption (or maximum amount subject to garnishment)
	of 40 times Federal minimum hourly wage.
PENNSYLVANIA	100% exemption except for 4 weeks board and lodging, support payments, taxes or alimony.
RHODE ISLAND	$50 per week exemption.
SOUTH CAROLINA	*Head of Household* — 100% exemption except for obligations for necessaries for which 15% of wages up to $100 may be taken.
SOUTH DAKOTA	No specific statute relating to exemptions on wages, but a general statute relating to executions in general permits a resident head of a household, exemptions up to $1500, ($600.. if single and not the head of a household).
TENNESSEE	*Head of Household* — Exemption greater of 50% of net weekly income, or $20; maximum, $50 per week, and 40% or $17.50 per week to a maximum of $40. per week for a resident who is not head of a family.
TEXAS	100% exemption as per State Constitution.
UTAH	*Head of Household or Married Men* — Minimum exemption $50, maximum 50% of earnings for 30-day period.
	Consumer transactions — Exemption equal to greater of 75% of disposable earnings or 40 times Federal minimum hourly wage.
VERMONT	Exemption, $30 of weekly wages plus 50% of wages in excess of $60.
VIRGINIA	Maximum garnishment, lesser of 25% of disposable earnings or excess of 30 times Federal minimum hourly wage.
WASHINGTON	Exemption, greater of 75% of disposable earnings or 40 times state minimum wage.
WEST VIRGINIA	Exemption, 80% of earnings for persons earning over $20 per week.
WISCONSIN	Exemption, greater of 75% of disposable weekly earnings or 30 times Federal minimum hourly wage.

State	Exemption (or maximum amount subject to garnishment)
WYOMING	Exemption, head of household, 50% of earnings for 60-day period before service.

Proposed Uniform Consumer Credit Code:
    Maximum garnishment, lesser of 25% of disposable earnings for one week or excess of 40 times Federal minimum hourly wage.

Consumer Credit Protection Act:
    Maximum garnishment, 25% of weekly disposable earnings, or excess of 30 times Federal minimum hourly wage.

Chart 4

WAGE ASSIGNMENTS

STATE

ALABAMA	Not permitted.
ALASKA	No provision.

ARIZONA — Assignment valid, payment for a loan:
1. Must be in writing.
2. Consent of spouse living with assignor must be given.
3. Assignment cannot exceed 10% of assignor's wages, salary or other compensation.
4. Assignment period cannot exceed 48 months.

ARKANSAS — Assignment must be consented to by wife in writing.

Assignment must be approved by employer and filed with county recorder.

CALIFORNIA
1. Must be in writing and transaction identified.
2. Must be consented to by spouse (or if minor, by parent or guardian.
3. Must state that there are no other existing assignments.
4. It must be notarized and filed with employer.
5. Except for certain deductions and withholdings by employer, as permitted by the Labor Code, an assignment of unearned wages can not be made except for necessities and cannot exceed 50% of the wages (25% if wages are needed to support a family).

COLORADO — Assignment void as to small loans. All other void and unenforceable can be honored by employer if in writing, for a fixed period of not more than 30 days and a copy mailed to employer and employee.

CONNECTICUT — Not permitted.

DELAWARE — Not permitted, with exception as to certain real estate transactions.

DISTRICT OF COLUMBIA	Not permitted.
FLORIDA	Not permitted.
GEORGIA	No provision.
HAWAII	Valid if in writing. Assignment in employment contracts permitted. Must be in form approved by the Department of Labor.
IDAHO	Not permitted, under Uniform Consumer Credit Code.
ILLINOIS	Permitted with qualifications as to disclosure, type of obligation, and notice. Limited to 15% of gross earnings.
INDIANA	Permitted with qualifications as to notice, consent of spouse and period of earnings covered.
IOWA	Permitted up to 10% of debtor's wages and with qualification as to writing, notice, and consent of spouse.
KANSAS	Limited to 10% of wages or other earnings with qualification as to notice. Employer is given the option whether or not to honor the assignment. Under Kansas Uniform Consumer Code, wage assignments are revocable at any time at the option of the consumer.
KENTUCKY	Permitted with qualifications as to form of assignment, appointment of agent, if non-resident employer consent and period covered. Small loan companies limited to 10% of borrower's wages.
LOUISIANA	Invalid unless employer consents.
MAINE	Employer must have actual notice; assignment must be recorded. Other limitations with respect to loans under $2,000. In Consumer transactions revocable at any time by the consumer.
MARYLAND	Limited to wages earned 6 months after assignment, allowed with qualifications as to writing, notice and consent of spouse. Prohibited in certain consumer transactions.

MASSACHUSETTS

Permitted with qualifications as to disclosures, writing, consent of spouse, and recording. Loans over $3,000 assignments limited to 2 years and 25% of wages; under $3,000 limited to 1 year and $10.

MICHIGAN

Permitted with qualifications as to signing and spousal consent. Householder with family subject to exemption of 60% per week but not less than $15. per week plus an additional $2 per week for a dependent other than a spouse.

MINNESOTA

Assignments of unearned wages for more than 60 days are void except for assignments in excess of $1500 per month for less than 5 years. Then permitted with qualifications as to writing, notice and consent of employer.

MISSISSIPPI

Permitted if notice is given to employer before consummation of contract or delivery of goods, and employer accepts.

MISSOURI

Void as to future earnings; assignments of past earnings must be in writing and make certain disclosures.

MONTANA

Permitted with qualifications as to consent of spouse, notice to employer, recording and period of wages covered. Consumer transactions limited to 10% of each wage payment.

NEBRASKA

Permitted with qualifications as to consent by spouse.

NEVADA

Not permitted.

NEW HAMPSHIRE

Permitted if in writing and recorded.

NEW JERSEY

Not permitted.

NEW MEXICO

Permitted with qualifications as to signing, recording and delivery to employer. Limited to 25% of disposable earnings.

NEW YORK

Permitted on indebtedness of more than $1000 with qualifications as to type of instrument, disclosures, filing and limitations as to liability of guarantor and effectiveness. No portion of debtors earnings may be withheld unless they amount to $30. per week (in cities over 250,000) or $25. per week elsewhere.

NORTH CAROLINA	Permitted with qualification of employer acceptance.
NORTH DAKOTA	No statutory provisions.
OHIO	Not permitted.
OKLAHOMA	Uniform Consumer Code adopted — permits revocation by assignor at any time.
OREGON	Not permitted unless assignor may revoke.
PENNSYLVANIA	Permitted if in writing, accepted by the employer and consented to by spouse. Wages payable semi-monthly may not be assigned.
RHODE ISLAND	For not more than one year are permitted if in writing, delivered to employer, and making certain disclosures. Recording required.
SOUTH CAROLINA	Employer must give written consent.
SOUTH DAKOTA	Permitted with qualifications as to acceptance by employer. Assignment is limited to 10% of each wage payment. Loans of $1,000 or less can only be for a period of 24½ months; loans over $1,000 to $2500 for 36½ months, loans of more than $2500 for 60½ months.
TENNESSEE	Employer must consent to assignment.
TEXAS	Employer must be given written notice immediately after the debtor's execution of the assignment.
UTAH	Employee can authorize payroll deductions if the authorization is revokable. (It appears Utah has adopted at least in part, the Uniform Consumer Credit Code.)
VERMONT	Permitted with qualifications as to wife's signature, service on employer and recording.
VIRGINIA	Permitted if employer consents and proper disclosures are made; limitation as to amount.
WASHINGTON	Permitted with qualification as to amount of

	obligation, notice, recording and consent of spouse.
WEST VIRGINIA	Limited for period of one year, qualification as to writing and disclosures and amount.
WISCONSIN	Permitted with qualifications as to consent of spouse and formalities of execution; limited to 6 months. consumer transactions assignment revocable.
WYOMING	Employer must accept, assignment must be recorded, spouse must consent. Consumer transactions, assignment revocable.

Chart 5

GROUNDS FOR ATTACHMENTS — STATE STATUTES

(NOTE: Recent rulings of the federal and state courts have placed in doubt the constitutionality of attachment (without giving defendant proper notice and opportunity to be heard), so it is possible that the laws relating to attachment will be in a state of flux for some time.)

ALABAMA
1. Defendant is a non-resident.
2. Defendant has absconded.
3. Defendant has secreted himself.
4. Defendant is about to leave the state.
5. Defendant is about to remove his property from the state.
6. Defendant is about to fraudulently dispose of his property.
7. Defendant has fraudulently disposed of his property.
8. Defendant is fraudulently withholding funds or property.

ALASKA
1. In any action on a contract for the payment of money when such contract is not secured or if secured, the security is insufficient to satisfy the debt.
2. The defendant is a non-resident and the action is one on contract.
3. The action is for collection of any state tax or license fee.

Debt Not Due
ARIZONA
1. Contract of obligation is unsecured.
2. Defendant is about to remove himself from the state.
3. Defendant secreted property to defraud creditors.
4. Defendant disposed of or is about to remove property with intent to defraud creditors.

Debt Due
1. The contract of obligation, express or implied, is not fully secured.
2. Defendant is a non-resident.
3. Defendant is a foreign corporation.
4. An executor or administrator failed to file a

verified account.
5. The obligation is upon a judgment of any state or District of Columbia.

ARKANSAS

1. Defendant is a foreign corporation or non-resident.
2. Defendant has been absent from the state for four months.
3. Defendant departed with the intent to defraud creditors.
4. Defendant left his county of residence or secretes himself to avoid service of summons.
5. Defendant is about to or has removed his property.
6. Defendant has sold or conveyed his property with the intention of defrauding creditors.

CALIFORNIA

1. Total amount claimed exclusive of interest, attorney's fees, is over $500.
2. Action is against a corporation, partnership or individuals engaged in business for a liquidated sum of money based on a loan, negotiable instrument, lease, or services rendered if claim is unsecured.
3. Monetary action against a non-resident person, unqualified corporation or foreign partnership which has not filed a designation, or,
4. Defendant cannot be found with due diligence.
5. Defendant has concealed himself to avoid service.

COLORADO

1. Defendant is a non-resident.
2. Defendant is a foreign corporation.
3. Defendant is a domestic corporation having its chief office out of state.
4. Defendant conceals himself or has been absent for four months.
5. Defendant removed property with intent to defraud creditors.
6. Defendant fraudulently conveyed or concealed property to delay creditors.
7. Defendant departed from the state with intent to remove his property.
8. Defendant refused to pay the price of articles delivered or work done.
9. Defendant fraudulently contracted the debt or procured money or property fraudulently.

CONNECTICUT — There are no special grounds. Any action for the recovery of money except actions for slander, libel or invasion of privacy may be started by attachment.

DELAWARE — Generally any action in contract or tort may be initiated by an attachment.

DISTRICT OF COLUMBIA
1. Defendant is a foreign corporation or non-resident.
2. Defendant has been absent for six months.
3. Defendant is evading service of process.
4. Defendant removed or is about to remove property to defeat creditor's claims.
5. Defendant assigned or secreted property or is about to do so to defraud creditors.
6. Defendant fraudulently contracted the debt.

FLORIDA
When Debt is Due
1. Defendant will fraudulently part with property.
2. Defendant is removing his property from the state.
3. Defendant is about to remove his property from the state.
4. Defendant resides out of the state.
5. Defendant is moving or is about to move from the state.
6. Defendant is absconding or concealing himself.
7. Defendant is secreting or disposing of his property.

When Debt is Not Due
1. Defendant is removing his property from the state.
2. Defendant is fraudulently disposing of his property.
3. Defendant is secreting his property.

GEORGIA
1. Defendant is a non-resident.
2. Defendant is removing or about to remove himself from the county.
3. Defendant has absconded or concealed himself.
4. Defendant has resisted arrest.
5. Defendant is removing property from the state.

HAWAII — Any action on an express or implied contract including those actions brought by non-residents or foreign corporations may be instituted by attachments.

IDAHO

1. In any action on a contract express or implied not secured or if secured, the property has become valueless.
2. Defendant is a non-resident.

ILLINOIS

1. Defendant is a non-resident.
2. Defendant conceals himself to avoid service of summons.
3. Defendant departed from the state with the intent of having his property so removed.
4. Defendant is about to depart from the state with intention of having his property so removed.
5. Defendant is about to remove his property to the injury of creditors.
6. Defendant has within two years fraudulently conveyed or assigned his property so as to hinder or delay his creditors.
7. Defendant has within two years fraudulently concealed or disposed of property to hinder or delay creditors.
8. Defendant is about to fraudulently conceal, assign or otherwise dispose of property so as to hinder or delay creditors.
9. The debt was fraudulently contracted.

INDIANA

1. Defendant is a foreign corporation or non-resident.
2. Defendant has secreted himself.
3. Defendant is about to leave the state.
4. Defendant is removing property from the state.
5. Defendant has sold or is about to dispose of property with the intent to defraud creditors.
6. Defendant's residence or whereabouts is unknown.

IOWA

1. Defendant is a foreign corporation or a non-resident.
2. Defendant is about to remove his property.
3. Defendant disposed of or is about to dispose of p erty with the intent to defraud creditors.
4. Defendant has absconded.
5. Defendant has removed himself and his property.
6. Defendant has removed his property.
7. Defendant has converted or concealed property.
8. Debt is due from property obtained under false pretenses.

KANSAS

1. Defendant is a non-resident or foreign corporation.
2. Defendant absconded or concealed himself.
3. Defendant is about to remove himself from the state.
4. Defendant is about to remove property from the state.
5. Defendant is about to convert property into money to put it beyond the reach of creditors.
6. Defendant has concealed, removed, assigned or conveyed property to hinder or delay creditors.
7. The debt was fraudulently contracted.
8. Damages sought are for injuries from defendant's commission of a felony, misdemeanor or seduction of a female.
9. Defendant failed to pay the price for articles delivered.

KENTUCKY

1. Defendant is a non-resident or foreign corporation.
2. Defendant has been absent for four months.
3. Defendant departed with intent to defraud creditors.
4. Defendant left the county to avoid service.
5. Defendant conceals himself.
6. Defendant is about to remove his property.
7. Defendant sold, conveyed, or disposed of property with intent to defraud creditors, or is about to do so.

LOUISIANA

1. Defendant has left state or is about to do so.
2. Defendant is a non-resident with no agent for service of process within the state.
3. Defendant has concealed himself to avoid process.
4. Defendant has mortgaged, assigned or otherwise disposed of his property to defraud creditors.
5. Defendant has converted his property to avoid creditors.

MAINE

Attachment may be had in any action in which claim, exclusive of costs, is twenty dollars or more.

MARYLAND

1. Defendant is a non-resident.
2. Defendant is a corporation having no agent but

where 2 attempts to serve him have been un-successful.
3. Defendant is a resident on whom two attempts at service have failed.
4. Defendant absconded or is about to or removed himself or is about to remove himself from his place of abode with intent to defraud creditors.
5. Defendant fraudulently contracted the debt or obligation.
6. Land of a decedent in the hands of a devisee may be attached.

MASSACHUSETTS   Plaintiff must show reasonable likelihood of his recovering an amount equal to, or greater than the property attached and above any liability insurance which defendant might have to cover the judgment. If attachment ex parte is desired, must also show that defendant is not subject to the jurisdiction of the court, that if defendant knew of the impending attachment he would remove the property from the state or conceal it, or that the property is in immediate danger of being destroyed by the defendant.

MICHIGAN   1. Defendant is not subject to the jurisdiction of the court.
2. Defendant cannot be served with process, even though a diligent effort has been made to do so.

MINNESOTA   1. The debt was fraudulently contracted.
2. Defendant is a foreign corporation or a non-resident.
3. Defendant departed the state or concealed himself to avoid services or to defraud creditors.
4. Defendant has assigned or disposed of his property (or is about to do so) in an attempt to defraud creditors.

MISSISSIPPI   1. Defendant is a foreign corporation or a non-resident.
2. Defendant removed himself or property or is about to do so.
3. Defendant absconds or conceals himself to avoid service.
4. The debt was incurred in conducting the business of a water craft in navigable waters of the state.
5. Defendant conceals or refuses to apply property to the debt.

6. Defendant assigned or disposed of property with intent to defraud creditors or is about to do so.
7. Defendant converted property to money to put it beyond the reach of creditors.
8. The debt was fraudulently contracted.
9. Defendant is buying, selling, or dealing in futures or has done so within the last six months.
10. The debt is due the state or sub-division thereof.
11. Defendant is a banker, banking company or corporation which received deposits while insolvent, or has given false statement as to financial condition.

MISSOURI

1. Defendant is a non-resident.
2. Defendant is a foreign corporation.
3. Defendant conceals himself to avoid service of summons.
4. Defendant has absconded or absented himself from his usual place of abode.
5. Defendant has removed his property with intent to defraud creditors.
6. Defendant is about to leave the state and change his domicile.
7. Defendant has fraudulently conveyed or assigned his property with the intent of defrauding creditors.
8. Defendant has fraudulently concealed, removed or disposed of his property with intent to defraud creditors.
9. Defendent is about to fraudulently convey or assign property to hinder, delay or defraud creditors.
10. Defendant is about to fraudulently conceal or remove or dispose of his property.
11. Where the cause of action accrued out of the state and defendant has absconded, or secretly removed his property into this state.
12. Where the damages sought arose out of defendant's commission of a felony, misdemeanor, or his seduction of any female.
13. Where the debtor has failed to pay the price or value of any article or thing delivered which by contract he was bound to pay upon delivery.
14. Where the defendant fraudulently contracted the debt.

MONTANA

Attachment is available in any action in contract, express or implied, for the direct payment of money where the contract is unsecured, or the security has become valueless.

Action upon statutory stockholders liability.

NEBRASKA

Debt Is Due

1. Defendant is a foreign corporation or non-resident.
2. Defendant absconded with intent to defraud creditors.
3. Defendant left the county to avoid service.
4. Defendant conceals himself.
5. Defendant is about to remove, or convert property to defraud creditors or put it beyond their reach.
6. Defendant concealed, assigned, removed or disposed of property with intent to defraud creditors or is about to do so.
7. The debt was fraudulently contracted.

Debt Not Due

1. Defendant sold, conveyed property with intent to defraud creditors.
2. Defendant is about to sell or remove property.

NEVADA

With Notice and Hearing

1. Action on judgment or unsecured contract (or in secured transactions where the security has become valueless).
2. Action where the court finds that extraordinary circumstances makes it impossible for plaintiff to execute on defendant's property.

Without Notice

1. Non-resident or unqualified corporation is defendant.
2. Action is upon a foreign judgment for a direct payment of money.
3. In recovery of personal property taken without owner's consent.
4. Defendant is about to remove his money from the state.
5. Defendant is about to assign or dispose of his property so that he would be unable to pay the judgment.
6. For recovery of money or property obtained through fraud or in an action brought under

the Uniform Reciprocal Enforcement of Support Act.
7. Where jurisdiction can only be obtained by attachment.

JEW HAMPSHIRE   Prejudgment attachments may be had in all actions upon notice to the defendant.

Without notice it must be shown:
1. There is substantial danger that the property would be lost, destroyed or removed from the state.
2. The attachment is necessary to obtain jurisdiction over the defendant.
3. In action for specific performance, where there is immediate danger of transfer to a bona fide third party.
4. Notice period under a bulk sale is about to expire.
5. Attachment is necessary to secure an important governmental or general public interest.

EW JERSEY
1. Where the fact would entitle the plaintiff to an order of arrest before judgment in a civil case.
2. Where the defendant has absconded or is a non-resident.
3. Where a cause of action existed against a decedent which action survives against the decedent's heirs, devisees, executors, administrators or trustees and any of such persons are non-residents.
4. In equitable claims where the defendant has absconded or is a non-resident.
5. Defendant is a foreign corporation but authorized to do business in the state and the home state of the corporation permits attachment on N.J. corporations qualified in the state.

EW MEXICO
1. Defendant is a non-resident.
2. Defendant concealed himself or can't be served.
3. Defendant removed, assigned, concealed or disposed of property with intent of defrauding creditors or is about to do so.
4. Defendant is a corporation whose principal place of business is out of the state and has no statutory agent in the state.
5. The debt was fraudulently contracted.
6. The debt is for work, labor, or services requested

by the defendant.
7. The debt is for necessities of life.

NEW YORK

1. Defendant is a foreign corporation or a non-resident.
2. Defendant is a resident but can't be served.
3. Defendant departed or keeps himself hidden.
4. Defendant assigned, disposed, or secreted property with intent to defraud creditors.
5. The debt was fraudulently contracted.
6. The debt arose from wrongful receipt, conversion or detention of property held or owned by any governmental agency.
7. Debt is due on judgment from another state.
8. There is a cause of action to recover damages for conversion of personal property or for fraud or deceit.

NORTH CAROLINA

1. Defendant is a non-resident, foreign corporation, or domestic corporation whose officers can't be found.
2. Defendant, with intent to defraud creditors, departed the state, concealed himself, removed, assigned, disposed of, or secreted property, or is about to do so.

NORTH DAKOTA

1. Defendant is a non-resident or foreign corporation.
2. Defendant absconded or concealed himself or is about to remove himself from the state.
3. Defendant sold, assigned, secreted, disposed, or removed property with the intent of defrauding creditors.
4. Defendant is about to remove property.
5. Defendant incurred the debt under false pretenses.
6. The action is for recovery of purchase price for personal property sold to defendant.
7. In an action against the owner of a motor vehicle for damages as a result of negligence, the motor vehicle may be attached.

OHIO

1. Defendant is a non-resident or an unqualified corporation.
2. Defendant has absconded to defraud creditors.
3. Defendant left or has concealed himself, to avoid service of summons.

4. Defendant is about to remove property to defraud creditors.
5. Defendant is about to convert property to defraud creditors.
6. Defendant is concealing property.
7. Defendant has or is about to assign, remove or dispose of his property.
8. Defendant has fraudulently or criminally contracted the debt.
9. The claim is for work, labor or necessaries.
10. Defendant has violated the Bulk Sales Act.

OKLAHOMA

1. Defendant is a foreign corporation or non-resident.
2. Defendant absconded, left the county or conceals himself to avoid service.
3. Defendant removed, converted, assigned, disposed of or concealed property with intent to hinder, delay or defraud creditors or is about to do so.
4. The debt was fraudulently contracted.
5. The debt arose from the commission of a felony, misdemeanor, or seduction of a female.
6. Defendant failed to pay the price of goods delivered.

OREGON

1. The action is one on contract where the creditor is unsecured or the debtor is a non-resident.
2. The action is one on breach of contract against a non-resident.
3. The action is one against a non-resident for injury to property.

PENNSYVLANIA

In general attachment will be permitted if defendant is a non-resident or an unregistered foreign corporation or a partnership or unincorporated association without a regular place of business in the state. A fraudulent debtors attachment may be obtained if defendant with intent to defraud plaintiff has concealed, transferred or removed his property from the state, or has concealed himself, absconded or left the state.

RHODE ISLAND

Allowed in action based on contract where damages may be estimated. Also allowed in tort actions, where defendant is a non-resident.

SOUTH CAROLINA

1. Defendant is a non-resident or a foreign corporation.

2. Defendant has departed the state with the intent to defraud creditors or to avoid service of summons or keeps himself concealed for such purpose.
3. Defendant has removed or is about to remove his property from the state with the intent of defrauding creditors.
4. Defendant has assigned, disposed or secreted his property or is about to do so with the intent of defrauding creditors.

SOUTH DAKOTA

1. Defendant is a non-resident or corporation which can't be served.
2. Defendant departed, removed, secreted, incumbered, transferred to disposed of property with the intent of defrauding creditors.
3. The debt was fraudulently contracted.
4. The action is one for the purchase price of personal property.

TENNESSEE

1. Defendant is a non-resident.
2. Defendant is about to or has removed himself or property from the state.
3. Defendant removed or is about to remove himself from the county.
4. Defendant conceals himself to avoid service.
5. Defendant absconded or is concealing property.
6. Defendant fraudulently disposed of property or is about to do so.
7. The claim is against a non-resident decedent leaving property in the state.

TEXAS

1. The debt is due for property obtained under false pretenses where seller relied upon the false pretenses as true and so parted with his property.
2. Defendant is a non-resident or foreign corporation.
3. Defendant secretes himself or is about to remove himself from the state.
4. Defendant has secreted his property with the intent of defrauding creditors, or is about to dispose or convert said property with that intent.

UTAH

1. Defendant is a non-resident or foreign corporation not qualified to do business in the state.
2. Defendant can't be served.
3. Defendant assigned, disposed of, or concealed property with intent to defraud creditors, or is

about to do so.
4. Defendant departed or is about to depart the state.
5. The debt was fraudulently contracted.
6. When plaintiff can show probable cause of being apprehensive of losing his claim unless attachment issues.

VERMONT   No specific grounds, any action or tort.

VIRGINIA
1. Defendant is a foreign corporation or a non-resident.
2. The defendant is removing or about to remove property from the state.
3. Defendant is converting or about to convert property to hinder, delay, or defraud creditors.
4. Defendant has assigned or disposed of, or is about to assign or dispose of his property.
5. Defendant has or is about to abscond from the state.
6. Defendant has or is about to conceal himself.
7. Defendant is a fugitive from justice.

WASHINGTON
Note: Defendant must be afforded a notice and a hearing.)
1. Defendant is a foreign corporation.
2. Defendant is a non-resident.
3. Defendant conceals himself to avoid service of summons.
4. Defendant has absconded or absented himself from his usual place of abode to avoid service of summons.
5. Defendant has removed or is about to remove property with the intent of delaying or hindering creditors.
6. Defendant has assigned, secreted, or disposed of property or is about to do so with the intent of defrauding, hindering or delaying creditors.
7. Defendant has converted his property to money.
8. Defendant fraudulently contracted the debt or obligation.
9. The damages sought in the suit are for injuries arising from the commission of some felony.
10. The object for which the action is brought is to recover on a contract.

WEST VIRGINIA
1. Defendant is a foreign corporation or a non-resident.
2. Defendant left or is about to leave with intent to defraud creditors.

3. Defendant conceals himself.
4. Defendant is removing, disposing of or converting property with intent of hindering or delaying creditors.
5. Defendant assigned or concealed property with intent to defraud creditors.
6. The debt was fraudulently contracted.

In actions on contracts or judgments

WISCONSIN

1. Defendant is absent from the state or concealed.
2. Defendant is a domestic corporation whose officers cannot be found.
3. Defendant disposed of or concealed property with intent to defraud creditors.
4. Defendant removed property from the state with intent to defraud creditors.
5. The debt was fraudulently contracted.
6. Defendant is a foreign corporation or non-resident.
7. Defendant, as a public officer, defaulted on an official bond.

In tort actions

1. Defendant must be a non-resident, or residence unknown.
2. Defendant must be a foreign corporation.

WYOMING

1. Defendant is a foreign corporation or non-resident.
2. Defendant absconded, left the county or concealed himself to avoid service.
3. Defendant removed, converted, assigned, concealed, or disposed of property with intent to defraud creditors, or is about to do so.
4. The debt was fraudulently contracted.
5. The action is on a contract, express or implied, for the direct payment of money not exceeding $1,500, which contract is unsecured or inadequately secured.

Chapter VII
JUVENILE LAW

The last two decades have resulted in many major decisions particularly by the Supreme Court, which have extended the protection guaranteed by the constitution to young people, notably in the fields of education and juvenile justice.

AGE OF MAJORITY

Traditionally the age of majority has been twenty-one. Since the 1971 constitutional amendment reducing the voting age to eighteen, most of the states have begun to regard those eighteen and over as adults.

Once a minor steps over the threshold of his majority, he is permitted to do many things, which before were prohibited. A guardian need no longer be appointed to bring legal suits for him; he can execute a will, give a deed to real property and marriage is now possible without parental consent.

There are however, some acts requiring a certain degree of maturity which may be performed by minors. They may drive cars. Subject to close scrutiny by the state, as to length of hours and type of work, a minor may get a job. Although the modern parent usually lets the child keep his wages, it is the parent, not the child, who has the legal right to these wages.

A minor can enter into a contract, but he can rescind it upon reaching his majority. The exception to this rule at common law, was that a minor is liable for necessaries furnished him. Modern day law has extended this rule to cover educational loans and certain banking transactions.

CHILD ABUSE LAWS

Parents have always had the right and duty to discipline their children and to use reasonable force to do so. In recent years, the public is becoming increasingly aware that in many cases children are being brutally abused by their parents.

Child abuse laws have been passed in many states. These laws set up procedures for reporting child abuse to the proper officials and permit these children to be placed under the supervision and care of the courts.

DESEGREGATION

In 1955, the United States Supreme Court, issued its now famous decision of *Brown v. Board of Education,* striking down the "separate but equal" doctrine, which had been the cornerstone of the southern educational system, since 1896. Speaking for the court Chief Justice Warren, stated that the doctrine of segregation "generates [in black pupils] a feeling of inferiority as to their status in the community that may affect their hearts and minds in a way unlikely ever to be undone." The effect of this decision rocked the South for several decades and its reverberations are still felt today, not only in the south but in many northern cities.

More than twenty years after the Brown decision, its goal still has not been reached. The focus of the desegregation has shifted to the north, to those cities where segregation is not caused because it is prohibited by law, but to other causes such as population shifts and normal residential patterns. Of prime concern to many today is the methods used to combat these population patterns. One in particular, that of busing children into schools located in districts some distance from their homes, has aroused the public interest.

The Supreme Court has always held busing to be a legitimate tool for implementin desegregation. This opinion was expressed in cases such as *Swann v. Charlotte-Mecklenberg Board of Education* and in *Davis v. School Commissioners of Mobile County,* both of which were decided in the early 70's. At the same time the court upheld a district court ruling that an anti-busing statute passed in North Carolina was unconstitutional (North Carolina State Board of Education v. Swann). The courts have continued to use busing in desegregation plans to the present time.

However, its ears attuned to public grumblings, the legislature has not always given its whole-hearted endorsement to busing, nor had the executive branch of the federal government, under Nixon, and continuing into the Ford administration. Many are agitating for a constitutional amendment prohibiting busing of students for the purpose of achieving racial equality in schools.

The aim of a nationwide desegregated school system is far from being realized. Undoubtedly the question of desegregation and how it is to be accomplished will be argued before the courts and in the legislature for some time to come.

JUVENILE CRIME

The rapidly increasing rate of juvenile crime, has resulted in a greater scrutiny and criticism of our prevailing system of juvenile justice. Some, alarmed at the increase in teen aged violence, complain that youthful offenders are being coddled under our present system and that more severe penalties are called for. Others maintain that under the system, youths are being denied certain fundamental rights guaranteed by the constitution.

Until the late 19th century, no distinction was made between the youthful or the adult criminal; they both received the same treatment and were placed in the same jails. Gradually, reforms were made in the state laws. Fearing that forcing juveniles to mingle with hardened criminals would merely entrench a child in a life of crime, separate systems were established to cope with juvenile crime. The rationale behind this system was that more attention should be paid to the prevention of future crimes than to the punishment of the one already committed.

The basic procedures are the same in most of the states.

The proceedings are usually started by a petition or complaint. This complaint is then referred to the proper department for investigation. If it is found that the youth has been wrongly accused the complaint will be dismissed. The child may be placed on probation, if the investigation discloses that the act complained of was not serious enough to constitute juvenile delinquency. If it is found that there is a possibility of delinquent behavior, a hearing will be held in front of a judge. Usually the child is put into his parents' custody until the hearing.

To protect the youth and to prevent him from having a criminal record, the hearing before the judge is an informal one, closed to the public. Usually only the child, his parents and if desired, his lawyer, are present as well as the probation officer and witnesses.

It was the very informality of this type of hearing that led to the landmark decision of the Supreme Court, *In re Gault,* in 1967. The case involved a fifteen year old boy, accused by one of his neighbors of making a lewd phone call to her. Ultimately the boy was confined to the Arizona State Industrial School, for the rest of his minority (6 years). Upon appeal to the U.S. Supreme Court, the court found that Gault had not received proper notice of the delinquency charge, nor was he informed of his right to counsel, or of his privilege against self-incrimination. Also the complaining witness was not present, thereby denying the boy his right to confront her and cross examine her. Such flagrant violations of constitutional rights would never be allowed in the trial of an adult accused of a crime. Juveniles, the court held, were also entitled to these rights.

In the wake of the Gault decision, many state laws were amended to safeguard a juvenile's constitutional rights. Since then the Supreme Court has ruled that the criterion of guilt in juvenile proceedings is the same as that in adult criminal trials, — guilt must be proven beyond a reasonable doubt. (In re Winship (1970)). In McKeiver v. Pennsylvania (1971), however, a divided court held that the right to trial by jury did not exist in a state juvenile delinquency proceeding.

It is evident that the present system of juvenile justice has not been as successful as hoped. Many are disillusioned by it and it is possible that in the years to come it may be drastically changed or discarded completely.

PARENTAL RESPONSIBILITY FOR DAMAGES CAUSED BY CHILDREN

As a general rule parents are not responsible for damages caused by their children unless the children were acting as their agents or under their direction. If it can be shown that parents were aware of a continuing pattern of wrongful behavior on the child's part, or if the parents themselves were negligent (e.g. gave the child a dangerous toy), they will also be held liable for their children's acts.

In recent years however, states have begun to pass laws holding parent's liable for wilfull and malicious acts of their children, even in the absence of the elements listed in the preceeding paragraph. The laws are primarily aimed at vandalism, although some few states extend the liability to willful assaults. Most of the states have a monetary ceiling on the liability ranging from $300 in states such as Delaware to $2,000 in Ohio.

STUDENT RIGHTS

The political activism of students in the past few decades has been paralleled by an increasing number of court decisions holding that students, as well as their elders, are entitled to those rights and freedoms guaranteed by the Constitution.

Throughout the years, schools have been regarded as substitutes for parents and entitled to their rights. Their rulings were unquestioned, all actions taken by the school being assumed to be for the benefit and welfare of the children.

In 1961, the United States Supreme Court upheld an appellate court ruling that two students were denied the right of due process when they were expelled from a state university without being given notice or opportunity for a hearing.

In cases dealing with personal appearance of students and their right to protest and express their opinion, the courts have held that students are entitled to the constitutional right of freedom of speech and expression. The school may not arbitrarily deprive students of these rights and has the burden of proving that its reason for suspending these rights is a valid one, e.g. for reasons of health and well being of the student or to prevent undue disruption of the educational process.

Chapter VIII

WOMEN AND THE LAW

In the late sixties and seventies, "Women's Lib", became a household word. The phrase has come to mean many things to many people. Numerous books and articles have been written on its meaning and it is not within the scope of this chapter to discuss the nature and aims of this movement. Suffice it to say that one of its prime aims is or should be that women must be treated as individuals with the basic right to determine for themselves what they will do with their lives, whether it be a career in the professions or the business world, or to become a homemaker and mother.

In order to achieve this freedom and develop all their potentials, women must receive help from the law. Traditionally the courts have always regarded women as inferior to men and usually accorded them the same treatment as children, seeking to protect them from themselves and others.

Throughout the years various individual women have sought not to be protected, but to be treated as man's equal. As with the Civil Rights movement for blacks and other minorities, it has been a long and discouraging battle. Gradually, the walls of inequality are beginning to crumble. What follows is an attempt to show the status of women in the eyes of the law today and what may be expected for the future.

CREDIT AND WOMEN

For some time now women's groups have been denouncing credit policies which have been practiced throughout the nation.

Women, particularly married and divorced women have been discriminated against solely on the basis of their sex. Most of their applications for loans had to be countersigned by another person (usually a male). Obtaining a mortgage, for most women was almost impossible, even if they possessed a relatively high paying job. Particularly disheartening was the difficulty that working married couples experienced in obtaining a mortgage. Lending institutions would not consider the combined salary of the husband and wife in determining eligibility for a mortgage. Unless the wife was over child bearing age, or could furnish proof of a hysterectomy, usually only the husband's salary was considered.

For the past several years, some banks and federal lending companies have begun to discontinue this type of discrimination. Several states, such as New York, began to pass legislation out-lawing discriminatory credit practices.

Perhaps the greatest impetus will come from the "Equal Credit Opportunity Act", effective October 1975. That Congress has become aware of the problem is clear from the statement of pupose of the act, which reads as follows:

"The Congress finds that there is a need to insure that the various financial institutions and other firms engaged in the extensions of credit exercise their responsibility to make credit available with fairness, impartiality, and without discrimination on the basis of sex or marital status. Economic stabilization would be enhanced and competition among the various financial institutions and other firms engaged in the extension of credit would be strengthened by an absence of discrimination on the basis of sex or marital status, as well as by the informed use of credit which Congress has heretofore sought to promote. It is the purpose of this Act to require that financial institutions and other firms engaged in the extension of credit make that credit equally available to all creditworthy customers without regard to sex or marital status."

Under the act it is unlawful for any creditor to discriminate against any applicant on the basis of sex or marital status with respect to any aspect of a credit transaction. A creditor may inquire into the marital status only for the purpose of ascertaining the creditor's rights and remedies with respect to any aspect of the transaction.

Any creditor who fails to comply with the provisions of this action is subject to a civil suit, and liable for the amount of damages actually sustained as a result of the credit rejection. If the aggrieved applicant brings the suit individually, punitive damages may also be granted by the court in an amount not greater than $10,000.

As of this writing, there have been no reported cases relating to this relatively new law.

CRIME AND WOMEN

The emergence of women's rights organizations has also focused attention on some of the inequalities suffered by women in the field of criminal law.

One aspect of this inequality has been discrimination in the sentencing and imprisonment of women who have been guilty of the same offenses as men. It has been pointed out by one author that this differentiation is quite common in the field of juvenile justice where many girls all over the country are sent to reform school because they engage in sexual activity. If their male counterparts engage in the same type of activity, they are said to be acting like healthy, normal males.

For some years it has been common for women who have been convicted of a crime to be sentenced for a longer period of time than would be a man who committed the same crime. Courts are beginning to strike down statutes permitting this, as violative of the fourteenth amendment and legislatures have begun to repeal such laws. Undoubtedly the Supreme Court will finally rule on the question.

The inconsistency in the enforcement of prostitution laws is also inveighed against by many women's organizations. Women prostitutes are heavily fined and sometimes imprisoned, while the men who have used their services are often not prosecuted. Some women's groups feel that because of this prostitution is a discriminatory crime and should be eliminated from penal codes altogether. It is doubtful that they will be successful in obtaining this goal, but it is possible that more will be done to punish the males who really are just as essential to the crime of prostitution as the female prostitute.

For nearly every women the possibility of rape is a fearsome thing; when the possibility becomes an actuality, the experience is a traumatic one. For years many of the states required the corroboration of an independent witness before a conviction for rape could be obtained. Realizing the great burden that this places on the rape victim, most of the states have eliminated this requirement.

In signing the New York bill, repealing this requirement, former Governor Wilson succinctly stated the arguments that have been proffered against the corroboration rule as follows:

"Presently, New York is one of a very few states that prohibit the conviction of a defendant for rape and other sex crimes unless there is some evidence independent of the complainant's testimony to establish that the sex act was committed and that force was used. The very nature of a sex offense and the isolated circumstances under which such crimes are normally committed most often makes it impossible to obtain such independent evidence. Consequently, each year many serious sex offenses, in which a reliable complainant's testimony is completely credible must be dismissed because of a failure to meet the corroboration requirement, and the alleged sex offender set free."

The Governor then touched on what has always been a sensitive issue for those in the women's rights movement. He stated, "the implicit suggestion in the corroboration rule that the testimony of women, who are most often the complainants in sex cases is inherently suspect and should not be trusted without the support of the independent evidence is without justification and contrary to our strong belief in the principle of complete equality for women in our society."

He dismissed the usual argument that false charges in matters such as these are easily brought, by pointing out that our legal system protects innocent persons by many procedural safeguards, such as the presumption of innocence and the requirement that guilt must be proven beyond a reasonable doubt, as well as through the "normal screening process, in our criminal justice system whereby unwarranted charges may be dismissed before trial by the district attorney, jury or judge."

EMPLOYMENT AND WOMEN

Gather together a group of women of different age groups, educational and family backgrounds and you will probably hear divergent views on "women's lib" and what its aims should be. They would all be unanimous on one point, however, and that is that one of the chief aims of the movement should be to end existing discriminatory practices in the hiring and paying of male and female employees.

Traditionally women have been given the lower paying jobs and have not been given the same advancement opportunities as men. Presumably one reason for this has been that many of the women have been married women and their pay checks supplement the earnings of their husbands. Today with the prevalence of divorce, and more women choosing to remain single, women are demanding equal employment opportunities and equal pay with their male counterparts.

In the sixties and seventies, courts have begun applying to the issue of discrimination between the sexes in employment, those principles used in combating racial discrimination.

Two powerful weapons which women may use to combat employment discrimination are the federal Equal Pay Act and Title VII of the 1964 Civil Rights Act. Many of the states have similar statutes, but for the purpose of this chapter, comments will be confined to the federal legislation.

Wage discrimination is prohibited by the Equal Pay Act. Under the provisions of this act, which is enforced by the Wage and Hours division of the U.S. Department of Labor, a woman has two alternative remedies to pursue, should she feel she is the subject of discrimination. She may request an investigation of the alleged violation by the Department of Labor who, if they find she is being discriminated against, will bring a suit in her behalf to recover the unpaid wages.

If she so desires, she may bring her own suit, and if successful, recover twice the amount of unpaid wages plus attorneys fees and court costs. At first glance, the second alternative may seem to be the better, but few women can assume the risk of losing the suit and being personally liable for the legal fees.

In addition the act provides fines for violations of the act. It should be noted that the act prohibits discrimination not only on the part of employers, but also on the part of unions.

To establish a case under the Equal Pay Act, a woman must prove that her work is substantially equal to work done by her male counterpart, i.e. the work requires equal skills and effort, and is performed under similar working conditions.

In the Wheating Glass Co. case and the Corning Glass Works case, two leading decisions in this area, over 45 million dollars were paid back to women workers who had been discriminated against. These cases also established that equalization in pay could not be accomplished by lowering men's salaries. The women's salaries had to be raised on a par with the men.

Title VII of the Civil Rights Act, originally applied to cases of racial discrimination, is now being applied to discrimination between the sexes. The Equal Employment Opportunity Commission is empowered to enforce the act which is applicable to employment agencies, and unions as well as private businesses with the specified number of employees. Executive Order 11478 prohibits discrimination on the basis of sex (as well as race, color, religion or national origin) in all federal agencies. Executive Order 11246 does the same with respect to federal contractors and sub-contractors or anyone holding a federal contract of $10,000 or more. These orders are enforced by the U.S. Civil Service Commission and the Office for Federal Contract Compliance, respectively. Both these agencies as well as the Equal Opportunity Commission have issued Sex Discrimination Guidelines.

As in the case of the Equal Pay Act, under Title VII, a woman has a choice of remedies. She may notify her regional office of the EEOC, who will then investigate and if necessary take steps to end the discrimination. If this fails, she may bring her own suit.

In addition to Title VII, there are several executive orders, requiring that discrimination with regard to sex be ended with respect to federal employees and those employed by holders of certain government contracts. In some instances not only is discrimination forbidden, but affirmative action must be taken to end it. Standards have been given to determine whether enough women are being hired, e.g. the number of available women within the neighborhood, and the proportion employed in the particular instance. If discrimination can be proven, the company involved can lose the contract.

Guidelines have been issued relating to discrimination because of sex. Jobs can no longer be arbitrarily classified as "men's jobs" and "women's jobs", either in offices or in newspaper advertisements. Pregnancy may no longer result in the termination of employment, nor can a company refuse to hire a married woman.

If the basis for sex discrimination is "a bona fide occupational qualification reasonably necessary to the normal operation of that particular business or enterprise", it would not be outlawed by Title VII. Of course the question arises, what is a "bona fide occupational qualification provision". The courts are still deciding the issue. The fact that customers or clientele might show a preference for one sex over another is not considered a legitimate reason for sex job discrimination. A case in point was the Diaz case where a male sought to be hired by Pan Am as a flight attendant, a position held only by women. Although the lower court denied he was discriminated against, on appeal he won his case, the court holding that refusal to hire him because of his sex was discriminatory and that the fact that Pan Am's passengers would probably prefer feminine stewardesses, should have no effect on its decision.

The burden of proving that sex is "a bona fide occupational qualification" is on the employer against whom a charge of discrimination is made. In one oft quoted case of Rosenfeld v. Southern Pacific Railroad co., the court commented that perhaps the only two jobs for which sex is a bona fide qualification are sperm donor and wet nurse.

The EEOC guidelines list modelling, acting or jobs in the entertainment industry for which sex appeal is an essential qualification, as instances where occupations may be limited to one sex. Others would be such occupations as rest-room attendants or lingerie sales clerk. They direct that discrimination may not be practiced simply because some or most members of one sex are unable or unwilling to do the job, or because the job involves heavy physical labor, late-night hours or because co-workers, employers, customers or clients prefer one sex over another.

Title VII also bars discrimination because of child care responsibilities. This question was raised in *Phillips v. Martin Marietta Corporation,* which finally reached the U.S. Supreme Court. The suit was brought by a mother who was refused employment because she had children of pre-school age. Since men with children of the same age were hired by the company, she claimed that she had been discriminated against. The EEOC agreed with her, but the lower courts held that she was not discriminated against, solely because she was a woman, but because she was the mother of pre-school children. The Supreme Court ruled that a woman can not be automatically refused employment because she had pre-school children. However to the chagrin of many women's rights advocates, some of the justices in separate decisions stated that while a woman could not automatically be denied employment for this reason, if it was felt that since the conflicting family obligations might have an adverse effect on a particular woman's work in certain instances, this could be a bona fide basis for not employing her.

Another controversial area is the so called "protective" legislation and decisions relating to women employees. Generally courts and legislatures tend to take a paternalistic attitude towards women. They tried to protect them from long work hours and heavier and more difficult labor. Many times, by so doing they were also "protecting" them from the higher wages that went with the longer hours and more difficult work.

Women began to challenge these protective laws, and are continuing to do so. Many states have struck down legislation limiting the number of hours a woman may work. So too, law suits are being brought to permit women to engage in occupations previously thought to be hazardous or laborious for women. In one, *Lorena Weeks v. Southern Bell & Telephone Co.,* a woman sought to become a telephone switchman. She finally won her court case on appeal when the federal appeals court held that she was being denied the job solely on the basis of her sex. In words, dear to the heart of the most rabid of "women's libbers", the court declared:

> "Title VII rejects just this type of romantic paternalism as unduly Victorian and instead vests individual women with the power to decide whether or not to take on unromantic tasks. Men have always had the right to determine whether the incremental increase in remuneration for strenuous, dangerous, obnoxious, boring or unromantic tasks is worth the candle. The promise of Title VII is that women are now to be on equal footing."

As time goes on and women continue to fight for equal employment opportunities, the old stereotyped ideas of the capabilities of the sexes will begin to crumble and a heretofore untapped reservoir of labor and talent will be placed at the nation's disposal.

EQUAL RIGHTS AMENDMENT

"Equality of rights under the law shall not be denied or abridged by the United States or by any State on account of sex.

The Congress shall have the power to enforce by appropriate legislation, the provisions of this article."

It's not very long and it is simply stated, but the above proposed amendment to the U.S. Constitution, known as the Equal Rights Amendment (ERA), is one of the burning issues of the 70's, hotly debated, its critics and supporters arguing with equal vehemence.

Most people think that it is a new proposal, but the ERA was first introduced into Congress in 1923, and had been introduced sporadically during the ensuing years, until it was finally approved by the House in August, 1970 and the Senate in March, 1971. In order to become a Constitutional amendment, it must be ratified by 3/4 of the states (38) or before March 22, 1979. So far the ERA has been ratified by 35 state. See chart at the end of this chapter. Idaho, Nebraska and Tennessee have voted in their state legislatures to rescind their approval of the amendment, but most legal authorities consider this action to be invalid. Similar efforts to rescind ratification were attempted in several other state legislatures such as Vermont and Kentucky, but so far these efforts have been unsuccessful.

In addition to voting on the referendum for an amendment to the United States Constitution, some states have added the equal rights amendment to their own state constitutions. See chart at end of this chapter.

Until the amendment is adopted, women enforcing their rights will have to depend on existing legislation, such as the equal pay, employment and credit laws, mentioned elsewhere in this chapter.

Now, if the discrimination complained of, is not prohibited by a specific statute and appropriate remedies given, women have to rely on the constitutional guarantees of the fifth amendment (due process) or the fourteenth (equal protection under the law) amendment. Many women's groups have felt that even given these constitutional rights, they are not fully protected, because in many cases, the burden of proof has been placed on the female complainant to show that she has been discriminated against rather than the defendant having to prove that the act was not discriminatory. In recent years, particularly in the actions brought under the Civil Rights Act, the burden has been shifted to the defendant, but many women feel that the passage of the ERA will remedy the situation by placing the equality of women in the category of a "preferred right", which can be denied for only the gravest of reasons.

There are some that fear that the passage of the amendment would result in the loss of many protections and privileges women now have under the law. The most frequent example given is that women would be expected to serve in the armed forces and be eligible for the draft. Proponents of the amendment maintain that while this may be true, women have been serving voluntarily in the armed services for years, that it is unlikely that women would be expected to fight on the front lines of battle and that there are many fringe benefits (educational, travel, etc.) to being a member of the armed services.

Chart 1

STATES WHICH HAVE ADOPTED A STATE ERA AMENDMENT OR RATIFIED A U.S. CONSTITUTIONAL AMENDMENT

STATE	State ERA Amendment	Federal ERA Amendment
ALABAMA	No	No
ALASKA	Yes	Yes
ARIZONA	No	No
ARKANSAS	No	No
CALIFORNIA	No	Yes
COLORADO	Yes	Yes
CONNECTICUT	Yes	Yes
DELAWARE	No	Yes
DISTRICT OF COLUMBIA	No	No
FLORIDA	No	No
GEORGIA	No	No
HAWAII	Yes	Yes
IDAHO	No	Yes
ILLINOIS	Yes	No
INDIANA	No	Yes
IOWA	No	Yes
KANSAS	No	Yes
KENTUCKY	No	Yes
LOUISIANA	No	No
MAINE	No	Yes
MARYLAND	Yes	Yes

STATE	State ERA Amendment	Federal ERA Amendment
MASSACHUSETTS	No	Yes
MICHIGAN	No	Yes
MINNESOTA	No	Yes
MISSISSIPPI	No	No
MISSOURI	No	No
MONTANA	Yes	Yes
NEBRASKA	No	Yes
NEVADA	No	No
NEW HAMPSHIRE	Yes	Yes
NEW JERSEY	No	Yes
NEW MEXICO	Yes	Yes
NEW YORK	No	Yes
NORTH CAROLINA	No	No
NORTH DAKOTA	No	Yes
OHIO	No	Yes
OKLAHOMA	No	No
OREGON	No	Yes
PENNSYLVANIA	Yes	Yes
RHODE ISLAND	No	Yes
SOUTH CAROLINA	No	No
SOUTH DAKOTA	No	Yes
TENNESSEE	No	Yes
TEXAS	Yes	Yes

STATE	State ERA Amendment	Federal ERA Amendment
UTAH	Yes	No
VERMONT	No	Yes
VIRGINIA	Yes	No
WASHINGTON	Yes	Yes
WEST VIRGINIA	No	Yes
WISCONSIN	No	Yes
WYOMING	Yes	Yes

Chapter IX
ENVIRONMENTAL LAW

In the sixties and seventies, we suddenly became aware that the world about us was beginning to show the detrimental effects of almost unrestrained technology. The quality of our air had greatly deteriorated; rivers and streams were becoming stagnant with pollution. It was obvious that something had to be done. Laws were passed and suits began to be brought by private individuals and groups concerned with preserving the environment, to stop the rampant pollution found around us. The area of environmental law therefore is a new one, still growing and constantly evolving. To attempt to write definitely on the topic is almost impossible, but a few general principles can be explored.

Usually, environmental concerns were the domain of state and local governments and because of this, laws regarding clean air, water, etc. were far from uniform. When it became clear that a workable environmental policy should be determined at the national level, federal laws were passed to curb environmental damage, notably the Federal Water Pollution Control Act as amended, the Water Quality Act of 1967, the Clean Air Act and the Air Quality Act. While it was a beginning, these laws did not solve the problem. Most of the earlier acts encouraged the individual states to eatablish environmental controls by supplying federal funding. Later acts establish minimum standards for clean air or water with which the states had to comply, but the implementation and enforcement of the laws was left to the individual states. In some cases, national standards were set and enforced. For example, the amendment to the Clean Air Act permitted national regulation of air pollution from new motor vehicles.

Many people felt that hope for the future was seen with the passage of the National Environmental Protection Act, which became effective January 1, 1970. It established an Environmental Protection Agency to administer the law, which reports directly to the President. One of its major provisions is to require agencies of the federal government (or those engaging in projects funded by the federal government) to file "impact reports" outlining the environmental effect of any new proposal endorsed by the agency. The law also permits individuals to bring private suits to force agencies to file such reports, or to clarify or expand those already filed or to challenge the accuracy of the reports.

The importance of suits by individuals and environmental groups cannot be overemphasized. If the environmental movement is to succeed, it will do so only if an informed and concerned public force the government to take effective steps to deal with the problem. One way to do this is through the courts.

A seeming blow to suits of this type appeared to be given by the U.S. Supreme Court in *Sierra Club v. Morton,* 405 U.S. 727 (1972). In that case, the Sierra Club sought a declaratory judgment that a plan to develop Mineral King Valley as a ski resort in California, violated federal laws governing the preservation of national parks etc. A restraining injunction was also sought. The lower court granted the injunction. The appeals court and eventually the U.S. Supreme Court held that the Plaintiff had no standing to sue. The Sierra Club sought to bring the suit on as a "public action" case, i.e. they were protesting harm to the general public, rather than alleging injury to the club directly or to one of its members. The high court held that for the plaintiff to succeed it must allege that it has suffered or will suffer an injury from the defendant's action. The injury, the court said quoting an earlier case, did not necessarily have to be economic, but "may reflect aesthetic, conservational and recreational as well as economic values". The injury must be to an interest which was to be protected by the statute claimed to have been violated. The question of the degree of injury which must be involved was not answered.

Many feel the question was answered in *U.S. v. Students Challenging Regulatory Agency Procedures,* 412 U.S. 669, decided a year later. There, recovery was allowed the plaintiffs who did allege an actual injury. SCRAP sought an injunction against enforcement of an ICC order allowing a temporary surcharge on freight rates, until the permanent rates were increased. The students charged that the order was unlawful because it failed to include an impact statement as required by the National Environmental Policy Act. They alleged that each of their members would be injured by the detrimental environmental impact that the increased rates would have on the forests and other natural resources in the Washington area, since they used such forests, mountains and streams. They based their claim of injury on the following chain of facts: the increase in freight rates would raise the cost of shipping recycled materials and discourage the use of recycled products; increased mining, lumbering and increased despoiling of natural resources would deprive the plaintiffs of their use. The court recognized that they had a valid claim and had alleged injury to themselves (which had not been done in the Sierra case). It seems then, that the allegation of any injury no matter how remote, will save an action from a similar result which befell the Sierra Club.

Another encouraging sign for those espousing the environmentalist cause, is that courts are beginning to award attorney fees to environmental groups who win their cases. It is very expensive to bring these suits. Also, it should be remembered that the plaintiffs rarely ask for money judgments. The usual suit requests either an injunction, mandamus or a declaratory judgment.

Environmental law is only in its infancy. What future laws will be passed cannot be predicted with accuracy. However, the need to protect our environment against misuse by consumers, industry and government, is one of the most urgent problems facing our country today.

Part Four

THE INDIVIDUAL AND SOCIETY

Chapter X
CITIZENSHIP, INDIVIDUAL RIGHTS AND DUTIES

Most of our fundamental rights as citizens come from the constitution, but that is only a starting place. In the last analysis it is the courts, particularly the U.S. Supreme Court, the interpreters of the Constitution who really decide our rights.

The Supreme Court of the last few decades have been under the leadership of Chief Justice Warren and later Chief Justice Burger.

The impact of the Warren Court on individual rights has been stunning. In its efforts to create racial and voting equality, it ventured into areas hitherto shunned by the judiciary. Its achievements have included an unprecedented extension of First Amendment Rights, as well as a "federalization" of the Bill of Rights by expanding the effect of the Fourteenth Amendment, particularly in the fields of civil rights and criminal law.

Although it has shown evidence of conservatism is some areas, notably criminal law, the Burger Court surprised some by continuing its predecessor's activist role in the desegregation of schools and achieving political equality as well as its interpretation of first amendment rights. However it remains for the future to see just how closely this court will follow the trail blazed by the Warren Court.

CITIZENSHIP AND VOTING RIGHTS

During the mid sixties the Supreme Court decided several cases dealing with the nature of citizenship. In one it held unconstitutional that section of the Immigration and Nationality Act, which imposed loss of citizenship on a naturalized citizen who had resided for three in the country of his birth. It violated the equal protection requirement of the Constitution, as native born citizens were permitted to reside in a foreign country without losing their citizenship. *Schneider v. Rusk,* 377 U.S. 533 (1964). In *Afroyim v. Rusk* 387 U.S. 253 (1967) it held that Afroyim had not lost his citizenship by voting in an Israeli election, thereby overrulling an earlier decision in the fifties.

The right to vote is essential for citizenship in a democracy such as ours. In the past decade or so, the right of suffrage has been enlarged by constitutional amendment, state and federal statutes and case law, particularly Supreme Court decisions.

Since 1960, there have been three amendments to the Constitution of the United States extending suffrage rights. The twenty-third amendment (ratified March 29, 1961), gave the residents of the District of Columbia the right to vote in presidential elections. The amendment reads as follows:

"SECTION 1. The District constituting the seat of Government of the United States shall appoint in such manner as the Congress may direct:

A number of electors of President and Vice President equal to the whole number of Senators and Representatives in Congress to which the District would be entitled if it were a State, but in no event more than the least populous state; they shall be in addition to those appointed by the states, but shall be considered, for the purpose of the election of President and Vice President, to be electors appointed by a state; and they shall meet in the District and perform such duties as provided by the twelfth article of amendment.

SECTION 2. The Congress shall have power to enforce this article by appropriate legislation."

The twenty-fourth amendment (ratified January 23, 1964) eliminated poll taxes. That amendment reads as follows:

"SECTION 1. The right of citizens of the United States to vote in any primary or other election for President or Vice President, for electors for President or Vice President, or for Senator or Representative in Congress, shall not be denied or abridged by the United States or any State by reason of failure to pay any poll tax or other tax.

SECTION 2. The Congress shall have the power to enforce this article by appropriate legislation."

Finally the twenty-sixth amendment granted the voting franchise to eighteen year olds. It reads:

"SECTION 1. The right of citizens of the United States, who are eighteen years of age or older, to vote shall not be denied or abridged by the United States or any state on account of age.

SECTION 2. The Congress shall have the power to enforce this article by appropriate legislation."

Besides these constitutional amendments federal legislation won the right for black people who were being disenfranchised, particularly in the southern states.

Perhaps the Voting Rights Act of 1965 lent the greatest impetus towards increasing these rights. It climaxed a series of legislation which began with the passage of the 1957 Civil Rights Act. This legislation sought to correct the practices that had been used to defeat the right conferred upon blacks by the fourteenth amendment. Some of these practices included employing "grandfather clauses" (a person could vote only if his grandfather could, thus eliminating many blacks whose grandfathers had been slaves); charging poll taxes and administering tests before one could qualify to vote. This last tactic was particularly insidious. Generally the question of whether one passed was in the discretion of the voting registrar. Such policies caused one justice, while commenting on the requirement that the prospective voter must give a reasonable interpretation of any section of the U.S. or state constitution, to declare that it was not a test but a trap! The 1957 Act authorized the Attorney General of the United States to bring civil suits for injunctions against either states or individuals to prevent discriminatory practices. Additional amendments, enacted in 1960, permitted a person to apply for an order stating that he was qualified to vote in an election. He was entitled to do this if it was shown that a pattern of discrimination existed towards any person of the same race in the area in which he lived. Federal referees could be appointed to speed up the process. The 1964 Civil Rights Act amending prior voting laws, provided that state officials had to have standard voting qualifications for white and black voters and that literacy tests must be wholly in writing and a copy of the test and the individual's answers to it made accessible to him. It also provided that completion of the sixth grade was a presumption of literacy.

The Voting Act of 1965 provided that no voting qualifications or procedures shall be imposed by any state or political subdivision thereof to deprive any citizen of the right to vote because of race or color. It forbade qualification tests for voting in those states found to have been using discriminatory practices concerning voting. Such states also had to obtain court approval for any change in their voting laws. The Attorney General was authorized to determine which states have had tests or other prerequisites for voting on a particular date. If the Bureau of Census showed that less than 50% of voting age residing in the state were registered or voted on a particular date or in the 1964 and 1968 presidential elections, then under the provisions of the act qualifying tests for voting would not be permitted in the area.

Such states would also be required to obtain the approval of the court before making any amendments to its voting laws.

The provisions of the 1964 Act were extended another five years by a 1970 amendment, which also eliminated literacy tests for the entire country and extended the right to vote in presidential elections to eighteen year olds. (As stated above, this provision later became a constitutional amendment.)

In recent years the legality of state and local durational requirements for voting have been questioned. It has always been held that before giving the right to vote, the state may insist that the voter is a bona fide resident of the state.

Earlier cases had held that durational limitations were permissible if the statutory requirement was "rationally related" to a legitimate legislative objective. In residency requirements, the objective was to insure that only those with a tangible interest in the outcome of an election would be entitled to vote.

In *Oregon v. Mitchell,* 400 U.S. 112 (1970), in passing upon the constitutionality of the 1970 voting amendments, the Supreme Court upheld the constitutionality of the provision abolishing state residence requirements for voting in presidential elections.

In *Dunn v. Blumstein,* 405 U.S. 330 (1972), the court took up the question of whether residence requirements for voters were invalid in state elections. The court held that such requirements are infringements upon the constitutional right to vote, the fourteenth amendment right of equal protection and the right to unrestricted travel (which the court believed to be a right within the penumbra of the first amendment). Since these constitutional rights are being limited by a statute, a compelling state interest must be shown to justify their infringement. It was contended that this residency requirement was necessary to preserve the "purity of the ballot," i.e. to prevent dual voting, or persons coming into the state temporarily and voting just to affect the outcome of a certain election. The state also claimed that the disputed one year residence requirement was necessary for a voter to become knowledgeable on the issues and candidates. The court held that these were compelling state interests but the court said that the relationship between the one year residency requirement and the intelligibility of the voter was a tenuous one, easily defeated by the threatened constitutional right. As far as election fraud was concerned, the state did have a compelling interest to prevent it but there were other means of doing this besides enforcing a one year residency requirement, particularly when it was merely established by having the prospective voter swear to it.

In Rosario v. Rockefeller (1973) a New York requirement that voters enroll in a party many months before the primary in order to vote in it, was held unconstitutional in a five to four decision. The dissenters claimed that party raiding could be prevented by a shorter enrollment deadline. In contrast, the court would not sustain an Illinois provision prohibiting a person from voting in a party's primary election if he had voted in the primary of another political party within the preceding twenty-three months.

For a long while voting and the procedures relating to it were considered solely within the realm of the individual states. When because of what it considered the gravest of injustices, the courts and the federal government entered into this realm of the law, it opened the door to controversies which will remain unsettled for some time.

DEFAMATION

Until the last decade, the law of defamation was based on common law concepts and was governed largely by statutes and decisions of the individual states. With its decision in the *New York Times Co. v. Sullivan,* the U.S. Supreme court entered the field, and in the words of Justice Powell (in *Gertz v. Robert Welch, Inc.,* 418 U.S. 323 (1974)). "has struggled for nearly a decade to define the proper accomodation between the law of defamation and the freedoms of speech and press protected by the First Amendment." That struggle has resulted in extensive changes in the law of defamation.

In the first of these decisions, *New York Times v. Sullivan,* 376 U.S. 254, a public official in Montgomery Alabama charged that an advertisement placed by civil right advocates in the New York Times, held him up to scorn and ridicule. The Supreme Court overruled the lower courts award of damages and held that a public official cannot receive damages for libel (even if the statements are false) unless actual malice on the part of the defendant is proven. The test for actual malice would be to show that the statement was made "with knowledge that it was false or with reckless disregard of whether it was false or not."

The rationale behind the court's reasoning was that to compel a publisher of official conduct to guarantee the truth of all his factual assertions would amount to an inhibition of the first amendment guarantee of freedom of the press. This case involved civil libel. The same principle was extended to criminal libel in *Garrison v. Louisiana,* 179 U.S. 64 (1964).

In 1967, the Times ruling was further extended to require that a showing of malice was required when the contested statement concerned a "public figure." The two companion cases in which the Supreme Court enunciated the rule were *Curtis Publishing Co. v. Butts* and *Associated Press v. Walker,* 388 U.S. 130. Neither case involved a public official, although they did involved persons known to the general public. Butts was the athletic director of the University of Georgia, accused in a magazine article of fixing a football game. Walker was a retired army General, at the time of the suit, having political prominence because of his interest and statements on the subject of federal government's intervention in the desegregation of schools in the south. A newspaper article accused him, among other things, of leading rioters against the federal marshals enforcing a federal court decree ordering that James Meredith, a black student, be enrolled in the University of Mississippi.

In considering the facts of the case, the court laid down the standard:

> "These similarities and differences between libel actions involving persons who are public officials and libel actions involving those circumstanced as were Butts and Walker, viewed in light of the principles of liability which are of general applicability in our society, lead us to the conclusion that libel actions of the present kind cannot be left entirely to state libel laws, unlimited by any overriding constitutional safeguard, but that the rigorous federal requirements of *New York Times* are not the only appropriate accomodation of the conflicting interests at stake. We consider and would hold that a 'public figure' who is not a public official may also recover damages for a defamatory falsehood whose substance makes substantial danger to reputation apparent, on a showing of highly unreasonable conduct constituting an extreme departure from the standards of investigation and reporting ordinarily adhered to by responsible publishers."

Applying the test of responsible reporting, the court upheld Butt's judgment against Curtis Publishing Co. and reversed Walker's judgment against the associated Press. It distinguished between the two cases on the basis of the Walker dispatch being a news release which had to be written and published quickly, whereas the Butts article, could be written more carefully and researched more thoroughly since it was for a magazine.

In 1968, in *St. Amant v. Thompson,* 390 U.S. 727, the Supreme Court again went into the question of what would be considered such reckless disregard as to constitute malice. Insufficient investigation or research would not be enough to warrant a finding of libel. In the words of the court, "There must be sufficient evidence to permit the conclusion that the defendant in fact entertained serious doubts as to the truth of his publication. Publishing with such doubts shows reckless disregard for truth or falsity and demonstrate actual malice."

The Supreme Court continued to expand the rule established in the Times case in the early seventies. (See *Greenbelt Publishing Association v. Bressler,* 398 U.S. 6 (1970), *Monitor Patriot Co. v. Roy,* 401 U.S. 265 (1971) and *Times, Inc. v. Pape.* 401 U.S. 279 (1971).

Then in 1971, the Supreme Court handed down a decision in *Rosenbloom v. Metromedia,* 403 U.S. 29, which had all the impact of the earlier New York Times opinion. The suit was brought by a Philadelphia magazine distributor for defamatory statements made in connection with a report of his arrest on an obscenity charge. The trial court's verdict for the plaintiff was overturned by the appellate court and an appeal was made to the United State's Supreme Court. This court denied the plaintiff's appeal and in so doing extended the requirement of the Times case that malice must be shown, to cases involving not just public officials and public figures, but also to private persons involved in matters of public concern. The court reasoned that "whether the person involved is a famous large scale magazine distributor or a 'private' businessman running a corner newstand has no relevance in ascertaining whether the public has an interest in the issue. We honor the commitment to robust debate on public issues, which is embodied in the First Amendment by extending constitutional protection to all discussion and communication involving matters of public or general concern, without regard to whether the persons involved are famous or anonymous . . .".

Within two years, the 'Supreme Court reversed the Rosenbloom case (or at least confined it to its facts), and refused to extend the protection of the Times case, when a private individual was defamed.

In 1974 it handed down its ruling in *Gertz v. Robert Welch, Inc.,* cited above, a defamation suit was brought by an attorney because of libellous statements printed about him in one of the defendant's publications. There was no dispute as to the libel, the statements were libel per se. The defendant claimed that by virtue of the Times and Rosenberg cases malice had to be proven.

Plaintiff had represented the family of a victim who had been shot by a policeman, in a civil suit against his assailant. There had been a well publicized criminal trial, in which the plaintiff did not participate. The defendant claimed that even though he was not directly involved with the criminal trial, his representation of the victim's family, tied him closely enough to a newsworthy event, to come within the pale of the Rosenbloom case.

The court did not agree. It distinguished between private and public persons. The latter type of persons by virtue of their activities should be expected to be covered by the media and in a sense assume the risk that an incorrect new story would be written about them.

Just as the court has a duty to preserve a free and uninhibited press, it also has the duty to see that private persons are given adequate means to seek redress when one of their most precious possessions, their reputation is impugned. Therefore it was the judgment of the court that the protection of the Times case should be extended only to publications concerning public officials and public figures.

While the court by its decision, curtailed the effect of the Rosenbloom case, it did not go back to the traditional common law doctrine of absolute liability for the tort of defamation.

The court felt that to impose on publishers an absolute liability for such publications, with truth the only defense to a defamation, did have the effect of inhibiting a free press. It therefore held that state laws could impose a liability for defamation, but it could not be an absolute one; some degree of negligence must be shown. It also declared that compensation can be allowed only for actual damages suffered by the plaintiff. *Gertz v. Robert Welch, Inc.,* is found at the end of this chapter. On reading the vigorous dissent by Justice White, the reader will obtain a general background in the common law rules on defamation and be able to judge for himself the impact of these recent decisions, on the traditional law.

DISCRIMINATION

During the last two decades the courts continued the task of desegregation, in schools, public accommodation, housing and employment.

As indicated in the chapter on Youth and the Law, courts are still continuing the assault on segregation in the schools which began with the famous *Brown* decision in 1954. Only now the battle is against de facto discrimination as well as de jure. While the majority of these cases have involved the rights of the black minority, some have dealt with discrimination against the other races.

In *Lau v. Nichols,* 414 U.S. 563 (1974) the Supreme Court agreed with the charge that the San Francisco Board of Education had violated the 1964 Civil Rights Act, by discriminating against non-English speaking Chinese school children in failing to furnish them with English language instruction classes.

Another interesting case is the DeFunis case. DeFunis, a white male was denied application to a law school, even though his grades and entrance scores were higher than some members of minority groups who had been accepted as students. The latter were accepted pursuant to a "quota system", whereby a certain proportion of students must be members of minority groups, even though their academic qualifications may not be as high as other students, denied admission. DeFunis brought a suit charging "reverse discrimination" and violation of his equal protection rights under the 14th Amendment. He won in the lower court and the school was ordered to accept him as a student. He lost an appeal and the case was headed before the Supreme court. The high court refused to hear it on the grounds that the issue before it was moot, as by the time the case came before the court, it was certain that DeFunis would graduate.

Although the Supreme Court did not have to rule on the issue of "reverse discrimination" this time, it is foreseeable that it will eventually have to do so.

Discriminatory housing and employment practices continue to occupy the attention of the courts. In 1968 the Supreme Court upheld the provisions of the 1968 Civil Rights Act prohibiting racial discrimination, private and public in the sale and rental of property, saying that "At the very least, the freedom that Congress is empowered to secure under the thirteenth amendment includes the freedom to buy whatever a white man can buy, the right to live where a white man can live. If Congress cannot say that being a free man means at least this much, then the thirteenth amendment made a promise the Nation cannot keep." *Jones v. Meyer Co.,* 392 U.S. 409.

Since then the courts have been alert to provide relief where it has observed a pattern or practice of discrimination in the sale or rental of housing. However in a recent 1977 case the Supreme Court refused to declare a zoning law unconstitutional even though it resulted in segregated housing in a suburb.

The Equal Employment Opportunity Act of 1972 expanded the 1964 Civil Rights Act coverage relating to federal employees and established an Equal Employment Opportunity Coordinating Council to implement and enforce equal employment opportunities and policies among the various federal government agencies.

Discriminatory employment practices continued to be the subject of litigation in recent years. Under attack are various educational requirements and testing programs, being used as a basis for hiring and promoting employees. It does not matter if discrimination is not the motive for these requirements. If they result in a discriminatory pattern, they are suspect. Then, as was stated in *Griggs v. Duke Power Co.*, 401 U.S. 424 (1971), it must be shown that the test or the educational requirement must be specifically related to the performance of the job. The burden of proof in these instances is upon the employer. The Guidelines of the Equal Employment Opportunity Commission set up ways in which the employer can demonstrate the usefulness of tests.

The last two decades saw a continuing effort to desegregate public accommodations, particularly in the South. Cases dealing with the interpretation of the public accommodations sections of the 1964 Civil Rights Act were heard by lower federal courts and the United States Supreme Court.

Many attempted to escape the purview of the statute by claiming to be a private club. Many failed, as in the case of *Daniel v. Paul*, 295 U.S. 298 (1969). Defendant attempted to evade the statute by advertising itself as a private club. Membership cards were sold for 25 cents. (However membership was given to all white applicants without exception and denied to all blacks.) The Supreme Court found that the operations of the club, particularly that of its snack bar, were so affected by interstate commerce that it fell within the provisions of the act. To be exempt from the Act, a club must be truly private, have a truly selective membership who control the club and services must be rendered only to its members and their guests.

The courts tried to solve some of these accommodations cases by applying the Fourteenth Amendment, which forbids unequal treatment of citizens by the state. (The Amendments to the Constitution are set forth at the end of this chapter.) To do this courts had to take a broad view of state action, not just limiting it to legislation passed by the state. See *Adickes v. Kress and Co.*, 398 U.S. 144 (1970) which held that the petitioner could show an abridgment of her right of equal protection, upon proving that she was refused service because of a state enforced *custom* of segregating the races in public restaurants. However in 1972, the concept of what constitutes state action was limited in the case of *Moose Lodge # 107 v. Irvis*, 407 U.S. 163 (1972), where in holding that the club in question was a private one, the court said: "Our holdings indicate that where the impetus for discrimination is private, the State must have significantly involved itself with invidious discrimination in order for the discriminating action to fall within the ambit of the constitutional prohibition."

This narrow view of state involvement was continued in *Palmer v. Thompson*, 403 U.S. 217 (1971) in which the court refused to force Jackson Mississippi to reopen its public swimming pools. The city had closed both white and black pools, rather than integrate them. The court declined to look into the motivation behind the law closing the pools stating that the facts show no state action affecting blacks differently from whites. However in 1974 in *Gilmore v. City of Montgomery,* 417 U.S. 356, the court refused to sanction the city's giving a private segregated academy exclusive use and control of a city-owned facility for athletic and recreation activities, saying that to do so would create enclaves of segregation within the city at a time when the city was under court order to desegregate its recreational facilities.

FREEDOM OF RELIGION

The first amendment states that "Congress shall make no law respecting an establishment of religion, or prohibiting the free exercise thereof . . " Throughout the years legal disputes concerning religion have fallen into two categories, those dealing with religious liberty and those concerned with the separation of church and state. In the past few decades most of the Supreme Court decisions have dealt with separation of church and state, usually taking up the problem of state aid to private schools. These will be discussed later on. First let us look at some of the cases relating to religious liberty.

The Viet Nam war was the occasion of several of these decisions. It was sought to be determined whether the term "conscientious objector" could be applied to one not a member of an established religion. In *United States v. Seeger*, 380 U.S. 163 (1965), it said one was entitled to an exempt status, provided the belief that prompted him to reject wars, was "a sincere and meaningful one which occupies in the life of its possessor, a place parallel to that filed by the God of those admittedly qualifying for the exemption."

In *Gillette v. U.S. and Negre v. Larsen,* 401 U.S. 437 (1971), the Supreme Court rejected the view that the exemption applied only to those who did not believe in any wars, holding that one who objected only to "unjust wars" was also entitled to a conscientious objector status.

Eventually the conscientious objection provision of the Universal Military Training and Service Act was amended to reflect the spirit of these decisions. A presidential order to draft boards resulted in objectors to the war being assigned to civilian work promoting the national interest for a period equivalent to that which they would have been obliged to serve in military service. A recent case would not extend veteran's education rights to those who had served civilian alternative to military service.

Conflict between religious beliefs and state statutes were explored in *Sherbert v. Verner*, 374 U.S. 398 (1963) and *Wisconsin v. Yoder*, 406 U.S. 205 (1972).

In the Sherbert case a Seventh Day Adventist was denied unemployment compensation because she refused to accept employment requiring her to work on Saturday, her religion's Sabbath. Repeating the fundamental principle that "only the gravest abuses, endangering paramount interests give occasion for permissible limitation" of religious freedom, the court declared that no one should be deprived of benefits from public warfare legislation because of their religious beliefs.

In the case of *Wisconsin v. Yoder,* members of the Amish sect refused to send their children to public high school, as required by law. They claimed that to do so would expose their children to wordly experiences which would diminish and destroy their religious beliefs. Instead they set up their own vocational schools within their own community to comply with the education law. The high court ruled that to require Amish parents to send their children to public schools would substantially interfere with their religious liberty. It stated that the Amish had a history of three centuries "as an identifiable religious sect" and a long history as successful and self-sufficient segment of American society and that they had convincingly demonstrated the sincerity of their religious beliefs and that their mode of life was essential to the practice of their religion. Noting that there was but a minimal difference between the state educational requirements and that required by the Amish in their schools, the court held that there was no compelling state interest in requiring the Amish children to go to state schools. Answering a contention in Justice Douglas' dissenting opinion that the state had a duty to protect children from parents who wished to impose their religious beliefs upon them, the majority stated:

> "Indeed it seems clear that if the State is empowered, as *parens patriae,* to 'save' a child from himself or his Amish parents by requiring an additional two years of compulsory formal high school education, the State will in large measure influence, if not determine, the religious future of the child . . . . Therefore, this case involves the fundamental interest of parents, as contrasted with that of the State, to guide the religious

future and education of their children. The history and culture of Western civilization reflect a strong tradition of parental concern for the nurture and upbringing of their children. This primary role of the parents in the upbringing of their children is now established beyond debate as an enduring American tradition."

Controversies concerning the separation of church and state doctrine centered around schools.

The most famous of these cases was *Engle v. Vitale*, 370 U.S. 421 (1962). In that case, the court held that a prayer adopted by the New York Board of Regents violated the establishment clause of the First Amendment. Stating that it was unconstitutional for a prayer to be prepared and sponsored by a governmental body, the court reasoned:

" . . . The First Amendment was added to the Constitution . . . as a guarantee that neither the power nor the prestige of the Federal Government would be used to control, support, or influence the kinds of prayer the American people can say. . . . It is no part of the business of government to compose official prayers for any group . . . to recite as part of a religious program carried on by the government. . . . Neither the fact that the prayer may be denominationally neutral, nor . . . that its observance . . . is voluntary can serve to free it from the limitations of the Establishment Clause. . . . It is neither sacrilegious nor antireligious to say that each separate government in this country should stay out of the business of writing or sanctioning official prayers and leave that purely religious function to the people themselves and to those the people choose to look to for religious guidance."

The following year in *Abington School District v. Schempp,* 374 U.S. 203 (1963), the Supreme Court held that Pennsylvania's statute requiring Bible reading in the public schools and Maryland's requirement for recitation of the Lord's Prayer or Bible reading at the start of the school day were unconstitutional. The Court stressed once again the necessity of the government retaining neutrality with respect to religious matters. It said:

"The place of religion in our society is an exalted one, achieved through a long tradition of reliance on the home, the church and the inviolable citadel of the individual heart and mind. We have come to recognize through bitter experience that it is not within the power of government to invade that citadel

. . . In the relationship between man and religion, the state is firmly committed to a position of neutrality."

Quite a furor was stirred up by these decisions. There was talk of amending the Constitution to permit prayer in the schools, but this amendment never materialized. It was thought that these decisions might result in suits seeking to ban other common practices with religious overtones such as opening legislatures with prayers, or depicting the Christmas Nativity scene in schools or other governmentally controlled areas. There have been assaults in the state and lower federal courts, with decisions going both ways. To date the Supreme Court has not ruled on any of these sensitive areas.

During the last decade the question of whether state aid could be given to private schools continued to plague the court. In *Everson v. Board of Education,* a case upholding the constitutionality of the state furnishing bus transportation to parochial schools the court devised the test to be used:

"The test may be stated as follows: what are the purpose and the primary effect of the enactment? If either is the advancement or inhibition of religion then the enactment exceeds the scope of legislative power as circumscribed by the Constitution. That is to say that to withstand the strictures of the Establishment Clause there must be a secular legislative purpose and a primary effect that neither advances nor inhibits religion."

Using this test, the court allowed loans of text books to private schools, but struck down proposed state plans to reimburse private schools for secular services furnished by them. Adding another test to that set forth in Everson, the avoidance of excessive entanglements between church and state, it upheld the giving of government aid in the construction of buildings, to private institutions of higher learning. Let's look at some of the cases.

New York had enacted a statute requiring local school boards to provide a free loan of books to students in grades seven through twelve in both public and parochial schools as well as other private schools. *In Board of Education v. Allen,* 392 U.S. 236 (1968) its constitutionality was challenged on the grounds that it violated the constitutional tenet of separation of church and state. The constitutionality was upheld on the "child benefit" theory which had been employed in earlier cases concerning loans of text books and bus transportation for children in non-public schools. Stressing that even though the principal of the school had the right to choose what books would be used, no evidence was given that any of the books used were for the purpose of teaching religion. Justice White who delivered the opinion of the court held that the law had a secular legislative purpose, and a primary effect that neither inhibits or advances religion. The law ran to the benefit of the children and their parents, not the school. Dissents were made by justices Black, Douglas and Fortas, who objected to the schools having the right to choose the books used and felt that they would pick books which would be in furtherance of religion.

However the Supreme Court struck down Pennsylvania and Rhode Island plans to reimburse private schools with state funds for secular services furnished by them in *Lemon v. Kurtzman, Early v. Dicenso* and *Robinson v. Dicenso* (403 U.S. 602 (1971)). These cases applied another test in addition to that previously mentioned, (i.e. that the primary purpose and effect of the legislation authorizing the state aid is secular). This test was that excessive entanglements between the state and religion must be avoided.

The "excessive entanglement" test was also used in *Waltz v. Tax Commission*, 397 U.S. 664 (1970). In that case, a tax payer brought a suit to prevent the state of New York from granting tax exemptions to religious organizations as such aid violated the first amendment's prohibition against establishing a religion. The majority of the court in an opinion given by Chief Justice Burger disagreed. He pointed out that "The court has struggled to find a neutral course between the two Religion Clauses, (prohibition against establishment of religion and the guaranteeing of religious freedom), both of which are cast in absolute terms and either of which, if expanded to a logical extreme, would tend to clash with the other. . . ." No individual religion was aided by the exemption; it applied to all relgions. The tax exemption did not result in the establishment of a religion, indeed, "the exemption created only a minimal and remote involvement between the church and state. . ." By restricting the fiscal relationship between the two, excessive entanglements are avoided.

In the Dicenso case, cited above, the Pennsylvania Statute authorized the State Superintendent of Public Instruction to purchase secular educational services from non public schools. The Rhode Island Statute provided for a 15% salary supplement to be paid to teachers in non-public schools where the payment per child on secular subjects was below the average paid in public schools. The court found that enforcing these statutes would require "excessive entanglement" of church and state. Tuition reimbursement plans were also struck down in Committee for *Public Education v. Nyquist* 413 U.S. 756 and *Sloan v. Lemon*, 413 U.S. 825 (1973).

However in *Tilton v. Richardson,* 403 U.S. 672 (1971), the Supreme Court found that aid given to non-public institutions of higher learning pursuant to a federal statute authorizing such assistance for the purpose of constructing educational facilities, was not unconstitutional, and would not result in excessive entanglements. There are several distinctions between this case and the tuition refund cases mentioned above. In this case the aid was for constructing facilities whereas the other was for paying teachers' salaries. Teachers would be apt to influence the minds of students; buildings would not. Another significant factor is, that this case involves institutions on the college and graduate levels. Students attending them would be less susceptible to influence than those on the primary and secondary level. The court also seemed to be influenced by the fact that payment of funds was made only once in this case, whereas in the reimbursement plans a series of payments was anticipated, and continued surveillance by the state would be required. Similar aid was held constitutional in *Hunt v. McNair,* 413 U.S. 734.

Undoubtedly the Supreme Court will continue to hear cases concerning religious liberty and the separation of church and state. The battle between those seeking aid to non-public schools and those who oppose it will continue, particularly now that many of the cities are undergoing a financial crisis. As the court said in *The Committee for Public Education v. Nyquist,* "We do not question the propriety . . . of New York's interest in preserving a healthy and safe educational environment for all of its school children. And we do not doubt — indeed we fully recognize — the validity of the state's interest in promoting pluralism and diversity among its public and non-public schools. Nor do we hesitate to acknowledge the reality of its concern for an already overburdened public school system that might suffer in the event that a significant percentage of children presently attending non-public schools should abandon those schools in favor of public schools."

FREEDOM OF SPEECH

The first amendment of the constitution of the United States reads in part,

"Congress shall make no law . . . abridging the freedom of speech, or of the press; or of the right of the people to peaceably assemble . . . "

Freedom of speech is one of our most precious rights. Most courts are usually reluctant to place any limitations upon it. Yet there are some instances when it must be restricted. Freedom of speech will generally be curtailed if it defames, is obscene or if the public safety requires it.

Deciding when the public safety requires curtailment of speech, is sometimes difficult. Through the years various theories have evolved.

One was the "clear and present danger" theory expressed by Justice Holmes in an espionage case, shortly after World War I. Giving the famous example that a man is not free to falsely shout "Fire!" in a crowded theater, thereby causing a panic, he continued, "The question in every case is whether the words used are used in such circumstances and are of such a nature as to create a clear and present danger that they will bring about the substantive evils that Congress has a right to prevent. It is a question of proximity and degree. . . ."

There are some, such as Justice Douglas, who believe that the right to free speech is absolute and should never be curtailed.

Then there is the "balancing theory", which considers the question in each particular instance whether the benefit to the common good in suppressing the speech outweighs the individual's need to express himself.

Finally there is the "preferred freedom" concept, which holds that only a *compelling* state interest can justify restriction of speech. This concept can be seen in the so called "prior restraint" cases. The Supreme Court employed this concept when it refused to enjoin the publication of classified material showing United States involvement in Viet Nam. To take such drastic action, the court required a showing that the publication would result in direct, immediate and irreparable harm to the Nation or its people. A showing that this was *possible*, was not enough. *New York Times v. US.,* 403 U.S. 713.

Another question which the court has to consider is what is speech. In some holdings the court has classified certain actions as "symbolic speech" and grant them the same protection that is afforded to actual speech. Thus students wearing black armbands, protesting the Viet Nam war were protected. A conviction for offensive conduct was overturned, when the act complained of, consisted of wearing a jacket on the back of which was written a four letter word condemning the draft. *Cohen v. California,* 403 U.S. 15 (1971). The court regarded the act as one of symbolic speech.

In determining whether it is necessary for the public good to limit freedom of speech, the court usually takes into consideration the time, place and manner of speaking. Therefore a quiet vigil by protestors in a library was permitted, (*Brown v. La.,* 383 U.S. 131 (1966)) but a jail yard was not considered advisable as it was likely to cause a disruption among the prisoners. (*Adderly v. Florida,* 383 U.S. 39 (1966)).

The court will not protect "fighting words", that is, speech liable to start a riot. However, this must be clearly proven. In *Cox v. La.,* 379 U.S. 559 (1965) the arrests of peaceful demonstrators, was held unconstitutional. The defense that hostile bystanders might resort to violence did not justify their arrest. The statute under which they were arrested was so vague that it could result in arrests for expressions of any unpopular belief.

The prevalence of civil rights and anti-war demonstrations have focused upon the questions of whether demonstrations are permissible, where they can be held and to what extent may the government pass statutes curtailing them.

The government clearly has an interest in protecting the safety of its citizens and in maintaining an orderly flow of traffic on its streets. Therefore it is not in violation of the constitution to require permits to be obtained to march in the streets. However the requirements for obtaining these permits must be specific and the granting of them may not be arbitrary. *(Shuttleworth v. City of Birmingham,* 394 U.S. 747, (1969) and *Gregory v. City of Chicago,* 394 U.S. 111 (1969)).

Generally speaking if a demonstration is quiet and orderly and does not obstruct the flow of traffic, it may be conducted in a public place.

While upholding the right to assemble or hand out leaflets in public areas, the courts have been reluctant to grant this right with respect to private areas. However, in the Logan Valley Plaza case, the court did hold it was proper for picketers to distribute leaflets on the streets of a privately owned shopping center, reasoning that the center served the same purpose as a public business district (391 U.S. 308 (1968). Yet it would not extend this ruling in *Lloyde Corp. v. Tanner,* which it heard a year later (407 U.S. 551). In that case it held that anti-war protesters were not deprived of their constitutional rights when they were prohibited from distributing leaflets in a privately owned shopping center. The two cases were distinguishable, because since the first case involved picketing of the businesses in the shopping center, it was essential to the success of the picketing that it take place in that area. The anti-war demonstration could have been just as effective in any other area.

In *Roth v. U.S.,* 354 U.S. 476 (1957), the Supreme Court stated that obscenity was not protected by the First Amendment, thus beginning a struggle, which has continued to the present day — to devise tests that can be applied to determine when material is obscene.

The Roth cases itself attempted to lay down some principles. "... sex and obscenity are not synonomous", it said. "Obscene material is material which deals with sex in a manner appealing to prurient interest. The portrayal of sex, e.g. in art, literature and scientific works, is not itself sufficient reason to deny material the constitutional protection of freedom of speech and press. Sex, a great and mysterious motive force in human life, has indisputably been a subject of absorbing interest to mankind through the ages; it is one of the vital problems of human interest and public concern."

The standard to be applied, for determining obscenity was whether "to the average person, applying contemporary community standards, the dominant theme of the material as a whole appeals to prurient interest."

Another test was given in *Memoirs v. Massachusetts,* 383 U.S. 413 (1966), the court reversed a lower court's decision that the book, Fanny Hill was obscene, holding that the book was not utterly without redeeming social value. Three elements must be found for a work to be obscene, "It must be established that (a) the dominant theme of the material taken as a whole appeals to a prurient interest in sex; (b) the material is patently offensive because it affronts contemporary community standards relating to the description or representation of sexual matters; and (2) the material is utterly without redeeming social value.

In *Ginzburg v. United States,* 383 U.S. 463, the court made methods of advertising part of the criteria for obscenity. In this case the material disseminated was not of itself obscene but the advertising accompanying the publications deliberately pandered to the baser interests of the reader. As put by the court, "Where an exploitation of interests in titilation by pornography is shown with respect to material lending itself to such exploitation through pervasive treatment or description of sexual matters, such evidence may support the determination that the material is obscene even though in other contexts the material would escape such condemnation. . ."

In *Stanley v. Georgia,* 394 U.S. 557 (1969) it was held that persons had a constitutional right to view obscene material in the privacy of their own home. However the court refused to extend this protection to the distribution of obscene material through the mails to adults who have requested it, (*U.S. v. Reidel,* 407 U.S. 351 (1971)). The court had also ruled that the state had the power to enjoin showing of obscene materials in "adult" theaters and importation of obscene films even if only for private use may be prohibited. *Paris Adult Theater I v. Slaton,* 189 S. Ct. 2628 and *U.S. v. 12,200 Reels,* 93 S. Ct. 2665).

Finally in *Miller v. California,* (1973), the Supreme Court reviewed the rulings on obscenity and acknowledging "the inherent dangers of undertaking to regulate any form of expression", ruled that state statutes designed to regulate such material must be carefully drawn. The court noted that the Oregon and Hawaii statutes were drawn in a careful manner. It established a new test for obscenity. The court said: "We now confine the permissible scope of such regulation to works which depict or describe sexual conduct. The conduct must be specifically defined by the applicable State law. . . A state offense must also be limited to works which, taken as a whole, appeal to the prurient interest in sex, and portray sexual conduct in a patently offensive way, and which, taken as a whole, do not have serious literary, artistic, political or scientific value." In determining whether obscenity exists, contemporary community standards, not national ones are to be applied. It is interesting to note that Justice Brennan, who wrote both the Roth and Memoirs decisions, dissented commenting on the futility of trying to define obscenity and still give adequate first amendment protection. Whether the court will ever be successful in devising an adequate test for obscenity remains to be seen. Certainly most would agree that minors, at least should be protected from hard core obscenity, but in a world of changing morals it is very difficult to define obscenity in a way which would be satisfactory to everyone.

PRIVACY

In 1890, an article appeared in the *Harvard Law Review,* entitled, "The Right to Privacy." In it the authors, Warren and Brandeis, maintained that there was a common law right of privacy which had evolved through the years. The article is a classic, and the laws relating to privacy are still evolving today. New technological advances have made it possible to invade on one's personal privacy in ways undreamed of by Warren and Brandeis. Privacy may be invaded by either the individual or the state.

There are many facets to the law of privacy. Some as indicated before regard it as a common law right. This is usually the theory invoked when privacy is invaded by private persons rather than the state. There are some that maintain that there is a constitutional right of privacy. They base this contention on the provisions of the fourth amendment which grants persons the right to be secure in their persons, houses, papers and effects against unreasonable searches and seizures. This aspect of privacy will be covered in another chapter relating to criminal law. Another theory holds that although the right of privacy is not specifically guaranteed by the Constitution, it falls within the shadow of several of its amendments. Justice Douglas set forth this "penumbra theory" in *Giswold v. Connecticut.*

The common law right of privacy differs from state to state. Some states, such as Texas do not recognize the common law right of privacy at all. In others such as New York, Virginia and Oklahoma, the right is a statutory one. Usually the statute enjoins the use of a person's name, photograph etc. being used for commercial purposes. The New York Civil Rights Law reads as follows:

"Right of privacy
A person, firm or corporation that uses for advertising purposes, or for the purposes of trade, the name, portrait or picture of any living person without having first obtained the written consent of such person, or if a minor of his or her parent or guardian, is guilty of a misdemeanor." (Sec. 50)

"Personnel records of police officers
1. All personnel records, used to evaluate performance toward continued employment or promotion, under the control of any police agency or department of the state or any political subdivision thereof including authorities or agencies maintaining police forces of individuals defined as police officers in section 1.20 of the criminal procedure law shall be considered confidential and not subject to inspection or review without the express written consent of such police officer except as may be mandated by lawful court order.

2. Prior to issuing such court order the judge must review all such requests and give interested parties the opportunity to be heard. No such order shall issue without a clear showing of facts sufficient to warrant the judge to request records for review.

3. If, after such hearing, the judge concludes there is a sufficient basis he shall sign an order requiring that the personnel records in question be sealed and sent directly to him. He shall then review the file and make a determination as to whether the records are relevant and material in the action before him. Upon such a finding the court shall make those parts of the record found to be relevant and material available to the persons so requesting.

4. The provisions of this section shall not apply to any district attorney or his assistants, the attorney general or his deputies or assistants, a grand jury, or any agency of government which requires the records described in subdivision one, in the furtherance of their official functions." (Sec. 50-a)

"Action for injunction and for damages

Any person whose name, portrait or picture is used within this state for advertising purposes or for the purposes of trade without the written consent first obtained as above provided may maintain an equitable action in the supreme court of this state against the person, firm or corporation so using his name, portrait or picture, to prevent and restrain the use thereof; and may also sue and recover damages for any injuries sustained by reason of such use and if the defendant shall have knowingly used such person's name, portrait or picture in such manner as is forbidden or declared to be unlawful by the last section, the jury, in its discretion, may award exemplary damages. But nothing contained in this act shall be so construed as to prevent any person, firm or corporation, practicing the profession of photography, from exhibiting in or about his or its establishment specimens of the work of such establishment, unless the same is continued by such person, firm or corporation after written notice objecting thereto has been given by the person portrayed; and nothing contained in this act shall be so construed as to prevent any person, firm or corporation from using the name, portrait or picture of any manufacturer or dealer in connection with the goods, wares and merchandise manufactured, produced or dealt in by him which he has sold or disposed of with such name, portrait or picture used in connection therewith; or from using the name, portrait or picture of any author, composer or artist in connection with his literary, musical or artistic productions which he has sold or disposed of with such name, portrait or picture used in connection therewith" (Sec. 51)

"Televising, broadcasting or taking motion pictures of
  certain proceedings prohibited

No person, firm, association or corporation shall televise, broadcast, take motion pictures or arrange for the televising, broadcasting, or taking of motion pictures within this state of proceedings, in which the testimony of witnesses by subpoena or other compulsory process is or may be taken, conducted by a court, commission, committee, administrative agency or other tribunal in this state; except that the prohibition contained in this section shall not apply to public hearings conducted by the public service commission with regard to rates charged by utilities, or to proceedings by either house of the state legislature or committee or joint committee of the legislature or by a temporary state commission which includes members of the legislature, so long as any testimony of witnesses which is taken is taken without resort to subpoena or other compulsory process, if (1) the consent of the temporary president of the senate or the speaker of the assembly, in the case of the respective houses of the state legislature, or the chairman, in the case of such a committee or commission, and majority of the members thereof present at such proceedings, shall have been first obtained, provided, however, that in the case of the public rate hearings of the public service commission, it shall be sufficient to obtain the consent of the presiding officer, (2) the written consent of the witness testifying at the time shall have been obtained, prior to the time of his testifying, and (3) it has been determined by such presiding officer or chairman and such majority of the members that it is in the public interest to permit the televising, broadcasting or taking of motion pictures." (Sec. 52)

The law of privacy is still developing and is still somewhat in the nebulous stage, and it is sometimes difficult to predict the outcome of a suit. There are some tests that may be used. The court sometimes examines the motives behind the invasion. Usually if it is for commercial exploitation as opposed to offering newsworthy information to the public, an invasion of privacy will be found. It also examines the method of invading the privacy, and usually if the methods are found to be unscrupulous, or if the plaintiff is found to be physically or psychologically harrassed by them, again it is fairly safe to assume that an invasion of privacy will be found.

There are certain areas where the law of privacy and defamation overlap. While truth is a justification in a defamation suit, it is not in a privacy suit. Defamation involves injury to one's reputation. Privacy is not concerned with this, but merely seeks to enforce the individual's right to be left alone.

Many of the problems arise when the person claiming invasion of privacy is a public figure. Granted that he has assumed the risk of the invasion of privacy by becoming a public figure. However there are two types of public figures, those who actively seek the limelight and those who are drawn into it by circumstances beyond their control.

With regard to the first type of person there are certain private intimate details of their lives about which the public is not entitled to know. Even this area of protection is changing, as the public mores change. In former years to state that a couple were living together without the benefit of the laws of matrimony would be an invasion of privacy. Today, where this is beginning to be regarded as permissible in some segments of our society, perhaps it might not be so regarded.

Problems also arise with respect to the second type of person, the one who is thrust into the glare of publicity through no effort of his own. In *Hill v. Time Inc.*, a family who had been held hostage by fugitives from the law, tried to enjoin a publication concerning a play, supposedly fictitious but obviously based on their experience. Their recovery was denied because the court applying the same rules followed in defamation cases, regarded them as public figures and held that to recover malice must be proven. See the discussion of this rule under the Defamation section of this chapter.

A question also arises as to how long a public figure remains one for the purpose of bringing suit with respect to invasion of privacy. A famous case on this point involved a former child prodigy. An article was written twenty years later telling of the author's visit with the former prodigy, who now led a rather reclusive life and commented on certain of his eccentricities. The court refused to compensate the plaintiff for invasion of his privacy. Apparently the court felt that the former child prodigy was still newsworthy.

Another aspect of the law of privacy is that of "privileged communications". There are some conversations about which one can not be compelled to testify.

Traditionally the common law has always recognized that conversations between husband and wife or attorney and client are privileged. Communications between priest and penitent are also privileged. This dates back to the Roman Catholic doctrine of the seal of the confession, whereby the priest is forbidden to divulge any information obtained in the confessional. Most states have codified these three ancient privileges. In the case of the latter immunity is not confined to confessional matters but applies to any communication to a clergyman by one seeking his aid. Although not privileged at common law, communications between physician and patient are privileged in some states. Some states have statutes granting this privilege to communications between psychologists and accountants and their clients.

In recent years there has been a growing belief that information obtained by newsman should be regarded as a privileged communication and that he should not be compelled to testify concerning it. The first amendment of freedom of the press is considered the basis of this privilege. The theory is that if newsmen are required to divulge information given them in confidence by their sources, they will cease receiving such information and thus the freedom of the press could be diminished. Lower court cases seemed to go both ways on this point. However in *Branzburg v. Hayes,* 408 U.S. 665 (1972), the Supreme Court held that newsmen could be compelled to testify before a grand jury as to information received in confidence.

The law relating to privacy is in a transitional stage. It will undoubtedly be litigated for some years to come. The trend towards recognizing a right of privacy will inevitably come into conflict with a growing trend towards less restrictions on the freedom of the press. It will be interesting to see what the outcome will be.

Chapter XI
PROTECTION THROUGH THE LAW: CIVIL

COMPARATIVE NEGLIGENCE

For years, many states have followed the contributory negligence theory of law. Under this theory, before a plaintiff can recover in a negligence action, he must prove not only that the defendant was negligent towards him and that such negligence was the proximate cause of his injury, but his own negligence could not have been a contributing cause to the accident. Even one percent negligence on his part could bar recovery.

In most states, contributory negligence can be pleaded as a defense to a negligence action by a defendant. However, in some states (such as in New York several years ago), a harsher rule was followed. The plaintiff had the burden of proving freedom from contributory negligence in order to sustain a cause of action in negligence.

Gradually, states have been turning away from the contributory negligence rule to that of comparative negligence. Basically, comparative negligence means that even though the plaintiff has himself been negligent he may recover in his suit, but his damages will be reduced in proportion to his negligence. A few states such as Nebraska and South Dakota permit recovery only if the defendant is grossly negligent and the plaintiff only slightly negligent.

CONSORTIUM, LOSS OF

Usually when a wife was injured, the husband was granted the right to sue for loss of consortium (loss of services and companionship). Women were not given the same right. Today, many states now permit the wife to sue for loss of consortium.

EMOTIONAL DISTRESS, RECOVERY FOR

In the past, courts have been reluctant to grant recovery for emotional distress. Gradually, recovery for such damages is being allowed.

At first, some courts allowed recovered for emotional distress only if it was accompanied by a physical impact no matter how slight. Courts felt it was necessary to require proof of some sort of impact to avoid a flood of fraudulent suits.

Gradually, courts are abandoning the impact theory in favor of another theory, sometimes referred to as "the zone of danger" principle. Under this latter principle, recovery is allowed even without physical contact, if plaintiff was placed in actual foreseeable danger by the negligence of the defendant. An example would be: A and B were walking along a highway; the defendant's negligently driven car bears down upon them, hitting A and barely missing B. In a jurisdiction adhering to the "zone of danger" theory, B would be entitled to recover for emotional distress, since the driver of the car had placed him in a position in which he was in grave fear of physical injury.

Some courts, before awarding a judgment for emotional distress, require a finding of physical injury as a result of the stress, e.g. a heart attack, or at least some physical manifestation of stress, such as vomiting as a result of the shock. Some courts also emphasize, that the plaintiff should be a person of normal sensibilities and not someone readily susceptible to shock.

Some courts have also taken up the question of whether someone can recover for emotional distress intentionally inflicted. (The cases referred to above were concerned with distress caused by the negligence of the defendant.) Some courts have permitted recovery if the conduct inducing the distress was such that it could be considered extremely outrageous and humiliating to the plaintiff. Whether defendant's conduct meets such criteria has been held to be a question of fact for the jury.

Will recovery be allowed for emotional distress suffered by a third party as a result of witnessing an accident resulting in injury to another. So far courts have been divided on the subject.

Waube v. Warrington, 216 Wis 604, an earlier leading case on the subject decided in 1935, pinpointed the problems involved in such cases. It refused to grant damages to a mother for the emotional shock sustained as a result of witnessing the death of her child. The mother was in no danger herself. The court held that to extend liability to include such emotional distress to a third party would be "wholly out of proportion to the culpability of the negligent tort feasor and would put an unreasonable burden upon users of the highway, open the way to fraudulent claims and enter a field that has no sensible or just stopping point."

Since then, some courts have tried to determine how some of these obstacles could be avoided. One such case was *Archibald v. Braverman,* 275 Cal App 2d 253 (1969). The defendant had sold plaintiff's son some explosives which plaintiff alleged were defective due to defendant's negligence and which exploded, amputating part of the boy's arm and inflicting other injuries. Plaintiff arrived moments later and as a result of viewing her son suffered severe emotional shock which resulted in later being confined for mental illness. The court allowed plaintiff's recovery, relying on the rules set forth in an earlier case, *Dillon v. Legg,* 68 Cal 2d 728 (1968), which ruled that recovery should be allowed in such cases if plaintiff was near the scene of the accident, the shock suffered by plaintiff resulted from actually seeing the accident, and the plaintiff was a close relative of the victim. In the *Archibald* case, even though the plaintiff was not there at the exact moment of the explosion, she arrived only moments later and the court considered the shock to be contemporaneous enough with the action to fulfil the test noted above.

Not all courts would arrive at the same results. In *Tobin v. Grossman,* 301 N.Y.S. 2d 554, a New York court reached the opposite conclusion on a similar set of facts. One essential element of a negligence action is that it was foreseeable (or should have been) that defendant's negligence would harm the plaintiff. To allow a recovery of this type to a third party, (even if a parent) seemed to New York to stretch the limits of foreseeability too far.

Courts are divided both ways on the issue of granting relief for emotional distress. This is undoubtedly an issue which will be litigated in the years to come.

LANDOWNERS—LIABILITY FOR NEGLIGENCE

In common law, when someone was injured while on another's property, the extent of the landowner's liability was based primarily on the status of the injured party. Most states still continue to base liability on the common law distinctions, but as we shall see, recently, the law has undergone some changes.

An owner (or person in possession of the premises) was not liable to a trespasser on his land, even if it was in unsafe condition. There were some exceptions to this general rule. If the owner had knowledge of frequent trespassing, he had to keep his land safe and if he actually knew that a trespasser was on his land and could be warned of an unsafe condition, he was required to do so.

In recent years, the greatest exception to this rule has been "the attractive nuisance" doctrine which has been accepted by a great many states. This rule applies to children who are trespassers. Simply stated, the rule is that if anyone has something (e.g. swimming pool, or deserted well), which is particularly enticing to children, he has a duty to take reasonable precautions to be certain that trespassing children will not be harmed by it. In deciding such cases, courts usually take several factors into consideration, such as whether children are likely to trespass upon the property, whether they would be unaware of the danger, whether the condition would involve unreasonable risk of serious harm to children and whether the advantages of having this dangerous condition on the land outweigh its possible risk to children.

The other types of persons entering the land of another are variously described as licensees or invitees. When one just takes a short cut through the land or is not on the land for a business purpose, the owner has a duty to warn them of hazardous conditions they would not know about. The highest duty of all was to the invitee, particularly the business invitee. As to these, the owner must not only warn them of actual dangers he knows about, but also of dangers he should have known about had he exercised reasonable care.

Recently courts have begun to reject the stringent applications of these rules too many of which smack of feudalism and seem too artificial to be applied in the twentieth century. Instead, the general negligence rule of reasonable care is being applied. Nevertheless, the old common law distinctions as to the types of visitors are not discarded completely. Even those courts which believe that a reasonable standard of care should be the criterion, find that the status of a visitor is a factor to be determined in establishing what would be reasonable care.

NO FAULT AUTOMOBILE INSURANCE

Since the first use of automobiles in America, until recent times, the legal result of an accident causing personal injury was that the person held to be legally liable by reason of his negligence would be required to pay damages to the injured party. To provide against such contingencies, most people carry automobile liability insurance. In many states they are compelled to do so.

As the costs of such insurance has risen over the years, and as court calendars became increasingly crowded, it became clear that revolutionary changes in the automobile insurance laws would be required.

This step was taken by the enactment of the so called "no fault automobile insurance". Under the old law an injured person was required to sue the driver (and his insurance company). Recovery would be denied unless the drive was negligent or "at fault".

Under the new law it is not necessary to prove any negligence or fault to be successful in your claim. The person, who is injured will receive his benefits, not from the other drivers insurance company, but from his own. This eliminates the possibility of going to court to sue the party at fault. Thus the term, "no fault insurance."

However, suits are allowed by statute in states that have enacted no fault insurance laws against the party at fault if the medical bills exceed a specified figure. Such medical amounts range between $400 and $1,000 as a general rule. In addition, most states require that there be some permanent injury or disfigurement in order to collect against the party at fault.

So far, less than half of the states have adopted no fault insurance laws, but its proponents expect more to do so in the future. See charts at the end of the chapter.

To best illustrate how a no fault law works, let's examine the New York statute.

The New York no fault law is designed to cover personal injuries. There has been no change in the law with regard to property damages. If a car is destroyed in an accident, the owner will be paid by his own insurance company if he carried collision insurance. The party at fault may also be sued for the damage to the vehicle.

In general, the new law provides for certain basic policy benefits which vehicle owners (except motorcycles) are required to carry. In addition, certain options may be obtained if it is desired to have such optional benefits.

As a general rule, the basic policy benefits follow the car and, if purchased, the optional benefits follow the driver and resident relatives living with the insured.

The basic benefits which can be collected under the New York law are as follows:

1. All reasonable and necessary medical and rehabilitation expenses up to $50,000 for the driver and any passengers or pedestrians involved in the accident.

2. Payments up to $1,000 a month (less 20%) will be paid up to three years. Such benefits shall be non-triable in New York.

3. Twenty-five dollars a day for a year shall be paid for other reasonable and necessary expenses such as a seeing eye dog for a person who became blind in an accident, or the expense of a housekeeper for an injured housewife.

4. All benefits are to be paid regardless of the injured person's health insurance plan. Payments to be made under workmen's compensation and social security disability benefits shall be

paid to the insured person first and no fault insurance shall pay the difference.

While a drunk or drugged driver may not be eligible for no fault benefits, this will not bar passengers in the car from benefits.

The right to sue by an injured party is preserved against the negligent party if medial damages for the personal injury exceed $500 for a permanent injury, a serious fracture, serious disfigurement or death.

The optional benefits, which may be obtained under New York law are as follows:

1. Out of state coverage is available. This would extend the same benefits that would be received in New York to an accident occurring in some other state. In addition to the insured, such benefits would apply to all resident relatives living in the household of the insured. One unusual example of the application of this option follows in the case where the policyholder or other beneficiary is injured walking across the street in a state other than New York. Such person could collect under the out of state option against his insurance company because the policy applies to the individual who was injured by the automobile. The no fault benefits would follow the individuals covered under the out of state provisions.

2. Higher policy limits for no fault benefits for medical bills and economic losses may be obtained.

3. Additional out of state medical benefits may be obtained as well as benefits for funeral expenses.

4. To reduce premiums slightly, a $200 deductible policy may be obtained for a lower premium than the regular policy.

Since the New York no fault law provides for the right to sue in certain cases, automobile owners are still required to carry minimum liability insurance for bodily injury in the amounts of $10,000 per person or $20,000 per accident and property damage coverage of $5,000. Higher policy coverage may be obtained by those who wish it.

PRODUCTS LIABILITY

As pointed out in the chapter "The Consumer and the Law", in our modern society it is becoming increasingly difficult for a consumer to enforce his rights. A case in point is a consumer's remedy for a defective product. Traditionally he could sue either on the theory of breach of warranty or the negligence of the seller, manufacturer etc. Due to the complexity of many products sold, and the multiplicity of persons handling them before they reach the consumer, it has sometimes become quite difficult to sue under either of these theories of law. Many states have evolved another theory, that of strict liability for defective products.

Let us examine the traditional theories first. Every product sold carries with it a warranty of fitness for use from the seller to the buyer. Hence, if a product is defective, the warranty is breached. However, it is not as simple as it seems. First of all, the warranty is only between the buyer and the immediate seller. It does not extend back to the manufacturer or the middle men in the situation. It is usually these people which one wishes to sue, particularly if there has been extensive injuries.

An even greater difficulty is encountered when the injury is suffered by a third party (e.g. a guest or member of a family), and not the buyer of the product. The seller can usually raise the defense of lack of privity of contract with the injured third party.

Some states have abolished this requirement of privity if food or drugs are involved. This means that not only may third parties recover but any one who has come in contact with the defective product is liable to the consumer. The U.C.C. also contains a provision to provide that the warranty will run to consumer's family and guests. Sec. 2-318 reads as follows:

§ 2-318. **Third Party Beneficiaries of Warranties Express or Implied.**— A seller's warranty whether express or implied extends to any natural person who is in the family or household of his buyer or who is a guest in his home if it is reasonable to expect that such person may use, consume or be affected by the goods and who is injured in person by breach of the warranty. A seller may not exclude or limit the operation of this section."

Damages for negligence may also be had in the case of injuries due to defective products. Under this theory, no privity of contract is required and anyone who has processed the product, the manufacturer, the wholesaler, sellers etc. may be sued. As in the case of all negligence actions, it must be proven that a reasonable standard of care was not used by the defendant. This is where the difficulty arises, under this theory. The manufacturer can always allege that he was not negligent, but that the defective product was the result of negligence on the part of one of the middlemen. It is especially hard and expensive in many cases for the plaintiff to sustain this burden of proof.

Gradually the courts and legislatures began to see the relative unfairness inherent in these two doctrines, given the facts of modern living. More states, therefore have been adopting the strict liability standard for manufacturers in product liability cases. Approximately half the states now follow this rule, and some of those that do not, apply the rule to defective food products and drugs. Although the manufacturer cannot use the defense (acceptable in negligence cases) that he exercised reasonable care in the manufacture of the goods, he does have some defenses. If the plaintiff has inspected the product, discovers the defect, but uses it anyway, he may not recover from the defendant. A plaintiff may not recover if he is injured because he has not used the product in a way one would normally expect him to.

It seems relatively certain that in the future more states will continue to adopt the strict liability theory when confronted with the problem of injuries from defective products.

Chart 1
STATE THEORY OF LAW—CONTRIBUTORY OR COMPARATIVE

STATE	CONTRIBUTORY NEGLIGENCE	COMPARATIVE NEGLIGENCE
ALABAMA	X	
ALASKA		X
ARIZONA [1]	X	
ARKANSAS		X
CALIFORNIA		X
COLORADO		X
CONNECTICUT		X
DELAWARE	X	
D. C.	X	
FLORIDA		X
GEORGIA		Plaintiff is barred from any damages he could have avoided by using ordinary diligence, but where plaintiff only contributed to the injury damages are apportioned.
HAWAII		X
IDAHO		X
ILLINOIS	X	
INDIANA	X	
IOWA	X	
KANSAS		X
KENTUCKY	X	
LOUISIANA	X	

STATE	CONTRIBUTORY NEGLIGENCE	COMPARATIVE NEGLIGENCE
MAINE		X
MARYLAND	X	
MASSACHUSETTS		X
MICHIGAN	X	
MINNESOTA		X
MISSISSIPPI		X
MISSOURI	X	
MONTANA		X
NEBRASKA		X
NEVADA		X
NEW HAMPSHIRE		X
NEW JERSEY		X
NEW MEXICO	X	
NEW YORK		X
NORTH CAROLINA	X	
NORTH DAKOTA		X
OHIO	X	
OKLAHOMA		X
OREGON		X
PENNSYLVANIA		X
RHODE ISLAND		X
SOUTH CAROLINA		X
SOUTH DAKOTA		X
TENNESSEE	X	
TEXAS		X
UTAH		X
VERMONT		X
VIRGINIA	X[2]	
WASHINGTON		X
WEST VIRGINIA	X	

STATE	CONTRIBUTORY NEGLIGENCE	COMPARATIVE NEGLIGENCE
WISCONSIN		X
WYOMING		X

---

[1] Arizona. The rule of contributory negligence is not followed in suits brought under the Employers Liability Law. In such cases the theory of comparative negligence is followed.

[2] Virginia. Contributory negligence is the standard except for railroad crossing cases.

Chapter XII

CRIMINAL LAW

In the field of criminal law, there always exists a tension between individual rights guaranteed by the Bill of Rights and the duty of the government to protect its citizens from crime. It is usually the duty of the courts to maintain the delicate balance between these sometimes conflicting forces, in a manner consistent with a workable Democracy such as ours.

Under the influence of the Supreme Court, particularly the Warren Court, the rights of defendants in criminal cases were greatly expanded. Landmark cases such as the Miranda and Escobedo decisions, *in re Gault* and *Katz v. U.S.*, to mention a few, restricted pretrial techniques used by the police, protected the constitutional rights of juveniles and curtailed abuses of the Fourth Amendment. In recent years, with a rising crime rate and a concerned and sometimes fearful public, the Burger Court gives evidence of veering somewhat from the course began by the Warren Court.

ARREST

One of the most important things to be decided is whether an arrest is legal. If it is not, it can be almost as damaging to the state as to the individual, whose freedom has been curtailed, since evidence obtained as a result of an illegal arrest can not be used as evidence in a later trial.

Usually the arresting officer has obtained a warrant to make the arrest. Under the constitution, a warrant may only be issued on probable cause. See discussion of warrants, below.

Under certain circumstances, which vary from state to state, an arrest may be made without a warrant. Usually an officer may make an arrest without a warrant for any crime committed in his presence, and for a felony, even if it was not committed in his presence provided he has reasonable grounds to believe that the person arrested committed the felony. A policeman may search a suspect pursuant to a lawful arrest, but the search may be made only in the interest of self defense, i.e. a search for concealed weapons, or to prevent evidence from being destroyed. Searches are discussed more fully later on in this chapter.

Sometimes a policeman may observe what he considers suspicious actions by persons. He does not arrest them but merely questions

379

them as to their identity and what they are doing. This is not an arrest. Can a policeman search such a person? The courts generally have held that a quick search may be made for weapons, to safeguard the police officer's safety. The United States Supreme Court examined this question in *Terry v. Ohio*, 392 U.S. 1 (1968). In that case a plain clothes policeman, while patrolling a downtown area of Cleveland, observed the actions of the defendant and two other men. It seemed that their behavior indicated they were "casing" the area for either a robbery or a holdup. The policeman asked them their names and what they were doing. They mumbled something. The officer thereupon spun them around and felt them to see if they were armed. The Supreme Court held that the police have a right to ask questions of people on the street, and if they have a reasonable belief that the person might be armed, they have a right to search them for weapons, for their own self protection.

In the Terry case, the basis for stopping the suspects was the officer's own observation. In *Adams v. Williams,* 407 U.S. 143 (1972), a police officer was told by an informant that a suspect was concealing narcotics and a gun in a car. The officer asked the suspect to open the door. He then frisked the suspect, found the gun and then searched the car, and found the narcotics. The Supreme Court upheld the whole proceeding as legal. The officer was justified in stopping the suspect, since he knew the informant to be trustworthy. Once the gun was discovered, the officer had probably cause for an arrest. Since the arrest was valid, he could then make a warrantless search for the narcotics.

To take the guesswork out of when a police officer may stop a suspect and interrogate him on the street, many states have so called "stop and frisk" laws, setting forth the specific circumstances and conditions under which this may be done. New York's "stop and frisk" law reads as follows:

"1. In addition to the authority provided by this article for making an arrest without a warrant, a police officer may stop a person in a public place located within the geographical area of such officer's employment when he reasonably suspects that such person is committing, has committed or is about to commit either (a) a felony or (b) a misdemeanor defined in the penal law, and may demand of him his name, address and an explanation of his conduct.

2. A court officer of the criminal courts of this state or a court officer of any court of the unified court system within the city of New York may stop a person in or about the court-

room to which he is assigned when he reasonably suspects that such person is committing, has committed or is about to commit either (a) a felony or (b) a misdemeanor defined in the penal law, and may demand of him his name, address and an explanation of his conduct.

3. When upon stopping a person under circumstances prescribed in subdivisions one and two a police officer or court officer, as the case may be, reasonably suspects that he is in danger of physical injury, he may search such person for a deadly weapon or any instrument, article or substance readily capable of causing serious physical injury and of a sort not ordinarily carried in public places by law-abiding persons. If he finds such a weapon or instrument, or any other property possession of which he reasonably believes may constitute the commission of a crime, he may take it and keep it until the completion of the questioning, at which time he shall either return it, if lawfully possessed, or arrest such person." CPL 140.50

CRIME AND PUNISHMENT

In the United States most crimes are statutory, that is they are defined by the various state codes. As with all our laws, the roots of our criminal laws are found in the English common law. The criminal laws of each state therefore are similar in nature, although there are variations from state to state. This is illustrated in the charts found at the end of this chapter outlining the state laws relating to homicide and burglary.

One of the most notable developments in the field of criminal law has been concern over the imposition of the death penalty. In a long awaited decision, the Supreme Court took up the question in *Furman v. Georgia*, 408 U.S. 238 (1972). In a 5-4 decision, a divided court (each of the justices wrote separate opinions) held that in the case before it the imposition of the death penalty was unconstitutional pursuant to the Eighth Amendment prohibiting cruel and unusual punishment and the Fourteenth Amendment which makes the Eighth binding on the states. Only two of the Justices (Brennan and Marshall) felt that the death penalty was unconstitutional per se. The other justices believed that the manner in which the death penalty was imposed, was unconstitutional. In many cases it is imposed capriciously, sometimes in ways that are discriminatory to the poor and minority groups. Some believed that the question of the validity of capital punishment was a legislative one and that state statutes should be amended to include specific guidelines for use by judges and juries in imposing the death penalty.

Although the Furman decision still left many doubts as to the status of capital punishment, it did cause many of the states to amend their laws concerning the imposition of the death penalty.

In 1976 the Supreme Court was asked to rule on the constitutionality of the laws of five states, Florida, Georgia, Louisiana, North Carolina and Texas. It ruled favorably on the Georgia law, pointing out that it did not permit wanton imposition of the death penalty. In the words of the court, Georgia's new law set up guidelines which focused the jury's attention on the particularized nature of the crime and the individual characteristics of the defendant and required that at least one statutory aggravating factor must be present before the death penalty could be imposed.

The laws of Florida and Texas were also found constitutional. The Supreme Court struck down the Louisiana and North Carolina laws. They did not lay down specific guidelines for the jury, giving them arbitrary power to impose the death penalty.

The issue of capital punishment is far from settled and will probably be with us for some time to come. In the 1976 case, the Court pointed out that between its Furman ruling in 1972 and the present case, the states had ample opportunity to pass laws abolishing capital punishment. The fact that they did not do so indicated to the Court that they did not consider capital punishment a cruel and unusual punishment. It will be the method of imposing that sentence that will now continue to be under the scrutiny of the courts.

EXCLUSIONARY RULE

In an effort to enforce the provisions of the Fourth Amendment, guaranteeing privacy to citizens, the Federal courts established the rule that evidence obtained as a result of unlawful searches and arrests would not be admitted as evidence. The rule was extended even further by the so called "fruit of the poisoned tree" doctrine, which also excludes evidence later found as a result of information obtained during the course of an illegal search or arrest.

Until 1961, only the federal courts observed this rule; state courts did not. (In some instances evidence uncovered by federal officials and not able to be used by them in federal trials, was turned over to state officers, for use in state courts.) This dual standard was abolished in *Mapp v. Ohio,* 367 U.S. 643.

The main purpose of the exclusionary rule has been to deter the police from using illegal methods to obtain evidence. In recent years commentators have voiced disillusionment with regard to the rule pointing out that it does not seem to have acted as a deterrent on illegal searches and many times results in the guilty party being set free. In his dissent in *Bevans v. Six Unknown Agents*, 403 U.S. 388 (1971) Chief Justice Burger stated ". . Although I would hesitate to abandon it until some meaningful substitute is developed, the history of the Suppression Doctrine demonstrates that it is both conceptually sterile and practically ineffective in accomplishing its stated objective. Some clear demonstration of the benefits of the Exclusionary Rule is required to justify it in view of the high price it extracts from society — the release of countless guilty criminals . . ." Many feel that the time has come to find an alternative to the exclusionary rule.

PRE-TRIAL RIGHTS, CONFESSIONS, ETC.

In the now famous *Miranda v. Arizona,* 385 U.S. 436 (1966), the Supreme Court focused its attention on the pre-trial rights of defendants. It found that the rights given by the Fifth and Sixth Amendment exist even before the trial. Although these rights may be waived, the waiver must be voluntary and the suspect can waive these rights only if he has knowledge of them.

In the Miranda case the court studied several instances where confessions were obtained as a result of police interrogation, while the suspect was being held incommunicado. The court stated that under such circumstances it was possible to coerce a confession by psychological means. Noting that in each of the cases, "the defendant was thrust into an unfamiliar atmosphere and run through menacing police interrogation procedures . . . where the potentiality for compulsion is forcefully apparent. . " Confessions obtained under such circumstances will be suspect unless the individual is advised of his constitutional right to remain silent and to obtain counsel and is warned that anything he says may later be used against him.

The rationale of the Miranda case, requiring suspects to be warned of their rights was extended in *Mathis v. United States,* 391 U.S. 1 (1968) to include admissions made to an internal revenue agent about prior tax returns while in jail. In *Orozco v. Texas,* 394 U.S. 324 (1969) defendant was questioned by four policemen in his boarding house bedroom. Statements given by him were held to be inadmissible because he was not given the Miranda warnings. The state claimed that the warnings were not required since defendant made the admissions in familiar surroundings. The Supreme Court disagreed. Even though there would have been greater coercion at a stationhouse, nevertheless the warnings must be given whenever and wherever a suspect is in custody or has his freedom of action limited. In this case defendant had been placed under arrest and his freedom had certainly been limited.

In recent years, a curtailment of the Miranda doctrine can be noted. In *Oregon v. Hass*, 95 S. Ct. 1215 (1975), the Court considered the question of whether a confession made by the defendant before his attorney was present could be used at a trial for impeachment purposes. The Court held that while under the Miranda doctrine the confession could not be introduced as evidence that the crime had been committed, it could be introduced to reduce the credibility of the defendant. However in *U.S. v. Hale*, (1975), the Court would not permit defendant's silence to be introduced in the trial for impeachment purposes. At the trial the defendant who had been accused of robbery gave an alibi for his having a particular sum of money in his pocket. On cross-examination he was asked why he did not give this story to the police when they questioned him, instead of remaining silent. The court did not decide it on the constitutional question. In order for impeaching testimony to be admitted, it must have probative value. Defendant's silence here was of little probative value, particularly since the Miranda warnings he had just received specifically told him that he had a right to remain silent.

In a 1977 case, the defendant, a parolee came to the police station, at the request of one of the officers. There he was confronted with evidence linking him to a crime. He then confessed to the crime. At that point he was arrested and the Miranda warnings given. The defendant contended that the confession could not be used against him, as the police were not timely in giving the Miranda warnings. The Supreme Court, in a 6-3 decision, held summarily, without hearing arguments that the warnings were not necessary since the suspect had appeared at the station voluntarily and had not been arrested at the time the confession had been made. The warnings are necessary "only when there has been such restriction on a person's freedom as to render him in custody!" In the present case, the suspect was not under such restriction.

In view of these later cases, an abridgement of the Miranda decision is indicated. Just how severe the erosion will be remains to be seen.

RIGHT TO COUNSEL

The sixth amendment provides that the "accused shall enjoy the right . . . to have the assistance of counsel for his defense." This right of counsel has been the center of many significant Supreme Court decisions in the immediate past.

One of these was *Gideon v. Wainwright,* 372 U.S. 335 (1963). Before this ruling, while it was well settled that indigent persons had the right to court-appointed counsel in federal criminal cases. Whether he had the right in state cases depended on the laws of a particular state. An earlier Supreme Court case, *Betts v. Brady,* decided in 1942 had held that this right to counsel was not one of those rights concerning due process, which must be guaranteed by the individual states pursuant to the Fourteenth Amendment. The Gideon case overruled the Betts decision and now the poor as well as everyone else are entitled to counsel in state courts as well as federal.

The Gideon case dealt with a defendant accused of a felony. What of the defendant involved in a misdemeanor? While over half the states had statutes authorizing the appointment of counsel for indigents charged with a misdemeanor punishable by imprisonment, the Supreme Court had never ruled on the question. It finally did in *Argersinger v. Hamlin,* 407 U.S. 25, decided in 1972, and held that the right to counsel exists in cases of misdemeanors which could entail a jail sentence. If the defendant could not afford counsel, he must be furnished one.

Lower courts had long debated whether an individual has a constitutional right to defend himself. The Supreme Court studied the question in *Faretta v. California,* (1975). There, the defendant had requested permission to act as his own counsel. The trial court denied his request and appointed a court counsel to represent the defendant. The Supreme Court decided that defendant has the right to act as his own counsel. As long as he is made aware of the dangers of self-representation, he may waive his right to court-appointed counsel and defend himself. Quoting an earlier case the court said:

"The defendant, and not his lawyer or the State, will bear the personal consequences of a conviction. It is the defendant, therefore, who must be free personally to decide whether in his particular case counsel is to his advantage. And although he may conduct his own defense ultimately to his own detriment, his choice must be honored out of that respect for the individual which is the lifeblood of the law.' "

The question of when this constitutional right to counsel arises was considered in the Miranda decision (referred to above in Pre-Trial Rights) and *Escobedo v. Illinois,* 378 U.S. 478 (1964). In both these cases, the right to counsel was pushed back in the pre-trial process. Escobedo, while being questioned after his arrest, but before his indictment, asked to see his lawyer. His request was refused. Incriminating statements made by him at this time were later introduced at his trial which resulted in a conviction. The Supreme Court overturned this conviction holding that he had been deprived of his constitutional right to counsel. The court held that it did not matter that the questioning took place prior to indictment. Nevertheless the court contended that what happens at a police investigation could affect the whole trial and that the accused might have rights which "may be as irretrievably lost, if not then and there asserted, as they are when an accused represented by counsel waives a right for strategic purposes." The dissenting minority felt that the right to counsel arose at the time of the indictment. The majority did however limit its ruling to those instances where the questioning is no longer a general inquiry, but where an actual police investigation has begun. The court said:

> "We hold, therefore, that where, as here, the investigation is no longer a general inquiry into an unsolved crime but has begun to focus on a particular suspect, the suspect has been taken into police custody, the police carry out a process of interrogations that lends itself to eliciting incriminating statements, the suspect has requested and been denied an opportunity to consult with his lawyer, and the police have not effectively warned him of his absolute constitutional right to remain silent, the accused has been denied "the Assistance of Counsel" in violation of the Sixth Amendment."

There had been some doubt as to whether a person was entitled to counsel while appearing in a police lineup. In 1967 in *U.S. v. Wade*, 388 U.S. 218, the Supreme Court held that the suspect had the right to counsel when the identification via a line up took place after the indictment. State courts had been ruling that counsel was required for lineups prior to the arrest. However in *Kirby v. Illinois,* 406 U.S. 682 (1972), the court sharply split on the question, but at least four of the majority Justices felt that the right to counsel, arises only after adversary judicial proceedings have begun. If police procedures were arbitrary or unfair, the defendant had recourse to other rights guaranteed by the Fifth Amendment, e.g. his privilege against self-incrimination. However in *United States v. Ash* (1973), the Supreme Court held that counsel need not be present when photographs are displayed to witnesses for identification, *after* the indictment. The Court pointed out that even the suspect usually was not present during this procedure.

SEARCHES, WARRANTS, WIRETAPS

It is the Fourth Amendment which guarantees that the people will be free from unlawful searches by government agents. The extent of this constitutional protection has been the subject of much controversy over the years.

One issue has been what governmental agents must abide by the Fourth Amendment. Obviously federal agents come within the purview of the amendment. State agents are subject to its restrictions also. In 1949 in *Wolf v. Colorado*, 388 U.S. 25, the Supreme Court decided that the prohibition against unlawful searches was included in the rights relating to due process protected in the Fourteenth Amendment and hence, binding on the states. However it was not until 1961 that evidence obtained by an illegal search by state officials was excluded in state courts. See discussion of *Mapp v. Ohio*, under the heading "Exclusionary Rule." It should also be noted that the illegality extends only to searches by *governmental* agents. So far the courts have held the protection against illegal searches does not extend to searches by private individuals. Thus incriminating evidence uncovered as a result of a private search and later turned over to the government is admissible at a trial, unless the search by the private individual had been made at the request of a governmental agency.

Searches may be made pursuant to a warrant or without one. Both types of searches are discussed below.

Search Warrants

To be certain that an arrest or search is legal police officers usually obtain a warrant, an order signed by a judge stating that the search or arrest may be made because there is probable cause for it. The United States Constitution provides in the Fourth Amendment that persons shall be secure from unreasonable searches and seizures and that no warrant, "shall issue but upon probable cause, supported by oath or affirmation, and particularly describing the place to be searched, and the person or things to be seized."

In recent years the Supreme Court has carefully studied the contents of the affidavits which form the basis for the issuance of a warrant by a magistrate.

In *Aguilar v. Texas,* 378 U.S. 152 (1966), the affidavit prepared by the police as the basis for obtaining the warrant stated that they had received reliable information from a credible person and that they believed that narcotics were being kept at a certain address, for unlawful purposes. The United States Supreme Court held that the affidavit was improper. It had failed to inform the magistrate of some of the underlying circumstances which led the affiant to the conclusion that the narcotics were present and were to be put to an illegal use. It is the magistrate who must ultimately determine if probable cause exists, not the police. The affidavit was based on hearsay (information furnished by an informant). This does not render the affidavit invalid, provided the police officer states some of the underlying circumstances that led the informer to believe that the narcotics were there and what facts enable the police to conclude that the informer was reliable.

The question was again raised in *Reggan v. Virginia*, 384 U.S. 152 (1966). In that case the supporting affidavit stated that the police believed that premises were being used for an unlawful lottery because of personal observation and information received from reliable sources. Again the Supreme Court in a 5-4 decision, held the affidavit defective because, as in the Anguilar case, not enough factual information was given the magistrate. The dissenters would have distinguished the two cases, in that the former was based wholly on hearsay, while in the latter case, the affidavit was based partly on the affiant's personal observation.

In a 1967 case, the Supreme Court was asked to rule whether an informant's identity must be revealed for the court to rule on the question of probable cause. In *McCray v. Illinois,* 386 U.S. 300, the Supreme Court answered this question in the negative, holding that the arresting officers were available as to cross-examination to show that the informant actually existed, that he had been reliable in the past and that the information he gave concerning the defendant was specific enough to give rise to probable cause. The dissenters felt the informant should be produced. Justice Douglas, in his dissent declared:

> "Unless he [the informer] is produced, the Fourth Amendment is entrusted to the tender mercies of the police. What we do today is to encourage arrests and searches without warrants. The whole momentum of criminal law administration should be in precisely the opposite direction, if the Fourth Amendment is to remain a vital force. Except in rare and emergency cases, it requires magistrates, to make the findings of 'probable cause'. We should be mindful of its command that a judicial mind should be interposed between the police and the citizen . . ."

In *U.S. v. Ventresca,* 380 U.S. 102 (1965) and *Spinelli v. U.S.,* 393 U.S. 410 (1969), the Supreme Court continued to examine supporting affidavits for warrants. In the Ventresca case, the affidavit, while giving ample facts to support probable cause, failed to state in detail the source of this information. The Supreme Court held that it was obvious that most of the facts stated in the affidavit resulted from the officer's own investigation and observation. It pointed out that affidavits of this sort were made by non-lawyers, usually hurriedly and in the midst of a criminal investigation. To hold the affidavit invalid simply for failure to spell out in more detail the affiant's sources would be overly technical and unrealistic. Those who regarded this case as a harbinger of a lessening of surveillance of police methods by the Court, were probably disappointed by the Spinelli ruling, which more or less reiterated the Court's earlier rulings, requiring affidavits to supply enough facts to support a finding of probable cause by a court. For the effect of illegally obtained evidence, see the heading "Exclusionary Rule."

Once a search warrant has been obtained, the police are permitted to search the premises described in the warrant, for the type property specified in the warrant. When the police have a search warrant, must they request admittance or may they enter the premises unannounced? Common law precepts and most case laws require the police in most instances, to identify themselves before entering. If after a reasonable length of time, they are not admitted they may make a forceable entry, using only that amount of force necessary to effect an entrance. However this rule of law has been qualified by the so-called "No-Knock" laws which provide that in the warrant the police may be given permission to enter without giving notice. More than half the states have such laws. They have been the subject of much controversy. Proponents claim that such laws are necessary to obtain evidence in narcotic arrests, while opponents of the law feel it is the first step towards a police state.

Not all searches are made with a warrant. In some instances searches may be made without a warrant and still be legal.

A search may be made without a warrant if it is consented to. However the consent must be given by the proper person. The requirement of consent is not satisfied by a landlord consenting to the search of a tenant's room (*Chapman v. U.S.,* 365 U.S. 610 (1961)) nor by a hotel clerk permitting the search of a guest's room (*Stoner v. California,* 376 U.S. 483 (1964)). In *Bumper v. N.C.,* 391 U.S. 543 (1968), a woman permitted the police to search her grandson's room, believing that they had a proper warrant to make the search. In fact they did not. The Supreme Court ruled that it was an invalid search, the women gave her consent only because she believed the police had a warrant to do so. Even so, the Court noted she did not have the authority to permit the search of her grandson's room. It is generally held that in the case of persons sharing living quarters, each is competent to consent to a search of those areas they use in common but may not give a valid consent to search areas used privately by the other.

In emergency situations (as most courts phrase it, in "exigent circumstances") a search may be made without a warrant. For example there is the "moving vehicle exception". If a law officer has probable cause that he will find incriminating evidence therein, he may search a moving vehicle, without a search warrant. The reason is obvious. The officer does not have time to obtain a warrant; if he stops to do so the vehicle will undoubtedly not be available for searching upon his return.

For many years searches by municipal agencies for fire, health and housing violations were assumed not to be within the purview of the fourth amendment and were permitted without a warrant. In 1967 in *Camara v. Municipal Court,* the Supreme Court held to the contrary, stating that such inspections of personal residences required a warrant. However, the Supreme Court ruled that visitations in connection with the Aid to Dependent Children Program, could be made without a warrant, in *Wyman v. James,* 400 U.S. 309 (1971). The court distinguished between the two cases saying that the first one involved a possible criminal prosecution, whereas in the second involved loss of money payments.

If a valid arrest is made, then it is permissible for a police officer to search the suspect and the area within his immediate control. Theoretically the reason for this is twofold: First, for his own safety, the policeman should be allowed to search for concealed weapons. Secondly he should be able to confiscate evidence before the accused has an opportunity to dispose of it. Just how extensive the search may be and what constitutes the "area within the control" of the suspect has been the subject of controversy in many courts.

For many years it has been questioned whether a legal arrest can justify a warrantless search of a person's home. Earlier Supreme Court cases seemed to indicate that this was possible, but two recent cases, *Chimel v. California,* 395 U.S. 752 (1969) and *Vale v. Louisiana,* 399 U.S. 30, negate this. In Chimel, the Court made it clear that an arrest can not be made an excuse for a warrantless search of a house.

> "When an arrest is made, it is reasonable for the arresting officer to search the person arrested in order to remove any weapons that the latter might seek to use in order to resist arrest or effect his escape. Otherwise, the officer's safety might well be endangered and the arrest itself frustrated. In

addition, it is entirely reasonable for the arresting officer to search for and seize any evidence on the arrestee's person in order to prevent its concealment or destruction. And the area into which an arrestee might reach in order to grab a weapon or evidentiary items must, of course, be governed by a like rule. A gun on a table or in a drawer in front of one who is arrested can be as dangerous to the arresting officer as one concealed in the clothing of the person arrested. There is ample justification, therefore, for a search of the arrestee's person and the area "within his immediate control" — construing that phrase to mean the area from within which he might gain possession of a weapon or destructible evidence.

There is no comparable justification, however, for routinely searching any room other than that in which an arrest occurs — or, for that matter, for searching through all the desk drawers or other closed or concealed areas in that room itself. Such searches, in the absence of well-recognized exceptions, may be made only under the authority of a search warrant."

The advent of the age of electronics and sophisticated listening devices ushered in additional problems relating to governmental intrusion on individual privacy. However it was not until the sixties that electronic surveillance was regarded as a potential violation of the Fourth Amendment.

Earlier cases had held that for a violation of this amendment, an actual physical trespass by government agents. In a 1928 case, *Olmstead v. U.S.,* the Supreme Court held that tapping the telephone of a bootlegger during the prohibition period did not violate his Fourth Amendment rights. It is noteworthy that Judge Brandeis wrote a dissent advocating the concept of a constitutional right of privacy, which while not accepted by the majority then, would be in later years.

Courts continued to base their decisions involving electronic surveillance on the "physical intrusion" test until a series of cases, beginning with *Wong Sun v. U.S.* (1963), which held that verbal communications were protected by the fourth amendment. In 1967, in *Berger v. New York,* the court found that evidence based on conversations recorded by concealed devices in defendant's office should have been inadmissible since they were obtained in violation of the Fourth Amendment. It also declared the New York Statute permitting such surveilance unconstitutional, since it sanctioned indiscriminate listening to private conversations, without any particular evidence in mind.

Another major case was that of *Katz v. U.S.,* 389 U.S. 347, also decided by the Supreme Court in 1967. The FBI had tapped a public phone booth from which a gambler transacted his illegal dealings, and introduced the recordings as evidence against him. The Supreme Court found that this evidence was unconstitutional as it violated the fourth amendment. The Court said, the Fourth Amendment protects people, not places. What a person knowingly exposes to the public, even in his own home or office is not a subject of Fourth Amendment protection but what he seeks to preserve as private, even in an area accessible to the public may be constitutionally protected."

After this ruling, state and federal statutes were enacted to conform with the case. Restrictions were placed on wiretapping and other methods used to intercept oral communication. Permission to use such devices must be obtained from a judge, usually for a specific purpose for a defined period of time. Some are dissatisfied with these laws claiming that they are an unnecessary abridgement of the individual's right of privacy. Others claim that such laws are required to aid in stopping the crime which seems to them, to be permeating our nation. Again we have the conflict between the tensions, mentioned at the start of the chapter. Only time will tell what is the best way of resolving them.

Chart 1

MURDER AND MANSLAUGHTER DEFINITIONS AND PENALTIES

ALABAMA

Murder—First Deg.: Perpetrated by poison, lying in waiting or any other kind of willful, deliberate, malicious and premeditated killing; or committed in perpetration or attempt to perpetrate any arson, rape, robbery or burglary; or from a premeditated design unlawfully and maliciously to effect the death of any human other than one killed; or by act greatly dangerous to lives of others and evidencing a depraved mind regardless of human life. [Death or life imprisonment.]

Second Deg.: Every other homicide, as would be murder at common law. [Not less than 10 years.]

Manslaughter—First Deg.: Voluntary depriving a human of life. [1-10 years.]

Second Deg.: Manslaughter under any other circumstance. [Up to 1 year and up to $500.]

ALASKA

Murder—First Deg.: Killing another out of deliberate and premeditated malice, or by means of poison, or in perpetrating or attempting to perpetrate rape, arson, robbery, or burglary. [20 years to life.]

Second Deg.: Killing another purposely and maliciously. [Not less than 15 years.]

Manslaughter: Unlawfully killing another. [1 to 20 years.]

ARIZONA

Murder—First Deg.: Perpetrated by poison, lying in wait, torture or other kind of willful, deliberate and premeditated killing, committed in perpetration or attempt to perpetrate of arson, rape, robbery, burglary or mayhem. [Death or life imprisonment.]

Second Deg.: All other kinds of murder. [Not less than 10 years.]

Manslaughter: Unlawful killing of human being without malice.

Voluntary: Upon sudden quarrel or heat of passion.

Involuntary: In commission of unlawful act not a felony or a lawful act which might produce death in an unlawful manner, or without due caution. [Up to 10 years.]

ARKANSAS

Capital murder: Kills a public official, policeman, fireman, prison guard, etc.; while intentionally and with premeditation kills one person and causes the death of another in the same criminal episode; killing committed under circumstances, evidencing extreme indifference to the value of human life during the perpetration of rape, kidnapping, arson, hijacking, robbery, burglary or first degree escape; killing occurs while killer is in prison under a sentence of life imprisonment or death, killer is hired or defendant hired someone to kill another. [Death or life imprisonment without parole. (Statute specifies aggravating and mitigating circumstances which must be considered by the jury at a special hearing before the death penalty can be imposed).]

First Deg.: (1) killing occurs during a felony other than those enumerated for a capital murder. (2) killing is intentional and premeditated. [5-50 years and/or up to $15,000.]

Second Deg.: kills one person while intending to kill or cause serious physical harm to another or kills another under circumstances manifesting extreme indifference to the value of human life. [3-20 years and/or up to $15,000.]

Manslaughter: murder committed under extreme emotional disturbance for which there is reasonable cause, (2) aids or causes another to commit suicide, (3) recklessly causes the death of another, (4) during a felony negligently causes the death of any person resisting the felony. [1-5 years and/or up to $10,000.]

CALIFORNIA

Murder: Unlawful killing of a human being, with malice aforethought.

First Deg.: Perpetrated by means of a destructive device or explosive or by poison, or lying in wait, torture, or by any other kind of willful, deliberate, and premeditated killing, or which is committed in the perpetration or attempt to perpetrate arson, rape, robbery, burglary or mayhem. [Death or life imprisonment.]

(Note: Statute specifies those conditions under which the death penalty may be imposed, after a special finding — e.g. hired killings, previous conviction, for first or second degree murder, etc.)

Second Deg.: All other kinds of murder. [5 to 7 years.]

Manslaughter: Unlawful killing of a human being without malice.

1. Voluntary: upon a sudden quarrel or heat of passion.

2. Involuntary: in the commission of an unlawful act, not amounting to felony; or in the commission of a lawful act which might produce death, in an unlawful manner, or without due caution and circumspection; provided that this subdivision shall not apply to acts committed in the driving

of a vehicle.

3. In the driving of a vehicle — (a) In the commission of an unlawful act, not amounting to felony, with gross negligence; or in the commission of a lawful act which might produce death, in an unlawful manner, and with gross negligence. (b) In the commission of an unlawful act, not amounting to felony, without gross negligence; or in the commission of a lawful act which might produce death, in an unlawful manner, but without gross negligence. [2-4 years for voluntary or involuntary manslaughter.]

Motor Vehicle deaths: up to 1 year in county jail uless conviction is under 3(a) above in which case imprisonment may be in either state prison or county jail.

COLORADO
Murder: Unlawful killing of a human being.

First Deg.: With intent and deliberation causes the death of another, or alone or with others commits arson, robbery, kidnapping, etc. and kills in furtherance of the crime, or causes the execution of an innocent person by giving perjured testimony, or killing evidences an extreme indifference to the value of human life. [Death or life imprisonment. (Special proceeding to determine if death penalty justified).]

Second Deg.: Death is caused intentionally but without deliberation, or defendant had intent to inflict serious bodily injury. [10 to 50 years.]

Manslaughter: Death caused by recklessness of defendant; killing occurred in the sudden heat of passion caused by a serious and highly provoking act of the intended victim; intentional aiding or provoking of another to commit suicide. [Minimum - 1 year and/or $2,000. Maximum - 10 years and/or $30,000.]

CONNECTICUT
Murder: With intent to cause a person's death kills that person or another.

Felony Murder: Killing another in furtherance of the crime of robbery, burglary, kidnapping, arson, rape, etc. [Minimum 10-25 years up to a maximum of life.]

Capital Murder: Murder of law enforcement officer, corrections officer, fireman, etc.; murder for hire (either the actual killer or the one who hired him) defendant had previously been arrested for murder (intentional or felony); the murder was committed while in prison; murder by kidnapper of his victim; death results from use of drugs, illegally sold. [Life imprisonment or death. (Death penalty imposed unless a mitigating factor [specifically outlined by statute] is determined to be present at a special hearing held for that purpose).]

Manslaughter: First—Deg. With intent to do serious bodily harm, causes another's death; intends to kill but was acting under the influence of an extreme emotional disturbance; under circumstances evidencing an extreme indifference to human life, defendant recklessly engages in conduct endangering the life of another. [From 1 to 1½ years up to 20.]

Second Deg.: Recklessly causes another's death or causes or aids another to commit suicide. [From 1 or 1½ years up to 10.]

DELAWARE
Murder—First Deg.: Intentional killing; recklessly causes the death of another while committing a felony; recklessly causes the death of a law enforcement officer, fireman, corrections officer, etc.; death caused by bombing; by criminal negligence causes the death of another person during a rape, kidnapping, first degree arson or robbery, or while fleeing therefrom; kills another to prevent a lawful arrest or to aid in escaping. [Death (or if declared unconstitutional, life imprisonment without parole).]

Second Deg.: Recklessly causes death of another under conditions indicating a cruel and depraved indifference to human life or causes death by criminal negligence, during felonies not enumerated under murder first degree. [Life imprisonment.]

Manslaughter: Recklessly causing the death of another person; while intending to cause serious physical injury to another, employ as means to do so, that which could reasonably result in death; causes anothers death while under the influence of extreme emotional disturbance; cause the death of a female by an abortion, unless death did not result from reckless conduct of defendant or the abortion was therapeutic. [3-30 years.]

FLORIDA
Murder—First Deg.: When perpetrated from a premeditated design to effect the death of the person killed or any human being, or when committed in the perpetration or attempt to perpetrate any arson, rape, robbery, or burglary, kidnapping, hijacking, bombing, or the unlawful sale of drugs by a person over 18, which results in the death of the user. [Death or life imprisonment (must serve 25 years before eligible for parole). Special proceeding must be had to determine if death penalty is to be imposed. Statute lists aggravating and mitigating factors to be considered.]

Second Deg.: By act imminently dangerous to another, evincing a depraved mind regardless of human life. [Up to life; optional fine of $10,000.]

Third Deg.: Killing occurred during the commission of one of the felonies enumerated above, but defendant did not perform the actual killing. [Up to 15 years; optional fine of $10,000.]

Manslaughter: By act, procurement or culpable negligence of another, in cases where such killings are not justifiable or excusable homicide nor murder. [Up to 15 years; optional fine of $10,000.]

GEORGIA
Murder: Unlawful killing of a human being by a person of sound memory and discretion, with malice aforethought, either express or implied; felony murder. [Death or life imprisonment.]

Voluntary Manslaughter: Murder committed as a result of sudden, violent and irresistible passion resulting from a serious provocation sufficient to excite such passions in any reasonable person. [1 to 20 years]

Involuntary Manslaughter: Committed, without an intent to kill during the commission of an unlawful act, other than a felony. [1 to 5 years.]

Without intent to kill, during the commission of a lawful act performed in a manner likely to cause death or great bodily harm. [As for misdemeanor.]

HAWAII
Murder—First Deg.: Killing without authority, justification or extenuation of law, with deliberate premeditated malice aforethought, with malice aforethought and with extreme cruelty or atrocity, or in connection with crimes or attempt to commit crime of arson, rape, robbery, burglary or kidnapping. [Life imprisonment at hard labor without parole.]

Second Deg.: Killing with malice aforethought. [Hard labor for not less than 20 years.]

Manslaughter: Killing without malice aforethought. [Hard labor for not more than 10 years.]

IDAHO
Murder—First Deg.: Perpetrated by means of poison, or lying in wait, torture, or by any other kind of willful, deliberate and premeditated killing, killing of a police officer, any murder by a person sentenced for 1st or 2nd degree murder. [Death.]

Second Deg.: All other kinds of murder. [10 years to life.]

Manslaughter: Unlawful killing without malice.

Voluntary: Upon sudden quarrel or heat of passion. [Up to 10 years, or $2,000 or both.]

Involuntary: In perpetration or attempt to perpetrate unlawful act, other than arson, rape, robbery, kidnapping, burglary, or mayhem; or in commission of unlawful act which might produce death, in an unlawful manner, or without due caution and circumspection; operation of motor vehicle in reckless, careless manner, or operation of any deadly weapon in reckless, careless manner. [Up to $1,000 and/or up to 10 years.]

ILLINOIS

Murder: Killing without lawful justification if in performing the acts which cause death, the killer intends to kill or do great bodily harm to that person or knows such acts will cause death, or strong probability of death, or killing while committing felony other than voluntary manslaughter. [Death or imprisonment not less than 14 years. (Before the death penalty is imposed, three judges must determine that the killing falls into one of the categories specified in the statute; e.g. victim was a police officer, murder occurred during a hijacking, etc.).]

Voluntary Manslaughter: Killing without lawful justification under sudden or intense passion resulting from serious provocation by the individual he attempts to kill, negligently or accidentally causing death to another; intentionally or knowingly kills one believing circumstances if they existed would exonerate him, but such belief is unreasonable. [1 to 20 years.]

Involuntary Manslaughter: Killing without lawful justification if acts lawful or unlawful are such as are likely to cause death or great bodily harm, and he performs them recklessly. [1 to 10 years (except in the case of motor vehicle death in which the penalty is 1-3 years).]

INDIANA

Capital Felony: Intentional killing of a judge, law enforcement officer, fireman, etc. in the line of duty; a killing by bombing; killing during a kidnapping; a hired killing; a killing by one who has a prior unrelated conviction of murder, or is serving a life term. [Death.]

Murder: Intentionally kills another; kills during felony (kidnapping, arson, burglary, rape, robbery or unlawful deviate conduct) [20-50 years]; person causes another to commit suicide (same punishment as voluntary manslaughter).

Voluntary Manslaughter: Intentionally kills another while under intense passion resulting from adequate provocation. [10 years with not more than 10 years added for aggravating circumstances, nor more than 4 subtracted for mitigating circumstances - Optional fine up to $10,000.]

Involuntary Manslaughter: Kills while committing an offense. [2 years with no more than 2 years added for aggravating circumstances; optional fine up to $10,000 (may alternatively sentence as a Class A misdemeanor).]

Reckless Homicide: Recklessly kills another. [5 years with no more than

3 years added or subtracted for aggravating or mitigating circumstances - optional fine up to $10,000.]

Reckless Driving: Same penalty as involuntary manslaughter.

IOWA

Murder: Malice aforethought, either express or implied.

First Deg.: Kills willfully, deliberately; kills another while participating in a forcible felony; kills another while escaping from lawful custody; intentionally kills a peace officer, correctional officer, hostage, etc. while imprisoned. [Life imprisonment.]

Second Deg.: Any murder not first degree [up to 25 years.]

Voluntary Manslaughter: Act would be murder except that accused acted as a result of sudden, violent and irresistible passion resulting from a serious provocation which would affect any reasonable person in the same manner. [Up to 10 years; optional fine up to $5,000.]

Involuntary Manslaughter: Unintentionally causes another's death by the commission of a public offense other than a forcible felony or escape. [Up to 5 years and may be fined up to $1,000.]

Unintentionally causes the death of another by the commission of an act in a manner likely to cause death or serious injury. [Up to 2 years and/or up to $5,000.]

KANSAS

Murder—First Deg.: Malicious, willful, deliberate, premeditated killing of another or murder committed during the perpetration of a felony. [Death or life imprisonment.]

Manslaughter—Voluntary: Unlawful killing without malice, but done intentionally upon a sudden quarrel or in the heat of passion. [Minimum, 1-5 years; maximum, 20 years; optional fine up to $10,000.]

Involuntary: Done unintentionally during the commission of an unlawful act (not a felony) or while doing a lawful act in an unlawful manner. [1-5 years; optional fine up to $5,000.]

KENTUCKY

Murder: With intent to kill someone, causes that persons death or another's, or under circumstances manifesting extreme indifference to human life, engages in actions creating a grave risk of death to another. [20 years to life.]

Capital murder: A hired killing; killing was intentional and occurred during the commission of arson, robbery, burglary, rape; intentional killing of a prison employee by a prisoner; intentional killing by bombing; intentional killing resulting in multiple deaths; intentional killing of police officer, sheriff or deputy sheriff in the line of duty. [Death.]

Manslaughter—First Deg.: Kills another with intent to cause serious bodily injury; intends to kill but does so under the influence of an extreme emotional disturbance. [10-20 years.]

Second Deg.: Wantonly causes the death of another. [5-10 years.]

(*Note:* If defendant has been convicted of a felony and granted a sentence of probation or conditional discharge, he may be sentenced to pay a fine, in an amount not to exceed $10,000, or double his gain for the commission of the offense, whichever is greater.

LOUISIANA

Murder—First Deg.: Killing with specific intent to kill or inflict great bodily harm. [Death or life imprisonment without parole.]

Second Deg.: When the offender is engaged in the perpetration or attempted perpetration of aggravated arson, aggravated burglary, aggravated kidnapping, aggravated rape, armed robbery, or simple robbery, even though he has no intent to kill. [Life imprisonment (not eligible for parole for 40 years).]

Manslaughter: Committed in sudden passion or heat of blood immediately caused by provocation sufficient to deprive an average person of his self-control and cool reflection; homicide committed without any intent to cause death or great bodily harm when the offender is engaged in perpetration or attempted perpetration of any felony (not included in the list under murder) or any intentional misdemeanor directly affecting the person, or when offender is resisting lawful arrest, in a manner not inherently dangerous. [Up to 21 years.]

MAINE

Criminal Homicide—First Deg.: Same as second degree (see below) with one or more of these elements added: committed by one who has been convicted of first or second degree homicide; defendant knowingly created a great risk of death to four or more persons; homicide was for the purpose of preventing arrest or escaping; it was committed for pecuniary gain; defendant knowingly inflicted great physical suffering on the victim. [Life imprisonment.]

Second Deg.: Intentionally causes death or knows that death will almost certainly result from his conduct; causes another to commit suicide by force, duress or deception. [Any term of years, not less than 20.]

Third Deg.: Kills during the commission of a Class A crime. [Up to 20 years.]

Fourth Deg.: Recklessly causes another's death or kills under circumstances that would be 2nd degree homicide except that defendant was under an extreme mental or emotional disturbance upon adequate provocation. [Up to 10 years; optional fine - $10,000. If reckless driving - up to 5 years; optional fine - $1,000.]

Fifth Deg.: Causes death by criminal negligence. [Up to 1 year; optional fine - $500.]

Sixth Deg.: Aids another to commit suicide. [Up to 1 year; optional fine - $500.]

MARYLAND

Murder—First Deg.: Perpetrated by means of poison, or lying in wait, or by any kind of willful, deliberate and premeditated killing; in perpetration of arson; in burning of any structure having tobacco, hay, horses, goods, etc.; in perpetration of rape, sodomy, mayhem, robbery, burglary or escape from Penitentiary. [Death or life imprisonment. (Statute specifies the conditions under which death must be imposed, e.g. accused actually committed the act of murder, was over 18 and additional elements must be present; murder committed while accused in prison; victim was a law enforcement officer or correctional officer; victim was a kidnapping victim; hired killing; accused has a previous 1st degree murder conviction; occurred during a robbery).]

Second Deg.: All other murders. [Not more than 30 years.]

MASSACHUSETTS

Murder—First Deg.: With deliberately premeditated malice aforethought or with extreme atrocity or cruelty, or in the commission or attempted commission of a crime punishable with death or imprisonment for life. [Death or life imprisonment.]

Second Deg.: Other murders. [Life imprisonment.]

Manslaughter: Not defined. [Up to 20 years, or up to $1,000 fine and imprisonment up to 2½ years. (If bombing is involved, may be imprisoned for life or any term of years).]

MICHIGAN

Murder—First Deg.: Perpetrated by means of poison, or lying in wait, or any other kind of willful, deliberate and premeditated killing, or which shall be committed in the perpetration or attempt to perpetrate any arson, rape, robbery or burglary, larceny of any kind, extortion and kidnapping. [Life imprisonment.]

Second Deg.: All other kinds of murder. [Life imprisonment or term of years.]

Manslaughter: Not defined. [Up to 15 years and/or up to $7,500.]

MINNESOTA

Murder—First Deg.: When perpetrated with a premeditated design to effect the death of the person killed or of another, or while attempting to commit first or second degree criminal sexual conduct, with force or violence. [Life imprisonment.]

Second Deg.: When committed with a design to effect the death of the person killed or of another, but without deliberation and premeditation, or when causing death while committing or attempting to commit rape or sodomy with force or violence. [Not more than 40 years.]

Third Deg.: Without intending to cause death, perpetrates an act eminently dangerous to others, without regard to human life and evidencing a depraved mind or during the commission of a felony other than those enumerated above under first degree murder. [Up to 25 years.]

Manslaughter—First Deg.: When intentionally causing death in the heat of passion provoked by words or acts of another that would provoke person of ordinary self-control under like circumstances; or causing death of another in committing or attempting to commit crime with such force and violence that death or great bodily harm is reasonably foreseen and murder in first or second degree was not committed thereby; or intentionally causing death of another because actor is coerced by threats and believes his act is only means of preventing his imminent death or death to another. [Up to 15 years or $15,000 or both.]

Second Deg.: Causing death by culpable negligence, shooting person believing him to be deer or other animal, setting spring gun, pitfall, death fall, etc., or negligently knowingly permitting dangerous animal to roam or confine it properly when victim was not at fault. [Up to 7 years or $7,000 or both.]

MISSISSIPPI

Murder: When done with deliberate design to effect the death of the person killed, or of any human being; when done in commission of an act eminently dangerous to others, and evidencing a depraved heart, regardless of human life, although without any premeditated design to effect death; when done without any design to effect death, by person engaged in commission or attempt to commit the crime of rape, burglary, arson, or robbery. [Death or life imprisonment.]

Manslaughter: Killing while slayer was committing felony other than those specified for murder; killing while slayer committing misdemeanor, where such killing would be murder at common law; killing in heat of passion, without malice, but in a cruel or unusual manner; killing in heat of passion, without malice, by use of a dangerous weapon, without authority of law, etc. [Not less than $500 and/or up to 20 years.]

MISSOURI

Murder—First Deg.: Committed by means of poison, or by lying in wait, or by any other kind of willful, deliberate and premeditated killing, and every homicide in the perpetration or attempt to perpetrate any arson, rape, robbery, burglary, or kidnapping. [Death or life imprisonment.]

Second Deg.: All other kinds of murder except manslaughter or justifiable homicide. [Not less than 10 years.]

Manslaughter: By act, procurement or culpable negligence of another, not murder or excusable or justifiable homicide. [$500 or more; or 6 mos. in the county jail or 2-10 years in the penitentiary; or $100 or more and not less than 3 months.

MONTANA

Deliberate Homicide: Committed purposely or knowingly or during the perpetration of a felony of robbery, rape, arson, burglary, kidnapping or any felony involving the use of threat of physical force or violence. [Death or up to 100 years.]

(*Note:* Statute specifies when the death penalty may be imposed, absent any mitigating circumstances.)

Mitigated Deliberate Homicide: Would be deliberate homicide except committed under extreme mental or emotional stress for which there is a reasonable explanation. [Up to 4 years.]

Negligent Homicide: Up to 10 years.

NEBRASKA

Murder—First Deg.: Purposely and of deliberate and premeditated malice, or in the perpetration of or attempt to perpetrate any rape, arson, robbery or burglary, or by administering poison, or causing the same to be done; or, by willful and corrupt perjury or subordination of the same, purposely procure the conviction and execution of any innocent person. [Death or life imprisonment. (After a conviction of 1st degree murder, a hearing is had for the purpose of determining the sentence to be imposed. The statute specifies the aggravating and mitigating factors to be considered in determining whether the death penalty should be imposed).]

Second Deg.: Purposely and maliciously, but without deliberation and premeditation. [10 years to life.]

Manslaughter: Unlawfully kill, without malice, either upon a sudden quarrel, or unintentionally, while the slayer is in commission of some unlawful act. [1 to 10 years.]

NEVADA

Murder: Unlawful killing of a human being, with malice aforethought, either express or implied.

Capital Murder: Is perpetrated by: killing a police officer or fireman in the line of duty; killing by a person under sentence of life imprisonment, without parole; hired killing; bombing; killing more than one person, willfully deliberately and with premeditation as the result of single plan, scheme or design. [Death.]

First Deg.: Perpetrated by means of poison, or lying in wait, torture, or by any other kind of willful, deliberate and premeditated killing, or which shall be committed in the perpetration, or attempt to perpetrate, any arson, rape, robbery, or burglary, kidnapping, sexual molestation of child under 14 or committed to avoid lawful arrest or effect an escape. [Life imprisonment, with or without parole (if parole permitted, a minimum of 10 years must be served).]

Second Deg.: All other kinds of murder. [Definite term not less than 5 years.]

Manslaughter: Unlawful killing, without malice express or implied, and without any mixture of deliberation. It must be voluntary, upon a sudden heat of passion caused by a provocation apparently sufficient to make the passion irresistible; or, involuntary, in the commission of an unlawful act, or a lawful act without due caution or circumspection. [Voluntary manslaughter - Up to 10 years.]

Involuntary Manslaughter: Killing during the commission of an unlawful act or during a lawful act performed in an unlawful manner. [1 to 6 years in state prison or for not more than 1 year in the county jail and/or up to $5,000.]

NEW HAMPSHIRE

Capital Murder: Killing of a law enforcement officer in the line of duty; killing during a kidnapping; hired killing. Defendant must be 17 years of age or over. [Death.]

First Deg.: To purposely cause the death of another or knowingly causes the death of another while committing felony of rape, deviate sexual relations, or arson or while armed, committing robbery or burglary or kills any of the public officials designated in the statute. [Life imprisonment without parole.]

Second Deg.: Knowingly causes the death of another or causes death recklessly under circumstances evidencing an extreme indifference to human life. Such recklessness is presumed if the killing occurs during the commission of a Class A felony. [Life imprisonment or such term as court orders.]

Manslaughter: Would be murder except defendant acted under the influence of an extreme mental or emotional disturbance or kills in a reckless manner. [Up to 15 years; optional fine up to $2,000.]

NEW JERSEY

Murder: Killing a person by someone committing or attempting to commit arson, burglary, kidnapping, rape, robbery, sodomy, or while avoiding or preventing arrest, or fleeing from legal custody; or killing any official in execution of his duty; or killing police officer or private individual helping him to suppress an affray or to apprehend criminal. [Death or life imprisonment.]

Any other kind of murder. [Imprisonment for not more than 30 years.]

Manslaughter: Not defined. [Not more than $1,000 or imprisonment up to 10 years or both.]

NEW MEXICO

Murder: The unlawful killing of a human being, with malice aforethought, either express or implied.

First Deg.: Perpetrated by means of poison or lying in wait, torture, or by any kind of willful, deliberate and premeditated killing, or which is committed in the perpetration of or attempt to perpetrate any felony, or perpetrated from a deliberate and premeditated design unlawfully and maliciously to effect the death of any human being, or perpetrated by act greatly dangerous to lives of others, and indicating a depraved mind regardless of human life. [Death, or if underaged - life imprisonment.]

Second Deg.: All other kinds of murder. [10-50 years and/or up to $10,000.]

Manslaughter: Unlawful killing of a human being without malice.

Voluntary: Upon a sudden quarrel or in the heat of passion. [2-10 years and/or up to $5,000.]

Involuntary: In the commission of an unlawful act not amounting to felony, or in commission of lawful act which might produce death, in an unlawful manner or without due caution. [1-5 years and/or up to $5,000.]

NEW YORK

Murder—First Deg.: Acting with intent to kill, kills police officer, prison employee in the course of duty or at time of crime dependant was over 18 years and in prison or custody for life. [Death]

Second Deg.: Intentionally kills another, kills while engages in reckless conduct under circumstances evidencing depraved indifference to human life; felony murder [Maximum life - minimum 15-25.]

Manslaughter—First Deg.: Acting with intent to cause serious physical injury to another person, and causing death of such person or of a third person; or, with intent to cause the death of another person, causing death under circumstances which do not constitute murder because of acting under influence of extreme emotional disturbance, mitigating circumstances reducing murder to manslaughter first degree; or, committing abortional act on female pregnant for more than 24 weeks which is not justified pursuant to 125.05 section 3. [Maximum - 25 - minimum up to 1/3 of maximum sentence]

Second Deg.: Recklessly causes another's death or aids another in committing suicide or commits abortional act not justified under 125.05(3). [Maximum - 15 years.]

NORTH CAROLINA

Murder—First Deg.: Perpetrated by means of poison, lying in wait, imprisonment, starving, torture or by any other kind of willful, deliberate and premeditated killing or killing committed in perpetration of, or attempt to perpetrate, arson, rape, kidnapping, robbery, burglary or other felony. [Death.]

Second Deg.: All other murders. [2 years - life.]

Manslaughter: No definition. [4 mos. to 20 years.]

Involuntary Manslaughter: Fine and/or imprisonment at discretion of court.

NORTH DAKOTA

Murder: Kills intentionally or knowingly kills under circumstances manifesting extreme indifference to the value of human life or kills another during the commission of treason, robbery, burglary, kidnapping, arson, etc. [20 years and/or $10,000.]

Manslaughter: Recklessly causes another's death or kills under circumstances that would be murder, except that defendant acted under an extreme emotional disturbance. [Up to 10 years and/or up to $10,000.]

Negligently causes the death of another. [Up to 5 years and/or $5,000.]

OHIO

Aggravated Murder: Purposely and with prior calculation and design and premeditated malice, or purposely kills while attempting to perpetrate rape, arson, robbery or burglary; maliciously places an obstruction on railroad, etc. [Death or life imprisonment. (Statute specifies the aggravating circumstances mandating the death penalty).]

Murder: Purposely and maliciously kills another, except as provided for murder in first degree. [15 years to life imprisonment. May be fined up to $15,000.]

Voluntary Manslaughter: Kills under great amount of emotional stress. [4-7 years up to 25 years. May also be fined up to $10,000.]

Involuntary Manslaughter: Causes another's death while committing a felony, not specified under murder. [4-7 years up to 25 years. May be fined up to $10,000.]

Causes another's death while committing a misdemeanor. [1-3 years up to 10. May be fined up to $10,000.]

OKLAHOMA

Murder—First Deg.: Kills another unlawfully and with malice aforethought or kills another while committing rape, armed robbery, kidnapping, burglary or while escaping from life imprisonment. [Death or life imprisonment.]

Second Deg.: Unpremeditated act imminently dangerous to human life, evidencing a depraved mind or killing occurring during a felony not enumerated above. [10 years - life.]

(*Note:* Jury decides whether death penalty should be imposed - statute specifies aggravating circumstances to be considered.)

Manslaughter—First Deg.: Kills without a design to effect death during the commission of a misdemeanor or kills in the heat of passion and in a cruel and unusual manner or by means of a dangerous weapon or kills unnecessarily while resisting a crime. [Not less than 4 years.]

Second Deg.: Culpable negligent act. [2-4 years and/or up to $1,000.]

OREGON

Murder: Intentional killing by one not under the influence of an extreme emotional disturbance: felony murder during first degree arson, burglary, kidnapping, rape, robbery, sodomy. [Life imprisonment.]

Manslaughter—First Deg.: Killing committed recklessly under circumstances manifesting extreme indifference to the value of human life: intentional killing under circumstances not constituting murder. [Up to 20 years.]

Second Deg.: Murder committed recklessly or causes or aids another to commit suicide. [Up to 10 years.]

PENNSYLVANIA
Murder—First Deg.: An intentional killing. [Death or life imprisonment. (Statute specifies aggravating and mitigating circumstances which the jury must consider before imposing the death penalty.)]

Second Deg.: Death of victim occurred while defendant engaged as principal or accomplice in perpetration of a felony. [Life imprisonment.]

Third Deg.: All other kinds of murder. [Up to 20 years and/or up to $10,000.]

Manslaughter: Not defined.

Voluntary Manslaughter: Felony. [Up to $6,000 and up to 12 years.]

Involuntary Manslaughter: Happening in consequence of an unlawful act, or doing of lawful act in unlawful way. [Up to $2,000 and/or up to 3 years.]

RHODE ISLAND
Murder: Unlawful killing of a human being with malice aforethought.

First Deg.: Perpetrated by poison, lying in wait, or any other kind of willful, deliberate, malicious and premeditated killing, or committed in perpetration of or attempt to perpetrate any arson, rape, burglary or robbery, or while resisting arrest, or perpetrated from a premeditated design, unlawfully and maliciously to effect the death of any human being other than him who is killed. [Life imprisonment. (If murder is committed in prison, the penalty is death).]

Second Deg.: Any other murder. [10 years to life.]

SOUTH CAROLINA
Murder: Killing of any person with malice aforethought, either express or implied. [Death or life imprisonment.]

(Note: Statute specifies those instances when the death penalty is to be imposed, e.g. if murder is committed during the commission of rape, assault, kidnapping, burglary, robbery, etc.; murder for hire; murder of policeman or corrections officer; previous conviction of murder).]

Manslaughter: Unlawful killing of another without malice, express or implied. [2 to 30 years.]

Involuntary Manslaughter: Criminal negligence to reckless disregard of other's safety. [3 months to 3 years.]

SOUTH DAKOTA

Murder: When perpetrated with a premeditated design to effect the death of person killed or of any human being, perpetrated by act imminently dangerous to others and evincing a depraved mind, regardless of human life, although without any premeditated design to effect death of any individual; perpetrated without design to effect death by person committing felony. [Life imprisonment or death.]

Manslaughter—First Deg.: Perpetrated without design to effect death by person engaged in commission of misdemeanor involving moral turpitude; perpetrated without design to effect death and in heat of passion, but in cruel and unusual manner or by means of dangerous weapon; perpetrated unnecessarily either while resisting attempt by person killed to commit a crime or after such an attempt has failed. [Not less than 4 years.]

Second Deg.: Killing by act, procurement or culpable negligence which is not murder nor manslaughter in the first degree. [2-10 years or 1 year and/or up to $1,000.]

TENNESSEE

Murder: Unlawfully kill any reasonable creature in being, and under the peace of the state, with malice aforethought, either express or implied.

A willful, deliberate, malicious and premeditated killing; a willful, deliberate, malicious killing of (a) an employee of a state prison, having custody of defendant (b) a co-inmate in prison (c) an on duty policeman or fireman (d) judge acting in the course of his judicial duties (e) an elected official: a hired killing and defendant is either the one who hires or who is hired; the killing occurred while defendant was attempting to escape law enforcement officials; committed during perpetration of arson, rape, burglary, larceny, kidnapping, aircraft piracy or bombing. [Mandatory death.]

Second Deg.: All other kinds of murder. [10 to life.]

Manslaughter: Unlawful killing of another without malice, either voluntary upon a sudden heat, or involuntary, but in the commission of some unlawful act.

Voluntary Manslaughter: 2 to 10 years.

Involuntary Manslaughter: 1 to 5 years.

TEXAS

Murder: Intentional killing; with intent to cause bodily harm commits an act clearly dangerous to human life and does cause another's death; during the commission of a felony commits an act clearly dangerous to human life and which does result in the victim's death. [5 to 99 years.]

Capital Murder: Killing of a police officer or fireman; intentionally commits murder while perpetrating the felony of kidnapping, burglary, robbery, aggravated rape or arson; defendant is either a hired killer or has hired a killer; murder is committed while in prison or escaping from prison. [Life imprisonment or death.]

Voluntary Manslaughter: Killing would be murder except defendant was under the influence of sudden passion arising from an adequate cause. [2-20 years and may be fined up to $10,000.]

Involuntary Manslaughter: To recklessly cause the death of an individual; to cause death by accident or mistake, or driving while intoxicated. [2-10 years and may be fined up to $5,000.]

UTAH

Murder—First Deg.: Intentional and knowing killing; while in jail; another homicide committed by defendant, at the same time; defendant knowingly created a great risk of death to others; felony murder during a robbery, aggravated robbery, rape, forcible sodomy, or aggravated sexual assault, aggravated arson, arson, burglary or kidnapping; killing was committed to avoid or escape arrest; killing was done for pecuniary gain; defendant had been previously convicted of first or second degree murder; killing was committed to prevent a witness from testifying. [Death or life imprisonment. (Statute provides for a special hearing and lists mitigating circumstances which must be present to impose life rather than death penalty).]

Second Deg.: Under circumstances not amounting to first degree murder or manslaughter, defendant intentionally kills another or intending to cause serious bodily injury to another, commits an act clearly dangerous to human life and causes the death of another while engaging in any of the crimes enumerated under first degree felony murder. [5 years to life and/or up to $10,000.

Manslaughter: Recklessly kills another; kills under extreme emotional or mental disturbance or believing that the killing was morally or legally justified, when in fact it was not. [1-15 years and/or up to $10,000.]

VERMONT

Murder—First Deg.: Murder committed by means of poison, lying in wait or by deliberate and premeditated killing, or committed in perpetrating or attempting to perpetrate arson, rape, robbery, or burglary. [Life imprisonment.]

Murder of prison employee or law enforcement officer. [Death or life imprisonment as jury determines.]

Second Deg.: All other kinds of murder. [Life or term as court shall order.]

Manslaughter: Not defined. [1 to 15 years and/or $1,000.]

VIRGINIA

Capital Murder: Willful, deliberate, premeditated killing during the course of abduction (for pecuniary gain); killing for hire or killing by an inmate in a penal institution. [Death.]

Murder—First Deg.: A murder (not a capital) caused by poison, lying in wait, imprisonment, starving, or by any willful deliberate and premeditated killing, or killing in commission of, or attempt to commit, arson, rape, abduction, robbery or burglary. [20 years - life.]

Second Deg.: All other murder. [5 to 20 years.]

Manslaughter: Not defined.

Voluntary Manslaughter: 1 to 10 years or up to $1,000 and/or up to 1 year.

WASHINGTON

Murder—First Deg.: With premeditated intent to kill, causes death of intended victim or another; kills another while engaging in risky conduct evidencing extreme indifference to human life; felony murder during robbery, rape, burglary, arson, kidnapping. (If acting with confederates is not guilty of first degree murder if did not actually commit the murder, was not armed and had no reason to believe the others were armed. [Life imprisonment.]

Aggravated Murder: Same as defined above plus any of these additional elements; victim was on duty policeman or fireman; defendant was an inmate of a prison; murder for hire; murder committed to conceal crime or obstruct justice; multiple murders; murder committed during the course of a rape or kidnapping. [Mandatory death sentence.]

Second Deg.: Committed with design to effect death, but without premeditation; perpetrated by person committing or attempting to commit, or withdrawing from scene of felony other than those enumerated for murder in the first degree. (If committed with confederates same exceptions as above). [Not less than 20 years and/or up to $10,000.]

Manslaughter: Other homicides, not excusable or justifiable. [Up to 20 yrs. or up to 1 yr. and/or up to $1,000.]

First Deg.: Recklessly causing the death of another; intentionally and unlawfully kills unborn quick child by inflicting injury on the mother. [Up to 10 years and/or up to $10,000 fine.]

Second Deg.: Criminal negligence. [Up to 5 years and/or up to $5,000.]

WEST VIRGINIA

Murder—First Deg.: By poison, lying in wait, imprisonment, starving, or by any willful, deliberate and premeditated killing, or in commission of, or attempt to commit, arson, rape, robbery, or burglary. [Life imprisonment.]

Second Deg.: All other murder. [5 to 18 years.]

Manslaughter—Voluntary: 1 to 5 years.

Involuntary: Up to 1 year and/or up to $1,000.

WISCONSIN

Murder—First Deg.: Causing death with intent to do so. [Life imprisonment.]

Second Deg.: Causing death by act imminently dangerous to others, evidencing depraved mind, regardless of human life. [5 to 25 years.]

Third Deg.: Killing of human being without any design to effect death, by person engaged in commission of any felony. [Up to 15 years more than the maximum penalty for the felony.]

Manslaughter: Causing death by any one of the following: without intent to kill and while in the heat of passion; unnecessarily, in exercise of privilege of self-defense; coerced by threats which make person believe his act is only means of preventing death to himself or another; pressure of natural physical causes makes person believe that his act is the only means of preventing public disaster or imminent death to himself or another. [Up to 10 years.]

WYOMING

Murder—First Deg.: With premeditated malice and purposely or in perpetration of, or attempt to perpetrate, rape, arson, robbery or burglary, or by poison. [Life imprisonment. (Statute specifies those circumstances under which the death penalty should be imposed, e.g. killing of police or fireman; hired murder; intentional murder with explosives; defendant had been convicted of first or second degree murder or murder is committed while defendant is under a sentence of life imprisonment; murder occurred during a rape, arson, burglary or robbery and defendant had previously been convicted of the same; murder occurs during a kidnapping or hijacking; the purpose of the murder was to conceal evidence of a crime or the murder of two or more persons in one series of related events).]

Second Deg.: Purposely and maliciously, but without premeditation. [20 years to life.]

Manslaughter: Unlawfully kills without malice, express or implied, either voluntarily, upon sudden heat of passion, or involuntarily but in commission of unlawful act or by any culpable neglect or criminal carelessness. [Up to 20 years.]

Chart 2
FIRST DEGREE MURDER PUNISHMENT

ALABAMA	Electrocution
ALASKA	Life imprisonment
ARIZONA	Gas
ARKANSAS	Electrocution
CALIFORNIA	Gas
COLORADO	Gas
CONNECTICUT	Electrocution
DELAWARE	Hanging
DISTRICT OF COLUMBIA	Electrocution
FLORIDA	Electrocution
GEORGIA	Electrocution
HAWAII	Life imprisonment
IDAHO	Hanging
ILLINOIS	Electrocution
INDIANA	Electrocution
IOWA	Life imprisonment
KANSAS	Hanging
KENTUCKY	Electrocution
LOUISIANA	Electrocution
MAINE	Life imprisonment
MARYLAND	Gas
MASSACHUSETTS	Electrocution
MICHIGAN	Life imprisonment
MINNESOTA	Life imprisonment
MISSISSIPPI	Gas
MISSOURI	Gas
MONTANA	Hanging
NEBRASKA	Electrocution
NEVADA	Gas
NEW HAMPSHIRE	Hanging
NEW JERSEY	Electrocution
NEW MEXICO	Life imprisonment
NEW YORK	Life imprisonment
NORTH CAROLINA	Gas
NORTH DAKOTA	Life imprisonment
OHIO	Electrocution
OKLAHOMA	Electrocution
OREGON	Life imprisonment
PENNSYLVANIA	Electrocution

RHODE ISLAND	Life imprisonment
SOUTH CAROLINA	Electrocution
SOUTH DAKOTA	Electrocution
TENNESSEE	Electrocution
TEXAS	Electrocution
UTAH	Hanging or shooting
VERMONT	Life imprisonment
VIRGINIA	Electrocution
WASHINGTON	Hanging
WEST VIRGINIA	Life imprisonment
WISCONSIN	Life imprisonment
WYOMING	Life imprisonment

Chart 3

BURGLARY AND ARSON, DEFINITIONS AND PENALTIES

ALABAMA

Burglary—First Deg.: In nighttime with intent to steal or commit felony, breaks and enters any inhabited dwelling or building. [Death or not less than 10 years.]

Second Deg.: Daytime, breaks and enters inhabited dwelling; nighttime or daytime breaks and enters uninhabited dwelling or shop, store, etc., where goods are kept. [1 to 10 years]

Arson—First Deg.: Willfully or with intent to defraud sets fire or aids in burning of dwelling.

Second Deg.: Burning of shops, store, etc., or other building or sets fire or aids burning of own property.

2 to 10 years (death or life imprisonment if death or maiming occurs).

ALASKA

Burglary: Breaking and entering dwelling house with intent to commit crime, or armed with dangerous weapon breaks and enters, or assaults person lawfully therein. [1-10 years, unless at nighttime, up to 15 years. If human being there, night or day, up to 20 years. Not dwelling house, 2-5 years. Breaking out of dwelling after committing, or attempting to commit crime, 1-3 years.]

Arson—First Deg.: Willfully and maliciously setting fire to or burning or causing to be burned or aiding, counseling or procuring burning, of dwelling house, whether occupied, unoccupied or vacant, or part of or belonging to or adjoining dwelling, whether his property or that of another. [2-20 years.]

Second Deg.: Building not described above. [1-10 years and/or $5,000.]

Third Deg.: Personal property of value of $100 or more. [1-3 years and/ or $3,000.]

Fourth Deg.: Attempted arson. [1-2 years and/or $1,000.]

Defrauding insurer: 1-5 years and or $3,000.

ARIZONA

Burglary: Entering building, house, office, etc., vessel, railroad car, motor vehicle, etc., with intent to commit grand or petit larceny or any felony.

First Deg.: In nighttime, 1 to 15 years.

Second Deg.: In daytime, up to 5 years.

Armed Burglary: 1st offense, not less than 5 years. 2nd offense, not less than 10 years. 3rd offense, not less than 20 years.

Arson—First Deg.: Sets fire, willfully and maliciously or aids burning of dwelling house, occupied or unoccupied, property of himself or another. [2 to 20 years.

Second Deg.: Burning any other property not included in first degree. [1 to 10 years.]

Third Deg.: Burning of property of value of less than $25 and property of another. [1 to 3 years.]

Fourth Deg.: Attempts to burn, 1 to 2 years or up to $1,000.

Burning to defraud insurer, 1 to 5 years.

ARKANSAS

Burglary: Entering or remaining in an occupiable structure of another with the intent of committing any offense punishable by imprisonment. [3-20 years and/or up to $15,000.]

Arson: Causes damage by fire or explosion (1) to an occupiable structure belonging to another (2) to property of another, if negligently creates risk of death or serious physical injury to any one (3) to a vital public facility. [3-20 years and/or up to $15,000.]

CALIFORNIA

Burglary: Enters any house, room, apartment, shop, warehouse, store, etc., or other building, vessel, railroad car, etc., with intent to commit grand or petit larceny or any other felony.

First Deg.: Burglary of inhabited dwelling or building in nighttime; either in day or night, by person armed with deadly weapon; in commission of burglary, assaults any person. [2-4 years]

Second Deg.: All other kinds of burglary. [up to 1 year.]

Arson: Willfully and maliciously sets fire to or burns any dwelling house, property of himself or of another. [3 or 4 years.]

Burning of building not dwelling house. [3 or 4 years.]

COLORADO

Burglary—First Deg.: Enters building or occupied structure intending to commit a crime, and is armed, or in the course of the burglary, assaults another. [5-40 years.]

> Second Deg.: Breaks and enters with intent to commit a crime but is not armed and does not assault anyone. [5-40 years (if a dwelling). 1 year or $2,000 - 10 years and/or $30,000 (any other building).]

> Third Deg.: With criminal intent breaks and enters vault safe, cash register, etc. [1 year or $1,000 - 5 years or $15,000.]

Arson—First Deg.: Intentionally, destroys by fire or explosives another's building or occupied structure [5 to 40 years]

> Second Deg.: Intentionally set fire to etc. any other building. If damages—$100 or more—1 day-10 years and/or $30,000. If less than $100—3 months &/or $250—12 months &/or $1,000.
> Third Deg.: With intent to defraud—1 day-10 years &/or $30,000.

> Fourth Deg.: Starts fire or explosion on own or another's property, placing another in danger of death or bodily injury 1 day-10 years &/or $3,000 or endangers the occupied structure or property of another property more than $10 3 months &/or $250 to 12 months &/or $1,000. Under $100—$50 to 6 months &/or $750.

CONNECTICUT

Burglary—First Deg.: Enters with criminal intent, is armed or carried explosives and intentionally or recklessly inflicts or attempts to inflict bodily harm. [1 year to ½ of maximum sentence imposed—20 years. (Armed burglary has a minimum of 5 years).]

> Second Deg.: Enters or remains at night with a criminal intent.

> Third Deg.: Enters or remains in building with criminal intent.

Arson—First Deg.: Willfully starts a fire or explosion knowing some one is in the building or close enough to the building to be put in danger. [1 year to ½ of maximum sentence imposed—20 years.]

> Second Deg.: Willfully starts fire or explosion with intent to destroy another building or collects insurance for himself or another and there is substantial risk to another person or another building. [Penalty same as above.]

> Third Deg.: Recklessly causes damage by fire or explosion to his own or another's building.

DELAWARE

Burglary—First Deg.: With criminal intent, enters a dwelling at night and is armed with a weapon or explosives or causes physical injury to another. [3 to 30 years. Enters during the day and is armed or injures another, 2-20 years.]

Second Deg.: Enters a building with criminal intent. [10 years.]

Third Deg.: Breaking and entering dwelling of another in circumstances not amounting to first or second degree burglary. [Up to 15 years.]

Fourth Deg.: Entering building with intent, or committing crime, and breaking out. [Up to 5 years.]

Arson—First Deg.: Intentionally damages by fire or explosion a building in which there shall be some human being or circumstances are such that there is a possibility of another being present. [3-30 years.]

Second Deg.: Where no human being is present. [2 to 20 years.]

Third Deg.: Recklessly damages a building. [7 years.]

FLORIDA

Burglary: Enters or remains in a building with criminal intent, and is armed with a dangerous weapon or assaults someone therein. [Life imprisonment or term of years at court's discretion.]

If not armed or with explosive, and does not assault anyone, but enters a dwelling or a human being is in the building. [up to 15 years with an optional fine up to $10,000.]

All other burglaries. [up to 5 years and optional fine of $5,000.]

Arson—First Deg.: Willfully and maliciously damages a structure, his own or another's, by fire or explosive knowing, or having reasonable grounds to believe, that a human being is therein. [up to 30 years, $15,000 (optional fine).]

Willfully and maliciously damages by fire etc. under any other circumstances. [up to 15 years, optional fine - $10,000.]

GEORGIA

Burglary: Enters or remains in dwelling or any other building of another person, with intent to commit a felony or larceny. [1 to 20 years.]

Arson—First Deg.: By means of fire or explosives, one damages a dwelling or a building designed for a dwelling, belonging to another or any building or structure under circumstances that it could have reasonably been foreseen that human life might be endangered. [1 to 20 years.]

Second Deg.: Burning or bombing of any other building. [1 to 10 years.]

Third Deg.: Burning of personal property of value of $25 or more. [1 to 3 years.]

HAWAII

Burglary: Entering by night or day dwelling house, room, building, store, mill, vessel, with intent to commit larceny in first or second degree, or any felony.

First Deg.: Nighttime or any time when committed by one armed with deadly weapon or when place entered has occupant, without right to be there. [Up to 20 years.]

Second Deg.: All others. [Up to 10 years.]

Arson: Willfully and maliciously burning dwelling house of another.

First Deg.: Burning at nighttime of occupied dwelling house. [Life imprisonment without parole, or life.]

Second Deg.: Burning in day or night dwelling house of another. [Life imprisonment or any number of years.]

IDAHO

Burglary: Entering any house, room, ship, warehouse, store, etc., or any other building, vessel, railroad car, etc., with intent to commit grand or petit larceny, or any felony.

First Deg.: Burglary committed in the nighttime. [1 to 15 years.]

Second Deg.: Burglary committed in the daytime. [Up to 5 years.]

Arson—First Deg.: Willfully and maliciously setting fire to, aiding burning of any dwelling, occupied, unoccupied or vacant, property of self or another. [2 to 20 years.]

Second Deg.: Burning of building other than dwelling. [1 to 10 years.]

Third Deg.: Burning of personal property of value of $25 or more. [1 to 3 years.]

Fourth Deg.: Attempted burning. [1 to 2 years, or up to $1,000.]

ILLINOIS

Burglary: Knowingly without authority entering or remaining without authority in a building, house, trailer, watercraft, aircraft, motor vehicle, with intent to commit felony or theft. [1-20 years.]

Arson: Damaging by fire or explosive real or personal property of value of $150 or more, of another, without his consent or with intent to defraud insurer. [1-20 years.]

INDIANA

Burglary: Entering a building or structure of another with intent to commit a felony. [2 years (not more than 2 years added for aggravating factors; optional fine, $10,000).]

If armed with a deadly weapon. [5 years - no more than 3 years added or subtracted for aggravating or mitigating factors - Optional fine, up to $10,000.]

If results in bodily injury to another person. [10 years - not more than 10 years added for aggravating circumstances nor more than 4 years subtracted for mitigating factors - optional fine up to $10,000.]

Arson: Damages by fire or explosives a dwelling of another without his consent; any property of another under circumstances that endanger human life; if monetary loss is at least $20,000. [5 years with no more than 3 years added or subtracted for mitigating circumstances; optional fine up to $10,000.]

With intent to injure person or damage property. [Same penalty as above.]

If results in personal injury to another. [10 years with no more than 10 years added for aggravating factors or more than 4 years subtracted for mitigating factors; optional fine; up to $10,000.]

If commits arson for hire. [Same penalty as above.]

If results in bodily injury to another. [20-50 years.]

IOWA

Burglary: Break and enter dwelling house in nighttime with intent to commit any public offense; or, after entering, with such intent, break any dwelling in nighttime.

Armed burglary, or if assaults any person, or has confederate aiding in burglary. [Life imprisonment or term of years.]

Otherwise than armed, etc. [Up to 20 years.]

Burglary: With intent to commit a felony, assault or theft, to enter an occupied structure or an enclosed area provided for keeping valuable property from theft, or to remain therein with criminal intent, or to break an occupied structure or other place where anything of value is kept.

First Deg.: During burglary is armed with weapon or explosive or intentionally or recklessly inflicts physical injury on someone. [up to 25 years.]

Second Deg.: All other burglaries. [up to 10 years; optional fine up to $5,000.]

Arson: Causing fire or explosion with intent to destroy or damage property.

First Deg.: Presence of persons on the property could be reasonably anticipated. [up to 25 years.]

Second Deg.: Property is a building, structure or real property of any kind, standing crops, or personal property worth over $500. [up to 10 years; optional fine of $5,000.]

Third Deg.: All other arson. [up to 2 years and/or up to $5,000.]

KANSAS

Burglary: Entering or remaining in any building or structure with intent to commit a felony or theft. [Minimum penalty, 1-3; Maximum, 10 years; Optional fine up to $5,000.]

Aggravated burglary — human being is in building. [Minimum, 1-5 years; Maximum, 20 years; Optional fine, up to $10,000.]

Arson—First Deg.: Damaging by fire or explosives, building or property of another without his consent, or damaging property with intent to defraud an insurance company. [Minimum penalty, 1-5 years; Maximum, 20 years; Optional fine, $10,000.]

Aggravated arson, human being in the building. [Minimum, 5-15 years; Maximum, life; Optional fine, $10,000.

KENTUCKY

Burglary—First Deg.: At night, with intent to commit a crime, knowingly enters, or remains unlawfully in a dwelling and is armed with explosives or a deadly weapon or causes physical injury to a person, not a participant in the crime or uses or threatens to use a dangerous weapon against anyone not a participant of the crime. [10-20 years.]

Second Deg.: Same as first, except it occurs in the day. [5-10 years.]

Third Deg.: Knowingly enters or remains in a building with criminal intent, but none of the other elements are present (e.g. not armed, does not threaten or cause harm). [1-5 years.]

Arson—First Deg.: Intentionally damages a building by fire or explosives, knowing, or having reason to know that there is another person in the building. [10-20 years.]

Second Deg.: No threat to a person involved. [5-10 years.]

Third Deg.: Wantonly damages a building by intentionally starting a fire. [1-5 years.]

LOUISIANA

Burglary—Aggravated: Unauthorized entering of any inhabited dwelling or any structure, watercraft, or movable where a person is present, with intent to commit a felony or any theft, if armed with dangerous weapon, or committing battery upon any person while in such place, or entering or leaving. [1 to 30 years.]

Simple burglary: Not armed or without battery. [Up to 9 years.]

Arson—Simple: Intentional damaging by any explosive substance or setting fire to any property of another, damage $500 or more. [Up to $500 value, $1,000 and/or 1 year; over $500, $5,000 and/or 10 years.]

Aggravated: Intentional damaging by any explosive substance or setting fire to any structure, water craft, etc., where it is foreseeable that human life might be endangered. [2 to 20 years.]

MAINE

Burglary: Enters or remains in building or structure with intent to commit a crime.

Class A — if armed with a firearm. [4-20 years.]

Class B — defendant intentionally or recklessly inflicts, or attempts to inflict bodily harm, or was armed with a weapon other than a firearm. [up to 10 years.]

All other burglary. [Up to 5 years.]

Arson: Starts or maintains a fire or explosion on the property of another, with the intent of damaging or destroying the property; or of defrauding an insurance company or with conscious disregard of a substantial risk that his conduct will endanger any person or damage or destroy the property of another. [up to 10 years.]

Aggravated arson: to intentionally start or maintain a fire or explosion that damages any structure which is the property of himself or of another, in conscious disregard of a substantial risk that at the time of such conduct a person may be at or near the structure. [If fire causes death or serious injury to any person — up to 20 years, otherwise up to 10 years.]

MARYLAND

Burglary: Breaking and entering any dwelling in nighttime with intent to steal, take or carry away personal goods of another. [Up to 20 years, and restitution.]

Breaking and entering in daytime, dwelling, with intent to commit felony, steal personal goods; or breaking storehouse, garage, etc., day or night, with intent to commit felony or steal goods of $100 or more. [Up to 10 years.]

Arson: Burning of dwelling, property of himself or another. [Not more than 30 years.]

Burning building other than dwelling. [Not more than 20 years.]

Burning personal property of value of $25 or more. [Not more than 3 years.]
Burning to defraud insurer. [5 years.]

Attempted burning. [Not more than 2 years or up to $1,000.]

MASSACHUSETTS

Burglary: Break and enter in nighttime, dwelling, with intent to commit felony, or after entering, breaks such dwelling, any person being therein and armed with a dangerous weapon, or assaults person therein. [Life imprisonment or term not less than 10 years.]

Break and enter in nighttime, dwelling, not armed, and no assault. [5-20 years.]

Break and enter building or ship in nighttime. [Up to 20 years.]

Entering dwelling in nighttime without breaking, or breaks and enters building or ship in daytime. [Up to 10 years.]

Breaking and entering either day or night with intent to commit a misdemeanor. [Up to 6 mos. and/or up to $200.]

Arson: Burning dwelling house, property of himself or another, occupied or unoccupied. [Up to 20 years and/or up to $10,000.]

Burning of other buildings. [Up to 10 years.]

MICHIGAN

Burglary: Breaking and entering, with intent to commit felony, or any larceny, any dwelling or other building. [Up to 15 years.]

Burglary, entering without breaking. [Up to 5 years or up to $2,500.]

Arson: Burning dwellinghouse, occupied, unoccupied, property of himself or another. [Up to 20 years.]

Burning of other real property, other buildings. [Up to 10 years.]

Burning of personal property, over $50 value. [Felony, up to 4 years and/or up to $2,000.]

Burning of personal property, less than $50 value. [Misdemeanor, up to 30 days and/or up to $100.]

Burning with intent to defraud insurer. [up to 10 years.]

MINNESOTA

Burglary: Enters building with criminal intent and has an explosive or other burglary tool; or the building is a dwelling and defendant has a weapon or assaults someone therein or the building is a bank or similar building and entry is by force and with intent to steal or commit a felony therein. [Up to 20 years and/or $20,000.]

If building is a dwelling and someone is inside. [Up to 10 years and/or $10,000.]

All others. [Up to 5 years and/or $5,000 (if felonious intent); 1 year and/or $1,000, if intends to commit a misdemeanor.]

Arson—First Deg.: Intentionally damages by fire or explosives a dwelling of himself or another therein, if anyone is in the building, or it is reasonable to assume this. [Up to 20 years and/or $20,000.]

Second Deg.: Any other building intentionally destroyed. [Up to 10 years and/or $10,000.]

Third Deg.: Intentionally damage by fire or explosives, his own or another's personal property. [Over $100. damage, intended or unintended, but could be foreseen - up to 5 years and/or $5,000.]

MISSISSIPPI

Burglary: Breaking and entering, day or night, dwelling of another, in which there is some human being, with intent to commit some crime either by forcibly breaking wall, window, door, or other manner, or by assistance of confederate, or unlocking with false keys, or picking lock. [7 to 15 years.]

Breaking and entering, in night, dwelling, armed, where human being is at time, with intent to commit some crime. [Up to 25 years.]

Breaking and entering dwelling, day or night, with intent to commit some crime; breaking out of dwelling; breaking any door of dwelling at night, having entered; breaking inner door of dwelling by one lawfully in house. [Up to 10 years.]

Breaking and entering building other than dwelling, in day or night. [Up to 7 years.]

Arson—First Deg.: Willfully and maliciously sets fire or aids burning of dwelling, occupied, unoccupied or vacant, property of himself or another, or school (state-supported building). [2 to 20 years.]

Second Deg.: Burning of property not included in first degree. [1 to 10 years.]

Third Deg.: Burning of personal property of value of $25 and belonging to another. [1 to 3 years.]

Fourth Deg.: Attempts to burn. [1 to 2 years or up to $1,000.]

Burning of insured property. [1 to 5 years.]

MISSOURI

Burglary—First Deg.: Breaking and entering dwelling in which human being is present with intent to commit crime or steal, by forcibly breaking wall, window, lock; or breaking in any other manner, armed with dangerous weapon, or with assistance of confederate, then present; or unlocking outer door by false keys or picking lock. [5 to 20 years.]

Second Deg.: Breaking and entering, with intent to commit crime or steal, under circumstances as are not burglary in first degree. [2 to 10 years.]

Arson: Willfully sets fire or burns any dwelling, boat or vessel, etc., in which a human being is present, or bridge or causeway upon any railroad, property of himself or another. [Not less than 2 years.]

Burning of shop, warehouse, factory, public building, etc. [2 to 10 years.]

Burning of other buildings, personal property of another, or burning of other buildings and personal property where he is owner with intent to injure or defraud; or burning of insured property; attempts to commit arson. [2 to 5 years.]

MONTANA

Burglary: Enters or remains in an occupied structure with felonious intent. [Up to 10 years.]

Aggravated burglary: If armed or carrying explosives or tries to inflict bodily harm. [Up to 40 years.]

Arson: Knowingly and purposely, by means of fire or explosive damages or destroys the occupied structure of another or places another person in danger of death or bodily injury. [Up to 20 years.]

Negligent Arson: Same as above, except done negligently. [Up to $500 and/or up to 6 months in the county jail.]

If another is placed in jeopardy. [Up to 10 years.]

NEBRASKA

Burglary: Breaks and enters dwelling, shop, office, etc., railroad car, etc., with intent to kill, rob, rape, or commit any other felony, or with intent to steal property of any value. [1 to 10 years or up to $500.]

In day or night, enters and attempts to kill, rob, steal, rape or commit arson, or enters armed with dangerous weapon, with intent to rob or steal and threaten to injure any person in building or with intent to rob or order any person to hand over money or property. [3 to 20 years.]

Arson—First Deg.: Willfully and maliciously sets fire or aids the burning of any dwelling, occupied, unoccupied or vacant, property of himself or another. [2 to 20 years.]

Second Deg.: Burning of other buildings or structure. [1 to 10 years.]

Third Deg.: Burning of personal property, of value of $25 or more, and property of another. [1 to 3 years.]

Fourth Deg.: Attempts to burn. [1 to 2 years, or up to $1,000.]

Burning to defraud insurer. [1 to 5 years.]

NEVADA

Burglary: Enters any house, room, apartment, etc., shop, warehouse, etc., or other building, vessel, railroad car, etc., with intent to commit grand or petit larceny, or any felony. [1 to 10 years.]

Arson—First Deg.: Willfully and maliciously sets fire or aids in the burning of dwelling, occupied or unoccupied or vacant, property of himself or another. [2 to 20 years.]

Second Deg.: Burning of other building. [1 to 10 years.]

Third Deg.: Burning of personal property, value of $25 or more and property of another. [1 to 6 years.]

Fourth Deg.: Attempted burning. [Up to one-half of longest term for offense attempted.]

Burning to defraud insurer. [1 to 6 years.]

NEW HAMPSHIRE

Burglary: Entering building or occupied structure with purpose to commit crime therein.

If at night or if bodily harm is inflicted or attempted, or person is armed. [Up to 15 years, optional fine up to $2,000.]

All other. [Up to 7 years, optional fine up to $2,000.]

Arson: Willfully and maliciously burn, or cause to be burned, dwelling house or outbuilding adjacent to it, or a part thereof. [Up to 30 years.]

Personal property, value of $25. [Up to 3 years or $1,000 and up to 1 year.]

Insured property. [Up to 5 years.]

Attempted arson. [Up to 2 years or $1,000.]

Knowingly starting a fire or causing an explosion which unlawfully damages the property of another.

If the damaged structure was an occupied structure and the perpetrator knew it was occupied. [Up to 15 years; optional fine up to $2,000.]
If intent was to defraud an insurance company or the fire or explosion was purposely started and another recklessly placed in danger of death or bodily harm or an occupied structure of another is placed in danger, or if damage is in excess of $1,000. [Up to 7 years; optional fine up to $2,000.]

All other arsons. [Up to 1 year; optional fine up to $1,000.]

NEW JERSEY

Burglary: Entering any church, dwelling, shop, vessel, or other building, etc., with intent to kill, rob, steal, commit rape, mayhem or battery. [Up to $2,000 and/or up to 7 years.]

Arson: Willfully or maliciously burning or aiding burning of any dwelling, his own or another's. [Up to $2,000 and/or up to 7 years.]

Burning ships and buildings other than dwellings. [Up to $2,000 and/or up to 7 years.]

Burning to defraud insurer. [Up to $2,000 and/or up to 7 years.]

NEW MEXICO

Burglary: Unauthorized entry of any vehicle, water craft, aircraft, dwelling or other structure with intent to commit any felony or theft therein. [A dwelling, 2-10 years and/or up to $5,000. Other buildings, 1-5 years and/or up to $5,000.]

Aggravated burglary: Unauthorized entry of any vehicle, water craft, aircraft, dwelling or other structure movable or immovable, with intent to commit felony or theft therein and person either is armed with deadly weapon or after entering arms self with one, commits battery upon person therein or while leaving. [10 to 50 years, and/or up to $10,000.]

Arson: Maliciously or willfully starting a fire or explosion which destroys or damages any building, occupied structure or property of another, bridge, fence or sign; or to defraud an insurance company. [If damage is $100. or less —up to 1 year and/or $1,000. $101-1,000—1-5 years and/or $5,000. Over $1,000—2-10 years and/or $4,000.]

Negligent arson: Recklessly starting a fire, or causing an explosion directly causing anothers' death or injuring another's property. [1-5 years and/or $5,000.]

NEW YORK

Burglary—First Deg.: With intent to commit crime enters or remains unlawfully in a dwelling at night and is armed with explosives or a deadly weapon, or causes physical injury to another person not a participant in the crime or threatens to use a dangerous weapon. [Indeterminate term, maximum up to 25 years; minimum up to 1/3 of the maximum sentence.]

Second Deg.: With intent to commit some crime, (1) at night enters or remains in a building or (2) while effecting entry or fleeing during the day is either armed with a deadly weapon or explosives or causes physical injury to anyone not a participant in the crime or threatens to use a dangerous weapon. [Indeterminate sentence—maximum up to 15 years; minimum, up to 1/3 of the maximum sentence.]

Third Deg.: To knowingly enter or remain in a building with intent to commit a crime therein. [Indeterminate sentence; maximum up to 7 years; minimum up to 1/3 of the maximum or alternatively the court may impose a definite sentence and fix a term of 1 year or less.

Arson—First Deg.: Intentionally starts a fire or causes an explosion in an inhabited building and accused knows or should have known that a person was in the building. [Indeterminate sentence—maximum up to 25 yrs.; minimum up to 1/3 of maximum sentence.]

Second Deg.: Intentionally sets fire etc., intending to unlawfully damage some building other than the perpetrator's. [Indeterminate sentence—maximum up to 15 yrs.; minimum up to 1/3 of maximum sentence.]

Third Deg.: (1) Intentionally damages by fire or explosives his own or another's (with his consent). (2) Intended to destroy building for a proper purpose and (3) Had no reasonable grounds to believe that another person or building would be endangered [Maximum 15 years; minimum up to 1/3 of maximum.]

NORTH CAROLINA
Burglary—First Deg.: If committed in dwelling house, and any person is in actual occupation of part of house at time of burglary. [Life imprisonment.]

Second Deg.: Committed in dwelling house, not actually occupied by anyone at time of crime. [Life imprisonment or term of years.]

Arson: Not defined. [Life imprisonment.]

Schools, public buildings, churches. [2-30 years.]

Attempted arson. [4 mos.-10 years.]

NORTH DAKOTA
Burglary: Willfully entering a building with intent to commit a crime therein. If occurs at night or in a dwelling place or defendant is armed, or inflicts (or attempts or threatens to inflict) bodily harm. [Up to 10 years and/or up to $10,000.]

All others. [Up to 5 years or $5,000.]

Arson: Starts a fire or explosion with intent to destroy an inhabited structure or building of another or a vital public facility. [Up to 10 years, and/or up to $10,000.]

Intentionally starts a fire or causes an explosion and thereby recklessly places another in danger of death or harm, or places a building or inhabited structure in danger of being destroyed; causes damages over $5,000. [Up to 5 years and/or $5,000. (If the actor places another in danger of death under circumstances manifesting an extreme indifference to the value of human life — up to 10 years and/or up to $10,000).]

OHIO
Aggravated burglary: Trespasses in an occupied structure with intent to commit a theft or a felony and either inflicts, threatens or attempts to inflict physical harm on another; or is armed; or the structure is a dwelling place and a person is, (or is likely to be) therein. [4-7 years to 25 years; optional fine up to $10,000.]

Burglary: Same as above without any of the additional elements, i.e. defendant is not armed and does not assault anyone, building is not a dwelling, etc.

Arson: By means of fire or explosives to knowingly cause or create a substantial risk of physical harm to another's property. [1-3 years to 10; optional fine $5,000 (if damage less than $150, up to 6 months and/or $1,000).]

With intent to defraud, to cause substantial risk to his own or another's property; to cause a substantial risk of physical harm to official buildings. [1-3 years to 10 years; optional fine up to $5,000.]

If defendant is hired to cause harm to his or another's property. [2-5 years to 15; optional fine up to $7,500.]

OKLAHOMA

Burglary—First Deg.: Breaking and entering in the nighttime the dwelling house of another, in which there is at the time some human being, with intent to commit some crime, either by forcibly breaking wall, outer door, window, etc.; by breaking in in some other manner, being armed with dangerous weapon or assisted by confederate actually present; or by unlocking an outer door by false keys or picking lock, or opening a window. [7 to 20 years.]

Second Deg.: Breaking and entering building or any part of any building, room, booth, tent, railroad car, automobile, truck, trailer, vessel, or other structure or erection, in which any property is kept; breaking into or forcibly opening any coin operated or vending machine or device with intent to steal any property therein or to commit any felony. [2 to 7 years.]

Arson—First Deg.: Willfully and maliciously setting fire to or burning or destroying in whole or in part, by the use of any explosive device or substance, causing to be burned or destroyed, or aiding, counselling, procuring, burning or destruction of any dwelling house or adjoining outhouse or garage or contents thereof, whether occupied, unoccupied, or vacant, the property of himself or another. [Up to 20 years and/or up to $25,000.]

Second Deg.: Willful and malicious burning of any building or structure, public or private, other than dwelling houses or contents thereof, property of himself or another. [Up to 15 years and/or up to $20,000.]

Third Deg.: Willful and malicious burning of personal property, automobiles, etc., standing farm crops, etc., of value of $20, property of himself or another. [Up to 5 years and/or $5,000.]

Fourth Deg.: Attempted burning of property mentioned in foregoing. [Up to 3 years and/or $2,000.]

OREGON

Burglary—Second Deg.: Enters or remains unlawfully in a building, with intent to commit a crime. [Up to 5 years.]

First Deg.: If the building entered is a dwelling or if defendant is armed with burglar's tools or a dangerous weapon or if he causes or threatens physical injury to another. [Up to 20 years.]

Arson: By fire or explosives, intentionally damages protected property of another or any property of his own or another if his act recklessly places another in physical danger or endangers another's property. [Up to 20 years.]

Second Deg.: By fire or explosion intentionally damages building of another that is not protected property. [Up to 5 years.]

NOTE: Protected property is defined as any structure, place, or thing customarily occupied by people.

PENNSYLVANIA

Burglary: At any time, willfully and maliciously, enters occupied building, with intent to commit any felony. [Up to $25,000 and/or up to 20 years.]

Arson—First Deg.: Intentionally starts fire or explosion and thereby places another in danger of death or bodily harm. [Up to 20 years and/or up to $25,000.]

Second Deg.: Starts a fire or causes an explosion with the intent of destroying a building or occupied structure of another; by starting a fire or explosion, recklessly places a structure or building of another in danger; intends to defraud an insurance company. [Up to 10 years and/or up to $25,000.]

RHODE ISLAND

Burglary: Not defined. [Life or term not less than 5 years.]

Breaking and entering any bank, shop, etc., public building, vessel, in nighttime with intent to commit murder, rape, robbery or larceny. [Up to 10 years.]

Break and enter at day or night any dwelling house, occupied or not. [Up to 3 years and/or up to $300.]

Enter any dwelling, day or night, with intent to commit murder, rape, robbery, arson or larceny; or with such intent, during the day, enter any other building, ship or vessel. [Up to 10 years and/or up $500.]

Arson: Not defined. [1 year to life.]

Wrongfully or maliciously sets fire or aids the burning of any dwelling, or dynamites, etc., the burning whereof is not arson at common law; or wrongfully sets fire to, dynamites, etc. any building not a dwelling. [2 to 20 years.]

Burning, etc., of personal property of another of value of $25. [1 to 3 years.]

Burning of personal property to defraud insurer. [1 to 5 years.]

Attempts to burn or dynamite. [Up to $1,000 and/or 1 to 2 years.]

SOUTH CAROLINA

Burglary: As at common law. [Life or 5 years and up.]

Break and enter, or break with intent to enter, in daytime, dwelling house, or in nighttime, with intent to commit felony or other crime of lesser grade. [Up to 5 years.]

Arson: Willfully and maliciously sets fire to or aids the burning of any dwelling, property of himself or another. [2 to 20 years.]

Burning of other buildings. [1 to 10 years.]

Burning of personal property to defraud insurer. [1 to 5 years.]

Burning of personal property. [1 to 3 years.]

SOUTH DAKOTA

Burglary—First Deg.: Breaks into and enters in nighttime dwelling of another, in which human being is at time present, with intent to commit crime therein, by forcibly breaking wall or door or window, etc., breaking in any other manner being armed with dangerous weapon or aided by confederate actually present or by unlocking door with false keys or picking lock. [Not less than 10 years.]

Second Deg.: Breaking into dwelling house in daytime under such circumstances as would have been burglary in first degree if at night; entered dwelling in nighttime through open door or window and breaking any inner door or window, etc., with intent to commit any crime; lawfully in dwelling house and breaking in nighttime inner door with intent to commit any crime, any building, inhabited or not and opening or attempting to open, safe vault, etc., by using explosives. [5 to 15 years.]

Third Deg.: Breaking into dwelling house in nighttime with intent to commit a crime, but not first degree burglary breaking or entering at any time any other building, railroad car, vessel, etc., with intent to commit larceny or any felony. [Up to 15 years.]

Fourth Deg.: Breaks and enters dwelling house, with intent to commit crime, where not burglary in any other degree or having committed crime in dwelling, breaks in nighttime outer door or window, etc., to get out. [Up to 3 years.]

Arson: Willfully sets fire to or aids the burning of any dwelling, property of himself or another. [Up to 20 years.]

Arson of building other than dwelling, property of himself or another. [Up to 10 years.]

Arson of personal property, property of another and of $25 value. [Up to 3 years.]

Arson with intent to defraud insurer. [For a term not exceeding the term for which arson on that particular property would be punished.]

Attempted arson. [Up to 2 years, or up to $1,000.]

TENNESSEE

Burglary: Breaking and entering dwelling house by night with intent to commit felony. [5 to 15 years. (If armed, 10-15 years).]

Second Deg.: Breaking or entering by day, with intent to commit felony. [3 to 15 years. (If armed, 10-15 years).]

Third Deg.: Breaking and entering business house or building other than dwelling, with intent to commit felony. [3 to 10 years. (If armed, 10-15 years).]

Breaking and entering, with criminal intent, into a dwelling or building, day or night and opening a safe or vault. [3-21 years. (If armed, 10-15 years).]

Breaking and entering freight or passenger car, motor vehicle, by day or night, with intent to steal anything of value or commit felony. [3 to 10 years.]

Arson: Willfully and maliciously setting fire to or aiding burning of any house or building, property of himself or another. [3 to 21 years.]

Burning bridge, railroad, vehicle, aircraft, etc. [1 to 10 years.]

Burning personal property, property of himself of another, of value of $25 or more. [1 to 10 years.]

Attempted arson. [1 to 5 years.]

TEXAS

Burglary: Enters or remains concealed in a building, and commits or intends to commit a felony. [2-20 years and may be fined up to $10,000.]

If the premises entered are a habitation or defendant is armed with a weapon or explosives or attempts to injure anyone. [5-99 years.]

Arson: Starts fire or causes explosion with intent to destroy or damage another's building or to defraud an insurance company. [2-20 years; may be fined up to $10,000.]

If anyone is injured. [5-99 years.]

UTAH

Burglary: Entering and remaining in building with intent to commit felony, theft or assault. [Up to 5 years and/or up to $5,000.]

If committed in a dwelling. [1-15 years and/or up to $10,000.]

Aggravated Burglary: Harms another during the burglary, threatens or uses a deadly weapon or is armed. [5-life, and/or up to $10,000.]

Aggravated Arson: Intentionally damages by fire or explosives any structure with a person therein or a habitable structure. [1-15 years and/or up to $10,000.]

Arson: Intentional damage to another's property by fire or explosives not amounting to aggravated arson; destroying any property with intent to defraud the insurer. [Up to 5 years and/or up to $5,000 (in case of insurance fraud).]

In other cases. [If damage exceeds $5,000 - up to 5 years and/or $5,000. Between $1,000-$5,000 - up to 1 year and/or up to $1,000. Between $1,000 -$250 - up to 6 months and/or up to $299. All others - up to 90 days.]

VERMONT

Burglary: In nighttime, breaking and entering dwelling, bank, shop, store, etc., vessel, railroad car, or other building in which personal property is situated, with intent to commit murder, rape, robbery, larceny or other felony. [Up to 15 years and/or up to $1,000.]

Burglary as above, but in daytime. [Up to 10 years, or up to $1,000.]

Arson—First Deg.: Willfully and maliciously setting fire to or aiding burning of dwelling house, occupied, unoccupied or vacant, property of himself or another. [2 to 10 years or up to $2,000.]

Death resulting — murder first degree.

Second Deg.: Burning of other buildings or structures, property of himself or another. [1 to 5 years or up to $1,000.]

Third Deg.: Burning of personal property not less than $25 value, and property of another. [1 to 3 years or up to $500.]

Fourth Deg.: Attempted arson. [1 to 2 years or up to $500.]

VIRGINIA

Burglary: Breaking and entering dwelling of another in nighttime with intent to commit felony or larceny. [5-20 years (if armed, 20 years to life).]

In night without breaking, or in daytime breaking and entering dwelling occupied, or office, shop, etc., railroad car, automobile (if used as dwelling place) etc., with intent to commit murder, rape, or robbery. [5-20; 20-life (if armed).]

As above, but with intent to commit larceny or other felony. [1-20 years, or up to 12 months and up to $1,000; 20-life (if armed).]

As above, but with intent to commit assault or other misdemeanor. [1 to 5 years, or up to 1 year and/or $1,000; 20-life (if armed).]

Arson: In nighttime, maliciously burning or using explosive, or aiding burning of any dwelling, property or himself or another. [20 years-life; 5-20 years (if jury or court finds that no person in the house).]

In the daytime (occupied or unoccupied). [2-5 years.]

Public building, meeting house, school, etc. [5-20 years.]

Burning any structure with a person therein or thereon. [5-20 years.]

Burning of personal property, maliciously or with intent to defraud insurer, of value of $100 or more. [2-5 years.]

Burning of personal property, maliciously or with intent to defraud insurer, of value of less than $100. [1 year and/or up to $1,000.]

Burning of other buildings, if no one present and property of value of $100 or more. [2 to 5 years.]

If no one present and property of less than $100 value. [1 year and/or up to $1,000.]

Threats. [1 to 10 years or up to 1 year and $1,000.]

WASHINGTON
Burglary—First Deg.: Enters or remains in building with intent to commit a crime and is armed with a deadly weapon or assaults anyone therein. [Not less than 20 years.]

Second Deg.: With intent to commit crime, where not burglary first degree. [Up to 10 years and/or up to $10,000.]

Arson—First Deg.: Causes fire or explosion manifestly dangerous to any human life, including a fireman; burns or causes an explosion in a dwelling or in any building where there is a human being present. [Not less than 20 years.]

Second Deg.: Willfully burns any other building or structure. [Up to 10 years and/or up to $10,000.]

WEST VIRGINIA
Burglary: In nighttime, break and enter, or enter without breaking, or in daytime break and enter, dwelling, with intent to commit felony or larceny. [1 to 15 years.]

In daytime, enter without breaking a dwelling, with intent to commit felony or any larceny. [1 to 10 years.]

Break and enter, or enter, building other than dwelling. [1 to 10 years.]

Break and enter, or enter, automobile, etc. [2 to 12 months and up to $100.]

Arson—First Deg.: Willfully and maliciously sets fire to or aids the burning of dwelling, occupied, unoccupied or vacant, property of himself or another. [20 years.]

Second Deg.: Burning of other building or structure. [10 years and/or up to $10,000.]

Third Deg.: Burning of personal property of another of $50 value. [1 to 3 years.]

Fourth Deg.: Attempts to commit arson. [1 to 2 years or up to $1,000.]

Burning insured property. [1 to 5 years.]

WISCONSIN
Burglary: Breaking and entering without consent, with intent to commit felony, any building, dwelling, railroad car, ship, etc. [Up to 10 years.]

If with dangerous weapon, explosive, battery on person therein. [Up to 20 years.]

Arson: By fire intentionally damaging building of another without his consent; doing so with intent to defraud insurer; or doing so by means of explosives. [Up to 15 years.]

Destroying property other than building, value of $100 or more. [$1,000 and/or up to 3 years.]

Damaging property other than building with intent to defraud. [$1,000 and/or up to 5 years.]

WYOMING
Burglary: Breaking and entering dwelling house, shop, office, warehouse, etc., or buildings, with intent to commit felony or steal property of any value. [Up to 14 years.]

If armed with dangerous weapon, or using explosives or committing battery. [5 to 50 years.]

Arson—First Deg.: Willfully and maliciously setting fire or aiding burning of any dwelling, occupied or vacant, property of himself or another. [2 to 20 years.]

Second Deg.: Burning of any other building or structure, property of himself or another. [1 to 10 years.]

Third Deg.: Burning of personal property, of value of $25 and property of another. [1 to 3 years.]

APPENDIX

APPENDIX

An American Legal Almanac, Summary and Update
of the following LEGAL ALMANACS:

Part One
LAW AND THE FAMILY

Part Two
LAW AND LIVELIHOOD

Chapter IV THE WORKER AND THE LAW

Legal Almanac No.: 7. *Labor Law*
19. *State Workmens Compensation Laws*
20. *Medicare*
39. *Arbitration - Precepts and Principles*
48. *Law of Retirement*
69. *Penalties for Misconduct on the Job*

Part Three
LAW AND LIVING

Chapter V LAW FOR HOMEOWNERS AND TENANTS

Legal Almanac No.: 4. *Law of Real Estate*
11. *Landlord and Tenant*
43. *Law for the Homemaker, Real Estate
Operator and Broker*
60. *Condemnation*
72. *Cooperatives and Condominiums*

Chapter VI THE CONSUMER AND THE LAW

Legal Almanac No.: 10. *Law of Credit*
52. *Legal Protection for the Consumer*
66. *Legal Protection in Garnishment and
Attachment*
70. *Legal Regulation of Consumer Credit*

Chapter VII JUVENILE LAW

Legal Almanac No.: 17. *Schools and the Law*   58980
22. *Law of Juvenile Justice*
46. *Youth and the Law*

Chapter VIII WOMEN AND THE LAW

Legal Almanac No.: 9. *Legal Regulation of Sexual Conduct*
53. *Legal Status of Women*